Public Policy in Transition Economies

Public policies are usually carefully designed to address a particular problem, but they are also shaped and influenced by the sociocultural heritage of a particular country. This volume explores the origins of economic and other public policies in Central and Eastern Europe.

This region makes for a particularly interesting case because after going through a major system change – transitioning from a command economy into a market economy – many of the key policies were written anew. The contributors to this book look at key policy areas at the intersection of state and private sectors, including industrial, pension, energy, and competition policies. The chapters examine key questions such as: how did these policies evolve from the time of transition to their final form? What were the main drivers of policy conduct and factors influencing major policy choices? How does the historical context impact contemporary policy space? Throughout the volume, an institutional approach is adopted, according to which policies are perceived as the outcome of top-down design, filtered through social institutions inherited from the past. With this approach, this book presents a long-running assessment, over 30 years, of policymaking in transition economies, which were subject to profound changes throughout the period.

This book will be of interest to readers in institutional economics, policy studies, transition economies, and the recent history of Eastern Europe.

Maciej J. Grodzicki is an assistant professor at the Institute of Economics, Finance and Management at Jagiellonian University in Krakow, Poland.

Anna Zachorowska-Mazurkiewicz is an associate professor at the Institute of Economics, Finance and Management and a director of the Doctoral School in the Social Sciences at Jagiellonian University in Krakow, Poland.

Routledge Advances in Economic Policy

In response to multiple crises, new impetus and energy have been directed at the development and implementation of progressive, or even radical, economic policies. From the Green New Deal to basic income, wealth taxation, and the living wage, new policy ideas are being generated around the world. The *Routledge Advances in Economic Policy* series provides a forum for the publication of monographs and edited volumes which explore the principles and theories behind these policies, analyse global case studies of trials and implementations, and propose new ideas and initiatives for how the economy might be improved or restructured for the greater good.

Technological Unemployment, Basic Income, and Wellbeing
Fabio D'Orlando

Public Policy in Transition Economies
An Institutional Perspective
Edited by Maciej J. Grodzicki and Anna Zachorowska-Mazurkiewicz

For more information in this series, please visit: www.routledge.com/Routledge-Advances-in-Economic-Policy/book-series/RAEP

Public Policy in Transition Economies

An Institutional Perspective

Edited by
Maciej J. Grodzicki and
Anna Zachorowska-Mazurkiewicz

Routledge
Taylor & Francis Group
London and New York

First published 2024
by Routledge
4 Park Square, Milton Park, Abingdon, Oxon OX14 4RN

and by Routledge
605 Third Avenue, New York, NY 10158

Routledge is an imprint of the Taylor & Francis Group, an informa business

British Library Cataloguing-in-Publication Data
A catalogue record for this book is available from the British Library

ISBN: 9781032546056 (hbk)
ISBN: 9781032546063 (pbk)
ISBN: 9781003425717 (ebk)

DOI: 10.4324/9781003425717

Typeset in Times New Roman
by codeMantra

Contents

Contributors

Maciej J. Grodzicki is an economist, researcher at the Jagiellonian University, member of the board of the Polish Economic Network, and trade union activist in the Employee Initiative. He conducts research on the international political economy, global supply chains, and the economy of shared resources, including forests. He seeks solutions for a sustainable and fair economy in the spirit of degrowth. He is a member of the Forum of Institutional Thought.

Ewa Gruszewska is an associate professor at the University of Bialystok, Faculty of Economics and Finance (Poland). Her research interests include analysis of institutions, economic growth, and entrepreneurship. She is a member of the Forum of Institutional Thought.

Jerzy Hausner is a professor of economic sciences, honorary professor of the University of Economics in Krakow, and founder of the Department of Economy and Public Administration of the University of Economics in Krakow. He is Chairman of the Open Eyes Economy Summit Program Council, former Deputy Prime Minister and Minister of Economy, Labor and Social Policy, member of the Monetary Policy Council of the 3rd term, and honorary doctor of the Warsaw School of Economics and Academy of Fine Arts in Krakow.

Katarzyna Kamińska is an assistant professor in the Department of German Economy Research of the Institute of World Economy at the Warsaw School of Economics. In 2016, she won the first place in the competition for the best doctoral thesis organized by the President of UOKiK for her thesis entitled "Ordoliberalism and Keynesianism – Two Contradictory Concepts in the Economic Policy of Post-War Germany". He is a member of the Forum of Institutional Thought.

Maciej Kassner is a political scientist and assistant professor at the Faculty of Politics and International Studies, University of Warsaw. His PhD dissertation was on the political philosophy of John Dewey. He is currently working on a book project devoted to the study of Karl Polanyi's social theory. He is a member of the Forum of Institutional Thought.

Adam Koronowski is currently professor of economics at Cardinal Stefan Wyszyński University in Warsaw and director of the Institute of Economics and Finance at the university. His main interests cover monetary policy, currency regimes, macroeconomic activity and fluctuations, and financial stability.

Črt Kostevc is a full professor of International Economics at the School of Economics and Business, University of Ljubljana. His research interests are in trade and firm heterogeneity, firm dynamics and innovation, productivity analysis, and foreign direct investment.

Yuriy Pogorelov, PhD in Economics, is a professor counselor in the Accounting Chamber, Kyiv (Ukraine). He has authored more than 200 publications in scientific journals in Ukraine and beyond.

Yevheniia Polishchuk, PhD in Economics, is an assistant professor at the Jagiellonian University in Krakow (Poland), and a professor at Kyiv National Economic University named after Vadym Hetman (Ukraine). She is a member of the Young Scientists Council at the Ministry of Education and Science in Ukraine and co-founder of Ukrainian Science Diaspora initiative.

Marek Ratajczak is a full professor in the Poznań University of Economics and Business from 2000. From 2018, he is the head of the Institute of Economics, and chair of the Department of Macroeconomics and Development Studies (from 2015). His research areas include history of economic thought, macroeconomics, and development of higher education. He is a member of the Forum of Institutional Thought Scientific Board.

Tjaša Redek is a full professor of economics at the School of Economics and Business, University of Ljubljana. Her research interests are in intangible capital, new technologies, firm performance, and human capital as well as labour market issues.

Fadil Sahiti, Ph.D., worked in the UK for Birkbeck, LSE, UCL, and Hult Business School before joining Rochester Institute of Technology in Kosovo. The author currently works as assistant professor at RIT Kosovo teaching various management and entrepreneurship courses. The author's research interests lie in the field of entrepreneurship in developing countries.

Sarolta Somosi, PhD in Economics (2012), is an assistant professor at the Faculty of Economics and Business Administration of the University of Szeged (Hungary). Her dissertation was about European gas market liberalization. She studies and lectures on the micro policies of the EU targeting competition, trade and industry, and energy markets and energy policy of the European Union.

Renata Śliwa is an academic economist working at the Institute of Law, Economics and Administration (Chair of Economics and Economic Policy) at the Pedagogical University of Krakow (Poland). She conducts research in the framework of the institutional approach , and is an author of publications on the telecommunications sector in Poland, as well as the institutional perspective of regulatory governance. She is a member of the Forum of Institutional Thought.

Karolina Trzaska is assistant researcher at the University of Bialystok, Faculty of Economics and Finance (Poland). Her research focuses on innovation, higher education, competences, and megatrends.

Anna Zachorowska-Mazurkiewicz is associate professor of economics and director of Doctoral School in the Social Sciences at Jagiellonian University in Krakow, Poland. She is a member of the Forum for Institutional Thought. Her main research interests focus on heterodox economic thought, especially institutional and feminist. She is a member of the Forum of Institutional Thought.

Anna Ząbkowicz is a faculty in the Department of Economics and Sociology at the University of Lodz and specializes in pensions and governance. She is co-founder of country-wide association of academics of Poland (Forum for Institutional Thought) and President of its Advisory Council. She is a member of the Forum of Institutional Thought Scientific Board.

Acknowledgements

The volume presented is an outcome of the vivid exchange of ideas and opinions by the members of Forum for Institutional Thought during the seminars, conferences, and less formal meetings. The Forum was established as an initiative of a group of representatives of social sciences united by the conviction that the institutional approach currently offers the best way to understand the world, and especially the changes taking place in economies undergoing systemic transformation. The Forum supported our efforts to share the vision of the institutional analysis of policy creation in transition economies with a grant that helped us to prepare the final version of the volume.

The person who directly triggered the first approach to the topic of the volume is Anna Ząbkowicz, who inspired us to work on the volume. Her efforts led to the establishing of Forum for Institutional Thought in which she served as the first president. She has been motivating us to undertake the topic, and eventually joined the team of authors herself.

We would also like to thank our colleagues who read the first versions of the chapters and shared with us their important insights. We are grateful to Judyta Lubacha, Zofia Łapniewska, and Rafał Wisła from Jagiellonian University, Tomasz Geodecki, Marcin Kędzierski, Tomasz Kwarciński, and Michał Możdżeń from the Krakow University of Economics, Sławomir Czech from the University of Economics in Katowice, and Michał Moszyński from Toruń University. We would especially like to thank our two colleagues, who shared their advice regarding the general direction of the volume and the introductory chapter of the book – Sławomir Czech and Michał Możdżeń.

We would also like to thank Jerzy Hausner, who pioneered writing about the institutional order and system transition. Professor Hausner joined us in our efforts and shared the opinion about the volume in the preface opening the book.

Foreword

Jerzy Hausner

I have become familiar with the herein publication with a huge deal of interest. The authors approached me with a request to write the preface. I was convinced by the fact that albeit the particular chapters are devoted to various public policies in Central and Eastern European countries, it is bonded together by the inspiring cognitive perspective of the authors, namely, the formation and functioning of the state in the process of the post-communist transformation. This in particular makes the aforesaid work both original and significant. However, I also appreciate the value of the case studies of public policies stipulated in this work. Nevertheless, I did not decide to discuss these as this has been done to perfection in the opening chapter by Maciej Grodzicki and Anna Zachorowska-Mazurkiewicz, the editors of the book.

In this case, I acknowledged that I would propose a review of the fundamental issue of the book, which is the evolution of the state in Central and Eastern European countries, in which the transition from a controlled economy to a market economy was conducted and later formed part of the EU.

Disintegration of command economy and a systemic vacuum

Under the socialist conditions, governance structures were built around the production function. Among other reasons, this resulted from the passive function of money and finance. Generally speaking, those structures reflected the main features of the socialist economy, namely, the extensive mode of growth and economics of shortage. They were mainly characterized by vertical integration as follows.

The notion of the command economy denotes only the formal principles and structures, within which the rules of the economic game gradually evolved and became entrenched involving discretionary decisions and bargaining mechanisms. Such rules began to emerge during a period of forced socialist industrialization. However, their full development occurred in the 1960s and 1970s, sometimes in conjunction with the consecutive attempts to reform the economy and decentralize management (Hungary, Poland).

As the discretionary/bargaining rules of the economic game became firmly established, the importance of branch corporations increased, which combined the features of huge bureaucratic and economic organizations, while also large social groups with an involved inner structure. It was the activity of such corporations that determined the mechanisms of allocation and distribution in practice and provided a framework for the development of governance structures.

The key features with respect to the mechanisms of resource allocation and distribution of value-added products were as follows:

i decisions about allocation taken first of all in response to current production bottlenecks;
ii short timespan of decisions on allocation;
iii shrinking range of available options in allocative decisions;
iv decisions concerning allocation reached by way of multi-level and multi-stage bargaining;
v dependence of the bargaining power of branch corporations on their productive potential;
vi relatively stable shares of branch corporations in the allocation of factors of production and distribution of payroll funds.

Socialist corporatism is without doubt the unintended consequence of the state's assumption of the function of a production organizer. It emerges through a gradual secondary adjustment of diverse mechanisms of the social division of labour and interest representation to the economic conditions imposed by the state. Socialist corporatism is neither state corporatism (as it is not a deliberately established institutional solution), nor is it a form of societal corporatism (as it does not emerge from the interaction and agreement between the state and non-state interest organizations). It is a product of the dysfunctional (pathological) adjustment of various groups and organizations to conditions imposed upon them, and which they cannot change.

It is a symptom of the erosion, rather than evolution, of the socialist economic system. Thus, it was not an institutional alternative that might create new possibilities and perspectives for communism. Instead, it was a polycentric, albeit hierarchical mechanism of interest concertation that was not fully conscious and controlled. As such, it allowed real socialism to survive at the cost of exhausting resources and a general decomposition, whose final stage was its gentle demise.

The combination of the representation monopoly and production monopoly on a nationwide scale led to a situation when social protest was efficiently contained, channelled, and dispersed by branch corporations, which at the same time strengthened their capacity for exerting political pressure and their position of a monopolist. Under such circumstances, any instance of corporatist, social protest oriented towards improving the living standards had a destructive effect on the economy: it blocked the possibility of a systemic reform, while at the same time it eroded the system. Both economically and socially the system of power "corrupted" the workers in order to prevent them from becoming citizens. This effectively blocked political development, but at the cost of slowing down the economy.

Definitely, at the final stage of the decay of the communist system structures, we encountered tempestuous events of a revolutionary nature. Nevertheless, it was fairly easy to notice that those events actually only marked the peak moment of progressing decomposition, and that despite loud declarations, the system was rather disintegrated than abolished (Hausner 1995a).

The final phase of the "gentle demise" was preceded by a long process of disintegration (protracted death – agony). Though this disintegration caused the system to collapse, it did not lead to the emergence of any alternatives for development. Neither within the system of power, nor within the opposition did any forces able to undertake strategic action have time to appear; forces which, with their own vision of the system and its formation, would not so much have taken over the old structures of power as initiated, but would have created and reproduced new ones in order to realize their own systemic project.

Therefore, the protracted disintegration and "gentle demise" led to a "systemic vacuum" and an absence of strategic forces, which could have mastered the situation relatively quickly. The communist state system was not really overthrown or transformed – it simply fell apart, leaving behind only ruins and an increasingly helpless and disoriented populace. The elites, without a structural project of their own, replaced it with an idealized academic model of an ideal market and democratic order.

However contrary to some interpretations, the notion of a "systemic vacuum" does not mean the destruction of all the elements which made up the hitherto existing system. Many continue to exist, such as for example, state enterprises and branch interest groups. The systemic vacuum is not an institutional void. The term "political void" is also doubtful here. This suggests the lack of political entities or political structures, which relates to the disappearance of the political system and the state in a systemic sense, thus the inability to realize strategic programmes by these entities and structures.

In these circumstances, even new structures are gradually emerging but do not constitute a system yet because the links between them (which normally transform the economy, politics, and culture into sub-systems of a whole that we call a social system) do not exist. These links consist of, amongst other things, the co-evolution, mutual penetration, and reciprocal adaptation of the various structures. It is only these kinds of relations between the various structures that shape a social order by providing special mechanisms of regulating the way this order functions. In the absence of these mechanisms, various segments of society function according to their own rules and separate logic. This leads to numerous horizontal and vertical discrepancies in the functioning of the economy (Eatwell et al. 1995) and society, which are reflected in the social consciousness in the form of dissonances.

The "systemic vacuum" was to first and foremost complete the shock economic therapy. In this case, the basis of the economic programme – the marketization and liberalization of the economy, the so-called "Washington consensus" – was adopted, which encompassed the following recommendations (Williamson 1990):

1. Fiscal discipline has to be restored.
2. Government subsidies need to be cut, while education and health care have to enjoy priority within public expenditures.
3. A tax reform aimed at broadening the tax base and moderating the marginal tax rates is necessary.

4 Interest rates have to be determined by the market and real interest rates must be positive.
5 Exchange rates have to be determined by the market as well.
6 There is need for liberalized, export-oriented trade regimes, while the liberalization of foreign financial flows is not required.
7 Restrictions of foreign direct investment should be abolished.
8 State-owned firms have to be privatized.
9 Economic activities are to be deregulated.
10 Property rights are to be protected and secure.

On the basis of these assumptions, the economic programme of transformation ("the Balcerowicz plan") was first of all incomplete and insufficient, while secondly, it was applied dogmatically, namely, without taking account of the specific conditions of the particular economy, which evoked a range of negative repercussions.

From a distance, it is currently generally acknowledged that the shock approach was justified and useful in the case of initiating market reforms, particularly when conducted in conditions of a macroeconomic crisis and the loss of control of the market, albeit insufficient for its advancement and consolidation. Simultaneously, significant responsibility lies with the great international organizations that released their resources in return for the uncritical implementation of their universal recommendations (Campbell and Pedersen 1996).

Between imperative and interactive methods of transition

The key to understanding the post-communist transformation is the grasping of the concept of the intricacy of the process of forming the new role of the state. It must withdraw from its hitherto function in order to gain the capacity to fulfil other functions. In a synthetic manner, it is possible to describe this process by referring to Schumpeter's differentiation between "owner state" and "tax state" (Schumpeter 1954).

In practice, the withdrawal by the state from its hitherto role, which was appropriate for the controlled economy, was carried out in a rapid and chaotic manner. The problem does not only lie in the fact of how fast and widespread the withdrawal of the state from its former role was, but first and foremost how fast it is capable of creating the new role, which incidentally takes time. From this viewpoint, the worst scenario is the situation whereby the state actually loses its ownership rights and acquires fiscal rights. This, in my opinion, constitutes the fundamental source of the occurrence of the "financial crisis of the state" in the post-communist process of transformation (Hausner, Jessop, and Owsiak 1993). Since the very beginning of the transformation, the structural problem of the lack of balance in public finances has existed, despite the successive attempts undertaken to rectify this matter.

Together with the existence of the financial crisis of the state, it is also necessary to connect this to the emergence of the populist threat in the process of the post-communist transformation (Hausner 1992). This did not lead to a populist revolt straight away, but rather appeared in the particular countries analysed with varying degrees of intensity and in different periods of time (e.g. Slovakia), whereby in certain countries this consequently led to the choice of authoritarianism.

Nevertheless, the fundamental significance for the perception of the dynamics of the post-socialist transformation is not attributed to the commonly discussed dichotomy, namely, shock therapy vs. gradualism, but rather the differentiation between the imperative and the interactive methods of transformation (Hausner 1995b).

The *imperative method* consists of forcing through the desired changes using the tools available. In this method, the transformation process is an experiment that is initiated and directed by the central authority, which in accordance with its theory applies specific methods to elicit certain reactions, whose appearance will bring about a new system, thus a qualitatively different reality. For the experimenter, the participants in the system are the active objects of his/her policy. The aim is to stimulate the desired changes in mentality and behaviour using the available means, while also to adjust them to the new rules of the game. To him/her, these rules are self-evident, given, while also exclusively correct, albeit the subjects of his/her policy need not understand or accept them. If they do, the experimenter's task becomes so much easier, whereas if they do not, then in order to accomplish the task (a moral, intellectual, and political imperative), he/she must weaken the resistance of the participants subjects and force them to adapt to the new rules. Taken as a whole, the rules constitute for him/her a coherent vision of social order whose realization will ensure some kind of desired state of social equilibrium.

The opposite approach is based on the *interactive method*. This involves eliciting the desired changes by generating a process of social innovation resulting from social interaction. In this method, the central authority, initiating and directing the changes, becomes a participant and treats the other participants as independent agents. The behaviour of each participant can only change as a consequence of mutual interaction. The task of the central authority initiating the transformation process is not to lay down the new systemic rules and force the participants to respect them, but rather to stimulate the process by which these rules are formulated and defined, thus allowing the participants to satisfy their needs and realize their interests. In this process, the role of the "central authority" is also subject to social definition and formulation.

The weakness of the imperative method fundamentally involves the fact that the change to the formal rules imposed from the top does not constitute a sufficient prerequisite to form a new institutional order (Raiser 1996, 12). In as much as it is relatively effective in restoring macroeconomic equilibrium, it turned out to be unreliable in the creation of a new social order. What is helpful at the stage of initiating market reforms, becomes a hindrance to their consolidation (Haggard and Kaufman 2018).

The imperative approach implies institutional mimicry, which is socially and economically costly. Even if it brings rapid gains in effectiveness (allocative effectiveness), it undermines the ability to adapt, which becomes a barrier to effectiveness in the longer term (dynamic effectiveness). The incorporation of the eastern regions after the German unification reveals the illusiveness of the imperative approach very well. This process has been perceptively analysed by Grabher, who shows that while the adopted approach may have led to the emergence of various new organizational forms in the East German economy, these forms are separated from one another and are not linked by the exchange of resources and information. Hence, their heterogeneity does not yet constitute a "genetic pool" for the evolution of more effective forms of organizing production and services (Grabher 1994).

The imperative method implies the perception of the state as the sole instrument of power whose control and subordination become intrinsic goals. The state is perceived statically as something that is fashioned according to the assumed pattern and simultaneously provided with the features of the perfect instrument for governing. Restrictions only stem from the fact there is no completely independent rule of power. This perception leads to the absolutization of the state and power.

In turn, the interactive method implies the view of the state at the level of civic discourse and coordination of collective actions that create the possibility of implementing and executing strategic undertakings by the state. The state ceases to be a space that is occupied and arranged and becomes a part of a broader sense of order (constitutional order), which, in one way or another evolves somehow and when all put together must be capable of mobilizing and directing collective efforts, which in turn, renews social legitimacy and provides it with an identity.

Administrative capacity and the soft state syndrome

Another key issue that is strictly associated with the formation and functioning of the state in the process of the post-communist transformation is that of the aspect of the organization of public administration. In this case, I shall directly relate to the Polish experience, albeit specific in terms of principles, it is similar to a multitude of other countries of Central and Eastern Europe.

Historically speaking, the Polish public administration inherited certain patterns that were binding in the partitioning states, which were culturally different. Subsequently, there was a problem with grouping them in a uniform organism. Following World War Two, a uniform state power was imposed on this incompletely developed structure, which arose from the doctrine of the steering role of the communist party. In the period of the political transformation, there was an attempt to implement solutions derived from various and contrasting approaches (paradigms) into the Polish public administration in a chaotic manner. Consequently, it is difficult to refer to this as a uniform organizational model and specific cultural pattern. We are dealing with an institutional conglomeration that managed to become resistant to the systemic changes implemented from the top by absorbing them and gradually neutralizing them.

Such a way of development is clearly different from the one that is related to public administration in highly developed countries. In their case, the solutions implemented in successive historical stages in the functioning of the state within the binding paradigms built up. Simultaneously, they evolved to form a strongly embedded administrative construction, in which the particular elements interact, thus creating a defined organizational structure and systemic order.

By way of consequence, the state is unable to execute what they promised and what society expects from them. The ruling authorities make promises they are unable to execute, while the citizens frequently expect what they cannot be given. Simultaneously, the state is incapable of doing what is necessary and what decides on the institutional conditions for socio-economic growth. This, in turn, is favourable towards the consolidation of the pattern of dependent development and sustains the peripherality of these countries. "Developmental drift" and falling into the "middle income trap" are clear and painful symptoms of this phenomenon.

In my hitherto works and journalism from the period of the end of the previous decade and the current decade, I referred to the notion of a "soft state" that was implemented by Gunnar Myrdal. In this way, I emphasized that Poland reflects features of the syndrome of a "soft state", whose presence was attributed by Myrdal to the states of the Third World, by perceiving the fundamental cause of the disaster of attempts at development. Notably, the term comes close to the definition of a "weak state" referred to by M. Ratajczak in this volume.

In my use of the term "soft state", it was a category describing a particularly low level of quality of governance, which gave rise to another term proposed by myself, namely, "institutionalized ir-responsibility", whose principal indications in the social, politica,l and administrative spheres were described by myself (in the work edited in cooperation with Mira Marody – Hausner, Marody 2001) as follows:

- Social ir-responsibility is: shifting the responsibility for the shape of social life to the state, while simultaneously the pursuit by entities and groups of the privatization of profits and announcing losses.
- Political ir-responsibility is: party-based colonization of the state apparatus, political clientelism, "indifference" of the political class with regard to the pathology of public life, acknowledgement by politicians of the right to "political rent", institutional corruption and the universality of quasi-public funds that are uncontrolled by the parliament.
- Administrative ir-responsibility is: administrative discretion, the lack of personal responsibility on the part of officials, the low quality of administrative decisions, low level of efficiency, and non-transparency of administrative procedures.

It is actually institutionalization of the perception of "ir-responsibility" that led to the creation of the syndrome of the "soft state". I have also underlined that exiting this syndrome will not be either autogenic, or easy as the "institutionalization of ir-responsibility" signifies the disappearance of the internal mechanisms of correcting policies, namely, the enhancement of the quality of governing.

Governance as a co-creation of institutional order

By way of conclusion, I would like to share a reflection that is also based on my own personal experiences in terms of conducting various public policies, particularly economic policies. In governing, we become systematic with regard to crisis situations or critical moments. Each situation of this kind consists of potentially multiple solutions, while also implying a range of different resolutions. The point here is that when making a choice, do we have a compass, or some profound vision of the institutional order or not? Thus, are we acting with the awareness of the rules that guide us, while also provide self-control, or are we guided by emotions or short-term impulses that give us the freedom of choice, yet also push us towards disorder? The choices previously made determine our possibilities to act in subsequent crisis situations (this is my perception of path dependency). Consequently, we have a gradual or greater, or even smaller basis of freedom and resources to react. If guided by some vision of institutional order, we can actually create this, then our possibilities of effective reaction increase, whereas if not, they become narrowed down and limited.

Creating the defined institutional order signifies the setting of the defined rules of procedure with regard to the actors participating in this. They are both bound and restricted by them, while simultaneously multiplying their resources, which in turn renders it possible and facilitates the solution of crisis situations. Weakening the institutional order means destruction of the normativeness, while also weakening communication and the ability to cooperate. Actors have more freedom of procedure, yet altogether their cooperation becomes more difficult, problematic, and significantly more costly. The possibilities of reacting to crisis situations become clearly lower.

When these possibilities become moot, then resolving crisis situations is a random situational balance of power, which is consequently less long-lasting, which in turn opens up opportunities for various types of quick fixes and pathological adjustments. These facilitate the functioning of organizations and actors, but create institutional dysfunctionality and lead to desystemization, namely, the erosion of order. If the scale of this process is significant, the consequence is the destruction of the constitutional order.

Hence, the national expectation with regard to the ruling party is that they can implement such segmental solutions as a reaction to critical moments, which by availing of the existing possibilities and resources would consequently lead to their multiplication on the scale of the social system. If they cannot do this, the chaotic action undertaken by them will in time lead to systemic blockades and the collapse of the particular order. Then its enactment as a new form is inevitable, while simultaneously essential and imposed. However, the social costs of such a formula of institutionalized change are very high, which consequently signifies civilizational retardation and peripheralization.

Thus, such an anachronism is the concept of building the power of the state by means of the implementation of the concept of the "technological sequence of power", which in its phraseology relates to the industrial organization from the era of mass production and the first factories of the Ford company. The appropriate reaction to the occurrence of the syndrome of the "soft state" is not the pursuit of monocontrol, forming monocentric order and strong arm government, but rather the formation of a heterarchical one, whose basis is that of "partnership management".

Instead of routine, repetition, and unreliability, this relates to innovativeness, while also the ability to adjust and participate. This is how modern economic organizations operate. In view of this fact, this is also how modern states should function. Otherwise, they lose the ability to regulate the economy and determine the course of development. They are powerless and become parasite organisms sucking on the resources and hindering growth.

As we are talking about the powerlessness of the ruling authorities, it is worth referring to the inspiring book by Jadwiga Staniszkis here (2006). The fundamental theme of Staniszkis is the acknowledgement that in contemporary times the political authorities must be perceived through the prism of the abilities of the political system to execute the strategic undertakings that lead to change in the institutional architecture of this system. In the case of economic policies, this signifies that its central issue is to conduct structural policies that initiate institutional change which is the prerequisite of competitive advantage over a long period of time. The role of the state in the economy involves the same fundamental element of resolving structural problems that create the institutional framework of the market, thus facilitating valorization for the participants and multiplication of its resources, as well as successive adjustments (restructuring).

Those who believe in the determinist power of the political authorities and the omnipotence of the state actually only lead to the fact that what is necessary becomes impossible, while simultaneously bringing about a systemic catastrophe. In order for what was impossible up to now to become probable, those in power must be capable of cooperation with a multitude of other actors by respecting their autonomy. This was written about in a convincing manner by M. Kassner (in this volume), by referring to the example of Hungary and Poland, in which the populist revolt led to questioning not only the market economy but also the constitutional democracy, while also the rule of law.

References

Campbell, J. L., & Pedersen, O. K. (Eds.) (1996). *Legacies of change: Transformations of post-communist European economies*. Transaction Publishers.

Eatwell, J. Ellman, M. J., Karlsson, M., Nuti, D. M., & Shapiro, J. (1995). *Transformation and integration: Shaping the future of Central and Eastern Europe*. Institute for Public Policy Research.

Grabher, G. (1994). Globalization, institutions and regional development in Europe. In: A. Amin and N. Thrift (eds.), *The disembedded regional economy: The transformation of East German industrial complexes into Western Enclaves*. Oxford: Oxford University Press.

Haggard, S., & Kaufman, R. R. (2018). *The political economy of democratic transitions*. Princeton University Press.

Hausner, J. (1992). *Populist threat in transformation of socialist society*. Polityka Ekonomiczna i Społeczna, no. 29. Warsaw: Friedrich Ebert Foundation.

Hausner, J. (1995a). Europe: Central and East. In: M. Mendell and K. Nielsen (eds.), *Contradictions and dilemmas in the development of post-socialist societies*. Montreal: Black Rose Books.

Hausner, J. (1995b). Imperative vs. interactive strategy of systemic change in Central and Eastern Europe. *Review of International Political Economy*, *2*(2), 249–266.
Hausner, J., Jessop, B., & Owsiak, S. (1993). The financial crisis of the post-socialist state: Principal causes and possible solutions in Poland. *International Journal of Political Economy*, *23*(2), 75–119.
Hausner, J., & Marody, M. (2001). *Polski talk show: dialog społeczny a integracja europejska. EU-monitoring V*. Kraków: Friedrich Ebert Stiftung, Małopolska Szkoła Administracji Publicznej AE w Krakowie.
Raiser, M. (1996). *Institutional developments during transition to a market economy*. Paper presented at UNU/WIDER Project Meeting "Transition Strategies, Alternatives and Outcomes", November 14–16, Helsinki.
Schumpeter, J. (1954).*Crisis of the tax state*. International Economic Papers, 4.
Staniszkis, J. (2006). *O władzy i bezsilności*. Kraków: Wydawnictwo Literackie.
Williamson, J. (1990). What Washington Means by Policy Reform. In: J. Williamson (ed.), *Latin American Adjustment: How Much Has Happened?* Institute for International Economics, Washington, 7–20.

Part I

Between institutions and policies – conceptual approaches

1 Institutionalization of economic policies in transition economies. Theoretical aspects and historical lessons

Maciej J. Grodzicki and Anna Zachorowska-Mazurkiewicz

1.1 Introduction

In the transition economies of Central and Eastern Europe (CEE), policymaking has been subject to profound shifts since at least the change of the political regime in 1989. Many of the key policies with respect to the economy were written anew. What was the nature and main directions of this evolution? What were the main drivers of policy fulfilment and factors influencing major policy choices? How does the historical context impact contemporary policy space? The focus in the volume is on the process of creating policies in diverse areas at the intersection of state and private sectors. The chapters in the presented collection are united by an institutional approach, according to which policies are perceived as the outcome of top-down design, yet filtered through social institutions inherited from the past.

CEE transition economies went through specific developments in the last several decades. After the Second World War, they were part of the Soviet bloc, which adopted the system of a command economy. In 1989, the process of the abrupt system transition from a centrally planned economy to a market one was implemented (Marangos 2004). The reform implied opening up the political monopoly of the ruling party and freeing the economy from state controls. The transition period was characterized by a very strong free market orientation, with its dimensions of deregulation, privatization, and growing economic openness. At the end of the last decade of the 20th century, some CEE countries started the process of the EU accession, which was completed in 2004. The forms of institutional integration into the EU, based on adopting peripheral positions, arguably determined further economic and political evolution, especially during and after the Global Financial Crisis (Gevorkyan 2018; Iwasaki 2020; Kozarzewski 2021). Contemporary assessments of this economic and institutional evolution range from the alarming threats of populist dependencies to optimistic appraisals of a "development miracle" (Piątkowski 2018; Bałtowski, Kozarzewski, & Mickiewicz 2022).

All these circumstances impact the current governmental policy choices in diverse socioeconomic areas, which may often appear as unexpected or chaotic. Such is the case of the recent populist shifts in some of the CEE economies, which, however, can be perceived as being embedded in the historical political economies of the region (Bohle & Greskovits 2019; Bluhm & Varga 2020). One could argue

DOI: 10.4324/9781003425717-2

that the political economy of CEEs is in a constant flux. Thus, the main objective of the monograph is to illustrate the historical and institutional embeddedness of contemporary policy choices in CEE economies, with the highlighted aspects of continuity and change.

The theoretical background of this volume is one of institutionalism. Thorstein Veblen presented a link between the central role given to institutions and the evolutionary approach that focuses on the process of economic change (e.g. Veblen 1898). In this perspective, the society in general and the economy in particular were evolutionary groupings of institutions. Institutions are derived from the past and are inherited from the past (Chavance 2009, pp. 10–11). Thus, institutionalists view society from a 'processual' perspective, in which social systems are perceived as dynamic, ever-developing entities, while all social activities occur in historical time and are accompanied by uncertainty regarding the future.

An important source of inspiration for the considerations in the volume lies in the thought of Karl Polanyi (Polanyi 2001 [1944]). Here, the socio-economic transformation in CEE countries may be perceived through the prism of the requirements of capital accumulation, which in turn leads to interrelated processes of commodification, privatization, and alienation. However, the expansion of markets and the growing disembeddedness of the economy from its social and environmental foundations leads to recurring crises when diverse social forces of the so-called counter-movement gain in significance (Fraser 2017; Kentikelenis 2018). Following other accounts of contemporary economies (Blyth 2002; Aulenbacher et al. 2019; Hann 2019), the Polanyian framework sheds light on the mechanisms and outcomes of the subsequent waves of institutional change in transition economies.

The proposed volume merges broad conceptual contributions with detailed historical and empirical analysis of the contemporary economies of CEE countries, mainly Poland. It consists of chapters analysing the selected sectors of the economy and policies availed of by the authorities. In the monograph, the analysis of contemporary policies and problems associated with them are put into institutional and historical contexts. The analysis presented in the volume will facilitate the observation of longue-durée patterns of institutional framework in Poland and some other CEE countries, as well as the endogeneity of certain changes (rather than mere shocks), while also their inertia, which often leads to unexpected consequences of the policies designed. It is divided into four sections covering the following topics: broad conceptual views of transition towards the market economy; involvement of organized interests into institutional change and policies; the role of formal institutional frameworks for policymaking; and also the specific case studies.

The introductory chapter discusses the contributions of the whole volume to the ongoing debates on transition economies. However, its main objective is to present the main categories and concepts of institutional economics which are essential to the analysis of transition and policymaking. Herein, four major recurring motives that are covered by the diverse chapters may be identified as follows:

1 The central, yet not unambiguous role of the state and its agencies.
2 Tensions and complementarities between formal and informal institutions in the course of policymaking.

3 The nature of radical institutional change, and the long-lasting effects of market transition for public policies.
4 The discussion on the factors of institutional continuity and path dependence in policymaking.

1.2 Theoretical understanding of institutions

Systemic transition in CEE was first and foremost a profound institutional change, followed by a cultural and economic one. Most formal rules and policies regulating the national economies in the region were radically redefined, while new market-promoting institutions replaced the old scheme of command and order that involved state-centred ones. This ignited a long co-evolution of policies, productive structures, while also informal norms, which is why the presented volume adopts an approach of institutional economics.

An institution is a cluster of social usages that designates the way of thought or action of some prevalence and permanence, which is embedded in the habit of a group or the customs of people (Hamilton 1932). Institutions are durable systems of established and embedded social rules and conventions that structure social interactions. They create stable expectations of the behaviour of others, since institutions enable ordered thought and action by imposing the form and consistency of human activities. Institutions are understood to be relatively uniform patterns of thought and action, namely, they are forms of human behaviour regarding other people in specific social situations (Kapp 2011, p. 50). Institutions do not stand alone in the group of individuals involved as they depend on individuals for their very existence, while also on their interactions and particular shared patterns of thought (Hodgson 2006, p. 7). However, institutions are not composed of individuals, but of behavioural patterns (Bush 2008, p. 161).

Seumas Miller (2011) offers an important distinction between atomistic and a structural-functionalist approach to institutions which is traceable in the afore-mentioned definitions (see also: Dai 2015). On the one hand, there are norms, conventions, and patterns which refer to individual behaviour. They constitute human life, namely, the way people think and act, pursue their goals, and gain their status in society. When aggregated, these "atomistic" elements may form complex systems coordinating human actions. In the presented volume, Gruszewska and Trzaska point at the role of diverse informal norms that jointly generate social trust, in terms of constituting entrepreneurship and innovativeness in Poland.

On the other hand, institutions are structures which consist of some set of interrelated rules and contribute to the construction of larger social entities, such as the state or society itself. These structures have logic of their own and are not reducible to simple human actions and preferences. Moreover, they tend to create social roles that need to be filled by individuals following specific norms and rules. Therefore, individual behaviour is often induced from the outside by society or a collective, even if there is the impression of making an individual decision. In her chapter, Katarzyna Kamińska writes about such a case. She analyses the competition policy and consumer protection in Poland and concludes that the development of strict regulations and strong policy bodies in this area facilitated shaping the market economy in Poland.

This dual view of institutions is valuable in interpreting tensions which appear between individuals and institutional structures, as well as in explaining how institutions evolve. A particular institution can be perceived through both viewpoints, namely, atomistic and structural-functionalist (Czech & Zachorowska-Mazurkiewicz 2020). An individual will evaluate a certain rule of behaviour through her/his own system of preferences and values. If the rule is beneficial both for this person and for the system itself, there is no reason why it should not be followed. However, if the rule is imposed on this person externally and is linked to certain costs, she/he is inclined to disobey the rule unless she/he acknowledges how the rule corresponds with other systemic goals or the coercion measures are effective enough for the rule to work. Thus, some institutions may be important for the functioning of a system, yet are rejected or criticized by individuals on various grounds. This conflict may either lead to silent contestation of certain norms and regulations, or outright attempts to change the rules of the game unless some other measures are taken to increase their legitimization and stability. As elaborated below, it shall be of particular importance to the evaluation of policymaking, i.e., organized, and purposeful actions of state and its diverse agencies, with influence over private actors, be it individuals, businesses, or entire social classes.

The philosophy of science that institutionalists employ is realistic, materialistic, pragmatic, and policy-oriented (O'Hara 2019, p. 172). It seeks to understand the world as it exists and as it has evolved and changed, while keeping "close to the ground", and trying to generalize about the structure and dynamics of real social economies evolving through historical time. It essentially tries to comprehend the changing ways of life that groups of people operate within economic systems to solve problems of production, distribution, exchange, and socio-economic reproduction. This generates a broad view of institutional-evolutionary trends, starting with the principle of historical specificity and evolution, where every serious problem or topic is required to be embedded in an historical inquiry. Economic life is the product of multiple determinations, since the economy is socially and culturally embedded, as well as being time and space bound. Ontologically speaking, economic complexity presupposes variety and multi-layering of influence (Amin & Hausner 1997).

According to Veblen, "institutions are products of the process of the past, which are adapted to past circumstances and are therefore never in full accord with the requirements of the present" (Veblen 1899, p. 126 cited by Chavance 2009, p. 11). Thus, historical factors undoubtedly help to explain the economy of today. Short-term changes are possible when they are compatible with a range of broad institutional constraints. Long-term change, on the contrary, involves the elimination of at least some of these constraints (Ramazzotti 2020a, p. 364). At the same time, in the long run and the short run concepts for mental experiments may be useful, but, as far as institutional change is concerned, they may be misleading

(Ramazzotti 2020a, p. 365). To properly understand the economy, one must take account of its historical and institutional context. Economic policy may change a historical-institutional context, as well as economic interaction itself (Ramazzotti 2021, p. 497). Economic inquiry should not be restricted to the understanding of the economy as it is, but, in so far as it needs to be a guidance for economic policy, it should try to envisage what change is possible. This involves considering not only how structural and institutional circumstances are likely to change over time due to historical and strictly economic circumstances. It also includes understanding how culture and identities may change because of economic policy, thereby affecting behavioural and economic outcomes.

According to Phillip A. O'Hara (2019, p. 172), the principle of the nexus between the system, institutions, habits, and also individuals links several levels of analysis to form a multilayered framework, while the principle of circular and cumulative causation includes the notion of interdependency between spheres and the amplified impact of changes. At the most general level, there is the world with its geopolitical environment, then at a lower level of capitalism as a system of production and distribution, while the microeconomic environment at an even lower level and individual human beings at the lowest level, who exhibit various habits of thought and behaviour (O'Hara 2019, p. 175, based on Veblen (1899, 1917, 1919)). These levels are all interconnected. Veblen pointed that it is essential to situate national forms of capitalism in a geopolitical, social, and environmental setting, with the focus on the dominant institutions, and how the individuals through groups link into this fabric. The core for Veblen was that these institutions evolve through historical time, and that their changing form must be comprehended in different historical contexts (O'Hara 2019, p. 175). The micro elements of the social economy (individuals, small groups) impact on the meso elements (sectors, institutions, and organizations), which in turn affect the macro and global elements (nations, global system), while reverse causation also occurs as the macro and global constituents impact on the meso and micro levels, and the meso also impacts on the micro (p. 176).

This evolutionary and emergent approach allows us to highlight the complexities embedded in diverse public policies. Interactions between different levels and spheres of society, including a cultural one, mean that there is no easy translation of the declared policy aims into actual outcomes. This observation was evident in the historical studies of institutional transformations by Karl Polanyi (1944), as well as his followers (Blyth 2002; Hann 2019). Social systems are perceived here as diversified and pluralist in terms of formal rules, while also informal ideas, norms, and values. Legal norms, regulations, and other instruments enacted by the government are only a subset of this entirety, while other social actors such as communities, trade unions, and business organizations may pursue and cultivate their own ones. Historically speaking, it often took on forms of counter-movements against the dominant course of market-oriented policymaking. The identification of such conflicts (potentially leading to contradictions and crises) is vital to properly understand institutional change.

1.3 Central and complex position of the state

The transition in CEE has been a broad and multi-dimensional process, affecting most social and economic relations, including the productive structures, industrial relations, and cultures. One of the spheres that has been affected most strongly by these changes was the state itself. However, the state has also been the only endogenous institutional nexus in the region that has been able to integrate diverse resources and govern complex processes (foreign capital being the dominant, yet exogenous one). In turn, we propose an insight from the perspective of the state in this volume.

The state may be perceived as a meta-institution in the broader institutional order. It means it has a pivotal directive and integrative role in relation to other institutions and their inter-relationships, even though the government is in itself simply one institution within a larger society (Miller 2011). It is, however, an actor with an extraordinary scope of agency, while also the power to influence other actors, as well as the entire spheres of social relations, including markets. This influence is practically organized into diverse policies, with their respective spheres, aims, and tools. Notably, policies can be at times perceived as institutions as well, in particular when they are stable and lasting. Yet, usually they are more flexible, open, and subject to sudden changes than other higher-level institutions, be it formal (constitutional rules or international regulations) or informal ones (prevailing ideas and cultural customs) (Rose 1990; Pierson 1993).

Agency does not mean state officials can act as they wish or that their actions can be perceived as fully exogenous with respect to the society and markets. In practice, these three large spheres are blended and intertwined with each other by dense networks of social and political relations. Diverse institutional arrangements within and outside the state constitute both capacities and constraints for policymakers. They span the legal systems, internal organization and bureaucratic capacity of state agencies, arrangement of major interest groups, as well as the rules of the international division of labour. The state itself is a sphere of politics and a forum for the interactions of diverse interests and ideas (Hausner & Możdżeń 2020). In this volume, Črt Kostevc and Tjasa Redek demonstrate that the government is only one of the actors of governance, and only by seeing other actors and different dimensions can we assess the effectiveness of policymaking.

Ramazzotti (2020b, pp. 140–141) presents two visions of the link between the policies and economy and society. In the first one, in the mainstream the economy is viewed as a closed system governed by its laws. Policy acts upon those laws exogenously, which is independent of any feedback of the economy on the policy itself. Policy outcomes are the result of the linear causation process (Ramazzotti 2020b, p. 139). Contrary to the mainstream, heterodox approaches stress that the economy is systematically open. Its coordination depends on historically determined circumstances, including the spheres of deliberation, and feedback on its outcomes as to how society is organized (Hausner, Możdżeń & Oramus 2021). Institutional economics consider the economy to be an open system that derives its organizing principles and dynamics from a larger, institutionalized whole, with which it is connected, and from which it derives its major impulses, which in turn are influenced by the economy (Kapp 2011, p. 17).

This has two implications (Ramazzotti 2020a, p. 364). First, a possible policy depends on the constraints arising from the existing institutional and cultural context and the time that it may take for that context to change. This is well illustrated by the chapter by Sahiti in which the author compares entrepreneurship policies in chosen economies in transition within and outside of the European Union and concludes that bureaucratic capacity and other nationwide institutions largely determine the quality of policymaking. Second, changes in that context affect both the institutional conditions for change and what people deem to be appropriate. Sarolta Somasi writes about this in her chapter in the context of energy policy in Hungary, where the shift in the national political regime resulted in averted goals and policy tools.

Early on in the mid-1990s, Amin and Hausner (1997, p. 22) wrote that in the wake of the collapse of the socialist system, the societies of CEE found themselves in a "systemic vacuum". To fill this vacuum, the formation of the state was required, and the state was formed in the course of negotiations and agreements between system representatives. Negotiations between such representatives had a double significance: on the one hand, they created an institutional framework and market rules, allowing particular economic projects to be realized (the meso and micro level), while, on the other hand, they used the resulting arrangements as a basis for defining and implementing a specific strategy to shape the economic system, thereby "building up" the state (the macro level). Notably, the resulting, newly transformed post-socialist economies were called "mutants" which were inconsistent with either the starting or the target model of the transition, but deeply embedded in their Soviet past (Amin & Hausner 1997, pp. 22–23).

This ambiguous and contradictory view of the post-socialist state is reflected in the transition economies under investigation in several chapters in the volume. The state as an institution has been subject to profound restructurings which consisted of a revolution of its main functions and forms of intervention. Central planning and direct oversight over production and social provisioning gave way to more indirect and implicit forms of governance of markets, as in the cases of product market regulation (See: the chapter by Renata Śliwa) or competition policy in Poland (Katarzyna Kamińska). In both these cases, high-level legal norms (constitution, EU regulations) provide a necessary balance between the authority of government agencies over the private sector, as well as a constraint for government opportunism. This means that the state evolved rather than withdrew from its intervention in the economy.

Nonetheless, the neoliberal mode of socioeconomic transition, motivated ideologically or by major internal and foreign business interests, led to the phenomenon of the so-called weak state (See: the chapter by Ratajczak). This formation was visible perhaps most strikingly in Ukraine, where weak institutions paved way for cronyism and multiple problems with the privatization of state-owned enterprises (Pogorelov and Polishchuk). Other vital examples are the energy policy in Hungary (Somosi) and the pension policy in Poland (Ząbkowicz). In both cases, foreign financial capital and domestic oligarchies went into a coalition with a weak, indebted state, while other social forces were not able to form an effective counter-movement. As a result, large rents were captured by narrow groups of vested interests. However, Marek Ratajczak and Sarolta Somosi demonstrate that the political processes in Poland and Hungary have brought the state to the fore again. This so-called neostatism is a patchwork formation that merges old Soviet institutions with new neoliberal ones with populist tendencies.

1.4 Co-evolution of formal and informal institutions

The relationship between institutions and political solutions in the transition economies might be also considered differently when we move beyond the state. Policymakers had direct control over formal institutions, which were designed and introduced into the legislative process. These, however, were often incompatible with the dominant informal institutions, which have sources in the culture and history of CEE societies. Institutional change was often radical and abrupt, rather than evolutionary and incremental (in particular in the early 1990s). In turn, the distinction between formal and informal institutions becomes essential in order to understand the dynamics and efficacy of policymaking in this region.

Helmke and Levitsky (2004, p. 728) specified four basic types of interactions between formal and informal institutions as follows: complementarity, substitution, accommodation, and competition, with various consequences for the effectiveness of policymaking (cf. Acemoglu, Johnson, & Robinson 2005; Voigt 2013; Grodzicki 2016).

Complementarity and substitution occur when formal regulations are consistent with informal institutions. In such a manner both types of institutions are compatible in terms of reinforcing each other. In the former case, informal rules enhance the effectiveness of formal regulations. In the latter one, informal institutions "fill in the gap" created by ineffective formal rules. In other words, if formal institutions fail for various reasons, they will be replaced by the activity of informal norms and rules (Helmke & Levitsky 2004, pp. 728–729; Voigt 2013).

The case of discrepancies between the formal and informal rules is more complicated. According to Stefano Fiori (2002), an inconsistency or even a conflict between informal customs and formal norms might erupt due to the fact that the two evolve in different timelines, with the latter one changing much faster. The outcome of such a clash is difficult to predict (Lissowska 2017, p. 119). According to Helmke and Levitsky (2004), there are two scenarios presented as follows: accommodation and competition. In the former, the informal rules create incentives to alter the effects of formal regulations, without violating them. In this case, the adjustment between institutions is possible, albeit it requires the passage of time, which results in a gradual, non-radical reform. The former scenario corresponds with the most dysfunctional type – a conflict between formal and informal rules. The risk of its occurrence increases especially in the case of radical reforms. In this scenario, the following rule means violating the other one. Thus, the society may not agree on a new institutional order and continue to act in accordance with the informal regulations. This means the failure of reforms and a high degree of uncertainty about the final social results (Helmke & Levitsky 2004, p. 729; Spranz, Lenger, & Goldschmidt 2012).

The transition period created special tensions in the process of institutional change. Formal rules changed abruptly, creating a lot of uncertainty and inconsistency with the informal rules shared by the society (Lissowska 2017, p. 122). In particular, the newly introduced market ties of competition, and provisioning based on privately owned means of production were met with suspicion, if not rejection by large sections of the societies. The transition of the 1990s resulted in growing instability, inequalities, and a decline in economic performance. Altogether, the experience of post-socialist states has made it clear that institutions do not change overnight and that national systems of policies need to evolve steadily in local cultural and political conditions (Voigt & Engerer 2002, p. 155; Dai 2015).

Such inconsistencies and negative effects have also been identified by the authors in the presented volume. According to Ratajczak, the differences between two cultures and institutional subsystems are still visible, while the transition is ongoing and incomplete. This co-existence of post-Soviet, state-centred forms of social functioning with capitalist, market-oriented ones, results in a chaotic, "patchwork" institutional order, in which policymakers attempt to realize diverse goals at once. Arguably, such co-existences appear in most contemporary market economies. However, the radical and chaotic nature of transition accentuated the competitive nature of both institutional subsystems, with many negative social and economic outcomes. New policy approaches were often copied automatically from the experiences of high-income economies of Western Europe, without the required adjustments to the historical and economic context of CEE periphery, as in the case of pension and innovation policies. Other scholars argue that the Polish cultural and institutional order fails to provide cohesion, equity (Koronowski), and social trust (Trzaska and Gruszewska). Such values, missing in the simplified rulebooks of market transition, are however essential for the proper functioning of market society, in order to ignite creativity and the high utilization of economic resources.

It is, however, Maciej Kassner who most evocatively argues in his chapter that transition in CEE was in fact a clash of different systems of values. He writes that:

> (…) the term market transformation refers to the change from an economy organized around the principles of redistribution or reciprocity to an economy where the market system becomes the primary form of institutional coordination of productive activities. (…) Market transformation is much more than a simple package of economic reforms such as price liberalization, privatization, and macro-economic stabilization. It affects the entire culture of a transformed society and has profound effects on the life worlds of ordinary people. The ability to cope with such disruptive social change depends on the material and symbolic resources people have at their disposal.
>
> (Kassner 2024, this volume)

This sheds new light on the persistence of cultural traits often coined "post-Soviet", such as life stability, solidarity, collaboration, or reliance on states and communities. Instead of barriers for capitalist development, they should be treated as vital for cultural and social endurance, especially for social classes marginalized during the course of state withdrawal and market expansion. It also allows for an assessment of reforms and policies introduced since the 1990s, which are vastly different from conventional ones, based on EBRD transition indicators or the Heritage Foundation's Index of Economic Freedom. Discrepancies with free market or business ideals should not be perceived as a policy failure, but rather as the prevalence of other norms and values.

1.5 Power struggles over the shape of policies

The relationship between formal and informal rules can also be perceived in terms of diverse interest groups, as well as their goals and values. This is most visible in the conflicting scenario when directions of policymaking clash with the prevailing social expectations, at least in the case of some social classes and economic sectors. Systemic transition in CEE countries resulted in many such clashes, in particular between the new market rules and the economic position of the working class, namely, its agency, incomes, and employment opportunities. Historical studies of this period documented massive social frustration and anger with the shape of transition, while also the distribution of its costs. These emotions, often realized in the form of strikes and protests, were however ignored by the political leaders (Kowalik 2012; Ost 2019). Hence, to properly explain the nature and sources of institutional change in CEE, we need to turn towards the category of power blocks and their evolution.

New formal institutions and policies do not need to be beneficial for the society as a whole. They could bring benefits only to individuals enjoying the position of power, thus weakening the social legitimization for the change. New formal rules are quite often not supported by society and become a battlefield between interest groups that benefit from them and the ones that lose out (Lissowska 2017, p. 121). Thus, institutional change becomes a question of political power, skills of persuasion, civic legitimacy, and social response.

Voigt and Engerer (2002) considered the link between institutions and transformation. They claim that institutional change and the establishment of the rules of the game of the market economy were seen as preconditions for the economic reforms programme, rather than as the centrepiece of it. It was assumed that the institutions of market economy could be established rapidly, as virtual copies of the Western order. They point out that the social acceptance or the appropriate match for the existing internal institutions was not an issue (p. 153). Even though there were two approaches to the transition, namely, the shock therapy introduced in Poland, with followers like Czechoslovakia and Bulgaria, and gradualism in Romania, Slovenia, and Hungary, in which both failed to offer a concrete process of institutional development (Marangos 2004).

Building up on the empirical contributions in the presented volume, policymaking may be perceived as a mechanism of radical institutional change in a broad sense. Transition in CEE introduced a specific type of political economy regime, namely, a dependent market economy (Nölke & Vliegenthart 2009). This meant the adoption of a peripheral position in the European division of labour, while internally it promoted neoliberal rules of liberalized markets, including the labour regulations (cf. Ratajczak & Koronowski – in this volume). The historical process of their introduction in practice consisted of several policies which transformed the respective spheres of social and economic life. They belonged to the same large ideational programme, yet each of them can be analysed separately to highlight specific factors that were relevant to the rivalry over policy goals and tools.

On the one hand, a view emerges that since the early 1990s policymaking has been largely subordinated to the interests of large capital, mostly of international origin. Such was the case of the pension reform in Poland described by A. Ząbkowicz, as well as the energy policy in Hungary in the description by S. Somosi. In the former case, foreign financial institutions were able to propose dominant ideas over the preferred policy direction in the form of funded pension schemes. In the latter one, the state guaranteed supplies of cheap energy to the industry and in that way supported the objectives of cost competitiveness, arguably relevant for the Hungarian export-oriented and FDI-based growth model.

On the other hand, there were exceptions to this pattern, which suggests that both state and social actors, apart from capital ones, are able to preserve some scope of agency and influence over policy directions. Renata Śliwa presents in her chapter the ongoing struggle between state and private companies over the shape of regulations of the telecommunications sector. The Polish government decided to privatize this industry, which has some characteristics of a natural monopoly. However, it maintained a substantial control over its functioning in terms of infrastructure and price setting. Similarly, the afore-mentioned energy policy in Hungary after a long period of submission to the goals of cost competitiveness was subject to a shift towards the social availability of energy, while also the inclusion of the perspective of households.

1.6 Mechanisms of path dependence and institutional lock-in

Finally, the past few decades in Poland and other CEE countries were not only distinguishable by radical shifts and institutional changes but also by long periods of continuity, during which major patterns of policymaking were stable. These were the times when mechanisms of institutional inertia and political and economic path dependence dominated over the will of decedents and agency to change (Lissowska 2017, p. 119). Initial choices at the beginning of the transition, in particular the quick liberalization of markets and the turn of direction towards economic openness, largely determined the further routes of development (Berend 2009; Kowalik 2012). This led to a sort of an institutional lock-in at the dependent modality of policymaking (Nölke & Vliegenthart 2009), thus leading to a pattern termed by Hausner and his co-authors as "a developmental drift" (Geodecki et al. 2012).

Such a phenomenon is widely described in institutional economics, probably most famously by the varieties of the capitalist approach (Hall & Soskice 2001), which perceives certain settings of the political economy as stable equilibria, due to its functionality for major actors, in particular the entrepreneurial sector and its international competitiveness. However, the overall evidence presented in this volume leads to a different sort of explanation, based on specific historical dynamics, in which diverse interests and ideas interact with each other that sometimes guarantee stability, while in other cases ignite abrupt change. This comes close to the reasoning of historical institutionalism, while also the concept of path dependence in politics and economics (Arthur 1994; Pierson 2000).

According to Pierson (2000), the mechanisms of increasing returns, which are well-established in economics, are also pervasive in politics. A policy regime – once legislated – has a tendency to stabilize, while the costs of switching to another regime grow in time. This trend is derived from a number of positive feedbacks within the sphere of state and politics, but also within economic structures and technologies. These include institutional complexity and power asymmetries of politics, weak mechanisms of learning, while also short-termism and the ideational stubbornness of policymakers. Altogether, it means that there is a lot of inertia and the preliminary choices of key formal institutions and policy traditions matter, since they function as the effective constraints to later policy choices.

In a similar vein, Howard Sherman (2003) identifies two sources of resistance to change. The first which he associates with David Hamilton (1970) and other institutionalists whom he labels "conservative" are those of myth, ignorance, and suspicion, which may be counteracted by education. The other – for which he credits Veblen, Dugger, and other "radical" institutionalists – refers to the use of power and influence by vested interests to protect their socio-economic status. Albeit, Sherman implies that these factors are mutually exclusive, they may work together to impede change by perpetuating the current cultural norms (Zalewski 2020, p. 298).

Elites may exploit the uncertainty that often arises in societies experiencing fundamental transformations by using propaganda and other forms of persuasion to reinforce or perhaps even establish nostalgic myths (Zalewski 2020, p. 298). Policymakers may reflect the vested interests or the interpretative frameworks that defend those interests. Similarly, the extant shared knowledge framework may preclude people from envisaging change. There is apparently no way to predict what path society may eventually follow (Ramazzotti 2007, p. 776).

Empirical studies of public policies in the presented volume provide detailed evidence of such mechanisms in transition economies. A positive example, according to Kamińska, is the policy of competition and customer protection in Poland, organized on the basis of strong ordoliberal ideas and constitutional norms. In particular, the latter ones which were already introduced in 1997, favoured strong anti-monopoly policy that was independent of partisan influence. On the more critical side, the authors observe substantial barriers to the quality of innovation (Trzaska and Gruszewska) and energy policy (Somosi), related to the phenomenon of a weak and dependent state. Other cases are more ambiguous and highlight the essential positive feedbacks between the capacity of state and its bureaucracy, while also the broad economic structures. Comparative studies by Satihi, Kostevc, and Redek demonstrate that strong bilateral ties exist between high-level political and macroeconomic factors, while also the efficacy of the respective entrepreneurial policy and intangible government investment.

However, this co-evolution of institutional frameworks, individual policies, and economic structures is indeterminate and there are certain limits to the mechanisms increasing returns and path dependence. The described cases also identify the phenomena of negative feedbacks and aggravated contradictions. These in time facilitate shifts in power relations in a dialectical manner. Dependent development and reliance on EU funds and regulations facilitates a slow, yet steady build-up of state capacity, as well as the upgrading of industrial structures. This in turn facilitates substantial improvements or even sovereign shifts in certain policies, such as entrepreneurial and energy ones. Such a perspective helps to explain the radical shift to neostatism observed in Poland and Hungary, while also analysed in the chapter by Ratajczak. Its new active policies of ownership (related to state-owned enterprises) were possible thanks to the utilization of certain traits hidden in the institutional framework of the past, but also due to the unsolved contradictions of the previous neoliberal regime.

1.7 Conclusions

The presented volume delivers a detailed, historical description of policy conduct in the transition economies of CEE region in recent decades. Likewise, it is meant to contribute to answering more general questions about the nature of policy evolution, while also its main drivers, and the ways the historical context impacts contemporary policy space. As stated by Możdżeń and Hausner (2020, p. 50), *the problem with the present time is that we live in a "post" period, in which the old does not work well anymore, but the new has yet to manifest itself clearly*. Since the transition period has been of a similar nature, the lessons drawn from this time seem to be indispensable.

The emerging picture is first of all one of an ongoing co-evolution of broad institutional frameworks, informal cultures, productive structures, and specific governmental policies. In this way, the historical choices of institutional change undertaken in the late 1980s and early 1990s still influence policymaking, either as direct constraints for policy choices or as more implicit determinants of games of interests, cultural evolution, or economic outcomes. For some authors, this is a sign of an incomplete ongoing transition, whereas for others this represents multiple transitions. Perhaps the best denomination is one of largely path-dependent processes (where initial choices matter, while positive feedbacks and continuity prevail), yet also indeterminate, open, and dialectic ones (where diverse negative feedbacks reveal hidden contradictions).

Second, it is a picture of a complex and internally diversified institutional order, whereby only one segment relates to the formal norms and official policies of the state. These always interact with the prevailing informal norms and ideas, resulting in dynamic and uncertain economic and political outcomes. The transition was, among others, a period of such an institutional clash, when new market rules stood in contradiction with the former norms of solidarity and collaboration. What is important to note is the fact that such normative clashes often coincide with conflicts of material interests and antagonism of social classes or other power blocks. In the recent history of the CEE region, it was particularly the conflict between the working class and capital, but also tensions between the diverse fractions of capital (including the financial and foreign ones), while also between the state and segments of the private sector. The proliferation of market relations had an asymmetric impact on these actors, with some of them losing their status and power (at least for the time being). Nevertheless, other modes of coordination and provisioning prevailed within the state and its policies, and one should still acknowledge the relevance of values other than market and business-friendly ones, such as social cohesion, economic democracy, and security.

Third, the state matters. Despite numerous theses of the state withering away or explicit claims for a government withdrawal from the economy, it still remains an exceptional institution, with the agency to mobilize resources and to constitute a governance and deliberation nexus for diverse interests and ideas. The CEE countries, though long perceived as dependent on and coordinated by foreign capital, are vital examples of the ongoing importance of the state and its policies, in order to frame, govern, and coordinate markets and private actors. Recent policy shifts in countries such as Poland or Hungary, even if often only partially effective, unprogressive, or politically conflicting, provide evidence of this agency in the globalized world.

References

Acemoglu, D., S. Johnson, and J.A. Robinson (2005). Institutions as the fundamental cause of long-run growth. In: P. Aghion and S. N. Durlauf (Eds.) *Handbook of Economic Growth, 1*, Amsterdam: Elsevier (pp. 385–472), 10.1016/S1574-0684(05)01006-3

Amin, A., and J. Hausner. (1997). Interactive governance and social complexity. In: A. Amin and J. Hausner (Eds.) *Beyond Market and Hierarchy* (pp. 1–31). Cheltenham: Edward Elgar. https://doi.org/10.4337/9781035303410.00008

Arthur, W.B. (1994). *Increasing Returns and Path Dependence in the Economy*. Ann Arbor: The University of Michigan Press. https://doi.org/10.3998/mpub.10029

Aulenbacher, B., R. Bärnthaler, and A. Novy. (2019). Karl Polanyi, the great transformation, and contemporary capitalism. *Österreichische Zeitschrift für Soziologie*, *44*, 105–113. https://doi.org/10.1007/s11614-019-00341-8

Bałtowski, M., P. Kozarzewski, and T. Mickiewicz. (2022). State capitalism in Poland and Hungary: Populist varieties. In: M. Wright, G.T. Wood, A. Cuervo-Cazurra, P. Sun, I. Okhmatovskiy, and A. Grosman (Eds.) *The Oxford Handbook of State Capitalism and the Firm*. Oxford: University Press (pp. 750–784). https://doi.org/10.1093/oxfordhb/9780198837367.013.33

Berend, T.I. (2009). *From the Soviet Bloc to the European Union: The Economic and Social Transformation of Central and Eastern Europe Since 1973*. Cambridge, UK: Cambridge University Press.

Bluhm, K., and M. Varga. (2020). Conservative developmental statism in East Central Europe and Russia. *New Political Economy*, *25*(4), 642–659. https://doi.org/10.1080/13563467.2019.1639146

Blyth, M. (2002). *Great Transformations: Economic Ideas and Institutional Change in the Twentieth Century*. Cambridge University Press.

Bohle, D., and B. Greskovits. (2019). Politicising embedded neoliberalism: Continuity and change in Hungary's development model. *West European Politics*, *42*(5), 1069–1093. https://doi.org/10.1080/01402382.2018.1511958

Bush, P.D. (2008). Culture, values and institutions. In: J. B. Davis, and W. Dolfsma (Eds.) *The Elgar Companion to Social Economics* (pp. 153–170). Cheltenham: Edward Elgar.

Chavance, B. (2009). *Institutional Economics*. London, New York: Routledge.

Czech, S., and A. Zachorowska-Mazurkiewicz. (2020). Institutional approach to gender bias in old age security systems: Comparative analysis of Swedish and Polish pension reforms. *Journal of Economic Issues*, *54*(3), 755–771. https://doi.org/10.1080/00213624.2020.1787050.

Dai, S. (2015). *Networks of Institutions: Institutional Emergence, Social Structure and National Systems of Policies* (Vol. 1). London and New York: Routledge. https://doi.org/10.4324/9781315796109

Fiori, S. (2002) Alternative Visions of Change in Douglass North's New Institutionalism, *Journal of Economic Issues*, 36 (4), 1025–1043. 10.1080/00213624.2002.11506534

Fraser, N. (2017). A triple movement? Parsing the politics of crisis after Polanyi. *Beyond Neoliberalism: Social Analysis after 1989*, 29–42.

Geodecki, T., G. Gorzelak, J. Górniak, J. Hausner, S. Mazur, J. Szlachta, and J. Zaleski. (2012). *Kurs na innowacje. Jak wyprowadzić Polskę z rozwojowego dryfu*. Kraków: Fundacja Gospodarki i Administracji Publicznej.

Gevorkyan, A.V. (2018). *Transition Economies: Transformation, Development, and Society in Eastern Europe and the Former Soviet Union*. London and New York: Routledge. https://doi.org/10.4324/9781315736747

Grodzicki, M.J. (2016). Construction of the development strategy versus informal constraints. *Jagiellonian Journal of Management*, 2 (1), 21–33, 10.4467/2450114XJJM.16.002.5323

Hall, P.A., and D. Soskice. (Eds.) (2001). *Varieties of Capitalism: The Institutional Foundations of Comparative Advantage*. Oxford: Oxford University Press. https://doi.org/10.1093/0199247757.003.0001

Hann, C. (2019). *Repatriating Polanyi: Market society in the Visegrád states*. Central European University Press.

Hamilton, D. (1970). *Evolutionary Economics: A Study of Change in Economic Thought*. Albuquerque, NM: University of New Mexico Press.

Hamilton, W. H. (1932). Institution. In: E. R. A. Seligman and A. Johnson (Eds.) *Encyclopedia of the Social Sciences* (vol. VIII, 84–89). New York: Macmillan.

Hausner, J., M. Możdżeń, and M. Oramus. (2021). Fragility of social and economic systems and the role of "modality". *Journal of Economic Issues*, *55*(4), 1118–1138. https://doi.org/10.1080/00213624.2021.1994790

Helmke, G., and S. Levitsky. (2004). Informal institutions and comparative politics: A research agenda. *Perspectives on Politics*, *2*(4), 725–740. https://doi.org/10.1017/S1537592704040472

Hodgson, G. H. (2006). What Ara Institutions? *Journal of Economic Issues*, 40 (1), 1–25. 10.1080/00213624.2006.11506879

Iwasaki, I. (Ed.) (2020). *The Economics of Transition: Developing and Reforming Emerging Economies*. London and New York: Routledge. https://doi.org/10.4324/9780429264979

Kapp, K.W. (2011).*The Foundations of Institutional Economics*. London, New York: Routledge. https://doi.org/10.4324/9780203827864

Kentikelenis, A.E. (2018). The social aftermath of economic disaster: Karl Polanyi, countermovements in action, and the Greek crisis. *Socio-Economic Review*, 16 (1), 39–59.
Kowalik, T. (2012). *From Solidarity to Sellout*. New York: Monthly Review Press.
Kozarzewski, P. (2021). *State Corporate Control in Transition*. Cham, Switzerland: Palgrave Macmillan. https://doi.org/10.1007/978-3-030-78562-8
Lissowska, M. (2017).Instytucje a polityka gospodarcza. In: J. Stacewicz (Ed.) *Perspektywy polityki gospodarczej* (pp. 111–135). Warszawa: SGH.
Marangos, J. (2004). Transformation to a market economy in Eastern Europe, the former Soviet Union and Asia. In: Ph. A. O'Hara (Ed.) *Global Political Economy and the Wealth of Nations: Performance, Institutions, Problems and Policies* (pp. 105–125). London, New York: Routledge.
Miller, S. (2011). Social institutions. In: E.N. Zalta (Ed.) *The Stanford Encyclopaedia of Philosophy*. Retrieved from http://plato.stanford.edu/archives/sum2019/entries/social-institutions/
Możdżeń, M., and J. Hausner. (2020). How ideas and institutions mutually affect each other. In: S. Mazur (Ed.) *Public Administration in Central Europe* (pp. 45–56).London: Routledge. https://doi.org/10.4324/9780429286452-5
Nölke, A., and A. Vliegenthart. (2009). Enlarging the varieties of capitalism: The emergence of dependent market economies in East Central Europe. *World Politics*, *61*(4), 670–702. https://doi.org/10.1017/S0043887109990098
O'Hara, Ph. A. (2019). History of institutional economics. In: A. Sinha, and A.M. Thomas (Eds.) *Pluralistic Economics and Its History* (pp. 171–190). London: Routledge.
Ost, D. (2019). *Defeat of Solidarity: Anger and Politics in Post-Communist Europe*. Ithaca and London: Cornell University Press. https://doi.org/10.7591/9781501729270
Pierson, P. (1993). When effect becomes cause: Policy feedback and political change. *World Politics*, *45*(4), 595–628. https://doi.org/10.2307/2950710
Pierson, P. (2000). Increasing returns, path dependence, and the study of politics. *American Political Science Review*, *94*(2), 251–267. https://doi.org/10.2307/2586011
Piątkowski, M. (2018). *Europe's Growth Champion: Insights from the Economic Rise of Poland*. Oxford: Oxford University Press. https://doi.org/10.1093/oso/9780198789345.001.0001
Polanyi, K. (2001[1944]). *The Great Transformation. The Political and Economic Origins of Our Time*. Boston: Beacon Press.
Ramazzotti, P. (2007). Policymaking and learning actors, or is a 'double movement' in cognition possible? *Journal of Economic Issues*, *41*(3), 765–781. https://doi.org/10.1080/00213624.2007.11507060
Ramazzotti, P. (2020a). Economic policy and the progressive idea. *Journal of Economic Issues*, *54*(2), 363–369. https://doi.org/10.1080/00213624.2020.1743583
Ramazzotti, P. (2020b). Economic policy, social identity and social consensus. *International Journal of Political Economy*, *49*(2), 139–152. https://doi.org/10.1080/08911916.2020.1778864
Ramazzotti, P. (2021). Foreshadowing change? Theories, policies, and COVID-19. *Journal of Economic Issues*, *55*(2), 492–498. https://doi.org/10.1080/00213624.2021.1909353
Rose, R. (1990). Inheritance before choice in public policy. *Journal of Theoretical Politics*, *2*(3), 263–291. https://doi.org/10.1177/0951692890002003002
Sherman, H. J. (2003). Evolutionary Economics from a Radical Perspective. *Journal of Economic Issues, 37*(1),75–83.

Spranz, R., A. Lenger, and N. Goldschmidt. (2012). The relation between institutional and cultural factors in economic development: the case of Indonesia. *Journal of Institutional Economics*, *8*(4), 459–488. 10.1017/S1744137412000124

Veblen, Th. (1898). Why is economics not an evolutionary science? *The Quarterly Journal of Economics*, *12*(4), 373–397. https://doi.org/10.2307/1882952

Veblen, Th. (1899 [1915]). *The Theory of Leisure Class: An Economic Study of Institutions.* New York: The Macmillan Company.

Veblen, Th. (1917). *An Inquiry into the Nature of Peace and the Terms of Its Perpetuation.* Los Angeles: Tutis Digital Publishing, 2008.

Veblen, Th. (1919 [1964]). *The Vested Interests and the Common Man.* New York: Kelley.

Voigt, S. (2013). How (not) to measure institutions. *Journal of Institutional Economics*, 9 (01), 1–26. 10.1017/S17441347412000148

Voigt, S., and H. Engerer. (2002). Institutions and transformation – Possible policy implications of the new institutional economics. In: K.F. Zimmermann (Ed.) *Frontiers in Economics* (pp. 127–184). Berlin, Heidelberg: Springer. https://doi.org/10.1007/978-3-540-24739-5_4

Voigt, S. (2013). How (not) to measure institutions. *Journal of Institutional Economics*, 9 (01), 1–26. 10.1017/S17441347412000148

Zalewski, D. (2020). Confronting the trilemma: Culture, institutions, and macroeconomic disequilibria. *Journal of Economic Issues*, *54*(2), 294–315. https://doi.org/10.1080/00213624.2020.1742061

2 Great transformations in historical perspective. Market and class in England, Algeria, and Poland[1]

Maciej Kassner

2.1 Introduction

History provides three examples of "great transformations" that involved turning non-market societies into market ones. The first one was described by Karl Polanyi as the birth of capitalism in 19th-century England and continental Europe. The second example concerns the inclusion of Africa and Asia into the global capitalist market by means of colonial conquest. Finally, the third example of "great transformations" is the post-socialist makeover that entailed

> Over thirty countries, stretching from the Elbe River to the Pacific Ocean, the territory of which is currently inhabited by over 1.8 billion people, which is more than one fourth of the world's population, which entered the path to a more or less liberal market and democratic transition.
>
> (Kołodko 2009, p. 176)

Certainly, differences between these experiences should not be diminished. The 19th-century transformation was driven by industrialization, whereas market changes in Eastern Europe actually led to the closing of factories. Undoubtedly, there are vast differences between feudalism, tribal societies, and the existing forms of socialism, which shaped the course of relevant transformations. Still, there are important similarities shared by various processes of market modernization. In all three types of transformations, the engagement of the state apparatus played a key role, while market changes were received by large portions of the population in "transformed" regions as an arbitrarily inflicted form of coercion. Each time, the clash with the modern market economy involved profound cultural changes and created traumatic effects. In this chapter, phenomena accompanying the creation of a market system are analysed using three works that represent three market transformations: the history of enclosures and industrial revolution, as presented by Karl Polanyi in *The Great Transformation*, the colonial modernization in Algeria described by Pierre Bourdieu, and the Polish discourse of transformation, especially the peculiar figure of *homo sovieticus*, best formulated in the study by Piotr Sztompka entitled *Trauma wielkiej zmiany* [The Trauma of Great Transformation].

DOI: 10.4324/9781003425717-3

In this essay, I follow the lead of Karl Polanyi in adopting the institutional approach to the political economy. Old institutionalism is unique among schools of economic thought in treating the economy as a part of a larger cultural totality (Mayhew 2008). Such a perspective has at least two advantages. First, it allows for fruitful cooperation between economics and other social disciplines, such as anthropology, sociology, and political science. Second, it encourages holistic investigations of the relationship between economic institutions and other aspects of culture. This is precisely what I shall attempt to do in the following pages. More specifically, I offer a detailed analysis of various discourses related to market and class in the three types of market transformation mentioned above. Particular emphasis will be placed on the fate of those classes that lack the resources needed for successful adaptation to the market regime. This chapter is organized as follows: The first section offers a conceptualization of the market transformation based on the writings of Karl Polanyi and other scholars inspired by his ideas. The following three sections are devoted to discussion narratives about the market and class in England, Algeria, and Poland. In the final section, I draw some conclusions from my own deliberations.

2.2 Theoretical approaches to market transformation

To conceptualize market transformation, we need to understand different types of economic regimes known from history. I will follow an approach offered by Ivan Szelényi, a Hungarian sociologist who builds his argument on a creative reinterpretation of Karl Polanyi's typology of institutional forms of economic integration (Szelényi 1991; Szelényi and Kostello 1998; Szelényi and Mihályi 2021). In his essay entitled *Economy as an Instituted Process*, Polanyi distinguished between three main institutional patterns capable of coordinating productive activities: reciprocity, redistribution, and market exchange (Polanyi 1957; Kassner 2017). Reciprocity is based on the pattern of symmetry. Gift exchange described by Marcel Mauss is a classic example of reciprocity. In a reciprocal transaction, there is no exact equivalence between the parties of exchange. By way of consequence, goods do not have a strictly defined "price". The only obligation entailed is to return a more or less similar gift in the future. Redistribution is associated with the pattern of centricity under which goods and services flow to and from the political centre. Redistributive coordination presupposes the existence of a hierarchy of power; however, temporary it may be. A simple case of redistribution may be illustrated by the practice of collecting the game from a successful hunt by a tribe chief and distributing it among the members of a tribe. Finally, market patterns refer to buying and selling goods and commodities based on the negotiated exchange rate. The political scientist, Charles Lindblom, in his excellent study of the market system called this simply a *quid pro quo* rule (Lindblom 2001, pp. 111–123). Both barter and monetary transactions fall under this theme. Nevertheless, the spread of this type of exchange is associated with the expansion of price-making markets.

Drawing upon Polanyi's typology of the forms of institutional integration, Szelényi modifies it in two ways. First, he maintains that all existing economies are mixed systems. The nature of a given economic regime is determined by an institutional mechanism that integrates the factors of production: labour, land, and capital. Second, he distinguishes between the dominant, secondary and tertiary forms of integration. A particular institutional pattern can be called dominant if it covers the bulk of the means of production used in a given society. The main task of secondary and tertiary forms of coordination is to supplement the dominant institution and correct the major deficiencies caused by its operations. In tribal societies, reciprocity was the main pattern of coordination with redistribution and markets playing subsidiary roles. Such societies relied primarily on a kinship network for the distribution of goods and services. The economies of ancient slave societies, such as Egypt, Greece, and Rome were mainly based on redistribution, although market trade played a significant role. The appropriation of surplus by slave owners can be described as a special case of a redistributive mechanism (Szelényi and Mihályi 2021, p. 449). Feudal societies were also organized around the pattern of redistribution. Landlords collected rent from serfs in exchange for military protection. However, the semi-autarkic household remained a notable institution in peasant societies. Starting from the late medieval and early modern period, markets steadily rose in prominence. With time, markets in land, labour, and capital had been established. For these reasons, some scholars regard peasant economies as "penny-capitalism" or semi-market systems (Dalton 1969, pp. 74–75).

The development of modern technology and the rise of the industrial revolution expanded the scope of economic activity. As a consequence of this, reciprocity becomes less important in comparison with market and redistribution. Only the market can operate on a global scale. For that reason, Charles Lindblom regards the market system as the largest institutional coordinator "without peer, in a class by itself" (Lindblom 2001, p. 41). Iván Szelényi and Petr Mihályi go even further and argue that "in a globalized, complex world, the dominant coordinating mechanism has to be the market" (Szelényi and Mihályi 2021, p. 454). However, within territorial boundaries, economies can be organized in different ways. State socialism is an economic system that relies on redistribution as the main institutional form of the coordination of productive activities. The process of the withering away of the official communist ideology led to a change of attitude towards markets and private property. As a result, markets, including black and grey markets, were increasingly tolerated. They were employed to remedy the shortages of certain goods (i.e. agricultural products) and services. Interestingly enough, quasi-market mechanisms were used to grant certain privileges to the party members. In the Polish People's Republic special "yellow curtain shops" existed where members of the nomenclature could buy otherwise inaccessible products and then resell them on the grey or black market (Ziółkowski, Drozdowski, Baranowski, and Rae 2021, p. 152).[2] On the contrary, industrialized societies that rely mostly on markets can be called capitalist. Under capitalism, the market system is the main institution for allocating productive assets. Market prices convey information about the relative scarcity of consumer and capital goods. They influence key investment decisions regarding what and how to produce. At the same time, state redistribution plays a major role in capitalist economies. The state provides public services, corrects income inequalities through taxes and transfers, while also addresses the problem of social costs, which are shifted by private enterprises to third parties and the society at large.

It is useful to supplement Szelényi's institutional approach with a more anthropological analysis of the impact of economic change as a larger cultural totality. Here, the typology offered by George Dalton, Polanyi's student and distinguished economic anthropologist, can be instructive. According to Dalton, the market transformation of society can lead to three types of results: degenerative change, growth without development, and socio-economic development (Dalton 1969, pp. 75–79). As Dalton explains, degenerative change refers to "a severe disruption of the traditional life of community over several generations with accompanying indicators of novel sorts and frequencies of personal and social malaise" (Dalton 1969, p. 77). The negative consequences of social degeneration include alcoholism, deprivation of widely shared values, and withdrawal from reality into a realm of fantasy. The second scenario involves the introduction of monetary transactions without the far-reaching transformations in the existing economic structures. In this scenario, the market economy and the traditional one (based on self-sustenance, often at a level barely supporting life) coexist side by side. The third option refers to economic modernization reconciled with basic social stability. Although Dalton refrains from giving specific examples, the rebuilding of Japan and Germany after World War II seems to fit this description. Market transformations analysed here oscillate between the first and the third scenario.

We can draw on Habermas's notion of life world to elucidate the human dimension of economic change (Habermas 1985, pp. 113–197). The term life world refers to society as it is perceived from the standpoint of actors engaged in ordinary situations. It is the world of practical plans and everyday communication. For the most part, it is treated as unproblematic and self-evident. According to Habermas, life world consists of a "culturally transmitted and linguistically organized stock of interpretative patterns" (Habermas 1985, p. 124). In other words, it refers to all linguistic resources people have at their disposal to construct their identities and make sense of their lives. However, a life world can disintegrate or even fall apart under the influence of external factors. In particular, radical economic transformation causes the structures of life world to collapse. Disruption can be observed on three distinctive levels identified by Habermas as culture, society, and personality. At the level of culture, the crisis manifests itself as a loss of meaning, delegitimization of the accepted forms of knowledge, and disorientation of individuals who cannot rely anymore on routine patterns of interpretation. At a social level, the crisis leads to a state of *anomie*. This term was originally coined by the French sociologist Èmile Durkheim and refers to the breakdown of accepted social norms. Overt manifestations of the anomic condition include the rise of criminal and morally illegitimate actions. At the level of personality, crisis leads to ego depletion and various psychopathologies. Individuals appear to be demotivated, undisciplined, unable to form rational plans, and prone to daydreaming. More severe symptoms include mental diseases and substance addictions (i.e. alcoholism). In sum, rapid economic change that disrupts the established forms of social life is likely to lead to the threefold crisis of cultural reproduction, social integration, and socialization.

If the disruption of the life world is a phenomenon almost universally associated with market transformation, then the question emerges how individuals can adapt to it. Here I believe that Pierre Bourdieu's theory of different forms of capital offers invaluable insights (Bourdieu 2002). Bourdieu distinguished between economic, social, and cultural capital. Economic capital is "directly convertible into money and may be institutionalized in the form of property rights" (Bourdieu 2002, p. 281). Cultural capital consists of skills and knowledge that can be "institutionalized in the form of educational qualification" (Bourdieu 2002, p. 281). Finally, social capital is "made up of social obligations" or "connections" (Bourdieu 2002, p. 281). Both cultural and social capital can be monetized under certain conditions and therefore transformed into economic capital. Individuals belonging to various social classes differ with respect to the amount of money, education, and valuable connections at their disposal. As Bourdieu's anthropological studies suggest, the more money, connections, or education one possesses, the easier it is to find a place in a newly emerging market order. Moreover, the development of some forms of capital (i.e. gaining valuable education or marketable skills) is virtually impossible without a fair dose of economic security. Hence, individual chances during the period of market transition are socially conditioned by the amount of different capitals they can command.

To sum up, the term market transformation refers to the change from an economy organized around the principles of redistribution or reciprocity to an economy where the market system becomes the primary form of institutional coordination of productive activities. In particular, markets with the factors of production are created. Market transformation is much more than a simple package of economic reforms such as price liberalization, privatization, and macro-economic stabilization. It affects the entire culture of a transformed society and has profound effects on the life worlds of ordinary people. The ability to cope with such disruptive social change depends on the material and symbolic resources people have at their disposal. In particular, access to economic, cultural, and social capital, or money, education, and social connections may increase the chances of successful adaptation to the market regime.

2.3 Karl Polanyi on enclosures and the industrial revolution

Let us begin with a reconstruction of Karl Polanyi's views on the nature of changes introduced by enclosures, industrialization, and the marketization of society (Polanyi 2001). The point here is not to verify the historical accuracy of his assessment, or to compare his account with competing analyses of the rise of capitalism.[3] What is at stake rather consists of highlighting those theses, observations, and concepts in Polanyi's argument that could help to grasp the general feature of market transformation. First of all, Polanyi holds that marketization could not proceed without state intervention. This perspective entails undermining the distinction between evolutionary and revolutionary paths towards the market economy. According to Polanyi, all market transformations involved some degree of shock. Second, he characteristically argues that economic change on such a scale must entail cultural change. Such a transformation is enforced under economic compulsion and the significant asymmetry of power between the social classes. Third, the social catastrophe brought about by market transformation is of a predominantly cultural nature, bringing about a crisis of accepted identities and models of interpretation. Fourth, by highlighting the cultural dimension of marketization, Polanyi was able to discern surprising parallels between market reforms and colonialism. This comparison reveals a vital analogy between the racist discourse about indigenous peoples and the language used to describe those who failed economically in the wake of market transformation. Fifth, Polanyi claims that successful coping with the market trauma requires recreating certain non-market institutions that would protect people and mitigate risks. Among them is class culture, which is of huge importance for hired workers because it provides models of solidarity and collective action indispensable for efficient adaptation to the market economy.

In *The Great Transformation,* Karl Polanyi compares two far-reaching social changes: enclosures and industrial revolution. "Enclosures", he claims, "have appropriately been called a revolution of the rich against the poor" (Polanyi 2001, p. 37). This process consisted of parcelling shared land and transforming it into private property. This led to expropriation, thus automatically turning peasants into hired workers. In retrospect, enclosures appear to be a decisive step towards the development of a competitive job market – an essential component of a capitalist economy. Thus, marketization entailed the destruction of the traditional economy based on sharing land. Intriguingly, Polanyi noted that analogous phenomena can be observed under colonial conditions:

> The natives are to be forced to make a living by selling their labour. To this end, their traditional institutions must be destroyed, and prevented from reforming. [...] Thus the colonists may decide to cut the breadfruit trees down in order to create an artificial food scarcity or may impose a hut tax on the native to force him to barter away his labour. Now, what the white man may still occasionally practice in remote regions today, namely, the smashing up of social structures in order to extract the element of labour from them, was done in the eighteenth century to white populations by white men for similar purposes.
>
> (Polanyi 2001, pp. 171–172)

Hence, colonial exploitation appears to repeat the events from the birth of capitalism. In a way, enclosures proved more gentle than the industrial revolution or economic colonization. Taking the opportunity of the rivalry between the nobility and the emerging middle class, royal authorities under the Tudors and early Stuarts were able to regulate the progress of enclosures. In this context, Polanyi formulates his famous thesis about interventionism being able to adjust the pace of change.

> The rate of change is often of no less importance than the direction of the change itself; but while the latter frequently does not depend on our volition,

> it is the rate at which we allow change to take place which may well depend upon us.
>
> (Polanyi 2001, p. 39)

Thus, one of the functions of the state's interventionism is to regulate the pace of market transformation.

The rise of the market system is seen by Polanyi as primarily cultural change. The emergence of the market economy, he argues, demanded to "annihilate all organic forms of existence and replace them with a different type of organization, an atomistic and individualistic one" (Polanyi 2001, p. 171). His analysis of the social consequences of market transition implies a critique of two intellectual traditions: economic liberalism and Marxism. Liberals would hold that in light of statistical gauges of living standards, such as real wages or demographic data, "the inferno of early capitalism [...] never existed" (Polanyi 2001, p. 163). Marxists, on the other hand, identified the main problem in the new regime as economic exploitation. In Polanyi's view, both accounts are too narrow and materialistic. As he argues, "a social calamity is primarily a cultural, not an economic phenomenon that can be measured by income figures or population statistics" (Polanyi 2001, p. 164). The category of exploitation is similarly fallible. "If exploitation is defined in strictly economic terms as a constant inadequacy of ratios of exchange, it is doubtful whether, as a matter of fact, there was exploitation" (Polanyi 2001, pp. 166–167). Even if we agree that under certain circumstances the concept of exploitation can be successfully deployed, it cannot be decisive. "Not economic exploitation, as often assumed", Polanyi argues, "but the disintegration of the cultural environment of the victim is then the cause of the degradation" (Polanyi 2001, p. 164).

In his account of the social catastrophe that accompanied the birth of the market economy, Polanyi further develops the analogy between the industrial revolution and colonialism, foregrounding the

> [...] Economic earthquake which transformed within less than half a century vast masses of the inhabitants of the English countryside from settled folk into shiftless migrants. But if such destructive landslides are exceptional in the history of classes, they are a common occurrence in the sphere of culture contact between peoples of various races. Intrinsically, the conditions are the same. [...] The economic process may, naturally, supply the vehicle of the destruction, and almost invariably economic inferiority will give the weaker yield, but the immediate cause of his undoing is not for that reason economic; it lies in the lethal injury to the institutions in which his social existence is embodied. The result is the loss of self-respect and standards, whether the unit is a people or a class, whether the process springs from the so-called culture conflict or from a change in the position of a class within the confines of a society.
>
> (Polanyi 2001, pp. 164–165)

According to Polanyi, the disintegration of culture means that it no longer provides individuals with legitimate goals and the motivation to work towards them. In Habermas' terms, such situations can be characterized as the breakdown of a life world. They display characteristic symptoms such as the loss of meaning, delegitimization of the accepted forms of knowledge, and individual disorientation, while also the spread of social malaises such as alcoholism, prostitution, and crime.

The analogy between the situation of the emerging working class in Britain and that of the colonized one has one more dimension that needs emphasizing. In an interesting note on sources to "Disraeli's 'Two Nations' and the Problem of Coloured Races", Polanyi observes that the language used to describe the British poor is comparable with the stigmatizing discourse about the colonized populations. In both cases, criticism is levelled against vices that "characterized coloured populations debased by disintegrating culture contact: dissipation, prostitution, thievishness, lack of thrift and providence, slovenliness, low productivity of labour, lack of self-respect and stamina" (Polanyi 2001, p. 303). Polanyi sees this as another form of proof of the cultural character of economic catastrophe. However, this issue can be approached from a different perspective. As Etienne Balibar asserts, racist discourse initially did not refer to ethnic differences, but to social classes or castes (Balibar 1995, p. 207). It was only later that the same language of condemnation and contempt was applied to people of different skin colour. Polanyi's true discovery, Balibar suggests, consists of revealing the discursive mechanisms of creating a class-based variant of racism. In my own view, these interpretations do not necessarily exclude each other. As shall become clear, the oppressive nature of market change can consist both of the disintegration of the cultural environment and in the discursive construction of identities, casting victims of transformation as lazy, undisciplined, irrational, and demoralized. Both processes dehumanize entire population segments in post-transformation societies. As Polanyi puts it, they become "degraded rabble" and "veritable human refuse" (Polanyi 2001, p. 165). The price of economic progress after the introduction of the market economy proved very high as it involved dehumanization of those who failed to succeed.

Polanyi's *The Great Transformation* offers two ways of healing from the trauma induced by market transformation. The first way consists of the afore-mentioned gradualism and conscious deceleration of the rate at which the market changes occur. The second way concerns the appreciation of the working-class culture. One model of the latter, described by Polanyi, is the "Red Vienna", where "in a purely capitalistic surrounding, a socialist municipality established a regime which was bitterly attacked by economic liberals" (Polanyi 2001, p. 298). In the economic dimension, Viennese municipal socialism relied on low rents, social housing, strong trade unions, and extensive unemployment benefits. In Polanyi's view, "the experiment from Vienna [...] achieved one of the most spectacular cultural triumphs of Western history" (Polanyi 2001, p. 299). Introduced during the chaotic aftermath of the First World War, it was an attempt to move outside the framework of the market economy by subordinating its operation to the imperative of social justice. As a result,

> 1918 initiated [...] a moral and intellectual rise in the condition of a highly developed industrial working class which, protected by the Vienna system, withstood the degrading effects of grave economic dislocation and achieved a level never reached before by the masses of people in any industrial society.
>
> (Polanyi 2001, p. 299)

As Polanyi claims, the British working class did not develop an equally elaborate culture, which proved decisive in worsening its experience of early capitalism.

2.4 Pierre Bourdieu on Algeria

Let us move on to Pierre Bourdieu's account of the economic transformation in Algeria, based on ethnographic studies carried out among the Kabyle in 1958–1961 (Bourdieu 1972; Goodman and Silverstein 2009). It is unnecessary to cover all aspects of Bourdieu's classic study. Suffice to highlight those areas that are crucial for the discussed perspective on economic change as cultural. Much like Polanyi, Bourdieu places his argument in opposition to Marxism and standard liberal theory since both of these approaches assume full compatibility between the economy's structure and the dispositions of individuals functioning in it. Neoclassical theory postulates universal rationalism of *homo oeconomicus*, whereas Marxism falsely assumes that individual dispositions are determined by the functional requirements of capitalism. Meanwhile, Bourdieu argues,

> In situations of transition between a pre-capitalist economy and a capitalist economy, the objectivist abstraction in which neo-marginalists join hands with structural-Marxists is so flagrantly inadequate that one has to be blind to reality to reduce the economic agents to mere reflections of the economic structures [...].
>
> (Bourdieu 1972, p. vii)

What really requires explication is the genesis of the economic habitus, or the sum of individual dispositions necessary in the context of market economy. Bourdieu discusses this in the following way:

> [...] the economic agents I was able to observe in Algeria in the 1960s had to learn or, more exactly, reinvent, with greater or lesser success depending on their economic and cultural resources, everything economic theory considers (at least tacitly) as a given, that is to say, everything it regards as an innate, universal gift, forming part of human nature: the idea of work as an activity procuring a monetary income, as opposed to mere occupation on the lines of the traditional division of activities or the traditional exchange of services [...] the notion of long term investment [...] lending at interest and the very

> idea of a contract, with its previously unknown strict deadlines and formal clauses, which gradually supplanted the honourable exchange between men of honour that excluded calculation and the pursuit of profit, and involved an acute concern with fairness etc.
>
> (Bourdieu 2005, p. 4)

Thus, economic transformation is a mass-scale reform of the habitus, which was enforced by economic necessity. Unlike Polanyi, Bourdieu emphasizes grassroots creativity as crucial for adaptation. Change involves innovative reconstruction of inherited dispositions and certainly does not follow accepted market patterns passively.

According to Bourdieu, the characteristic feature of the modern worldview is the ability to imagine the future as an objective reality that can be subject to rational calculation. Pre-modern societies treat the future as a repetition, to some degree, of what already happened. Drawing on Marxist terminology, Bourdieu writes in this context about simple social reproduction, which consists of the biological recreation of life and the perpetuation of accepted social order. Institutions of the traditional economy such as gift exchange and the autarkic household limit the range of market transactions, whereas the prevailing code of honour defines the socially permissible accumulation of capital. Colonial conquest initiated the destruction of the traditional order. As Bourdieu vividly puts it, "the economic system imported by colonization [...] has the necessity of a 'cosmos' (as Weber puts it) into which the workers find themselves cast and whose rules they must learn in order to survive" (Bourdieu 1972, p. 3). With the new cosmos meaning there also emerged a different understanding of time. The instruments of the market economy such as money, credit, and the striving to increase profit require the ability to envision the future as an object of prediction and calculation. In this way, the future is opened for individual and collective projects. Although originally the future becoming rife with possibility was connected with anticipation of huge gains, goals do not have to be strictly economic. The projected outcomes may involve not only business opportunities but also developing a life plan or even radically transforming the dominant social order. As it turns out, the market economy, individual emancipation, and socialist revolution all rely on the same experience of making the future an object of rational calculation.

Bourdieu's anthropological research demonstrates that the differing pace of adaptation to the market economy reflects social inequality. He rejects those explications of failure in the processes of modernization that refer to cultural heritage or its specific elements, for example the impact of Islam. His ethnographical studies and statistical analyses show that the ability to envision the future as the object of rational calculation is closely connected with the availability of economic resources, especially work and education. Unstable employment and irregular income limit the ability to develop rational courses of action. In Bourdieu's view, this is the situation of what he called the sub-proletariat. People in this social group live in the perpetual present since the future is only accessible to them as a fantasy. Proletarians, on the other hand, are able to make rational predictions, but their ability to formulate long-term plans is curbed by the looming unemployment and consequent declassation. Finally, along with increased education and income, plans made by individuals become more precise and better adapted to the objective possibility of their realization. Bourdieu draws an insightful conclusion regarding the perspectives of collective action in capitalist economy:

> With permanent employment and regular wages, an open and rational temporal consciousness is able to be formed; actions, judgements, and aspirations can be ordered in relation to a life-plan. Then, and then only, does the revolutionary attitude take the place of escape into daydreams or fatalistic resignation.
>
> (Bourdieu 1972, p. 62)

One does not have to embrace Bourdieu's revolutionary views to appreciate the accuracy of his findings. Indeed, glorification of pre-modern culture or attempts to embrace the lifestyle of subdued classes are counterproductive. Organizing a strike demands the ability to make rational predictions just as much as planning an individual career. Internalizing the basic coordinates of market habitus is necessary if individuals are to be able to organize collective resistance. Like Polanyi, Bourdieu is convinced that adaptation to the realities of the market economy ultimately has to take the form of a class-based self-organization with a view to fighting for collective goals.

2.5 The case of *homo sovieticus*

The term *homo sovietiucs* was first developed by the Russian thinker Alexander Zinoviev. It was introduced into Polish public discourse by Józef Tischner (2018).[4] In his view, this category describes a group of psychological traits inherited from real socialism, which are presented as a threat to the new capitalist system. The huge popularity of the term in public debates would not be possible if it had not been for critical articles on the condition of Polish society in real socialism penned by eminent sociologists. In this context, Krzysztof Tyszka lists sociological diagnoses that employ concepts such as "learned helplessness", "sociological void", "amoral familism", or the "culture of apparent action" (Tyszka 2009). When seen through the prism of these categories, Polish society emerged as demoralized, passive, and ill-adapted to modern life. At the onset of systemic transformation, the traits and habits developed under communism began to be considered as obstacles for the growth of capitalism and civil society. Poles had to make the utmost effort to internalize modern ways of thinking with their success depending on whether they would be able to shed the values and expectations originating in the previous system. Although the discourse of *homo sovieticus* was developed collectively, the most systematic outline of this category is contained in the book by Piotr Sztompka entitled *Trauma wielkiej zmiany* [The Trauma of Great Change].

Similarly to Polanyi and Bourdieu, Sztompka accentuates the cultural dimension of economic transformations (Sztompka 2000; Długosz 2019, p. 97). "Institutional reform", he argues, "is accompanied by cultural shifts that involve changes in mentality, attitudes and motives among the participating social actors" (Sztompka 2000, p. 54). Indications of failure to adapt to new conditions include symptoms of trauma such as increased suicide rates, dissolution of social bonds, and the disintegration of value systems. Basically, every change in the economy, technology, or culture may be potentially traumatic. The concept of trauma originates in medical discourse, where it is understood as "the long-term, destructive impact of a sudden event that affects the organism, disabling some of its vital functions" (Sztompka 2000, p. 20). Social trauma would involve situations where adaptation to new conditions poses a problem for entire collectives. In this sense, trauma is a pathology of social subjectivity. Shock-inducing events are not traumatic in themselves but can become such as a result of accepting a certain interpretation that accentuates their negative character. Consequently, every social trauma would have a cultural character since it depends on the accepted definition of a particular situation. However, the concept of cultural trauma can also have a more specific meaning: it emerges when social change undermines the prevailing system of values, along with the accepted beliefs and old habits. This would be the situation of Poland after 1989, Sztompka argues. On the one hand, there was a "stable repertoire of cultural regulations, inherited from the previous system and characteristic for its habitus", while on the other hand, "a new culture was budding – one that was functionally predefined by democratic and capitalist institutions" (Sztompka 2000, p. 55).

Relics of the past system, which thwart the efforts to overcome cultural trauma, are personified by *homo sovieticus*: a Soviet-style mindset that is at odds with *homo oeconomicus. Homo sovieticus* has no cultural competences necessary to function in the new system, which causes them to abide by old habits. Distrustful of intellectuals and elites, they are envious of those who succeeded, and strongly oppose individualism with a collectivist attitude. Further characteristics include the lack of interest in public matters, focus on private life, favouring justice and equality over merit and efficiency, as well as fatalism: belief in fate, tendency to look back, while also fear of the future. Consequently, they value security, avoid risk, and apply double standards in their unceasing judgements about close ones and others. According to Sztompka, the mentality of *homo sovieticus* is symptomatic of the trauma caused by the inability to adapt to the realities of the market economy. In his view, this trauma reinforces expectations regarding welfare state functions, prioritization of equality, justice, and security, as well as egalitarian paternalism and faith in social benefits (Sztompka 2000, pp. 73–74). Breaking away from egalitarian sentiments seems necessary to ensure that society can overcome trauma. "Only when the influence of homo sovieticus diminishes or disappears entirely can we be certain", Sztompka concludes, "that the Polish nation finally healed itself from the trauma of post-communism" (Sztompka 2000, p. 106).

Scholars of political ideologies will easily note that the discourse of *homo sovieticus* echoes themes displayed previously in the neo-conservative criticism of the welfare state. The rhetoric of this concept is based on naïve and highly politicized notions of capitalism. Real capitalist systems are a mix of market and non-market-based institutions, values, and practices. It is difficult to clearly indicate which attitudes and values shall ultimately become "functional" with regard to democratic and capitalist institutions. Many attitudes stigmatized by Sztompka, including the attachment to egalitarianism and security, are strongly represented in Scandinavian and Asian models of capitalism. The discourse of *homo sovieticus* did not account for the implications of inequality in access to various capitals for individual strategies of coping with change. Although Sztompka noticed that successful adaptation to the market economy is premised on resources such as education and economic capital, in his analyses he underlines mental barriers instead. However, such an emphasis seems entirely misguided. For example, studies carried out by Marta Kołodziejska and Mikołaj Hnatiuk demonstrate that the inclination to take risks does not depend on any mental traits, but on the available resources (Kołodziejska and Hnatiuk 2012, p. 130). For members of the lower class, taking risk entails a much higher probability of dire repercussions in case of failure than for the upper classes. Another shortcoming of Sztompka's approach is that he focuses only on individual adaptation strategies, referring to strike action, pickets, and protests as "ill-conceived" strategies (Sztompka 2000, p. 93). This is all the more astonishing because one of the consequences of the capitalist transformation was the development of worker movements and social democratic parties. As Kołodziejska and Hnatiukaptly note, the concept of *homo sovieticus* undermines the rationality of the lower class and parts of the middle class, preventing them from articulating their interests (Kołodziejska and Hnatiuk 2012, p. 137).

The discourse of *homo sovieticus* can also be interpreted as a special case of social racism, namely, a phenomenon that consists of representing lower classes as if they belonged to another, "lower" race. This perspective was developed by Michał Buchowski and Monika Bobako, who refer to Edward Said's concept of Orientalism and examine language-based images of otherness (Bobako 2010; Buchowski 2017). According to Buchowski, who is an anthropologist, describing entire social groups as lazy, demoralized, and suffering from civilizational incompetence is similar to how white colonizers would frame non-Europeans. However, it is not just a question of stylistic similarity. As Buchowski claims, we encounter here the same practice of casting the other as naturally worse and subordinate, the only difference being that classic Orientalism located the other in geographical space, whereas social Orientalism places otherness in the social sphere among the subdued classes. In this light, Piotr Sztompka, Jan Winnicki, and other popularisers of the *homo sovieticus* discourse emerge as internal colonizers who ascribe cultural inferiority to the lower classes that occupy subordinate rungs on the social ladder. It does not matter whether working classes really display any of these traits. Orientalist discourse has performative power: not only does it stigmatize and humiliate, but also perpetuates a negative image of contemptuous social classes. Ultimately, it serves to delegitimize any criticism of the market order, ascribing all difficulties experienced by individual and social groups in finding their place in the economic system to their own, insufficiently modern mentality.

The problem is similarly described by Monika Bobako, who interprets the formation of social classes in Poland after 1989 as a process of racialization, or ascribing of inherent traits to classes in order to legitimize newly formed power relations (Bobako

2010). From the perspective of my topic, particularly enlightening observations are contained in the study of *Privatizing Poland* by Elizabeth Dunn, which Bucholc quotes to support her argumentation. Dunn discusses how employees at Alima, a company producing baby food and other foodstuffs, were on the one hand divided by the new management into "individualists" and "flexible" workers of the new type, while on the other hand, "collectivist", "uncreative" workers whose mentality would be burdened with socialism. Moreover, exams in creativity and pro-market attitudes were not passed by some of the former management. Dunn's study shows that dividing workers into "creative" and "uncreative" was largely arbitrary and relied on no substantive criteria (Dunn 2004, pp. 58–129). Likewise, the former management did indeed grasp how markets function and how to manage a company. It was not the case that employees at Alima failed to learn the market language – they only had no mastery of its latest idiom borrowed from American handbooks of management. Knowledge of practices in transnational corporations became a tool of delegitimizing other forms of knowledge such as orientation in local markets or the ability to organize production in times of scarcity. It is also difficult to uphold that the management methods preferred by Americans are really more effective or better suited for the local business context. An abrupt imposition of management models may be regarded in this light as a form of cultural imperialism, which perpetuates the idea that local knowledge is in fact backward and illegitimate.

Writing about the Hungarian experience, anthropologist Chris Hann noted that

> The dramatic collapse of Soviet socialism meant the end of a moral order in this sense, comprising both the termination of practical ways of life and the sudden calling into question of Weltanschauung, of most people's taken-for-granted knowledge of the world in which they lived.
>
> (Hann 2011, p. 17)

To describe this experience Hann coined the term moral dispossession. Similar discrepancy concerning inherited moral expectations and new economic realities was observed in Poland. While I do not believe that the entire *Weltanschauung* associated with real socialism deserves to be preserved, it should not be dismissed altogether. In particular, concerns about equality and social cohesion voiced by the critics of the market transformation strike me as legitimate. As Wolfgang Streeck has argued, capitalist economies may benefit from moral and legal restrictions placed on unbridled profiteering (1997). Calls for more equality and social solidarity may be regarded as an attempt to establish potentially beneficial constraints, which make the economic system both more civilized and more efficient.

It is important to see the conflict between social values and market values in a proper perspective. As Erich Fromm rightly noted, virtually any moral philosophy known to humankind is likely to be at odds with the workings of the capitalist economy (Fromm 2008). Most religious and secular philosophies stress different values than individual aggrandizement and the quest for profits. Hence, the conflict between markets and morality exists in every society. During the period of market transformation, it only took a more dramatic form. Hence, it is a mistake to depict solidaristic and egalitarian attitudes as perverted forms of soviet mentality, even if the language in which they were expressed had been marked by the vocabulary of the previous era. Conflict between market values and social values can also be seen as a consequence of institutional pluralism (O'Neil 1997). Markets tend to promote a particular set of priorities such as efficiency, individual initiative, and entrepreneurship. However, other institutional spheres, such as the family, educational system, or the state, are based on different sets of values (i.e. love, solidarity, talent, and patriotism) that cannot be easily expressed in monetary terms. From this point of view, an attempt to delegitimize non-market values as relics of communism suggests a rather problematic ideal of a mono-institutional society consisting of the market system alone.

2.6 Conclusions

Karl Polanyi sensed that *The Great Transformations* contain important lessons for nations who had not experienced the market transformation of society. In a letter written in 1956, he declared: "My work is for Africa, for Asia, for the new peoples" (Polanyi 1958, as cited in Dulczyńska-Polanyi 1977). Since Polanyi wrote those words, we have witnessed several market transformations in post-colonial and post-socialist countries. What lessons can we draw from these experiences? As we have seen, Karl Polanyi offered two suggestions with regard to the task of mitigating negative repercussions of the market transformation of society. First, he advised an interventionist policy aimed at slowing the pace of economic change. Second, he put his faith in counter-movements and their ability to create non-market institutions that would shelter populations from the most adverse consequences of marketization. Interestingly enough, the idea of intervention aimed at slowing down the pace of change re-emerged in the debates between the proponents of gradualism and shock therapy (Przeworski 1991; Balcerowicz 1997). Yet a closer analysis reveals certain ambiguity in the very notion of gradual social change. In Polanyi's *The Great Transformation,* this concept is illustrated with the case of enclosures of common land, a process spread over two centuries. In comparison, even the most gradualist post-socialist would count gradual transformation as fairly rapid. Hence, it seems that the experience of Red Vienna and the idea of creating non-market social institutions hold greater promise for mitigating the adverse effects of market transformation.

Karl Polanyi, Pierre Bourdieu, and Piotr Sztompka rightly maintained that market transformation cannot be understood without taking cultural factors into account. For them, creating a capitalist economy is not simply a matter of introducing private property and competitive markets. It is a profound cultural change that affects virtually every aspect of human life. Moreover, it can disrupt established life worlds and distort human lives. Hence it is important to understand change in order to mitigate its negative consequences. In my view, Sztompka and his followers misunderstood market transformation at least in three important ways. First, it assumed a rather naïve notion of capitalism as a self-regulating market system that operates on the basis of individual initiative. As a consequence, the importance of moral and institutional constraints on markets has been overlooked. But, as Ivan Szelényi points out, modern economies are mixed systems that cannot rely on markets alone. Second, the discourse of Polish sociology employed racialized or otherwise simplified an image of groups who were regarded as unfit for the market society. However, as Pierre Bourdieu has demonstrated, success in adapting to the market regime depends on the resources available to individuals, such as money, education, and social connections. It is therefore extremely naïve to imagine that failure to adapt can be explained by purely psychological factors such as alleged post-soviet mentality. Third, Polish sociology overlooked the importance of class politics in mitigating the adverse consequences of economic change. This is particularly puzzling, since the emergence of capitalism has been accompanied by the rise of the working-class movement. As historical experiences demonstrate, without organized political action on behalf of the working class it is difficult to create stable social order necessary to maintain the market system.

One of the key moral problems of market transformation is the suffering it inflicts upon innocent populations. In *The Great Transformation*, Karl Polanyi suggested that the ideological function of classical political economy lay precisely in its ability to describe social pains, which accompanied the rise of capitalism, as an inevitable by-product of the iron laws of the economy (Polanyi 2001, pp. 116–136). Interestingly enough, in the case of the Polish market transformation, a similar ideological role was performed by sociological discourse with regard to *homo sovieticus*. Victims of the early years of the market transformation were described as lazy, passive, outdated, and otherwise deserving their fate. This situation can be aptly characterized by an English idiomatic expression "to add insult to injury". Even if the injury was to some extent inevitable, the insult was not. Overall, the historical comparison of three different market transformations attests to a certain poverty of sociological imagination among Polish and other Eastern European scholars. They assumed a somewhat naïve dichotomy between modern capitalism on the one hand, and traditional culture and egalitarian values on the other. What they failed to envisage is the possibility of a market transition that would be less culturally disruptive and more socially cohesive. Admittedly, this moral and intellectual error is of some consequence. It can be seen as one reason behind the illiberal backlash besetting contemporary Poland and Hungary, a backlash which puts into question not only the free market economy but also constitutional democracy and the rule of law.

Notes

1 The first draft of this paper was translated by Grzegorz Czemiel. I thank Dr Czemiel for his help in rendering the manuscript in English.

2 Under the Polish People's Republic, the term *nomenclature* (literally: list of names) referred to the policy of reserving key positions in factories and other workplaces for candidates supported by the communist party.

3 Readers interested in a critical discussion of Polanyi's theory of the genesis of the market economy should consult Allen Sievers book-length examinations of his views (Sievers 1949), as well as a more recent discussion by Gareth Dale (Dale 2010, pp. 45–88).

4 Original essays were written by Józef Tischner in the late 1980s and early 1990s.

References

Balcerowicz, L. (1997). *Socjalizm, kapitalizm, transformacja. Szkice z przełomu epok*. Warszawa: Wydawnictwo Naukowe PWN.

Balibar, E. (1995). Class racism. In E. Balibar and I. Wallerstein (Eds.), *Race, Nation, Class. Ambiguous Identities* (204–217). London: Verso.

Bobako, M. (2010). Konstruowanie odmienności klasowej jako urasowienie. Przypadek Polski po 1989 roku. In P. Żuk (Ed.), *Podziały klasowe i nierówności społeczne. Refleksje socjologicznie po dwóch dekadach realnego kapitalizmu w Polsce* (165–177). Warszawa: Oficyna Naukowa.

Bourdieu, P. (1972). *Algeria 1960. Essays by Pierre Bourdieu*. Cambridge: Cambridge University Press.

Bourdieu, P. (2002). The forms of capital. In N. W. Biggart (Ed.), *Readings in Economic Sociology* (280–292). Malden and Oxford: Blackwell Publishers.

Bourdieu, P. (2005). *Social Structures of the Economy*. Cambridge: Polity Press.

Buchowski, M. (2017). *Czyściec. Antropologia neoliberalnego postsocjalizmu*. Poznań: Wydawnictwo Naukowe UAM.

Dale, G. (2010). *Karl Polanyi. The Limits of the Market*. London: Polity Press.

Dalton, G. (1969). Theoretical issues in economic anthropology. *Current Anthropology*, 10 (1), 63–102. Retrieved from: https://www.jstor.org/stable/2740685

Długosz, P. (2019). Trauma transformacji w Europie Środkowo-Wschodniej. *Środkowoeuropejskie Studia Polityczne*, 1, 95–122. https://doi.org/10.14746/ssp.2019.1.6.

Dulczyńska-Polanyi, I. (1977). Karl Polanyi: Notes on his life. In K. Polanyi (Ed.), *The Livelihood of Man* (xi–xx). New York, San Francisco, CA, London: Academic Press.

Dunn, E. (2004). *Privatizing Poland: Baby Food, Big Business, and the Remaking of Labor*. Ithaca, NY: Cornell University Press.

Fromm, E. (2008). *To Have or to Be*. London and New York: Continuum.

Goodman, J. E. and Silverstein, P. (2009). Introduction. In J. E. Goodman and P. Silverstein (Eds.), *Bourdieu in Algeria: Colonial Politics, Ethnographic Practices, Theoretical Development* (1–62). Lincoln: University of Nebraska,

Habermas, J. (1985). *The Theory of Communicative Action*. Volume 2. Boston, MA: Beacon Press.

Hann, Ch. (2011). Moral dispossession. *InterDisciplines*, 2, 11–37. https://doi.org/10.2390/indi-v2-i2-36.

Kassner, M. (2017). Economic process as institutionalization of values. Karl Polanyi's institutional theory and its ethical consequences. *Annales. Etyka w ŻyciuGospodarczym*, 20 (6), 69–86. https://doi.org/10.18778/1899-2226.20.6.05.

Kołodziejska, M. and Hnatiuk, M. (2012). Pożegnanie z homo sovieticus: próba weryfikacji empirycznej kategorii oraz analiza jej obecności w socjologicznym dyskursie o transformacji. In M. Gdula and P. Sadura (Eds.), *Style życia i porządek klasowy w Polsce* (117–138). Warszawa: Wydawnictwo Naukowe Scholar.

Kołodko, G. (2009). The great transformation 1989–2029. *Society and Economy*, 31 (2), 175–191. https://doi.org/10.1 556/SocEc.3 1.2009. 2. 2.

Lindblom, Ch. (2001). *The Market System. What It Is, How it Works, and What to Make of It*. New Haven, CT and London: Yale University Press.

Mayhew, A. (2008). Institutions, culture and values. In J. B. Davis and W. Dolfsma (Eds.), *The Elgar Companion to Social Economics* (28–43). Cheltenham and Northhampton: Edward Elgar.

O' Neill, J. (1997). Value pluralism, incommensurability, and institutions. In J. Foster (Ed.), *Valuing Nature. Economics, Ethics, and Environment* (75–88). London and New York: Routledge.

Polanyi, K. (1957) The economy as instituted process. In K. Polanyi, C. M. Arensberg and H. W. Pearson (Eds.), *Trade and Market in Early Empires. Economies in History and Theory* (243–270). Glencoe, IL: The Free Press.

Polanyi, K. (2001). *The Great Transformation. The Political and Economic Origins of Our Time.* Boston, MA: Beacon Press.

Przeworski, A. (1991). *Democracy and the Market: Political and Economic Reforms in Eastern Europe and Latin America.* Cambridge: Cambridge University Press.

Sievers, A. M. (1949). *Has the Market Capitalism Collapsed? A Critique of Karl Polanyi's New Economics.* New York: Columbia University Press.

Streeck, W. (1997). Beneficial constraints: On the economic limits of rational voluntarism. In R. Hollingsworth and R. Boyer (Eds.), *Contemporary Capitalism: The Embeddedness of Institutions* (191–220). Cambridge: Cambridge University Press.

Szelényi, I. (1991). Karl Polanyi and the theory of a socialist mixed economy. In M. Mendell and D. Salée (Eds.), *The Legacy of Karl Polanyi. Market, State and Society at the End of Twentieth Century* (231–251). New York: St. Martin Press.

Szelényi, I. and Kostello, E. (1998). Outline of an institutionalist theory of inequality: The case of socialist and post-communist Eastern Europe. In M. Brinton and V. Nee (Eds.), *The New Institutionalism in Sociology* (305–327). New York: Russel Sage Foundation.

Szelényi, I. and Mihályi, P. (2021). Karl Polanyi: A theorist of mixed economies. *Theory and Society,* 50, 443–461. https://doi.org/10.1007/s11186-020-09403-3.

Sztompka, P. (2000). *Trauma wielkiej zmiany. Społeczne koszty transformacji.* Warszawa: Instytut Studiów Politycznych PAN.

Tischner, J. (2018). *Etyka solidarności oraz homo sovieticus.* Kraków: Wydawnictwo Znak.

Tyszka, K. (2009). Homo sovieticus' two decades later. *Polish Sociological Review,* 168, 507–522. Retrieved from: https://polish-sociological-review.eu/-Homo-Sovieticus-Two-Decades-Later,127045,0,2.html.

Ziółkowski, M., Drozdowski, R., Baranowski, M. and Rae, G. (2021). Commodification in an officially decommodified economy: Institutional contradictions and everyday practices in Poland's real-socialism. *Polish Sociological Review*, 218 (2), 145–167. https://doi.org/10.26412/psr218.01.

3 The state in a (post)transition economy

Between neoliberalism and neostatism

Marek Ratajczak

3.1 Introductory remarks

The transition from non-market economies to market economies and from non-democratic systems to democratic ones, especially with respect to countries that are already EU member states, is regarded as an essentially completed process. Their membership in the EU would not have been possible if it had not been determined that these countries had a market economy and a democratic political system. However, the author of this article is one of those economists who believe that this transition, while formally completed, has not finished, which explains the writing of the "post" suffix in brackets. Moreover, given what is happening in some countries of the former Soviet Union, especially Russia, as well as the phenomena and socio-political processes taking place in some other countries of the former Eastern Europe, it is reasonable to ask not only whether the process of the transition can really be regarded as a matter of the past but also whether we are actually observing symptoms of what can be described not so much as attempts to turn back time as rather a kind of a new stage of transition, which may result in significant systemic changes. In simplified terms, this will be referred to as the "new" transition in this paper. Generally, this "new" transition involves the idea of correcting the errors associated with the version of the transition, which, in the early 1990s, was presented as a solution without alternatives (Kowalik 2005). This version of transition, especially in the economic sphere, was based on the principles of what can briefly and with some degree of simplification be called neoliberalism. A considerable number of those who criticized the original political transition favour solutions advocating a more active role of the state, not only in the economy. In its extreme version, these solutions represent what can be referred to as (post)transition neostatism.

The discussion exploring the author's understanding of this "new" transition is preceded by a brief description of the idea and assumptions underlying the original transition, as well as what can be described as the institutional legacy of a centrally planned economy. The methodological part of this article is first of all based on developments in the field of institutional economics, both traditional institutionalism, and to a lesser extent on New Institutional Economics (NIE).

DOI: 10.4324/9781003425717-4

3.2 The main idea of the original systemic transition[1]

As regards the declared economic goals of the systemic transition that the former Eastern Bloc countries underwent at the turn of the 1980s and 1990s, the process essentially consisted of a departure from a centrally planned economy towards a market economy. In the political sphere, the transition involved shifting from an authoritarian, or even totalitarian regime to a democratic system. On the social level, it was the process of transforming a society based on the principles of state-imposed collectivism[2] into a society where individual activity plays a central role.

The beginning of the transition coincided with the period of evident dominance of neoliberal thought in economic theory and practice, which drew on the legacy of neoclassical economics. Therefore, in order to summarize what many external experts and advisors advocated as the right course of economic measures for the countries undergoing transition and what many internal decision-makers accepted, one would have to write about the neoliberal version of a market economy.

Speaking of the dominant perspective regarding the transition in the economic sphere, one should bear in mind that it was, by no means, the only perspective that existed at that time. Several scientific studies offering transformation formulae and written by mostly Western scholars, including immigrants from countries that functioned in the Soviet sphere of influence after World War II, were based on other trends of economic thought, such as contemporary Keynesianism or institutionalism (Kiss 1993). Nonetheless, studies whose theoretical foundations included ideas derived from heterodox economics usually remained nothing more than a rather interesting contribution to the discussion about political transition, without any real impact on economic practice. It was largely the consequence of the dominating role of experts and advisors representing such organizations as the World Bank, the International Monetary Fund, or the US Department of the Treasury, which were associated with the so-called Washington Consensus, a set of economic policy recommendations based on the then dominant economic theories. It is worth noting that in comparison to analysts without previous experience of the realities of the socialist system, the idea of a quick and radical transition to a market economy, or simply, to capitalism, was viewed with a lot more scepticism by "old-school" Sovietologists, i.e. scholars engaged in analysing the economies of real socialism at the time when it seemed like the Cold War and its socio-political and economic consequences were to determine the reality of the world for many years to come (Kiss 1993). To those representing the former group, the political transition, even in a country like the Soviet Union in a state of collapse, was just another case in a long list of developing countries struggling with economic and socio-political problems. Despite the apparent realization that, for various reasons, transitions and resulting challenges in Poland, Russia and, say, Kyrgyzstan, could not be treated equally, the dominant conviction was that socialist economies were, to a certain extent, homogenous, which means that the proposed reform measures were largely universally applicable (Bunce 1999).

In hindsight, one cannot help but wonder what would have happened if the opinions of old-school Sovietologists, backed by some economists with first-hand knowledge of the realities of the countries in transition, had been considered. This is particularly relevant today, when, following Russia's invasion of Ukraine, questions are being asked about how and why it happened and how it could have been avoided that Russia, which for a short period of time was regarded as a country capable of a relatively quick transition to liberal democracy, has become an authoritarian regime, where the military and police play a key role. It is also worth noting that a considerable part of Russian society is critical of the actions of Mikhail Gorbachev, who is respected and held in high esteem abroad on account of his key role in the process of perestroika and glasnost, which, while not designed to dismantle the centrally planned economy and its political superstructure, effectively contributed to the collapse of the Soviet Union.

In the author's opinion, during the period characterized by a certain euphoria associated with the end of the Cold War, the West was too quick to assume that Russia, or the Russian Federation, was just one of many cases of political transition, differing from others mainly in terms of scale, and, of course, due to the fact of having nuclear weapons. As a result, there was no serious discussion about whether and how one can minimize the risk of failure in the process of Russia's transition from a non-democratic regime, relying on the power of the military, security services, and the police, while also functioning in a centrally planned economy with virtually non-existent elements of civil society, to that of a post-imperial, liberal democracy, based on a well-functioning market economy with an emerging civil society. In addition, Russia was a country with a much smaller territory compared to the Soviet Union, whose citizens were expected to accept the fact that the formal borders, until recently separating republics of the USSR, became the symbol of the territorial integrity of sovereign states overnight, with all the economic and social consequences involved. Unfortunately, Russia quickly became a fertile ground for the emergence of political capitalism with elements of comprador capitalism, crony capitalism, or even criminal capitalism, while its citizens were affected even more than the inhabitants of other transition countries by what Piotr Sztompka referred to as the trauma of a great cultural change (Sztompka 2000). This trauma was partly connected with economic shock therapy, which was applied in Russia in the process of political transformations. According to some analysts, such as the severity of the Russian measures what is commonly described as Poland's shock therapy does not really deserve that name.[3] The only structures that turned out to be strong enough to survive the period of the great Russian transition almost unchanged were, unfortunately, the military and the police. This situation helped these sectors to play an increasingly stronger role, as exemplified by Vladimir Putin himself, and made it easier for a large part of the society to accept slogans promoting neo-imperialist ideas and emphasizing Russia's fundamental distinctiveness from the Western world, which was presented as the embodiment of "weaknesses and threats", including gender ideology, the LGBT+ movement and the "misconceived" notion of gender equality, or, worse still, as a force striving to colonize Russia culturally and economically.

A large section of the Russian population has succumbed to a form of social nostalgia and started to idealize past institutions, which is a pattern that can also be observed in other countries that for several decades functioned according to the principles of a socialist economy. This should not be surprising, given the fact that the system was much more strongly rooted in Russia and was in place for a much longer period. Social nostalgia is manifested by, among other things, a reluctance to accept institutional changes, which stems from the belief that the previous system failed not because its institutions were inherently ineffective, but because of unfavourable circumstances and the fallibility of the people in power, who were to blame for the fact that those institutions could not reveal their advantages. This leads people to idealize past institutions. Memories of the negative consequences of past institutions fade into the public consciousness of some sections of society, while their questionable or apparent positive effects are enhanced. Social nostalgia should decline along with demographic changes and the growing proportion of people without first-hand knowledge of the previous political system. It can, however, be intentionally sustained and strengthened by the state as an element of strengthening the system of power, which is exactly what happened under Vladimir Putin. Unfortunately, Russia is an example of a flawed transition posing a great risk, not only to other countries but also to Russia itself, a risk which has materialized into the war in Ukraine.

In the political sphere, liberal democracy was supposed to be a model of transition for the countries of the former Eastern Bloc. Unfortunately, for the majority of these countries, liberal democracy meant not so much a return to the tradition interrupted by a period of real socialism but was rather associated with the necessity to rebuild democratic institutions from scratch with limited possibilities of drawing on traditions from the inter-war period or earlier times. Once again, this situation was particularly difficult for most of the former Soviet Union, including Russia, which moved almost directly from Tsarist autocracy, reformed and weakened, but exceptionally enduring in the cultural sense to the dictatorship of the proletariat, which was a *de facto* mono-party system with the general secretary of the communist party essentially taking the role of a tsar. Neither the period between the Russian Revolution of 1905 and the February Revolution of 1917, when political reforms were initiated with the intention of making Russia a constitutional monarchy, nor the period of perestroika, which lasted only a few years from the mid-1980s to the collapse of the Soviet Union in 1991 and could have become an element of gradual transition, were all long enough for institutions typical of civil society and essential for the functioning of a democracy to take root.

The sphere of social changes, so crucial from the perspective of civil society, was the most underestimated dimension of the transformation. It was somehow assumed that the very transition from what Janos Kornai called "the economics of shortage" (Kornai 1980) to the abundance of goods in the market economy would facilitate the acceptance of *de facto* capitalist economic conditions and trigger social changes that strengthened new political institutional arrangements codified in the constitution. The problem of underestimating the social dimension of a political transition can be exemplified by the processes associated with the reunification of Germany and the frequently discussed division into Ossis (Easties) and Wessies (Westies), which eventually disappeared, but not as quickly as had been expected. While the process of reunification concerning institutional changes in the form of legal norms and organizational structures was practically completed, it was still incomplete in the sphere of public consciousness and traditions. It was largely the consequence of the social changes that had taken place during the period of over 40 years when two radically different political systems were in place in what is now the unified German state.

As a result of an insufficient understanding of the essence and importance of social changes, where informal institutions endure to play a crucial role, very little was done to foster the development of a civil society, which provides the best framework for the emergence of social individualism, i.e. a form of individualism in which the exercise of individual freedom is accompanied by the respect for and pursuit of what can be described as civic virtues. Shortcomings in the development of a civil society favour the emergence of various forms of dysfunctional, or even pathological individualism, which, in extreme cases manifests itself as the so-called amoral familism, a belief that ethical and moral norms should be obeyed above all or exclusively with respect to members of one's family, which can include company employees, a group sharing mutual interests or even members of a criminal organization (Leonardi 1995).

The dominance of negative forms of individualism can ultimately lead to the development of criminal capitalism (Abrams 2011). In the 1990s, Russia exhibited many characteristics of criminal capitalism mixed with crony capitalism, or even, as already mentioned, some elements of comprador capitalism, typically found in colonial countries and implemented by some of their political elites, which put their own interest and those of their principals above the interests of the country and its population.

Let us now turn to the question of how to interpret the notion of liberalism. Unfortunately, in the practice of the countries of the former Eastern Bloc and others as well, liberalism came to be identified with neoliberalism.[4] As a result, the greatly deserved criticism of neoliberalism leads to the rejection of liberalism as such (Ratajczak 2017). One should not, however, forget about social liberalism, whose principles are derived from, among other aspects, the tradition of John Stuart Mill and his thoughts on the mechanisms underlying the laws of distribution and the associated role of the state (Harvey 2008). Unlike neoliberals, who generally assume that the market determines a fair compensation for different factors of production, i.e. consistent with its actual value, J.S. Mill and his successors identified with social liberalism and recognise the need for the state to take measures aimed at correcting the primary distribution of income. Likewise, the idea of the social market economy, both in its traditional version originating from ordoliberalism, and in the form presented by Grzegorz W. Kołodko in his articles devoted to the idea of so-called new pragmatism (Kołodko 2013), which combines the acceptance of the principle of liberty that lies at the foundation of liberalism, with a much greater concern for the distribution of income than that demonstrated by radical advocates of the free market.

Obviously, according to the version of the political transition that was prevalent in the 1980s and 1990s, the role of the state was supposed to be maximally limited. For adherents of neoliberalism, the state is fallible and incapable of generating solutions that produce effects, which, if not better, then are at least comparable to those resulting from the operation of a free market. According to neoliberal ideas, the market is rarely fallible, and it is even doubtful whether any such exceptions can really be described as fallibility. By contrast, the state is inherently and universally fallible. A slogan, popular in Poland at one time, said that the best industrial policy is the lack of industrial policy, which is the quintessence of that original and dominant perspective on the role of the state in the economy. The vision of the state as an organization that, above all, damages the market rather than corrects it had an impact on different aspects of public policy ranging from infrastructure development to the system of education. For example, in Poland, the idea of limiting the role of the state in areas traditionally associated with public policy was manifested by overly optimistic expectations concerning public-private partnerships (e.g. the initial stage of the programme of motorway construction), the tendency to overestimate the possibilities of applying market solutions in the area of social policy (the programme of open, i.e. *de facto* private pension schemes) or a higher education policy with very low barriers to entry, thus posing serious risks to the quality of education, in favour of private institutions, officially referred to as "non-public" entities creating new educational institutions.

3.3 Weaknesses of the first original transition

In search of the causes of what the "new" transition entailed in countries, among others, such as Hungary and Poland, while also further exploring the idea of enduring institutions[5] and the concept of path dependence (Acemoglu, Johnson, and Robinson 2001), it is useful to provide a brief description of the reality and institutional legacy of a centrally planned economy,[6] with an emphasis on aspects concerning economic transformations.[7]

In a socialist economy, or, more accurately, a centrally planned economy, private property rights were either eliminated - or, in a less radical version, extremely restricted. The dominance of so-called collective ownership meant the disappearance of microeconomic impulses that ensured not only allocational efficiency but also X efficiency, which is associated with the use of one's own resources (Leibenstein 1988). Moreover, a non-market economic system was exceptionally good at fostering rent-seeking and free-riding behaviour, because of the relationship between the principal, i.e., the state, represented by its agents (officials), as well as the managerial staff of state-owned economic organizations. In a centrally planned economy, the state acted as a kind of general insurer, who assumed the risk associated with the economic activity of micro-entities. Such conditions provided no motivation to ensure the microeconomic efficiency of business operations and stimulated the development of attitudes typical of ex-post opportunism. The mechanisms of a centrally planned economy also triggered attitudes typical of ex-ante opportunism, which was associated with the stage of economic decision making at the central level, when executors of the central plan fought for the least challenging tasks and the biggest possible funds for their implementation. Through its actions and the system of propaganda, the state strengthened the citizens' belief that the main problem was not the production, but the distribution of goods and that the state was essentially an omnipotent institution, which only fails through the faults of those who act on its behalf and not as a result of its inherent inability to solve allocational problems, and consequently, also when it comes to the distribution of income.

A centrally planned economy and its solutions in the political and social spheres led to the development of phenomena that were symptomatic of the dysfunctionality of economic and social life. One such phenomenon was corruption, which was often perceived as a peculiar way of correcting the absurdities of central planning (Kamiński and Kamiński 2004). Corruption became a tool used to adjust the centrally planned division of outlays and effects to the actual needs. At the same time, this microeconomic adjustment of errors resulting from central planning gave rise to social tolerance of various types of pathological behaviour.

The institutional infrastructure developed in the conditions of a centrally planned economy and the associated vision of the role of the state in the economy were carried over to new conditions created by the transition. Among institutions inherited from the system of a centrally planned economy mantra-type dogmas played a particularly important role (van Brabant 1992). Mantra-type dogmas, such as the notion of social justice associated with the idea of equality and the distribution of wealth and opportunities, are still a component of the institutional path dependence of Eastern Europe. Of course, this is not true of all transition economies to the same extent. It seems to be less the case in the countries that do not belong to the former Soviet Union and is more so (apart from the former Baltic states) in the countries of the former USSR.

As a result of the institutional legacy of the former system and institutional inertia, particularly evident in enduring institutions, the transition is not a fully completed process, largely because of the nature of changes regarding informal norms and culture. Other symptoms of the institutional weakness of the first transition included the already-mentioned phenomena typical of state capitalism or political capitalism, where regulation, and frequent overregulation, contribute to the emergence of political clientelism and paternalism in state–citizen relations (Kochanowicz 2000). Political clientelism, crony capitalism, as well as criminal capitalism, are associated with a weak state. The state's strength as well as its sovereignty with respect to other economic entities should be distinguished from the idea of an omnipotent state. The state's strength is manifested by its ability to strengthen and promote norms and behaviour that are in line with the institutional system represented by formal rules. The state with a centrally planned economy created the impression of being an omnipotent institution, while in fact was weak, as evidenced by the discrepancy between the official norms and rules of economic life and those commonly observed in practice.

3.4 Idea of the "new" transition and (post)transitional neostatism

Along with the progress of the transition, significant positive changes should follow. In the economic sphere, one should expect elements of political and state capitalism to gradually give way to the development of a social market economy. This expectation stems from the belief that a social market economy provides the best chance of reconciling current ambitions and goals regarding economic growth with the concern for long-term conditions of development based on the principles of civil society and liberal democracy. In the political sphere, a weak and immature liberal democracy should be gradually replaced by a more mature and inclusive liberal democracy, guided by the idea of the common good. Finally, in the social sphere, a weak civic state should be slowly transformed into a mature civil society practically pursuing the ideal of equal opportunities, where relations between the state and its citizens are based on trust and subsidiarity.

However, when one observes the changes implemented for example in Russia,[8] a very different scenario can be imagined, which ultimately leads to the sharpening and fossilization of the weaknesses associated with the original transition. In this scenario of a "new" transition, political and state capitalism is strengthened. A weak and immature liberal democracy evolves in the direction of a non-liberal democracy with authoritarian elements and the tyranny of the majority, while the weak civil society grows even weaker with the development of apathetic individualism and paternalism in state–citizen relations.

The scenario described above is characteristic of the (post)transition neostatism.[9] It is a system in which the economy is formally based on market rules and where private property and competition play a key role. On the socio-political level, the rules of democracy are formally respected, and the idea of a civil society is also pursued. In reality, however, it is just a façade, which serves as a cover for solutions that from the political perspective, can even be perceived as authoritarian. In the economic sphere, the solutions may involve attempts to strengthen the state's role as a participant of economic life, which only pretends to respect market rules with respect to companies where it is a key shareholder. This, in turn, may result in a significant dependence of, and sometimes, actual attempts to subordinate the private sector to the state and its bureaucratic and strongly politicized structures (Mitrović 2007; Lukmanow 2013). The (post)transition neostatism is based on the belief that a "well" managed state, where power is exercised by the "right" people, embracing the "right" ideology, is capable of not only properly fulfilling regulating role – but can to a certain extent, replace the allocation function of the market. According to this vision, the state is also able to act as the initiator of "desirable" social changes, which contribute to the development of a more "civil" society according to the model of civil virtue largely determined and promoted by the system of education and state-controlled media. One typical feature of neostatism is that the state is imbued with a kind of omnipotence, which stands in contrast to what some Polish politicians describe as the state's impossibilism.[10] Under neostatism, the goal of the state's public policy is to strengthen its role as a policymaker and as an entity directly involved in managing organizations implementing this policy. These efforts are accompanied by centralization attempts seen as a way of improving the effectiveness of using public funds. Unfortunately, the experiences of the past political system implemented in countries such as Poland provide a lot of evidence to support the argument that excessive centralization incentivizes ineffectiveness on the part of lower-level task executors, who are largely free from the burden of economic responsibility, which cannot really be substituted by administrative responsibility. Of course, given the weaknesses regarding capital and those associated with the tradition of individual entrepreneurship, in post-socialist countries, the state's activity, while also in the field of allocation, is sometimes necessary as the only alternative to economic development based on foreign capital (Czaja and Fiedor 2021). However, there is a big difference between the approach where this activity is treated as a necessity associated with certain drawbacks and is gradually restricted as the scope of entrepreneurship expands, and dirigiste measures, typical of new statism, where the regulatory and allocative functions of the state are believed to be capable of actually replacing or directing the activity of the private sector.

With respect to the relationship between democracy and liberalism, it is worth noting that for quite a long time, these two concepts were treated as largely irreconcilable. For advocates of liberalism, the prospect of democracy understood simply as the implementation of the majority rule was associated with the threat of the tyranny of the majority, with all its consequences that go against the principles of liberalism. It was only the emergence of liberal democracy, combining the principles of majority rule with the protection of minority rights, which made it possible to reconcile democracy with liberalism.[11] Unfortunately, in the 1960s, the experiences of many countries, especially those classified as developing ones, were labelled as non-liberal democracies (Zakaria 1997). Generally, the term describes a system with certain typically democratic solutions that constitute what is usually referred to as an electoral democracy, but these mechanisms are used to create and/or strengthen the monopoly of power, which is sometimes based on the tyranny of the majority. For a long time, it was assumed, mistakenly as it later turned out, that non-liberal democracies were typically found in developing countries and, more generally, outside Europe. Unfortunately, as is obvious today, a non-liberal democracy may also exist in European countries, though, it must be stressed once again that only on the condition that a considerable section of the society is willing to accept this model of democracy.

As regards neostatism and non-liberal democracy, one should remember that at the start of the political transition, some key representatives of the earlier opposition believed that after dismantling the totalitarian system it was not possible to switch directly to a democratic system (Żelew 1993). Such opinions were consistent with assertions, formulated in literature, which state that periods of economic hardships accompanied by a strong need for development contribute to the strengthening of a market economy under conditions associated with authoritarian rule (Heilbroner 1985). In the economic and political spheres, such solutions have been implemented by countries known as the Asian tigers. Singapore, South Korea, Taiwan, and China or Vietnam are neither paragons of democracy but "tempt" potential emulators with the efficiency of their economic measures. One should not forget, however, about essential cultural, and, more broadly, the institutional differences between the societies of these Asian tigers and those of European countries.

The notions of paternalism in state–citizen relations and apathetic individualism have not been created only to be invoked in the discussion about the "new" transition. They appeared in connection with analyses focusing on some highly developed countries in the context of social and political changes that were taking place there. Both terms refer to the symptoms of the atrophy of a civil society and liberal democracy, with citizens becoming increasingly convinced of having no agency over the actions of the political class, and, consequently, over the functioning of the state, while also deluding themselves that by focusing on their individual goals and aspirations and abstaining from civic participation they will be able to retain their autonomy from the state while benefiting from its "protection" when it is considered useful. Unfortunately, the more widespread this apathetic individualism is, the easier it is for people in power to pursue their own objectives, which they justify as acting in the public interest.

The likelihood of the "new" transition resulting in the intensification and fossilization of the weaknesses associated with the original transition and the rise of (post)transition neostatism increases with the growing tendency of the ruling class to succumb to the temptation of a new kind of enlightened absolutism, with the erosion of liberal democracy and the market economy where the state plays a subsidiary role, and with the growing willingness of citizens to give up liberty in exchange for a more or less illusory sense of security. It should be stressed that neostatism can produce positive effects, but in the long run, they increase the risk of everybody and everything becoming dependent on the state instead of fostering innovation and growth.

As already mentioned, neither non-liberal democracy nor neostatism, which describes the possible consequences of the pessimistic scenario of the "new" transition, is phenomenon only to be observed in countries and societies that have found themselves back in the conditions of capitalism after going through a period of real socialism. However, it is in these countries, though obviously not in all of them to the same extent, that one can notice evident symptoms of processes that can give rise to the development of capitalism strongly affected by these phenomena (Berend and Bugaric 2015; Cianetti, Dawson, and Hanley 2018). When looking for the causes of this situation, one should obviously analyse past events and processes, such as the frequently late decline of the feudal system or marginal participation of the society in the socio-economic changes associated with the first, and especially, second industrial revolution, while also the weak and short-lived character of the relatively modern phase of capitalism in the inter-war period, or its complete absence, as in the case of the majority of the former Soviet Union. Special attention, however, should be paid to the period of real socialism and the frequently underestimated problem of its institutional legacy (Polski Kapitalizm 2016; Rapacki et al. 2018). Of course, one cannot forget about the evident errors and shortcomings of the first stage of the transition.

It seems that any analysis of the problems connected with the strengthening of non-liberal democracy and the growing role of the state attempting to control the process of social and economic changes can be facilitated by applying the idea of the narrow corridor, proposed by Daron Acemoglu and James A. Robinson (Acemoglu and Robinson 2019). Seeking to answer the question why some societies manage to achieve liberty and associated positive outcomes also in the sphere of socio-economic development while others fail in their attempts, the authors conclude that it is due to a combination of different circumstances, where the relationship between two actors plays a key role. One of them is the state, which must be strong, but in the sense explained in the previous sections of this chapter. This strength should manifest itself by the state's ability to perform certain functions, such as ensuring public order, and not by projecting an image of apparent omnipotence. The second actor without which liberty cannot be achieved is a strong society, whose role is to supervise the state. The authors argue that the state, described by Thomas Hobbs as a Leviathan in the absence of supervision, which can only be exercised by a strong society, always tends to become the so-called Despotic Leviathan. Liberty can only be achieved when the Leviathan has been shackled. Acemoglu and Robinson also describe two other forms of state, which they label as the Absent and Paper Leviathan. The former is associated with the threat of anarchy and a war of everyone against everyone. The latter only appears to be strong, while in fact, it is not only incapable of being despotic and effectively enforcing its decisions but even less so in terms of supporting positive grass-roots social initiatives. The analytical approach proposed by Acemoglu and Robinson, though not without certain weaknesses, is particularly interesting in the context of discussions about the case of Russia. One can agree with the authors that at the beginning of the political transition, Russia, such as most of the states that came into being after the collapse of the Soviet Union, was far away from the narrow corridor leading to liberty, mainly because of the absence of civil society. Over centuries of existence, with changing political systems, the despotic state was never counterbalanced by a strong society and as a result, the neo-imperial ideology and all its consequences have become the symbol of the new Despotic Leviathan.

3.5 Final remarks

Any systemic transition first and foremost involves a radical institutional transformation, and it is on the institutional level that one needs to look for the causes of many problems associated with the process of transitioning from a centrally planned economy to a market economy. Arguably, for the transformation process in the institutional sphere to be regarded as completed, the following conditions would have to be satisfied: (1) formal institutions sustaining the planned order must give way to a coherent and complete set of rules underlying the market order; (2) informal norms, conventions, and customs associated with a centrally planned economy must be replaced by a coherent system of informal market institutions; and (3) business units must internalise formal and informal rules, which means that their choices and patterns of behaviour are based on a set of market norms (Hockuba 2000, p. 127).

As has already been pointed out, it is easier to satisfy the aforementioned conditions (especially the first and the second ones) in states whose centrally planned economies were based on rules that were less orthodox and radical than the model of the Soviet economy. Throughout the period of the centrally planned economy in Poland, quasi-market entities existed that were engaged in individual economic activity, which, among other things, contributed to the successful development of individual entrepreneurship in the period directly following the end of real socialism. At the start of the transition, Poland was undoubtedly much closer than, for example, Russia, to the narrow corridor leading to liberty, which is the foundation of socio-economic life, though not close enough to eliminate the risk of restoring a version of the state with more features of a Despotic Leviathan than a Shackled one.

At present, it is difficult to make definitive predictions about future evaluations of the fascination displayed by some politicians and sections of society with non-liberal democracy with the state acting not only as a regulator – but also as a decision maker directly involved in the economy. Perhaps, it will be merely a transitional period to be followed by a return to the vision of the state, which, while having to regulate the market, as well as occasionally correcting its mechanisms and in extreme cases substituting it, cannot aspire to become a kind of alternative to the market. There is, however, another possibility, albeit rather unlikely at present, involving not only countries of former Eastern Europe – but of a world opting for a political system in which changes described in the pessimistic scenario of the "new" transition and strengthening the weaknesses of the original transition will become the characteristic feature of a new political standard. The case of China seems to indicate that the state can quite effectively shape socio-economic processes in the absence of democracy, and even more so when it is a liberal democracy. One should not forget, however, as has already been mentioned, that most Asian cultures are collectivist by nature and tend to de-emphasize the notion of a separate, autonomous self. Moreover, China has a long tradition of combining strong centralized power with a certain amount of respect, frequently expressed in a form, which is, admittedly, far from perfect, for the principles of meritocracy. This combination partly prevents excessive politicization of personnel decisions, and, consequently, economic activities (except for the period of the Cultural Revolution, which was an extreme departure from this meritocratic tradition).

In conclusion, one can only hope that the Despotic Leviathan will not be the symbol of the future of countries such as Poland or Hungary, and it will be possible to pursue policies enabling citizens to meet their aspirations and expectations in the conditions of an equilibrium between the power of the state and a strong society, and neostatism will not turn out to be the permanent form of political and economic systems.

Notes

1 This section and the following ones include elements of the author's previous article (Ratajczak 2019).

2 The use of the term "state-imposed collectivism" is motivated by the need to emphasize the non-voluntary nature of the process, which stands in contrast to strong elements of natural collectivism observed in some societies in East Asia because of a specific

understanding of the role and obligations of an individual, which differs from those typically found in European traditions.

3 According to one view, Russia is the only example of a real economic transition, a sort of an economic "big bang", i.e. the most radical version of a transformation, which led to, among other things, a considerable decline in the standard of living for a large percentage of the population, even compared to the already relatively low Soviet standards (Stiglitz 2004).

4 An interesting analysis of how the concepts of liberalism and neoliberalism became one is included in a book by Jadwiga Godłów-Legiędź (Godłów-Legiędź 2020).

5 The idea of enduring structures in history and social sciences is associated with Fernand Braudel (Braudel 1958). His article, originally published in French, was popularized after being translated into English. However, as Immanuel Wallerstein explains in his interesting article (Wallerstein 2009), the problem is that the apparently easy task of translating the French expression "la longue durée" proves to be a serious challenge – obviously not in semantic terms, but from the perspective of the idea that Braudel wanted to express. At this point, suffice to say that the history of how ideas put forward by various authors were distorted because of being translated into other languages could be the subject of a separate study.

6 It is beyond the scope of this article to discuss at length the elements of *path dependence* and the institutional legacy of the countries of the former Eastern Bloc that are associated with such historically distant phenomena as the first and second industrial revolutions. One cannot fail to notice, however, that some consequences of the generally marginal role of Eastern Europe in those historical processes can still manifest themselves, at least partially. The special significance of history, from the perspective of *path dependence*, in countries with non-democratic institutions is explored by Georgy Egorov and Konstantin Sonin (Egorov and Sonin 2020). In Poland, the discussion about the impact of distant past events on the present and the idea of enduring structures includes considerations about the consequences of the so-called grange culture (Hryniewicz 2004; Banach 2014; Kolasa-Nowak 2018).

7 There are several publications exploring the institutional dimension of the political transition, especially in the economic sphere, although most of them appeared within the first 20 years following the start of the debate on the topic. The following examples can be named as follows: Bałtowski and Miszewski (2007), Godłów-Legiędź and Legiędź (2009), Gruszewska (2013), Hare (2013), Kołodko (2014), Lissowska (1998, 2004), Piątek (2016), Wojtyna (2002).

8 Since the beginning of the Vladimir Putin era, Russia has been the best example of a "new" transition. Significant elements of references to the idea of a "new" transition can also be observed in countries such as Hungary from the beginning of Viktor Orban's rule or Poland after the elections in the autumn of 2015. Of course, there are some fundamental differences between the political and non-political realities of Russia and the two countries mentioned above.

9 Czaja and Fiedor (2021) provide an interesting analysis of the history of statism in Poland, including the phase that the authors describe as the seeds of nationalist-ideological statism, which corresponds to the idea of neostatism presented in the article.

10 The term "impossibilism" was introduced by Marek Jurek, Speaker of the Sejm in 2005–2007, to refer to the fact that the power of the authorities is limited by the law and the constitution.

11 In their article entitled "The Political Economy of Liberal Democracy", Sharun W. Mukand and Dani Rodrik make an argument, which many would find controversial, in that given all the conditions required for a liberal democracy to exist "the surprise is not that few democracies are liberal, but that liberal democracies exist at all" (Mukand and Rodrik 2020, p. 765).

References

Abrams, A. (2011). *From Criminal Communism to Criminal Capitalism*. Wilson Center. Retrieved from: https://www.wilsoncenter.org/publication/criminal-communism-to-criminal-capitalism.

Acemoglu, D., Johnson, S., and Robinson, J. A. (2001). The Colonial Origins of Comparative Development: An Empirical Investigation. *The American Economic Review*, 91(5), pp. 1369–1401. https://doi.org/10.1257/aer.91.5.1369.

Acemoglu, D., and Robinson, J. A. (2019). *The Narrow Corridor. States, Societies, and the Fate of Liberty*. New York: Penguin Publishers.

Bałtowski, M., and Miszewski, M. (2007). *Transformacja gospodarcza w Polsce*. Warszawa: Wydawnictwo Naukowe PWN.

Banach, W. (2014). Refleksja nad koncepcją folwarcznych korzeni polskiej kultury gospodarczej Janusza Hryniewicza. *Człowiek i społeczeństwo,* XXXVIII, pp. 49–65. https://doi.org/10.14746/cis.2014.38.4.

Berend, I. T., and Bugaric, B. (2015). Unfinished Europe: Transition from Communism to Democracy in Central and Eastern Europe. *Journal of Contemporary History,* 50(4), pp. 768–785. https://doi.org/10.1177/0022009415596845.

Braudel, F. (1958). Histoire et Sciences sociales: La longuedurée. *Annales. Économies, Sociétés, Civilisations*, 13(4), pp. 725–753.

Bunce, V. (1999). The Political Economy of Post-Socialism. *Slavic Review*, 58(4), pp. 756–793. https://doi.org/10.2307/2697198.

Cianetti, L., Dawson, J., and Hanley, S. (2018). Rethinking "Democratic Backsliding" in Central and Eastern Europe – Looking Beyond Hungary and Poland. *East European Politics*, 34(3), pp. 243–256. https://doi.org/10.1080/21599165.2018.1491401.

Czaja, St., and Fiedor, B. (2021). *Oblicza polskiego etatyzmu gospodarczego. Spór o miejsce państwa w okresie międzywojennym, powojennym i po 1990 roku. Liberalizm versus etatyzm*. Wrocław: Wydawnictwo Uniwersytetu Ekonomicznego we Wrocławiu.

Egorov, G., and Sonin, K. (2020). The Political Economics of Non-Democracy, National Bureau of Economic Research, Working Paper 27949. https://doi.org/10.3386/w27949. Retrieved from: https://www.nber.org/papers/w27949.

Godłów-Legiędź, J. (2020). *Polska transformacja w świetle sporów o rynek, sprawiedliwość i ekonomię*. Łódź: Wydawnictwo Uniwersytetu Łódzkiego.

Godłów-Legiędź, J., and Legiędź, T. (2009). Interakcja instytucji formalnych i nieformalnych w procesie transformacji od planu do rynku. In J. Godłów-Legiędź (Ed.). *Instytucje i transformacja.* Toruń: Wydawnictwo Adam Marszałek, pp. 64–73.

Gruszewska, E. (2013). *Instytucje, a proces tworzenia kapitału w Polsce.* Białystok: Wydawnictwo Uniwersytetu w Białymstoku.

Hare, P. (2013). Institutions and Transition: Lessons and Surprises. *Society and Economy*, 35(1), pp. 1–24. https://doi.org/10.1556/SocEc.35.2013.1.1.

Harvey, D. (2008). *Neoliberalizm. Historia katastrofy*. Warszawa: Instytut Wydawniczy Książka i Prasa.

Heilbroner, R. L. (1985). Ponad ekonomiczną rewolucją. In *Ponad ekonomią.* Warszawa: PIW, pp. 150–163.

Hockuba, Z. (2000). Transformacja jako zmiana porządku ekonomicznego. In J. Winiecki (Ed.). *Transformacja gospodarki postkomunistycznej a teoria ekonomii.* Warszawa: Towarzystwo Ekonomistów Polskich, pp. 121–133.

Hryniewicz, J. (2004). *Polityczny i kulturowy kontekst rozwoju gospodarczego.* Warszawa: Wydawnictwo Naukowe Scholar.

Kamiński, A. Z., and Kamiński, B. (2004). *Korupcja rządów. Państwa postkomunistyczne wobec globalizacji.* Warszawa: Wydawnictwo TRIO.

Kiss, K. (1993). *Western Prescriptions for Eastern Transition. A Comparative Analysis of the Different Economic Schools and Issues.* Budapest: Hungarian Scientific Council for World Economy.

Kochanowicz, J. (2000). Dwoista konsolidacja. Transformacja ekonomiczna i zmiana instytucjonalna. *Ekonomista,* 3, pp. 305–323.

Kolasa-Nowak, A. (2018). Od idei homo sovieticus do mentalności folwarcznej Polaków. O używaniu przeszłości w dyskursie socjologicznym i publicznym. *Res Historica,* 46, pp. 301–320. https://doi.org/10.17951/rh.2018.46.301-320.

Kołodko, G. W. (2013). *Dokąd zmierz świat, ekonomia polityczna przyszłości.* Warszawa: Prószyński i S-ka.

Kołodko, G. W. (2014). Instytucje i polityka a wzrost gospodarczy. In P. Kozłowski and M. Wojtysiak-Kotlarski (Eds.). *Grzegorz W. Kołodko i ćwierćwiecze transformacji.* Warszawa: Wydawnictwo Naukowe SCHOLAR, pp. 499–522.

Kornai, J. (1980). *Economics of Shortage.* Amsterdam: North-Holland Publishing Company.

Kowalik, T. (2005). *Systemy gospodarcze. Efekty i defekty reform i zmian ustrojowych.* Warszawa: Fundacja Innowacja.

Leibenstein, H. (1988). *Poza schematem homo oeconomicus.* Warszawa: PWN.

Leonardi, R. (1995). Regional Development in Italy: Social Capital and the Mezzogiorno. *Oxford Review of Economic Policy,* 11(2), pp. 165–179.

Lissowska, M. (1998). *Instytucje gospodarki rynkowej w Polsce.* Warszawa: Wydawnictwo C.H. Beck.

Lissowska, M. (2004). *Instytucjonalne wymiary procesu transformacji w Polsce.* Warszawa: Wydawnictwo SGH w Warszawie.

Lukmanow, A. S. (2013). Lobbism w Rossii: Analiz sovremennoj specyfiki. Sborniki konferencji NIC. *Socijosfera,* 45, pp. 153–158.

Mitrović, L. R. (2007). Immanuel Wallerstein's Contribution to Mondology and the Critical Theory of the Global World System Transition. *FACTA UNIVERSITATIS, Series: Philosophy, Sociology and Psychology,* 6(1), pp. 91–104.

Mukand, S. W., and Rodrik, D. (2020). The Political Economy of Liberal Democracy. *The Economic Journal,* 130, pp. 765–792. https://doi.org/10.1093/ej/ueaa004.

Piątek, D. (2016). *Instytucje państwa a wzrost gospodarczy w krajach postsocjalistycznych.* Poznań: Wydawnictwo UEP.

Polski kapitalizm. Jaki model gospodarki realizujemy? (2016). Polityka Insight, Komitet Dialogu Społecznego Krajowej Izby Gospodarczej. Retrieved from: https://www.politykainsight.pl/gospodarka/ryzykaitrendy/_resource/multimedium/20104895.

Rapacki, R., Gardawski, J., Czerniak, A., Horbaczewska, B., Karbowski, A., Maszczyk, P., and Próchniak, M. (2018). Wyłaniające się odmiany kapitalizmu w Europie Środkowo-Wschodniej: Przegląd badań. *Ekonomista,* 5, pp. 523–553.

Ratajczak, M. (2017). Liberalizm i neoliberalizm ekonomiczny w perspektywie historycznej. *Ekonomista,* 1, pp. 7–29.

Ratajczak, M. (2019). Instytucjonalne aspekty nowej transformacji ustrojowej. In E. Mączyńska (Ed.). *Ekonomia i polityka: wokół teorii Grzegorza W. Kołodko.* Warszawa: Wydawnictwo Naukowe PWN, pp. 221–239.

Stiglitz, J. E. (2004). *Globalizacja.* Warszawa: Wydawnictwo Naukowe PWN.

Sztompka, P. (2000). *Trauma wielkiej zmiany. Społeczne koszty transformacji.* Warszawa: Instytut Studiów Politycznych Polskiej Akademii Nauk. Warszawa.

van Brabant, M. (1992). *Privatizing Eastern Europe*. Dordrecht: Kluwer Academic Publishers.

Wallerstein, I. (2009). Braudel on the Longue Durée: Problems of Conceptual Translation. *Review (Fernand Braudel Center)*, 32(2), pp. 155–170.

Wojtyna, A. (2002). Nowe kierunki badań nad rolą instytucji we wzroście i transformacji. *Gospodarka Narodowa*, 10, pp. 1–24.

Zakaria, F. (1997). The Rise of Illiberal Democracy. *Foreign Affairs*, 76(6), pp. 22–43.

Żelew, Ż. (1993). Demokracja w społeczeństwie posttotalitarnym. *Gazeta Wyborcza*, 77, p. 8.

Part II

Organized interests

4 Interest-centred explanation of pension reforms in Poland

Anna Ząbkowicz

4.1 Introduction

The financialization and privatization of the pensions industry, which has been in progress since the turn of the millennium, received its material shape in capital-based pension funds. New institutional arrangements supplementing pay-as-you-go (PAYG) systems have invited financial entities such as banks, insurance companies, and investment funds into a domain that used to be managed by public agencies in Europe. This meant profound structural change, namely, in pension welfare this segment emerged or was visibly extended where pensions were capital-based and privately managed, with the risk of old-age poverty being borne basically by would-be pensioners. I claim that the nature of this transformation is by no means merely technical. During these reforms, values, motivations, and the institutional order itself have all changed.

Why have these courses of reforms been followed? The study proposes an explanation by providing insight into interests that drive and retard this institutional change.

This chapter draws on the language and concepts of institutional political economy. It starts from the following observation: The late 20th century saw fully fledged market economies with accumulated capital surplus which sought new non-industrial investments, thus empowering financial intermediaries, with the state becoming their best client due to its structural fiscal deficits and its borrowing requirements. In particular, pension systems became perceived as a relevant source of capital to be invested in treasury bonds and other securities traded on financial markets (Estevez-Abe 2001; Jackson and Vitols 2001).[1] From this perspective, the aforesaid reforms may be regarded as promoting certain interests rather than simply introducing another pension structure, as normally presented within pension economics (Mitchell and Utkus 2003; Beshears et al. 2006; Polakowski and Hagemejer 2018).

In this case, special concern is given to new interests that banks and other financial intermediaries have in the pensions industry. Traditionally, in European welfare states the segment of obligatory pension insurance was directly managed by a public institution on the PAYG basis, and financial companies (FCs) were engaged in voluntary old-age insurance with the aim of investing accumulated savings in

DOI: 10.4324/9781003425717-6

financial markets. In the 1990s, the state took interest in the "capital" segment as well, with balances of the PAYG segment continuously deteriorating and implicit public debt on the rise. It resulted in the visible extension of capital-based pensions in Western Europe (e.g. Germany) and facilitated capital-based pension funding in Eastern European countries where it was utterly new. Such reforms put new money into existing interests (such as in Germany) or gave rise to new interests (such as in EE) within the pensions industry.

The research presented in this chapter is limited to the case of Poland, which may be broadly associated with the Eastern European type of pension structure. An overview of reforms in the opening section identifies the course of institutional changes, in which it shows that Poland introduced capital-based pension funding both in its mandatory and voluntary forms. The following section takes an interest-centred approach by methodically outlining the matrix of major economic interests involved in pension reforms: the government, the financial sector, non-FCs, and trade unions (TUs), as well as prospective or the actual pensioners themselves. The main body of this chapter relies on country-specific policy papers and public statements in an attempt to delineate the narratives of the reforms. Subsequently, it strives to identify the substantive interests of the parties involved and their material positions. In conclusion, an explanation is offered that contradicts the official stance supporting the reforms in the name of the well-being of pensioners and points to the major driving force of the reforms.

4.2 A brief record of pension reforms

Contemporary pension reforms seem to tend towards what may be briefly described as the privatization of the management of funds, while also the capitalization of savings and the privatization of risk.

Under welfare capitalism, governments mandated individual employees and employers to participate in the pension schemes which were normally publicly managed. The pension-system structure in post-socialist Poland after 1990 followed this pattern. The method of financing was based on the PAYG system where the public administration of mandatory old-age insurance would continuously pay benefits from the pool of current revenues formed by contributions made to the system by the employed and/or their employers. The system was run with implicit state guarantees of retirement benefits.

The year 1999 and the subsequent years saw the architecture of the pension system profoundly transformed. The reform split the traditional pension system into publicly and privately managed pillars. Moreover, the mandatory contributions raised by the state agency ZUS (Social Insurance Institution) have since then been divided into funds run by ZUS and by privately licensed companies (PTEs), the so-called open pension funds. Thus, two pillars of mandatory insurance emerged, which were supplemented by funds raised on a voluntary basis and run by another category of private fund-managing firms (TFIs).[2] Hence, the state invited private firms into the area of old-age security.

Funded pensions are about capital-based financing of future benefits in the old-age insurance. According to this institutional arrangement, an accumulated fund built from contributions by or on behalf of its participants is in use as capital to be invested in financial assets (Barr and Diamond 2010). This method is utterly different from PAYG system where contributions are spent on current benefits with no investments in sight. In fully fledged market economies, reforms promote funded *voluntary* pension plans. In Poland, as in the case of many emerging market economies, they developed "greenfield" structures at the turn of the 20th and 21st centuries. As already said, *mandatory* pension funding was introduced there as well, not without the persuasion of the World Bank.

In effect, the privatization of pensions was accompanied by the expansion of capital-based pension funding. Moreover, in old-age insurance in Poland, the risk of old-age poverty was shifted to contributors in the system as a whole. The overall outcome of the transformation of pensions in Poland may be summarized in Table 4.1.

The 1999 transformation of the pension system still enabled welfare to be financed traditionally on a PAYG basis as the core of the system, albeit it introduced some relevant changes into it. The establishment of two tiers of capital-based pensions constituted the most spectacular change. The second pillar emerged as a hybrid at the intersection of the public and private sectors under the name of open pension funds (OFEs). Subsequently, the pension funding structure became extended with such schemes as the employee pension fund, saving investment fund, life insurance scheme, and the mutual saving fund which constituted the third pillar of the Polish system.

In the aftermath of 2008, major reforms were introduced regarding the two privately managed pillars in which pensions are funded on a capital basis (namely, the second pillar and the third pillar in Table 4.1).

In 2008, the first information about the excessive costs of maintaining OFEs was conveyed to the public, which was followed by the slow scaling down of the second pillar. The breakthrough moment occurred when by means of a new law passed in December 2013, OFE assets were cut down by half due to the

Table 4.1 Old-age insurance in Poland after the 1999 reforms

Pillar/tier	*I*	*II (hybrid)*	*III*
Management	Public (ZUS)	Private (PTEs)	Private (TFIs)
Contribution	Mandatory	Mandatory	Poluntary
Financing base	Pay-as-you-go	**Funded**	**Fully funded**
Retirement benefits	Basic	Basic	Premium
Funds/plans	FUS (reformed)	OFE	PPK, IKE, IKZE
Benefit/contribution formula	Defined contribution	Defined contribution	Defined contribution

Note: ZUS=Social Insurance Institution, FUS=mandatory contribution and social spending under ZUS management. Entries in bold indicate where pension funding is located in the system.
Source: Self-analysis.

obligatory transfer of treasury bonds and publicly guaranteed securities from their portfolios to a special account under the management of ZUS. After 2013, there have been hardly any new contributors to this pillar; moreover, the contributions of aged members are to be transferred to accounts administered by ZUS. The outflows of contributions from the second pillar have outpaced their inflows. The deficits have become even more profound due to the negative financial performance of OFEs.

As a result, the nominal value of OFE portfolios in December 2022 corresponded with the 2007 level and was lower than in December of the breakthrough year of 2013 (Chamber of Commerce of Pension Societies 2023). Still, the fate of the hybrid pension funds affects a large number of the adult population due to the assets, or basically stock, which remained in the second pillar after the scaling down of 2013. The policy regarding the hybrid pillar remains vague. The 2018 bill envisages the funds in the second pillar to be split again and transferred this time to individual accounts in the third pillar, or to a special account in the first pillar. The latter would be administered by ZUS. Transfers to the third pillar would be automatic, while transfers to the first pillar would require a declaration of consent from the owners of the savings (opt-out option) (Błaszczyk 2020). The level of determination here seems to fade in the face of real politics. For some reasons, the project, which has already found acceptance in the eyes of the government twice, remains stuck in the Polish Parliament. Since 2018, the law has never been voted on and according to the Polish high-ranking official Paweł Borys, the vote is to be postponed to post-election time, which means it will be presented in Parliament no sooner than in 2024.

Simultaneously, since 2014 projects to transfer considerable amounts of public money to the third pillar have been developed in order to stimulate individual (private) saving and company-based saving as well (Social Insurance Institution, 2016). The 2019 Employee Capital Plans Act has not only accommodated voluntary private schemes by transfers of public money but also imposed general automatic enrolment with an opportunity to opt out. This is a peculiar combination of automatism and individual choice. In this arrangement, employees no longer need to declare participation in the scheme as new regulations provide that each employee and each newly employed person is automatically enrolled in the employee capital plan (PPK). Declarations are necessary only to opt out. In such an event, however, an employee will be automatically enrolled after a period of time (GazetaPrawna.pl 2019). The general idea of imposing this peculiar automatism of enrolment is to provide new members. Therefore, it seems that despite the development of the hybrid pillar being stopped, capital-based pension funds might still have a bright future.

Along with the expansion of capital-based tiers, pension benefits increasingly rely on gains from financial operations. By way of consequence, besides social or generational solidarity underlying the core PAYG tier (or the first pillar in Table 4.1), the logic of investing in the securities market has been introduced into the pension system. This is not merely the technical question of how to maintain income after retirement. This component of the transformation seems to be deeply rooted in values. For this reason, it is appropriate to regard pension funding as an institutional change rather than merely a new design of the pension system. Prior to the reforms, the public PAYG system would prioritize functions of a mostly social and political nature, while current pension funding is governed by principles that definitely differ from ones aiming to counter poverty and exclusion. In capital-based tiers, pension benefits are paid out with no redistribution occurring between the current contributors and beneficiaries.

Moreover, the fundamental relationship between contribution and benefit was altered. The structural reform of 1999 introduced the Defined Contribution (DC) formula in the system as a whole, in order to equally embrace publicly managed, as well as privately managed funds (Table 4.1). I am going to undertake this issue again in the analysis to follow. Suffice to note here that the DC formula risk became privatized, which means that basically would-be pensioners or individual members of the funded-pension schemes take the consequences, while in the pre-reform system, with single public old-age insurance and Defined Benefit (DB) formula, the risk of financial failure was fully supported with public money. This is another major change since it determines risk sharing in the industry. Although it may seem to be a simple component of financial engineering, it must have had a profound impact on the institutional order. Together with the shift of risk, pension funding has made the well-being of beneficiaries dependent on corporate strategy and the performance of FCs investing in volatile capital markets. Perhaps because of distributional and political consequences, it is easily overlooked in public debate and the issue was rather not exposed by the reformers themselves.

4.3 Interests in action: the theoretical approach

The conceptual framework of subsequent analysis is provided by the institutional political economy. This cognitive approach to economic processes regards politics as an institutionally structured process and considers institutional change to be ultimately driven by political and economic interests. According to this strand of thought, on the one hand, individuals and organizations exploit their institutional environment in order to pursue political and entrepreneurial goals. In this perspective, institutions are areas of strategic social interactions and decision-making processes (Shepsle 2006, pp. 1032–1033). Some authors put it even stronger: Institutions provide modes of conduct that channel the actors' interests, while ultimately institutions constitute the formal and informal rules that actors *must* follow when pursuing their interests (Swedberg 2006, pp. 945–946). On the other hand, the influential Northian perspective says that institutions may reflect the outcome of struggles over interests. Douglas C. North (1990) suggested a game form of the conception of institution. Institutional change is seen as the outcome of interest-driven games. The game is played by organizations and "political entrepreneurs". According to Kenneth A. Shepsle (2006, pp. 1032–1033), these "political entrepreneurs" maintain companies, political parties, legislative committees, interest groups, public offices, while also military units, etc. The institutional political economy diverges from methodological individualism, arguing instead that "in the social environments common to human interactions, the self-regarding are often induced to act in the interest of the group" (Bowles and Gintis 2006, p. 954).

According to Richard Swedberg, the very notion of an institution is interest centred (Swedberg 2006). In economics and political science, the concept of interest describes goals pursued by actors. Those who believe that these goals are rooted in objective material positions often prefer to speak of interests, "while those who believe in the subjective nature of these goals tend to choose the term preferences" (Paster 2015). In this respect, again, the institutional political economy seems to be opposed to the mainstream economics, i.e. as the latter chose to speak about preferences or utility, rather than interest.

The aforesaid semantic difference hides an inspiring differentiation between these two worlds of economists which seems to be rooted in the Weberian concepts of formal and material rationality. Namely, "formal" means "the following rules" and "material" means "the following interests". While the former is related to monetary calculus, the latter relates to the distribution of goods and is more closely associated with the notion of "interests". While mainstream economics focus on the "formal" calculus, the political-economic approach chooses rather interests and social interaction. According to Max Weber, everyday life is governed by habits and material interests, while faith in formal rules (the law) is an additional, yet essential factor (Weber 2002, pp. 79, 158). According to this intellectual tradition, interest refers directly to the *material* resources necessary to meet human needs and distribute *goods*, while both the economic rationality based on *calculus* and the rule of *law* constitute the background.

Karl Polanyi seems to follow suit in his 1957 article "The economy as an instituted process", although he indicates Carl Menger's 1923 work as his inspiration when discussing cognitive approaches to economic processes. According to Polanyi, two approaches are possible: either formal "economizing", based on the logic of scarcity and choice, or a "substantive" approach taking into consideration human interactions with the natural and social environments in pursuit of tangible goods required to meet one's needs (Kassner 2017). This train of thought in social sciences offers an understanding that departs from the abstract formalized economic framework in favour of material and "substantive" dimensions, as in the case of the analysis presented in the next section.

Another important theoretical aspect of the analysis is to identify group interests involved in the game about pensions. In the field of pension reform, the following interests are at stake: (1) interest in winning and maintaining political power; (2) interest in increasing profits from the financial markets; (3) interest in employment and profits related to manufacturing, as well as the welfare of the employees; and last but not least; and (4) interest in social security.

Such a classification of interests, in association with specific actors, organizes the argumentation developed in this chapter. Interests of political nature are first of all associated with (1) the government, namely, the interest in winning and maintaining political and/or regulatory power is the concern of public executive authorities and/or public bureaucracy. The government acts in a double role capacity. Obviously enough, it is responsible for legal regulations affecting both the public and private pillars of the pension system. Due to the public core of the system, it also acts via a governmental agency as the administrator of public funds. Following the list from the previous paragraph, the earnings in the financial markets are a matter of interest of (2) this part of the financial sector which is engaged in the management of capital-based pension funds. Interests related to manufacturing are shared by (3) non-FCs and their employees who became involved either in the organization of, or contributions to occupational capital-based pension funds. The basis for pursuing interests named here as 1, 2, and 3 is constituted by contributors to a variety of pension funds. All participants and beneficiaries of pension funds and schemes are collective actor number 4.

This presentation of the basic material positions of socioeconomic actors provides the framework for the empirical analysis of the Polish case. Who is for and who is against capital-based pension funds? Whose interests are followed or harmed due to shifting the risk?

4.4 Rhetoric of the reforms

This section provides a review of arguments in favour of capital-based pension funds, drawing from media debates and official announcements with the aim of identifying the rational basis of pension funding. Here, I claim that direct interests remained somewhat in the shadow of the rhetoric.

As far as dynamics and orientation of reforms are concerned, the government's ideological and economic interests seem to be pivotal. The primary goal is the interest in winning and maintaining political and/or regulatory power. This is conditioned by the stimulation of economic growth. Macroeconomic growth is substantive since it feeds all other ends government can dream of, which include economic stability, social peace (with sustainable public deficits, high rates of employment, etc.), and, last but not least, sufficient public debt financing. I am going to show that Polish governments approached this challenge with a special rhetoric relying in essence on two statements:

- Supplementary capital-based tier is to create more security for prospective pensioners.
- Accumulation of capital in pension funds and/or expanding the financial services sector is a chance to accelerate economic growth.

4.4.1 Need for preservation of retirement income

Demography and security are widely exploited in publicity campaigns accompanying pension reforms. Due to the diminishing fertility rates and increased longevity in European welfare states, the ratio of insured people of retirement age with regard to contributors of a productive age has been consistently increasing. This, along with other factors, throws doubt upon the financial sustainability of the public PAYG system in Poland and elsewhere. For many years, the rising ratio implied increased spending on pension benefits with relation to current inflows of pension contributions. As a result, the balance would show current pension deficits, as well as net liabilities of the pension system that would increase in the long term. Instead of addressing the necessity to raise contributions in order to match deficits, the debate in Poland focused on preserving the living standard of the pensioners thanks to supplementary funded pensions.

At the turn of the century, the concept prevailed that a multi-tier system creates more income security for prospective pensioners, and the pensions provided are partly funded on a capital basis. Its logic was developed along the following lines: The traditional PAYG tier due to its structural deficits is able to pay lower and lower benefits, unless it is financed at the cost of state budget deficits. Neither of these two developments is desirable. Supplementary pension funds and schemes, based on a different mode of financing, will possibly increase their share of retirement income and improve the sum of benefits originating from different tiers, thus effectively constraining a further risk of poverty at old age. Investing in capital markets is at the very core of such reasoning. An important premise stated that funds managed by financial firms are to be invested in stock and securities with a return on stock turnover being positive in the long run. This reasoning made the concept of multi-tier financing attractive thanks to the suggestion of improving rather than deteriorating the outcome of the system as a whole. In Poland, "security through diversity" became the official policy. The individual proponents, as well as the institutional supporters of funded pensions implied what was rather acknowledged by the public, namely, that capital-based funds and schemes would possibly bring a positive return on investments, thus enlarging the sum of benefits originating from different pillars (Government Council for Socioeconomic Strategy 1997; Office of the Government Plenipotentiary for Social Security Reform 1997; Office of the Pension Funds Supervisory Commission 2000).

Polish experts and policymakers, such as Agnieszka Chłoń or Jerzy Hausner, who designed the 1999 reform together with the World Bank experts, were given the power to act on the basis of a broad political consensus (see: Chłoń, Góra, and Rutkowski 1999; Hausner 2002). The privatization of the pension system was based on a cross-party agreement supported not only by the post-communist and agrarian majority of SLD/ PSL but also by the liberal and conservative opposition, which implemented the reform in 1999 after taking power.

The pro-reform line of argumentation shows the explicit regard for the income of prospective pensioners. The social peace was a real concern indeed. However, the preservation of the retirement-income rhetoric was actually covering another substantive interest of the state which was the deep anxiety about the financial condition of the welfare state, including the implicit public pension debt, budgetary deficits, and public debt financing.

In order to reduce the pension deficits, the predicted pension benefit as related to the average or last wage was radically reduced (Wiktorow 2008, p. 36, Table 3). In pension-engineering slang, this index is called the rate of replacement. One of the authors of the reform claimed in 2002: "The reform apparently was just aimed at diminishing this index. In an aging society, this is the requirement of systemic solvency" (Hausner 2002). The foreseen constraint in rates of replacement needed to be somehow cushioned with regard to the public. Including the capital-based tier into the reform seemed to be of help, along with the multi-tier rationale attached. Actually, the 1999 reform avoided an increase in mandatory contributions, albeit, it cut relative benefits from PAYG pillar due to the changed accounting formula.

4.4.2 Financial capital considered as the main pro-growth factor

The rhetoric pointing to the welfare function of the new pension structure provided a smokescreen along with another aspect. Tadeusz Szumlicz made a good point that pension funding and OFE in particular were introduced not to secure future pensions, but to invest pension savings (Szumlicz 2002). Capital-based pensions were meant to generate continuous financial flows, via institutional investors, to the financial markets rather than to provide security for old-age income.

A special rhetoric put weight on the relation between pension funding, flourishing finance, and economic growth. The message exposed by reformers said in brief that pension savings, either mandatory or voluntary, if funded, contribute to the flourishing of public companies and capital markets (OECD 2003, p. 78). Some theories, widely accepted in the 1990s and backed, among others, by the authority of the World Bank (IBRD), carried a message that flourishing capital markets possibly mean macroeconomic growth. Empirical tests mostly confirmed the positive link between financial and economic growth in developed economies, particularly in the period between 1960 and 1989 (see, e.g., King and Levine 1993). As far as middle-income countries such as Poland were concerned, where domestic private capital was typically scarce, the World Bank argued that mandatory pension funds would contribute to the trade in long-term financial instruments and would become an instrument of growth by increasing capital accumulation (World Bank 1994). Finance-growth nexus theories due to their pro-growth premise had a chance to become popular and widely accepted, while also going hand in hand with the government's substantive interests as well. Based on the concept of the finance-growth nexus, policymakers could assume that the development of financial markets would accelerate economic growth and thus increase income, while also spending, and consequently tax revenues, as well as promising fiscal and electoral successes.

All goals of the government are more easily controlled under the promise of macroeconomic growth. However, this option could not have materialized since domestic savings in Poland were low by international standards. Actually, mandatory pension funding meant using the state apparatus to transfer the contributions of fund members to capital markets first and subsequently to public debt financing. Analogically, the introduction of the quasi-mandatory employee capital plans by the Polish government was described in 2017 by Paweł Borys, the CEO of the Polish Development Fund, as "de facto nothing more than a programme for the development of Polish financial markets" (Naczyk 2018, p. 558).

It is clear that the financial sector had a substantive interest in the privatization and financialization of pensions as well. This strand of the reforms received strong support from banks and numerous foreign bank subsidiaries, and was lobbied for by representatives of the interests of the financial sector, with the Union of Polish

Banks (ZBP) and the newly established Warsaw Stock Exchange taking the lead. The two waves of pension reforms – in 1999 and after 2008 – contributed considerably to the rise of financial firms as players in the game of capital-based pension funds in Poland. The creation of the mandatory second pillar led to the rise of a sizeable pension industry with a trade association of its own, the Chamber of Commerce of Pension Societies (IGTE), which launched a lobbying campaign against scaling down the hybrid funds. At the same time, the Chamber and some PTEs were proponents of automatic enrolment in the new company-based pension funding, emphasizing that programmes with opt-out arrangements have much better results in terms of coverage than the ones with an opt-in option (Chamber 2018).

4.5 Substantive interests

Thus, it seems that despite the fact that topics of demography and security were widely exploited in the promotion of the reforms, public-finance requirements and the development of financial markets, though much less exposed, actually constituted a substance. This section provides arguments for this hypothesis. The official arguments referred to the economic logic of scarcity and choice. Rather than taking this "economization" at face value, this section is considering social interactions occurring in pursuit of basic interests, such as being employed and/or secure. What is substantive for the actors emerges here as an important factor in identifying the forces that drive changes.

4.5.1 Public-finance requirements

The need to improve the country's fiscal position proved to be the most important argument for pension reforms in Poland (Polakowski and Hagemejer 2018). In the early 1990s, under the radical transformation of the political and economic system, the unemployment rate was on a dramatic rise and with the aim of reducing the social and political costs of mass unemployment, a large number of people acquired the status of early pensioners and official invalids instead of being unemployed. In consequence, the increased outlays from the pension system replaced social aid to a large extent. International comparisons for Poland revealed the results, which were significant pension spending and a record implicit pension debt (Impavido and Tower 2009, p. 41, Table 8). Public-finance instability, represented among others, by the current illiquidity and implicit insolvency of the publicly administered pension system explains the policymakers' positive interest in reforms.

A fundamental change in the contribution-benefit formula had obviously much to do with the substantive interest in diminishing the PAYG system deficits and/or broad fiscal deficit. Under the former formula (DB formula), the value of retirement benefits was calculated in accordance with the rules imposed by the state and was actually guaranteed by the state who ran the risk that inflows to the system do not balance the outflows which are due to the benefits outlays. Shifting to the new formula (DC formula) made the predicted pension benefit, related to the average or last wage radically reduced. The reform architects (namely, A. Chłoń, M. Góra, and K. Rutkowski) were unanimous in that the index was to fall (to 44.7% of the last salary, retirement age of 60 and 62.1% of the last salary, retirement age of 65) (Hausner 2002, p. 359). These predictions, made in the late 1990s, are significant when compared with the actual replacement rates of 70% in the early 1990s.

Originally, the risk of old-age poverty was to be prevented by the state. Basically, public insurers were entrusted with providing DBs due to financing on the basis of PAYG, since this system facilitated income redistribution. By abandoning the DB formula, the Polish state threw this great financial burden away. This meant improving the country's fiscal position, as discussed in previous paragraphs, while at the same time, the governments' responsibility for the maintenance of a decent retirement income diminished considerably.

4.5.2 Development of financial markets

It will be argued here that the shift to the DC formula was also on behalf of non-public interests. This is an interesting context and a good moment to discuss this accounting formula in more detail.

The shift to the DC rule occurred in Poland right at the same time as when pension funding on a capital basis was introduced. Pension funds are built from the contributions of their participants that are used as capital to be invested in financial assets. Along with these changes, the risk of varying rates of return on the pension assets appeared. Under the DC formula, the parameters of contributions are precise, and contributed savings are transparently registered on individual member accounts to be invested in securities and stock, in which the value of benefits depends on returns on capital, and therefore is uncertain (Bodie, Marcus, and Merton 1988). When pension fund operations witness shrinking pension capital due to failed investments, then the risk of default on liabilities appears.

Basically speaking, the risk of failed investments can be shared between contributors, fund management companies, and the state (Barr and Diamond 2009). It *may* be a risk to fund management, and it *is* a definite risk to contributors since, by way of consequence, the risk of low pension benefits arises. Under the new formula, the obligations against pensioners match the available funds. In effect, it is the individual contributor who mostly faces the risk of a failed investment. In the case of private insurance agents, the DC formula diminishes their responsibility for a return on capital. For public insurance agents, it eases the tension in their pension balances.

The Polish reform of 1999 made fund-managing companies free from any guarantees that pension capital would be undiminished as a consequence of a failed investment. Instead, the state undertook the obligation concerning the amount of the state-acknowledged minimum level of retirement benefit. Once the erosion of pension capital makes the total benefit from both mandatory pillars lower than this minimum level, the governmental budget covers the difference. In effect, it is the state not the PTE who bears the cost. In addition, the 2013 re-reform introduced regulatory arrangements that prevent losses from retiring when capital markets are down and/or price inflation is relatively high. However, these regulations are solely connected with the sub-account in the Social Insurance Institution (ZUS) where the former second-tier contributions and a portion of assets were directed (Polakowski and Hagemejer 2018, pp. 20–21). Paradoxically enough, private companies managing pension savings, which are mandatory, have not shared any responsibility for minimum benefits or capital preservation. With the DC formula replacing the Benefit Defined formula, notwithstanding moderate and selective guarantees, the bulk of the risk was shifted to the contributors.

This discussion of the risk question allows us to make the following points: The introduction of a new accounting formula met substantive material interests of both the state, who was an administrator and the actual sponsor of the PAYG pillar, and of FCs that were just entering the pensions industry. The consequent distribution of risk and outlays improved pension balances for the public fund-managing agency ZUS and must be regarded as extremely attractive to private actors engaged in old-age insurance, thus making their business unusually safe and lucrative. This was an important change on behalf of general interests lobbying for the development of financial markets.

4.5.3 Do the interests of governments and financial groups match or diverge?

The discussion of the risk question sums up in the statement that this institutional change actually met substantive interests both in terms of public-finance balances and the development of financial markets, which means that in this respect the government had a shared interest with the financial sector.

With regard to raising funds to be invested in stock, financial instruments, and securities, once again, the Polish state seemed to have a shared interest with the actors in financial markets. Mandatory saving with open pension funds (OFEs) and automatic enrolment in pension schemes (e.g. PPK) reveal the government's determination to have new funds raised and invested through capital-based pillars of the pension system. The other side, which is comprised of FCs, strives to expand the flows of financial assets because they constitute the basis for fees.

Thus, expanding pension funds was seen as a chance to accelerate economic growth on a macro-scale and to increase earnings on a micro-scale. As a result of this match, while the country's public tier struggled to constrain pension deficits, the private tiers of the country's pension system saw the inflow of new funds, thus creating more business opportunities for fund-managing companies.

However, as post-2008 reforms show, the case of mandatory funds turned out to be somewhat problematic (Ząbkowicz 2016). On the one hand, this institutional arrangement steadily fuelled the capital market and promised growth. On the other hand, OFEs were neither a solution to the implicit problem of insolvency in public pensions, nor a source of fiscal relief (Chełchowski 2001). One-third of mandatory contributions to the public pillar of old-age insurance were to be transferred to the privately managed OFEs. The transfers increased the deficit in the publicly managed fund FUS, while also enforced subsidies from the governmental budget and thus contributed to fiscal deficits. Although the public debt was rather moderate when the 1999 reform took shape, it could have been easily predicted that it would rise because of the subsidizing that the public pension deficit inevitably required (Impavido and Tower 2009, p. 41, Table 8). Capital pension funds could have been envisaged to offer possible fiscal relief only with respect to the third voluntary pillar, which has nevertheless remained underdeveloped. This ultimately gave rise to controversy about public debt financing.

Why then was such a costly institutional arrangement supported by a broad political coalition in the 1990s? First, the privatization of state-owned enterprises, which was initiated under the systemic transformation in the early 1990s, was officially recognized as a chance to increase budgetary revenues (Office of the Government Plenipotentiary for Social Security Reform 1997). Second, the change in the pension accounting formula discussed earlier diminished outlays from the public pillar. These two fundamental changes made the OFEs politically feasible at the turn of the century. Moreover, the idea was fuelled by a new interest of the financial sector in transferring mandatory retirement savings to private management and this was backed by organized financial sector groups. In Poland, FCs managed to build a powerful lobby whose strength and broad support among intellectuals and ordinary, mostly young people, was openly demonstrated around 2013 during the public campaigns against the re-reforms concerning OFEs.

However, after 2008 the vested interests of the Polish government and financiers seemed to diverge. From 1999, reform of mandatory savings had been channelled via OFEs towards purchasing treasury bonds, which in turn made public debt financing easier in the short run. However, in 2009, the Finance Minister Jacek Rostowski issued a communiqué to the public that the vicious circle, namely, the government incurring debt to finance transfers to OFEs, thus enabling them to buy its debts, was found to be unsustainable by the ruling liberal party known as Civic Platform (PO) (*Rzeczpospolita* 2009). Under the re-reform of 2013, all state bonds owned by the second-pillar funds, constituting half of their assets, were transferred to the fund administered by the Social Insurance Institution (ZUS), while the hybrid funds were no longer allowed to invest in state securities. The turnabout was backed by sound governmental analysis, which exposed the costs induced by funding the mandatory capital-based system (Ministry of Finance and Ministry for Labour and Social Policy, and Ministry of Finance 2013; Ministry of Finance 2013).

Nevertheless, the 2018 governmental project should be regarded as peacemaking with "war contributions" attached rather than the final eradication of OFEs. According to the 2018 "transfer" project, the total assets of OFE would be transferred either to new accounts (IKE+) in the third pillar managed by the same PTEs renamed as TFIs or under the management of the state agency ZUS. The proportion would result from OFE-member declarations of their will to opt-out from IKEs+. In effect, PTEs remain in business, albeit, renamed, but, the government takes its share. The aforesaid share partly consists of stock, having been shifted under ZUS management on behalf of one of the fiscal funds. Another part of this "war contribution" consists of the compulsory payment made by each person who did not opt out and was going to continue saving with IKE+. The so-called transfer fee worth 15% would be taken from the stock that would have remained under PTE-TFI's management. This is nothing more than a quasi-tax meant to improve the government's fiscal position, according to the former Minister of Finance Paweł Wojciechowski (https://www.prawo.pl/kadry/co-dalej-z-likwidacja-ofe,512452.html).

In spite of the determination to follow the fiscal line while destroying the OFE's pillar, some other regulations were however oriented towards the expansion of private pension funding. The explicit goals of the reform of 2014 and the reform project of 2018 were to make membership of the pension funding run by the TFIs as large as the one run by the PTEs once was. Consequently, the "split" with OFEs is by no means a battle against privileges in the privately managed tier of pension industry, but rather a struggle to constrain public deficits and debts.

The introduction and expansion of pension funding can be seen as an end in itself which is tightly related to interest in the development of a financial market. Basically speaking, the vested interests of the government and financial sector groups did not appear to be contradictory enough to ruin the coalition.

4.6 Driving forces

At the end of the day, the inherent interests in public-finance requirements and the development of financial markets seemed to go hand in hand as long as the Polish reforms took shape. On the one hand, the partial privatization of pensions, along with the introduction of a general DC formula was a chance to keep outlays for public pensions in check and, consequently, to constrain their subsidization by the state budget. Moreover, capital-based pensions were valued as a relevant source of investments in treasury bonds and other securities traded in financial markets up until the first decade of the 21st century at least. On the other hand, pension funding made capital in Poland more accessible. Even if the finance-growth nexus in a macro-dimension failed to pass the econometric tests anymore,[3] in a micro-dimension the increasing flows of financial assets still constituted the basis for abundant fees and commissions.

One may speculate that the non-financial sector, or at least the representatives of interests related to manufacturing, might have effectively opposed the privatization and financialization of pensions. Both businesses and/or TUs have had for some reasons developed an interest in welfare. The public provision of health care and education transferred costs from the employers to taxpayers. Social policy with the support of the publicly administered PAYG pension system acted as a cushion and diminished the risk of conflict on wage costs and/or employment. In particular, institutional arrangements leading to early retirement and increased retirement benefits supported a rather smooth transition from work to welfare. Early retirement accommodated rising unemployment in an economic recession or job reductions in the face of intensified international competition, the outcome of which was valued equally by both business and labour unions.

The systemic change at the turn of the 1980s and 1990s, backed as it was by external advisers and finance providers, relied on institutional change that was neoliberal by nature. However, the social revolution that resulted in a transition to capitalism in Poland was in fact led by industrial labour unions, who bargained with the state authorities. The Polish TUs, who were extremely strong and militant when the transition began, could have been considered a social coalition that would naturally question the "insecure" privatization and financialization of pensions and defend the PAYG system's sustainability.

In the era of the financialization of pensions, the hypothesis about the manufacturing sector's institutional power and interest in welfare is not supported by evidence. The most powerful TUs actively supported reforms that introduced capital-based pensions to Poland, invited private firms into the pension industry and utterly changed the relation between contributions and benefits. Poland's biggest union, NSZZ Solidarność, very soon became a true ally of conservative governments. It supported pension reforms, with one prominent activist, Ewa Lewicka, heading the government agency that dealt with them. Two major TUs (NSZZ Solidarność and OPZZ) were even involved in establishing two open pension funds. Besides these facts, even if TUs were ready to defend their vested interests, they actually appeared to be rather weak. Very soon they saw dramatic losses in terms of their credibility and membership. TUs that once had real authority over their members, exercised much less influence under capitalism, as those members were increasingly tempted to defect.

Business attitudes in manufacturing during the transition period provide less clear evidence. For certain, the representation of businesses and employers was definitely weak because there was no tradition of corporate interest organizations in Poland. It is uncertain to what extent non-financial companies (NFCs) might share interests with FCs. While FCs are engaged in managing market pension funds, NFCs are organizers and sometimes also managers of company-based pension schemes (occupational pensions). However, the vested interests of both pension savings management systems overlap. Manufacturing, as well as FCs can equally manage occupational pensions. The NFCs may be also tempted to make transactions in financial assets, and profit like FCs do by using funds accumulated in occupational pension schemes (Estevez-Abe 2001, pp. 207, 204). NFCs can also go to market-fund managers in order to make use of the capital and services offered by them. Thus, NFCs that issue corporate bonds or seek capital in the stock exchange are interested in the development of financial operations and markets like FCs are. For these reasons, alliances with regard to capital-based pensions between manufacturing corporations and financial institutions are possible.

Summing up, it seems that NFCs and labour unions had hardly any interests that would cause them to speak out firmly against pension funding.

At least prospective pensioners would have had reasons to protest against the outcomes of the financialization and privatization of pensions in Poland. First, capital-based pension funding, when combined with the PAYG system, involved the problem of double payments since it required that workers continue to finance the previous generation's retirement in the first pillar and simultaneously save on their own account in the second and third pillars. Second, prospective or actual pensioners could regard their social income security to be under threat. Along the lines of the reform, public pension benefits as related to the average wage were radically reduced, with the outcome even more radical than predicted. Actually, the net pension in Poland (in the case of men) amounted to over one-third (36.5%) of pre-retirement earnings in 2020, which is below the OECD average (OECD 2020).

Third, the capital-based funds offered volatile portfolios with DC plans, making the old-age well-being of the insured dependent on the performance of FCs investing in markets of capital and securities. Whether such a deal is acceptable for would-be pensioners depends on further legal and technical details. For instance, benchmarking which determines rewards for managing firms matters. Recent mechanisms have stimulated PTEs in their investment decisions to follow the leaders of the pensions industry rather than to maximize the capital of fund members. Thus, the threats posed were moderated by protective regulations to a limited extent. Guarantees on capital imposed on fund-managing companies make the value of fund-member contributions preserved notwithstanding losses on investments. Although such guarantees seem to constitute a decent minimum, the more so when the investments are drawn from mandatory funds, this rule has been absent in Poland. In effect, what the amount of future benefits will be is uncertain. Many contributors may end up receiving minimum-level retirement benefits.

It is claimed (Polakowski and Hagemejer 2018, pp. 22–23) that in Poland the expertise while promoting pension funding presented overly optimistic assumptions and manipulated results. Under the reforms, the interests of prospective pensioners and welfare recipients turned out to be inferior to the interests of other parties. By way of consequence, the reformers were not trusted by the public. Nevertheless, the bargaining position of a massive social group of pensioners is weak as they are hardly organized as a group at all. After TUs had lost their power and esteem, prospective pensioners became either powerless or simply indifferent. It can be assumed that they only matter as voters.

The examination carried out in the current section showed there were no retarding forces strong enough to resist the privatization and financialization of pensions. Insight into the interests of the actors of the game revealed the coalition of the indebted state and its actual or eventual creditors from the financial markets as the pivotal force driving the change.

4.7 Conclusion

This analysis presented an interest-centred explanation of the Polish pension reforms, after having considered four parties engaged in the socioeconomic game seen in a historical perspective. Among the arguments in favour of capital-based pension funds, both demographic developments and social security were widely exploited in the publicity surrounding the reforms. However, general concern about public-finance requirements and the development of the financial markets, though rather not exposed to the public, constituted more direct interests than any other involved in the process. It was argued that both the introduction of pension funding and the DC formula served these major interests well.

Public-finance requirements and the development of the financial markets fulfil the material interests of the government and financial sector groups. Their shared interests in economic growth, growth of finance, and risk shift (away from private and public insurance agents) allowed me to consider the two collective actors as powerful forces driving change. In this coalition government, backed by the expertise of international institutions could be regarded as the leader, while private banks, insurers, and funds engaged in managing pension assets as its enthusiastic supporters.

As far as retarding forces are concerned, the picture remains blurred. Non-financial employers and would-be pensioners, represented mostly by TUs, who might be considered as vested interests, seemed to be prone to enter coalitions either with polity or with financiers. The proposition that the non-financial sector might be capable of effectively opposing change has not been confirmed. Since the turn of the millennium, non-financial sector groups have exerted little power or were generally incapable of organizing a demonstration of popular discontent.

The explanation of Polish pension reforms offered here contradicts the official stance of those supporting reforms in the name of the well-being of pensioners. The rational attitude, reconstructed on the basis of official announcements, would be that saving and earning help capital-based funds to achieve a significantly higher old-age income and preserve the living standard of retirees in the face of decreasing benefits from the publicly managed pillar, which is unavoidable because of demography. This analysis asserted that it is the state's material position rather than the pensioners' welfare that might be at stake and that privatized and funded pensions were meant to generate continuous financial flows to the financial markets rather than to provide the security of old-age income.

In Poland, we can observe more clearly than elsewhere how the state's power was used to exert influence on behalf of some companies interested in expanding their business into the pension industry. Here, organized financial interests were rewarded to the extent that suggests a position of a dominating player among interests involved in a political and ideational game about the pension policy. As pointed out above, the Polish policymakers' stance combined two contradictory aims, namely, suppressing budget subsidies to public pensions and expanding financial markets by diverting part of pension contributions to OFEs. The conflicting goals of this plan suggest that the experiment with hybrid funding was backed by powerful driving forces interested in transferring mandatory retirement savings under private management.

This observation can be associated with Polanyi's ideas of the instituted process and double movement. Using Polanyi's framework, under pressure from the "market forces", the pensions industry in Poland underwent profound transformation. The development of capital-based pensions promoted market *values* where the utterly non-market objective of social security was at stake. It invited individualism, calculation, and risk where principles of social solidarity once prevailed. Its seductive mirage of rationality and choice helped to implant and extend a new *distribution* of risk and income in the old-age insurance industry. In Polanyi's glossary, this would be termed as a creeping "economization" of the social sphere. The state, which in Polanyi's vision represents the social ability for self-organization, provided counter-action. Having found the hybrid pension funds problematic, the government authored the 2013 encounter and the 2018 "war" project. This story, however, cannot be presented as a fine empirical demonstration of countermovement in Polanyi's terms, which might be a smart closing point to this chapter. Alas, I find no argument to support the eventual claim that the corresponding state's action resulted from the Polish society's ability for self-dependence.

Notes

1 These developments found a critical description i.a. in Oręziak (2022).
2 The TFIs and the PTEs are private companies founded mainly by banks and some insurers
3 For a summary of critical arguments, see, e.g., Stolbov (2012). According to Mikhail Stolbov, in recent years we have seen financial turmoil and partial erosion of the previously documented positive link between finance and growth. Some studies find no statistical significance of financial depth regressors for later periods, e.g., the years 1989–2004. Other research has revealed signs of publication bias, i.e., the fact that papers supporting the finance-growth nexus are more likely to be published rather than those yielding contrasting results.

References

Barr, N., and P. Diamond. (2009). Reforming pensions: Principles, analytical errors and policy directions, *International Social Security Review*, 62(2), 5–29.
Barr, N., and P. Diamond. (2010). *Pension Reform. A Short Guide*. New York: Oxford University Press.
Beshears, J., J. J. Choi, D. Laibson, and B. C. Madrian. (2006). *The Importance of Default Options for Retirement Saving Outcomes: Evidence from the United States*. National Bureau of Economic Research Working Paper No. 12009. Cambridge, MA: National Bureau of Economic Research. Accessed at: https://www.nber.org/system/files/working_papers/w12009/w12009.pdf.
Błaszczyk, B. (2020). Filar kapitałowy w polskim systemie emerytalnym. Od OFE do PPK. *Gospodarka Narodowa (The Polish Journal of Economics)*, 301(1), 9–54. https://doi.org/10.33119/GN/116616
Bodie, Z., A. J. Marcus and R. C. Merton. (1988). Defined Benefit versus Defined Contribution Pension Plans: What are the Real Trade-offs?. NBER Chapters. In: *Pensions in the U.S. Economy* (139–162). National Bureau of Economic Research, Inc.
Bowles, S., and H. Gintis. (2006). The evolutionary basis of collective action. In B. R. Weingast and D. A. Wittman (Eds.). *The Oxford Handbook of Political Economy* (951–970). Oxford: Oxford University Press.
Chamber of Commerce of Pension Societies. (2018). *Biuletyn IGTE No. 14*. Warszawa: Izba Gospodarcza Towarzystw Emerytalnych.
Chamber of Commerce of Pension Societies. (2023). *Analizy Online S.A: Podsumowanie rynku funduszy emerytalnych* (December 2022), IGTE, www.analizy.pl 2, January 4th. Accessed at: https://igte.pl/wp-content/uploads/2023/01/OFE202212.pdf.
Chełchowski, A. (2001). *Strategie Inwestycyjne Funduszy Emerytalnych: Reforma Emerytalna—Sukcesczy Porażka*. Export Development Bank (BRE Bank) and Center for Social and Economic Research (CASE) Working Paper No. 57. Warsaw: BRE Bank/CASE. Accessed at: https://www.case-research.eu/files/?id_plik=3640.
Chłoń, A., M. Góra, and M. Rutkowski. (1999). *Shaping Pension Reform in Poland: Security through Diversity*. Social Protection Discussion Paper Series no. 9923. Washington,

DC: World Bank. Accessed at: https://www.researchgate.net/publication/254456162_Shaping_Pension_Reform_in_Poland_Security_Through_Diversity.

Estevez-Abe, M. (2001). The forgotten link: The financial regulation of Japanese pension funds in comparative perspective. In B. Ebbinghaus and Ph. Manow (Eds.). *Comparing Welfare Capitalism: Social Policy and Political Economy in Europe, Japan, and the USA* (190–216). London: Routledge.

GazetaPrawna.pl. (2019). *Pracownicze Plany Kapitałowe (PPK)—co to takiego i kiedy wejdzie w życie.* July11. Accessed at: https://www.gazetaprawna.pl/ppk/artykuly/1315274,ppk-pracownicze-plany-kapitalowe-kiedy-wejda-w-zycie-skladki-wyplata.html.

Government Council for Socioeconomic Strategy. (1997). *Reforma Systemu Emerytalnego w Polsce: Bezpieczeństwo dzięki Różnorodności.* Raport Rady Strategii Społeczno-Gospodarczej przy Radzie Ministrow (RSSG) no. 24. Warszawa: Council for Socio-economic Strategy.

Hausner, J. (2002). Poland: Security through diversity. In M. Feldstein and H. Siebert (Eds.). *Social Security Pension Reform in Europe* (349–364). Chicago, IL: Chicago University Press.

Impavido, G., and I. Tower. (2009). *How the Financial Crisis Affects Pensions and Insurance and Why the Impacts Matter.* IMF Working Paper No. WP/09/151. Washington, DC: International Monetary Fund. Accessed at: https://www.imf.org/external/pubs/ft/wp/2009/wp09151.pdf.

Jackson, G., and S. Vitols. (2001). Between financial commitment, market liquidity and corporate governance: Occupational pensions in Britain, Germany, Japan, and the USA. In E. Bernhard and Ph. Manow (Eds.). *Comparing Welfare Capitalism: Social Policy and Political Economy in Europe, Japan, and the USA* (171–189). London: Routledge.

Kassner, M. (2017). Gospodarka jako zinstytucjonalizowany proces. Instytucjonalizm Karla Polanyiegoi jego etyczne konsekwencje. *Annales Etyka w Życiu Gospodarczym* [Ethics in Economic Life], 20(2), 45–61.

King, R., and R. Levine. (1993). Finance and growth: Schumpeter might be right. *Quarterly Journal of Economics,* 108(3), 717–737.

Ministry of Finance. (2013). *Uzasadnienie Zmian w Systemie Ubezpieczeń Społecznych z dn. 10/10/2013.*Warszawa: Ministerstwo Finansów.

Ministry for Labour and Social Policy, and Ministry of Finance. (2013). *Bezpieczeństwo dzięki Zrównoważeniu.* Warszawa: Ministerstwo Pracy i Polityki Społecznej oraz Ministerstwo Finansów.

Mitchell, O. S., and S. P. Utkus. (Eds.) (2003). *Pension Design and Structure: New Lessons from Behavioral Finance.* Oxford: Oxford University Press.

Naczyk, M. (2018). When finance captures labor's capital: Dominant personal pensions, resurgent occupational provision in Central and Eastern Europe. *Social Policy & Administration,* 52(2), 549–562.

North, D. C. (1990). *Institutions, Institutional Change and Economic Performance.* New York: Cambridge University Press.

OECD. (2003). *Financial Market Trends—OECD Journal* 84. Paris: Organization for Economic Co-operation and Development.

———. (2020). *Net Pension Replacement Rates.* Accessed at: https://data.oecd.org/pension/net-pensionreplacement-rates.htm#indicator-chart.

Office of the Government Plenipotentiary for Social Security Reform. (1997). *Bezpieczeństwo dzięki Różnorodności: Reforma system emerytalnego w Polsce.* Warszawa: Biuro Pełnomocnika ds. Reformy Zabezpieczenia Społecznego.

Office of the Pension Funds Supervisory Commission. (2000). *Bezpieczeństwo dzięki Konkurencji. Ocena Realizacji Reformy Emerytalnej — Analiza II Filara.* Warszawa: Urząd Nadzoru nad Funduszami Emerytalnymi (UNFE).

Oręziak, L. (2022). *Pension Fund Capitalism. The Privatization of Pensions in Developed and Developing Countries*. Milton Park, Abingdon: Routledge.

Paster, Th. (2015). *Bringing Power Back in: A Review of the Literature on the Role of Business in Welfare State Politics*. MPIfG Discussion Paper No. 15/3. Cologne: Max Planck Institute for the Study of Societies. Accessed at: https://pure.mpg.de/rest/items/item_2157421/component/file_2157419/content.

Polakowski, M., and K. Hagemejer. (2018). *Reversing Pension Privatization: The Case of Polish Pension Reform and Re-reforms*. Extension of Social Security (ESS) Working Paper No. 68. Geneva: Social Protection Department of the International Labour Office. Accessed at: https://www.ilo.org/wcmsp5/groups/public/—ed_protect/—soc_sec/documents/publication/wcms_648632.pdf.

Rzeczpospolita. (2009). Rząd chce zdemontować II filar. November 4. Accessed at: https://www.rp.pl.

Shepsle, K. A. (2006). Old questions and new answers about institutions. The Riker objection revisited. In D. A. Wittman and B. R. Weingast (Eds.). *The Oxford Handbook of Political Economy* (1031–1049). Oxford: Oxford University Press.

Social Insurance Institution. (2016). *Przegląd Emerytalny: Bezpieczeństwo dzięki Odpowiedzialności. Białaksięga*. Warszawa: Zakład Ubezpieczeń Społecznych (ZUS).

Stolbov, M. (2012). *The Finance-Growth Nexus Revisited: From Origins to a Modern Theoretical Landscape*. Kiel Institute for the World Economy Discussion Paper No. 2012-45. Kiel, Germany: Kiel Institute for the World Economy. Accessed at: http://www.economics-ejournal.org/economics/discussionpapers/2012-45.

Swedberg, R. (2006). The tool kit of economic sociology. In D. A. Wittman and B. R. Weingast (Eds.). *The Oxford Handbook of Political Economy* (937–950). Oxford: Oxford University Press.

Szumlicz, T. (2002). System zabezpieczenia emerytalnego. In A. Kurzynowski (Ed.). *Polityka Społeczna* (186–200). Warszawa: Instytut Gospodarstwa Społecznego SGH.

Weber, M. (2002) [1922]. *Gospodarka i społeczeństwo. Zarys socjologii rozumiejącej*, trans. D. Lachowska. Warszawa: Wydawnictwo Naukowe PWN.

Wiktorow, A. (2008). Ryzyko załamania systemu ubezpieczeń społecznych. *Zarządzanie ryzykiem*, 28, 32–42.

World Bank. (1994). *Averting the Old Age Crisis. Policies to Protect the Old and Promote Growth*. Washington, DC: World Bank.

Ząbkowicz, A. (2016). A paradox of reforming pensions in Poland. *Equilibrium: Quarterly Journal of Economics and Economic Policy*, 11(3), 585–602.

5 Labour incomes and economic activity in Poland

Adam Koronowski

5.1 Introduction

The purpose of this chapter is to consider the impact of labour incomes on economic activity and growth in Poland. Labour incomes – and their share of GDP – are shaped by market forces and by public policies and regulations that determine the institutional environment of economic processes. The proportion of labour incomes to the product in turn exerts an influence on the structure and the value of the aggregate demand and thus it has an effect on economic activity.

The social distribution of incomes – the falling share of labour incomes in GDP or more generally income inequality – has become a hot issue in economics in recent years. The downward trend of the share is now a well-established fact with respect to many major economies, which in turn evokes opinions that capitalism has become more aggressive again. It seems that the problem may be particularly acute in Poland where the share of wages and salaries (labour incomes) of GDP is low by European standards and has been falling in recent years.

A consistent and useful theoretical paradigm that relates the share of labour incomes to economic activity is the hypothesis of under-consumption; a proposition that low wages undermine consumption spending and eventually lead to a persistent stagnation. The hypothesis, respectively, claims that higher labour incomes might increase a deficient level of the aggregate demand and make it closer to the potential output.

In principle, wages, or more generally speaking, primary incomes, i.e. incomes received by the factors of net production of any later public redistribution, are determined by market forces. Market forces are not, however, free of public regulation and policies that create an institutional and legal economic environment and in particular determine the functioning of labour markets. As J. Berg (2015) states,

> Equitable societies with large middle classes are not the natural outcome of market forces. Equity, rather, is created by society, by the institutions – the laws, policies and practices – that govern the society, its economy and, in particular, its labour market.

In this context, it is reasonable to mention labour law, the actual role of labour unions, tax systems, or the degree of monopolization of the economy that should be

DOI: 10.4324/9781003425717-7

subject to legal rules and policies that promote competition. Institutional changes that have been taking place in some major market economies under the influence of supply-side economics in recent decades are a good example of how state policies create an economic institutional environment; in principle, economic conditions have been typically expected to be business friendly.

Poland, as other former communist countries, underwent the turbulent process of transformation. Particularly its first phase, often referred to as "Shock Therapy", meant a major institutional and systemic change that had important effects for economic activity, employment, incomes, and social distribution. As a result, Poland ultimately emerged as a middle-income and market economy. With respect to income distribution and income inequalities, which are measured with the Gini coefficient, Poland is placed among the ranks typical to other European countries, keeping in mind the differences among them. It is also natural that inequalities and their measure, Gini coefficient, evolve. In particular, inequalities rose during the Covid pandemic.

In this chapter, the subject of analysis relates to changes in real wages as compared to changes in real GDP as a factor that determines economic activity and (un)employment. Such analysis does not refer directly to income inequalities but to relative changes in labour incomes which, among others, determine inequalities. The main interest in this chapter is paid, however, to the question of what the impact of real wage dynamics on economic activity is when related to changes in real GDP. In simple terms, is economic growth wage-led or profit-led? The analysis confirms the thesis of this chapter; a decline in the share of labour incomes in terms of production has had a negative impact on economic activity in Poland.

During the analysed period, there were two-directional changes in the relation between real wages and real GDP. This suggests that the changes have been caused by current developments rather than being deeply rooted in past transformation. Clear identifying forces behind the developments is a challenge, and it is worthy of further research.

The subsequent second part of this chapter presents theoretical remarks that relate to the hypothesis of under-consumption, while the third part contains a discussion and provides an answer to the question of whether wages are too low in Poland in view of the hypothesis, as well as some remarks on factors that may drive changes in the social structure of incomes, and the final fourth part provides conclusions based on the research findings.

5.2 Some theoretical remarks

The issue of income and wealth inequalities has become an intensely discussed subject of the economic debate, in both theoretical and empirical terms in recent years. The popularity is in a sharp contradiction to an earlier elimination of the question of income distribution from mainstream economics (Lucas 2004). The new trend in economics is represented by the famous bestsellers of Stiglitz (2012) and Piketty (2014) and some other books, for example Rajan (2010), Zingales (2012), Atkinson (2015) and Milanovic (2016). There are important papers published under the auspices of IMF, which analyse the problem of rising inequalities (Kumhof and Ranciere, 2010; Berg and Ostry, 2011; Berg et al., 2014; Dabla-Norris et al., 2015), as well as official reports by international organizations that document the decline in the labour share of GDP (ILO, OECD 2015; OECD 2012). The decline is now a well-established fact.

Both the reasons for and even more so the consequences of rising income and wealth inequalities have not been sufficiently recognized yet. Among the reasons technological progress (automation) and globalization seem crucially important; employees in developed countries are subject to declining demand for labour when it is replaced with technologically advanced equipment in production processes and they must compete stronger with a cheaper labour force in emerging markets. With regard to the consequences, there are multiple social, political, and economic issues involved. Possibly the best analysis of social and political consequences continues to be the one provided by Stiglitz (2012). Recognizing the economic effects of rising income inequalities/a declining share of labour incomes is more challenging. Empirically speaking, Berg and Ostry (2011), Berg et al. (2014), and Dabla-Norris et al. (2015) document a negative correlation between inequalities and economic growth, while Kumhof and Ranciere (2010) find that rising inequalities impair financial stability.

There is no clear and broadly accepted theoretical paradigm that would provide well-established judgements on whether wages are too low or too high in economic terms. In economic theory, there are concepts of both profit-led and wage-led growth. Within the neoclassical school of thought, wages that emerge on the free market are always at the right level; such an attitude lies behind the earlier mentioned claim by Lucas. Within this paradigm, any forced rise of wages is harmful to the economy and to the society. However, the paradigm does not allow for any possibility that wages may be too low and that they may coexist with unemployment; this is a case that is important for this analysis.

In my opinion, the best paradigm that facilitates a comprehensive and consistent consideration of the problem of excessively low wages is the hypothesis of under-consumption; the hypothesis claims that low wages result in little consumption spending which does not support new investments. Ultimately, the economy stagnates at the level of production below its potential. Such a stagnation may be persistent and long-lasting or, as Hansen (1939) termed the phenomenon, it is a secular stagnation.[1]

The hypothesis of under-consumption is a version of the idea of deficient demand; the version is older, more concise, precise, and consistent than the Keynesian theory. The idea has its roots in the early 19th century when Sismondi and Malthus opposed the "optimistic" view of classical economists (Smith, Ricardo, Say) who shared a conviction that the economy is a self-regulating mechanism and that, in particular, there is always enough demand to meet the aggregate supply (the conviction expressed as the law of Say). This dispute has never really ended and was central to the Marxian school of thought. It evoked different and politically opposing recommendations, for example that the rich should consume more (von Kirchman), or that they should be taxed and the state should spend the money (pre-Keynesian ideas of fiscal intervention, Rodbertus). A solid ground stone for the hypothesis was put forward by Hobson in 1889 (Hobson and Mummery 2014).

> Hobson's economic heresies were based on his theory of distribution in which he rejected the orthodox marginal productivity theory and developed a theory of economic surplus, in which distribution is determined by economic power. This underlay his theory of under-consumption which in turn, was used to explain and analyze economic and social issues such as unemployment, the business cycle, the labour movement, imperialism and taxation.
>
> (Richmond 1978)

An example of a more recent reference to the hypothesis is a book by Wilcock and Scholtz (2016) who wrote:

> The characteristics of an under-consumption crisis are a recessionary climate, unused capacity, excessive debt and pessimistic expectations that block further accumulation. An under-consumption model has the hallmarks of a weakened negotiating position of labour, wages that have not kept pace with productivity increases, weak demand caused primarily by a lack of reinvestment and consumers preferring to save rather than spend, which is the situation in the West today.

In the situation of under-consumption there is no mechanism that would guarantee self-regulation. On the contrary, in terms of the game theory, it is easy to prove that microeconomic rationality that makes firms keep wage costs low results in non-optimum macroeconomic outcomes. Kalecki (1935, transl. A.K.) wrote that "if one entrepreneur cut wages, he could, ceteris paribus, increase the utilization of his factory, but if all entrepreneurs cut wages the result (…) would be quite different", as a group they would find it impossible to sell their product. The forces that could make wages rise and boost the deficient consumption spending must be of a social and political nature. Income distribution is to a certain degree determined by social and political factors (Koronowski 2016, 2022), for example, the power of labour unions. This statement is in sharp contrast with marginal, neoclassical claims (that are in particular deeply rooted in the assumption of Cobb-Doulas production function (Koronowski 2018).

Another institutional aspect of economies that keeps profits high (and their share of GDP high) is the high degree of monopolization; competition does not provide forces that should reduce profits and their share of GDP. That is the reason why Kalecki paid so much attention in his work to the degrees of monopolization (Kalecki 1986). The problem of monopolization was also central to the analysis of the capitalist economy by P.A. Baran and P.M. Sweezy (1968), which was reflected in the title of their book. It is important to note that even a high degree of monopolization that is restricted to a few major sectors may be enough to poison the whole economy with under-consumption; more competition among those who would fight to survive in a milieu of deficient demand would not help a lot (Koronowski 2022).

Can the hypothesis of under-consumption be empirically tested? I mentioned above some papers that present conclusions of empirical analysis of the consequences of low shares of labour incomes in GDP. The conclusions are reassuring for the proponents of the hypothesis. However, for reasons that were first illustrated by Baran and Sweezy (1968), it may be difficult to decisively prove the hypothesis in an empirical sense. To put simply, the small share of wages of GDP may trigger processes of adjustment similar to what is the essence of the paradox of thrift; in this case savings are nothing else but excessive profits that cannot be spent on new investments due to a lack of demand for final consumer products. As in the case of excessive savings in the Keynesian paradox of thrift, profits that cannot be spent on new investments "evaporate" in terms of macroeconomic categories; the problem is that the process may hit rather competitive sectors more than monopolies that are responsible for the underlying mismatch in the relative structures of incomes and spending. Ultimately, the manifestation of under-consumption is that of persistent trends on the economy to remain below the potential level of production, which is reflected by high rates of unemployment. Capital would not be accumulated and invested in new productive assets, thus excessive capital resources would not necessarily emerge.[2]

The effects of low wage and consumption shares may be temporarily modified, weakened, or eliminated by public policies or market developments; which also makes empirical analysis complicated. An example of market developments that have an impact on the share of consumer spending in GDP is the rising role of consumer credit. In the US economy where the share of labour incomes in GDP has been continuously falling and income inequalities have been rising in recent decades, the share of private consumption in GDP has increased. Thus, it is impossible to argue that a lower share of labour incomes has led to a deepening under-consumption and it is also difficult to claim that the American economy has been persistently and considerably below its potential for the past few decades. A solution to this conundrum is the fast rise in private credit, namely, labour incomes are supplemented with more credit (Federal Reserve Bank of New York 2023). Rising debt was boosted by a lax monetary policy, financial innovations, and deregulation of financial markets ("privatized Keynesianism" (Crouch 2009)). This is an important aspect of excessive financialization. Capital incomes that are replaced in the flow of value in the economy with credit-financed consumption are spent on existing assets and fuel speculative bubbles. Financial instability follows, as documented by Kumhof and Ranciere (2010).

It is not easy, if at all possible, to decisively prove the validity of the hypothesis of under-consumption. It should also be obvious that the validity would never be universal; one cannot in principle exclude a case of excessively high wages. Every case is determined by the particular institutional features of the economy. However, there are observations compatible with the hypothesis of under-consumption; this is when the hypothesis provides a consistent theoretical basis for an analysis that has a strong explanatory power. The question that matters most in this chapter is whether this is the case of Poland; the following section contains a discussion of the issue and provides an answer to the case in point.

5.3 Labour incomes in Poland: facts and assessment

The evolution of the labour income share of GDP in Poland is in line with global trends, namely, the share has been declining. Indeed, the global trends are not overwhelming. In particular, in the European Union, the share of labour incomes in market prices in GDP remained fairly stable; in 1997 it was equal to 56.2% and in 2017 55.2%. At the same time in Poland, the share declined from 59.2% to 48.4%, which is one of the lowest in the European Union. Similar shares describe the situation in the Czech Republic, Slovakia, Romania, and Hungary. One could claim that this is characteristic of the post-transformation economies of central Europe which, irrespective of major differences among them, still have to preserve their competitive position due to low labour costs. However, this is not a rule; in 2017 the share was equal to 58.9% in Bulgaria and 61% in Slovenia, both among the highest numbers in the European Union. Hence, it seems that some idiosyncratic phenomena and processes play a major role.[3]

However, any judgements based on the share of labour incomes in GDP and on international comparisons may be misleading and are not sufficient to prove or dismiss the claim that the economy analysed is subject to under-consumption.

First, it is a matter of international data comparability. In particular, the share of labour incomes may be low in Poland due to the common and increasingly widespread "self-employment" of actual employees that are motivated to register their own firms for tax considerations, whereby their incomes are not wages and are not included in the statistics of labour incomes. There is no reason to believe that the phenomenon should be equally spread among a group of countries. Another factor that has a similar effect is the relatively high percentage of people working in Poland in agriculture (and the share of agriculture in GDP); whereby their incomes for the most part are not classified as wages. In fact, the positive difference between the share of private consumption and labour incomes is much higher in Poland than in the European Union as the data presented show. It might serve as an argument that a relatively low share of labour incomes is basically a legal and statistical phenomenon and does not justify the claim that Poland is experiencing the problem of relatively low consumer spending and under-consumption due to low wages.

Second, an alternative mechanism that may loosen the relation between labour incomes and private consumption, while also serve as an explanation why the decline in consumption was much slower than the fall in labour incomes might be the dynamic growth of consumer credit and fast increase in household debt, namely, the mechanism that was in operation in the US economy. In this case, the claim of under-consumption may be dismissed without any judgements with respect to labour incomes. Such a supposition is not confirmed in the data analysed. Although the rate of growth of consumer credit is high, the ratio of credit to GDP remains fairly low by European standards. This is typical for post-transformation countries and to a degree it determines the high rate of growth of credit. New consumer credit is not a crucially important source of financing of private consumption; this is not a factor that blurs the would-be relation between wages and private consumption.

However, there is another source of financing private consumption; social programmes. With regard to social benefits in Poland, a game changer was the 500+ programme introduced in 2016, which provides 500 PLN of a monthly benefit payment for a child. Its impact is well-presented in the National Bank of Poland (NBP 2017, transl. A.K.):

> Rising consumer demand only to a low degree was financed with credit. The balance of credit changes has remained positive since 2013 (more credit taken than paid back), but the rising trend of the ratio of new credit to consumption slowed down in the last six quarters and in the first quarter of 2017 it was equal to 1.1%. This phenomenon may be partly explained by social benefits of the 500+ programme replacing new liabilities.

Such observations might provoke opinions that even when wages are low there are alternative sources of household incomes that increase private consumption and allow for the avoidance of under-consumption.

Third, in accordance with the hypothesis, a low share of labour incomes in GDP should result in low consumption spending (and this link is subject to the reservations discussed above) and in trends of stagnation in the economy. However, as compared to other countries of the European Union, the economy of Poland grew fast and this growth was to a high degree fuelled by rising private consumption spending. The contribution of private consumption to market prices in terms of economic growth in the period 1997–2017 was equal to 2.24% on average in Poland as compared to 1.0% in the European Union. The share of private consumption in GDP (in market prices) decreased in Poland between 1997 and 2017 from ca. 62% to ca. 57%, but remained above the average for the European Union, which was equal to ca. 58% and ca. 56%, respectively.[4] Any conclusion drawn on the basis of observations concerning the dynamics of the economy and international comparison in this respect might be propitious and questionable. The observations are not sufficient to say that the economy and economies that serve as a comparison could not grow faster or attain higher levels of GDP and employment if a possible barrier of deficient consumer demand was lifted.

Summing up, in addition to difficulties to prove the validity of the hypothesis of under-consumption presented in the previous part of this chapter, there are other factors that make conclusions drawn on the basis of an analysis of shares of labour incomes in GDP and on broader international comparisons unreliable, irrespective of whether they seemingly support or dismiss the hypothesis of under-consumption.

In particular, the low share of labour incomes in GDP in Poland partly reflects the specific, structural, and legal features of the Polish economy, as it does not induce a particularly low share of consumption spending, and consumer demand is not financed in excess by new credit. Moreover, Poland's economy has been growing fast on average in comparison with other European countries. Thus, it seems that wages in Poland are not too low to claim that the hypothesis of under-consumption matters in this case. As I argued above, these arguments are not sufficient and the conclusion would be propitious.

At this juncture, I shall conduct an alternative analysis of domestic macroeconomic data. It speaks for the applicability of the hypothesis of under-consumption to the case of Poland. The earlier discussion in this part hopefully provides justification of the method I choose and it also dismisses some arguments that might be applied to counter the conclusion I draw.

I refer to a few macroeconomic categories from the period of 2012–2019; the period chosen seems relevant to provide a good, illustrative example of the dependencies that are the subject of interest in this chapter. I do not include more recent data, namely, for 2020 and later, as the impact of Covid blurred the picture.

The period chosen for analysis does not cover the early years of transformation. In fact, it relates to recent years. Since in the chosen period there were changes in the analysed data that mirrored opposing trends in different sub-periods, it is reasonable to say that the processes are not related in a determined, one-directional way to past transformation as they are subject to ongoing changes that are not rooted in earlier transformation. Respectively, there is no need to look back to the distant past (Table 5.1).

In 2010, there was very fast growth of real GDP per employee that was not reflected in similar growth of real wages or household consumption. The rate of real growth of GDP was fairly high, but the rate of unemployment was high, while also rising with respect to the previous year (a jobless growth). In 2011, the trends were similar; albeit, the rate of growth of GDP per worker was lower. The subsequent year and in 2013 positive rates of growth of real GDP per employee, real wages, real GDP, as well as private consumption were even lower and household spending on consumption stalled in 2013. Moreover, the slowdown was mirrored in falling investments; in 2012 and 2013 the impact of gross capital formation on GDP growth was negative[5]; weak consumer demand did not boost investments and the economy was on the brink of stagnation. The year 2014 marked a major change

Table 5.1 Growth rates of GDP per employee, real wages, real GDP, household consumption, and rate of unemployment

	Growth of real GDP per employee (yearly %)	*Growth of real wages (yearly %)*	*Rate of unemployment (Dec %)*	*Growth of real GDP (yearly %)*	*Change in household consumption (yearly %)*
2010	13.8	1.4	12.4	3.4	1.6
2011	5.9	1.4	12.5	5.0	2.5
2012	4.1	0.1	13.4	1.5	0.9
2013	3.0	2.8	13.4	0.9	0
2014	1.7	3.2	11.4	3.8	3.4
2015	3.1	4.5	9.7	4.4	3.8
2016	3.1	4.6	8.2	3.0	3.6
2017	3.4	3.4	6.6	5.1	6.3
2018	7.8	5.3	5.8	5.9	4.4
2019	5.7	4.8	5.2	4.5	3.5

Source of data: GUS and Krajowa Platforma Raportująca – SDG (https://sdg.gov.pl/statistics_glob/8-2-1/, accessed 16.01.2023).

in previous trends. Modest rates of growth of real GDP per employee started rising until 2019 and in every year of this period the rate of growth of real wages was even higher. Faster growth of wages than growth of productivity was accompanied by a change in the negative developments of the previous period; the rate of unemployment was falling and the rate of growth of real GDP and the rate of consumer spending were rising. Likewise, investment bounced back, albeit unsteadily. In 2016, the impact of gross capital formation on the rate of growth of GDP was negative again; albeit, in this case, as market surveys showed,[6] the problem was a very bad investment climate due to political and legal uncertainty. The data for 2019 suggests further change brewing, but due to the impact of Covid, any interpretation of later developments in terms of under-consumption would be difficult and risky.

The data provided clearly suggests – I do not dare to say they prove – that whenever the driving force of consumption stops propelling the economy, it slows down; the rate of unemployment increases and the rate of GDP growth falls. Ultimately, there are neither many profits to invest nor – probably even to a higher degree – sufficient incentives to invest. The economic slowdown ultimately gains solid supply-side foundations. However, this is not an argument for more profits at the expense of labour incomes and probably a faster profit-led growth, yet in contrast, it speaks for a more wage-led strategy. The relation between the rates of growth of productivity and wages is vital for a switch between two different types of economic dynamics; (1) under-consumption and weak investment and growth and (2) a strong consumer demand and a high level of business activity.

Summing up, there are strong indications that the Polish economy was at least periodically subject to a major constraint of under-consumption rooted in excessively low labour incomes.

At this stage of research other questions arise as follows: What factors drive changes in the remuneration of employees (in particular with respect to changes in productivity)? Are they market forces or institutional, legal, or policy developments? The reasons that lie behind a relatively slow growth of labour incomes have been shortly outlined earlier in this chapter. The important question now is what can revert this tendency and make the share of wages in the value of production rise?

What concerns market mechanisms is that it is important to notice that their operations might not provide a quick solution to the problem of under-consumption. Rising unemployment due to low labour incomes means even tougher labour market conditions; wages would not bounce back quickly. I also previously mentioned the contradiction between microeconomic optimizing decisions and good macroeconomic outcomes as noted by Kalecki. This is a paradox and a kind of a market failure that a disequilibrium may self-reinforce. There are probably less direct and more subtle market adjustments that restore conditions for higher economic activity, but if so, they have not yet been discovered. It would be risky to claim that the system is implosive.

However, it is also reasonable to look for explanations among institutional, legal, and policy factors. One of them, which is often indicated in economic journalism in Poland, is that of the rising minimum wage. The problem with this explanation is that the process was fairly smooth in the period analysed, so it cannot explain the dynamics observed.

In the period analysed, there were minor changes with respect to "junk job contracts", and they had no major impact on the labour market and it seems highly improbable that they should influence wages considerably and exactly at times when wages grew relatively fast.

Obviously, a factor that might have boosted the economy was the social programmes (above all, the 500+ programme), while also via the multiplier effect. The problem with this explanation is that economic activity rose before the programme started in 2016.

Another explanation might relate to salaries set in the public sector; however, salaries of public servants at best dragged behind other labour incomes, so they cannot serve as an explanation of a general rise (in periods) of labour incomes.

It is difficult to indicate any major institutional/legal/policy factors that might explain the dynamics of labour incomes in the period analysed. However, it does not mean that such factors do not deserve much attention as their role may be pivotal in keeping the economy at/close to full employment equilibrium. Even if it is difficult to trace their impact in the analysed case, there is no doubt that in principle, they may strongly influence the social (re)distribution of incomes.

5.4 Conclusions

After years of fast growth and positive institutional changes that meant a successful transformation into a middle-income market economy, Poland faces problems that need to be solved. The particular problem of a falling share of labour incomes in GDP is characteristic for many modern market economies, including the most developed ones.

The problem analysed in this chapter concerns the negative impact that a declining share of wages in production exerts on economic activity. Low labour incomes and, respectively, low consumer spending does not support full employment equilibrium, which is the phenomenon of under-consumption. This phenomenon may be difficult to trace by simple static judgements that refer to the shares of labour incomes and consumer spending in GDP, including international comparisons. However, the analysis applied in this chapter of changes in real production per employee, while also real wages, the rate of unemployment, the rate of GDP growth, and changes in household consumption spending strongly support the claim that low wages at least periodically are behind a demand constraint in the Polish economy. Even so, it is important to avoid a dogmatic attitude. The supply constraint may also matter and good policies should provide positive incentives to work and invest.

The reasons for a falling share of labour incomes, a major trend in developed economies in recent decades, are fairly well identified in subject-related literature, albeit, it is much more difficult to explain changes in the opposite direction that occasionally appeared in Poland and had a positive impact on economic activity. It is doubtful whether simple economic mechanisms could trigger such changes. However, it is also difficult to find any institutional/legal/policy factors that might explain them. The factors that determine the developments remain partly mysterious.

However, there is no doubt that the institutional evolution of an economy may have a great meaning for the social distribution of incomes. We should be ready to use legal and policy tools in the face of under-consumption as economists since the times of Keynes have used to intervene to overcome a more general problem of deficient demand. Of course, very different tools are needed in the specific case of under-consumption rather than ones needed only to mitigate a temporal slowdown.

Market developments may give birth to the problem of under-consumption that should be addressed with due diligence. The state has tools that could help mitigate the problem. As market economies evolve, institutions must follow. It should be a kind of a general and constant transformation of market economies and not just a phase of a post-communist transformation.

Notes

1 More on the hypothesis of under-consumption in, for example: (Koronowski 2018) and on contemporary discussion of secular stagnation in, for example: (Teulings, and Baldwin 2014, Backhouse, and Boianovsky 2016, Koronowski 2020).

2 In practice, it would be a bold simplification to identify macroeconomic savings with profits. Savings can be also made from other kinds of household incomes, including wages. In general, high savings by definition mean lower consumption and they can cause the problem of under-consumption. Consumer sentiments – waves of optimism or pessimism matter. In this chapter, emphasis is placed on the structural aspects of incomes and spending. In any case, any savings "evaporate" with a fall in spending and incomes, so the analysis of savings would not illustrate the problem of under-consumption.

3 The source of the data; AMECO.

4 Own calculations, source of data; AMECO.

5 The source of the data on investment/gross capital formation; https://stat.gov.pl (accessed 29.05.2023).

6 For example: https://rynekinwestycji.pl/spadek-inwestycji-w-2016-roku/, https://www.wirtualnemedia.pl/artykul/jaki-wzrost-pkb-w-2016-r-konsumpcja-zapasy (accessed 29.10.2023).

References

Atkinson, A. B. (2015). *Inequality – What Can Be Done?* Cambridge, MA, London: Harvard University Press.

Backhouse, R. E., and M. Boianovsky. (2016). Secular stagnation: The history of a macroeconomic heresy. *The European Journal of the History of Economic Thought,* 23(6), 946–970.

Baran, P. A., and P. M. Sweezy. (1968). *Monopoly Capital, an Essay on the American Economic and Social Order.* New York, London: Modern Reader Paperbacks.

Berg, A. G., and J. D. Ostry. (2011). Inequality and Unsustainable Growth: Two Sides of the Same Coin? IMF Staff Discussion Note, April 2011.

Berg, A., J. D. Ostry, and C. G. Tsangarides. (2014). Redistribution, Inequality, and Growth, IMF Staff Discussion Note, April 2014.

Berg, J. (Ed.) (2015). *Labour Markets, Institutions and Inequality, Building Just Societies in the 21st Century.* Cheltenham, Northampon, MA: Edward Elgar Publishing and Geneva: ILO.

Crouch, C. (2009). Privatized keynesianism: An unacknowledged policy regime. *The British Journal of Politics & International Relations*, 11(3), 382–399.

Dabla-Norris, E., K. Kochhar, N. Suphaphiphat, F. Ricka, and E. Tsounta. (2015). Causes and Consequences of Income Inequality: A Global Perspective, IMF Staff Discussion Notes No. 15/13.

Federal Reserve Bank of New York. (2023). Household Debt and Credit Report.

Hansen, A. H. (1939). Economic progress and declining population growth. *American Economic Review*, March 1939.

Hobson, J. and J. A. Mummery. (2014, reprint). *The Physiology of Industry*. New York: Routledge.

ILO, OECD. (2015). *The Labour Share in G20 Economies*, Report prepared for the G20 Employment Working Group (Turkey, 26–27 February 2015).

Kalecki, M. (1935). Istota poprawy koniunkturalnej, reprined in: K. Łaski, and J. Osiatyński (Eds.) *Michał Kalecki, Kapitalizm: dynamika gospodarcza i pełne zatrudnienie*. Warszawa: iTONSociety.

Kalecki, M. (1986). *Teoria dynamiki gospodarczej* (3rd ed.). Warszawa: PWN.

Koronowski, A. (2016). Technological progress and unemployment: Luddism and beyond. *Gospodarka Narodowa,* April 2016.

Koronowski, A. (2018). Czy niski udział płac w PKB prowadzi do stagnacji?; hipoteza niedostatecznego popytu konsumpcyjnego. *Gospodarka Narodowa*, April 2018.

Koronowski, A. (2020). Epistemologia, aksjologia i ideologia w ekonomii; przypadek funkcji Cobba-Douglasa. *Ekonomista*, May 2020.

Koronowski, A. (2022). *Stagnacja sekularna – stara herezja czy nowy paradygmat*. Warszawa: Wydawnictwo Naukowe UKSW.

Kumhof, M., and R. Ranciere. (2010). Inequality, Leverage and Crises, IMF Working Paper WP/10/268.

Lucas, R. E., Jr. (2004). *The Industrial Revolution: Past and Future, 2003 Annual Report Essay*, The Federal Reserve Bank of Minneapolis.

Milanovic, B. (2016). *Global Inequality, A New Approach for the Age of Globalization.* Cambridge, MA: Harvard University Press.

NBP (A. Kolasa) (2017). Sytuacja finansowa sektora gospodarstw domowych w I kw. 2017 r.

OECD. (2012). *Labour Losing to Capital: What Explains the Declining Labour Share*? OECD Employment Outlook 2012.

Piketty, T. (2014). *Capital in the Twenty-First Century*. Cambridge, MA: Harvard University Press.

Rajan, R. (2010). *Fault Lanes: How Hidden Fractures Still Threaten the World Economy.* Princeton, NJ: Princeton University Press.

Richmond, W. H. (1978). John A. Hobson: Economic heretic. *The American Journal of Economics and Sociology*, 37(3), 283–294.

Stiglitz, J. (2012). *The Price of Inequality.* New York: W. W. Norton.

Teulings, C. N., and R. E. Baldwin. (2014). Secular stagnation: Facts, causes, and cures- a new Vox ebook. *VoxEU.org*, September 10, 2014. https://voxeu.org/article/secular-stagnation-facts-causes-and-cures-new-vox-ebook (accessed 5.01.2023).

Wilcock, N., and C. Scholtz. (2016). *Hartmut Elsenhans and a Critique of Capitalism. Conversations on Theory and Policy Implications.* London: Palgrave Mcmillan.

Zingales, L. (2012). *A Capitalism for the People: Recapturing the Lost Genius of American Prosperity*. New York: Basic Books.

6 Path of privatization and its risks for Ukraine

Yuriy Pogorelov and Yevheniia Polishchuk

6.1 Introduction

1991 was a turning point in the development of the modern economy of Ukraine. After the collapse of the Soviet Union, Ukraine inherited many facilities that were then under state ownership. The transition from a planned to a market economy meant, i.e. the transfer of state property into private ownership. The process of changing ownership from state-owned to private individuals or companies is considered to be privatization. Over the past three decades, Ukraine has undergone several waves of privatization, with a significant proportion of the country's state-owned assets sold to private investors. The privatization process has been shaped by a range of political, economic, and institutional factors, including the legal and regulatory framework for privatization, the role of the government in managing the process, and the investment climate in Ukraine.

All interested parties should, in principle, benefit from this process: the replenishment of the state budget with additional financial resources; improving the quality of the manufactured products and services under the influence of market instruments; revival of competition; departure from monopolization, etc. At the same time, the actions of the Ukrainian government regarding the implementation of the privatization process can hardly be called successful and it has high risks for its security.

First of all, it should be mentioned that privatization as changing ownership for any entities is totally normal despite the ownership form of such entities – private, public, state, municipal, etc. The processes of buying and selling stocks and shares, mergers and acquisitions are usual, normal, and common in any market-oriented economy. Enterprises emerge, grow, develop, but also degrade, deteriorate, or become bankrupt. Such phenomena are commonly witnessed all over the world (Beraho, 2008, 2011; Buttwill & Wihlborg, 2004; Hudson, 1997; Tomczak, 2018).

Moreover, the experience of many countries including post-soviet ones, as well as countries of Europe proved that privatization is not only a normal economic process as such a process, can intensify economic growth, increase productivity, as well as satisfy social needs, etc. (Abarbanell & Bonin, 1997; Balfour & Crise, 1993; Bellas et al., 1994; Bochniarz, Jermakowicz & Meller,

DOI: 10.4324/9781003425717-8

1994; De Fraja & Roberts, 2009; Lipton & Sachs, 1992; Ord, Walker & Hunt, 2016).

Third, as a complicated multi-dimensional process, privatization may cause both positive and negative consequences. Attention relating to the changing of the ownership and ownership structure in a national economy is mostly paid in economic science to some positive consequences of such changes (Balfour & Crise, 1993; Bochniarz et al., 1994; Botis, 2013; Collett, 2015; Gugler et al., 2003; Jackson & Miyajima, 2007). It is shown that changes of the ownership structure may cause a lot of positive consequences, such as the involvement of foreign direct investments (because of the increasing investment attractiveness and profit rate of the local economy), while also the adoption of new technologies and buying some new equipment, employment creation, making positive social changes due to the massive involvement of households in the processes of property distribution and management (because of successful privatization).

However, there are some risks and threats that emerge because of the changes of the ownership structure in the national economy. Such risks should be taken into account while planning privatization and creating institutional conditions of the transition of property rights. The key condition for the "normal character" of changing ownership because of buying and selling stocks, mergers, and acquisitions is its *voluntary* nature. If anyone can be forced to sell shares with the artificially lowered price and by illegal pressure, there are a lot of negative consequences, namely, there is first and foremost no motivation to do and develop any business (if any enterprise can be seized and taken away); the costs of any enterprise grow because of the necessity to protect such an enterprise from the frequent illegal actions of raiders; increasing the costs causes a decrease in the competitiveness of any enterprise and the national economy as a whole; insecurity for minor investors causes low investment attractiveness of the enterprise and the national economy as a whole; whereas low investment attractiveness limits the access to investments and loans and in this way limits the necessary financial resources for the enterprise; while there is also the phenomenon of capital outflow in the national economy, etc. Hence, historical analysis of changes of the ownership structure in Ukraine facilitates defining risks and threats that emerge because of such changes. Additionally, it is useful to know such risks and threats to avoid them in the future in other countries and to provide measures to overcome them in the Ukrainian economy. Hence, the **aim** of the study is to provide an overview of the privatization process in Ukraine and its risks, with regard to its historical development, while also the institutional framework for privatization.

Based on the research objectives provided, the most important/general ones may be as follows:

- Analysing the effects of privatization on the Ukrainian economy, including its impact on economic growth, employment, and income inequality.
- Evaluating the effectiveness of the legal and regulatory framework for privatization in Ukraine, including the transparency and the risks of the process, the protection of property rights, and the prevention of corruption.

These objectives are closely related and will provide an understanding of the privatization process in Ukraine, its impact on the economy, and the effectiveness of the legal framework that governs the process.

6.2 Theoretical background of privatization

The institutional framework for privatization refers to the set of laws, regulations, and institutions that govern the process of transferring ownership of state-owned assets to the private sector. Based on the studies of institutional theory (Berle & Means, 2017; Demsetz, 1967; Eggertsson, 1990) the general institutional framework for privatization and our analysis of the privatization process in Ukraine may be considered with the following components:

Legal component: This includes the laws and regulations that define the scope of privatization, while also establishing the procedures for asset valuation and sale, and ensuring transparency and fairness in the privatization process. It also includes the legal protection of property rights for buyers and sellers, and the prevention of corruption and conflicts of interest.

Organizational component: This includes the government agencies responsible for managing the privatization process, such as the State Property Fund, and the supervisory bodies that monitor the process, such as the Anti-Monopoly Committee. It also includes other institutions that support privatization, such as legal and financial advisors, while also accounting and auditing firms. Likewise, it also includes the instruments of privatization (e.g. certificate of privatization).

The effectiveness of the institutional framework for privatization is critical to the success of the privatization process. It determines the degree of transparency and fairness in the process, the protection of property rights, and the prevention of corruption and other abuses. A well-designed and implemented institutional

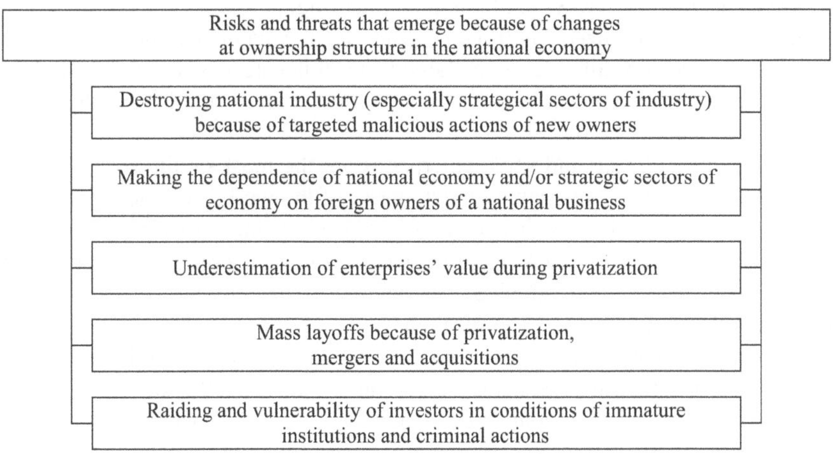

Figure 6.1 Risks and threats that emerge because of changes at ownership structure in the national economy (on the example of Ukraine).

framework may help ensure that privatization contributes to economic growth and development, while minimizing the negative impacts on society.

While exploring the privatization structure in Ukraine, it is important to consider the key risks and threats that emerge because of property ownership changes (Figure 6.1).

It is worth mentioning that this is a generalized view of the type of risks of privatization in Ukraine and there are many other smaller risks, including those arising from wartime privatization, albeit, these need to be further explored.

6.3 General picture of ownership in Ukraine (structure of ownership/oligarchs/SMEs)

Before considering the peculiarities of privatization in Ukraine, we suggest considering how the ownership structure of micro, small, medium, and large-scale businesses in Ukraine has changed in recent years. As we can see from Table 6.1, Ukraine has a diverse range of enterprises, including micro, small, medium, and large-scale enterprises.[1] Here is an overview of the characteristics of each category of enterprise in Ukraine.

In Ukraine, the share of the *large companies* (state and private) is low and averages out around zero. Large enterprises are often involved in high-tech manufacturing, while also heavy industry and other complex activities. Large enterprises account for less than 0.1% of all businesses.

However, the situation with *medium-sized business* is not much better in terms of the percentage indicators and the latest trends show less than 1%. In Ukraine, medium-sized enterprises account for less than 1% of all businesses. Medium-sized enterprises are often involved in more complex activities, such as manufacturing, construction, and professional services.

Small enterprises (in the last three years around 3%) are often involved in activities such as retail, services, and light manufacturing.

In Ukraine, *micro-sized* enterprises account for the majority of businesses, with an estimated 96% of all enterprises falling into this category. Micro-sized enterprises are often involved in low-skilled activities, such as retail, agriculture, and small-scale manufacturing.

Overall, micro-sized and small enterprises are the most significant part of the Ukrainian economy. They employ the majority of the workforce and significantly contribute to economic growth. A total of 95.5% of all enterprises in the Ukrainian economy were SMEs, and 4.4% of all enterprises in the Ukrainian economy were medium ones in 2018 (Miroshnik & Prokopieva, 2020). The share of all employed workers in Ukraine for small and medium-sized enterprises is 75%, or 4.8 million Ukrainians. The remaining 25% (or 1.6 million Ukrainians) worked in large enterprises (Lyvch, 2022; State Statistic Service in Ukraine, 2019). At the same time, the contribution to the economy's development is the other way round. In 2019, *large and medium-sized* enterprises in Ukraine constituted more than 73% of GDP, which means that *micro and small enterprises* in Ukraine constituted only 16% of GDP. However, there are challenges facing small and medium enterprises in

Table 6.1 Characteristics of ownership in Ukraine according to the size of the enterprises, 2010–2021

	Large business, *units*	*In % to the total of business entities*	***Medium entrepreneurship entities,*** *units*	*In % to the total of business entities*	***Small*** *entrepreneurship entities, units*	*In % to the total of business entities*	*Of which micro-entrepreneurship entities, units*	*In % to the total of business entities*
2010	586	0,0	21343	1,0	68311,0	3,1	2093688	95,9
2011	659	0,0	21059	1,3	71083,0	4,2	1608819	94,5
2012	698	0,0	20551	1,3	68102,0	4,3	1510776	94,4
2013	659	0,0	19210	1,1	65021,0	3,8	1637180	95,1
2014	497	0,0	16618	0,9	55159,0	2,8	1859887	96,3
2015	423	0,0	15510	0,8	47555,0	2,4	1910830	96,8
2016	383	0,0	15113	0,8	49298,0	2,7	1800736	96,5
2017	399	0,0	15254	0,9	52324,0	2,9	1737082	96,2
2018	446	0,0	16476	0,9	57934,0	3,2	1764737	95,9
2019	518	0,0	18129	0,9	58965,0	3,1	1864013	96,0
2020	512	0,0	17946	0,9	56217,0	2,9	1898902	96,2
2021	610	0,0	17811	0,9	56969,0	3,0	1880858	96,1

Source: Own preparation based on State Statistic Service in Ukraine.

Ukraine, including limited access to finance, high taxes, and a challenging regulatory environment. Efforts are underway to support the growth and development of micro, small, and medium-sized enterprises in Ukraine, including the provision of financial and technical assistance, the simplification of regulations, while also the promotion of entrepreneurship and innovation.

6.4 Privatization in Ukraine

6.4.1 Beginning and development of privatization in Ukraine

Privatization in Ukraine has been a complex and ongoing process since the country gained independence from the Soviet Union in 1991. There have been several phases of privatization in Ukraine, each with its own unique characteristics and goals. Here are some of the key phases:

First wave of privatization (1992–1994): This phase involved the privatization of small enterprises, such as shops and restaurants, through auctions and tenders. The government hoped to stimulate economic growth by transferring state-owned assets to private ownership.

Second wave of privatization (1995–1998): This phase focused on larger enterprises, including heavy industry and energy companies. The government used a combination of auctions, tenders, and voucher privatization (where citizens could buy vouchers that could be used to buy shares in state-owned companies) to sell off state-owned assets.

Third wave of privatization (1999–2004): This phase involved the privatization of the remaining state-owned assets, including land and infrastructure. The government also encouraged foreign investment and the participation of international financial institutions.

Fourth wave of privatization (2005–2010): This phase focused on the privatization of strategic assets, including ports, railways, and power plants. The government aimed to attract foreign investors and improve the efficiency of these sectors.

Fifth wave of privatization (2011–2021): This phase has focused on the privatization of small and medium-sized enterprises, as well as the consolidation of state-owned assets into larger companies. The government has also sought to improve transparency and reduce corruption in the privatization process. It is worth mentioning that in 2021, the State Budget of Ukraine received UAH 5.1 billion from privatization, which is a record for revenues in a decade. The amount of revenues in 2020–2021 exceeds the previous seven years in total (State Property Fund in Ukraine, 2021).

It is also worth noting that privatization in Ukraine has been a contentious issue, with some arguing that it has led to the concentration of wealth in the hands of a few oligarchs and has not resulted in the expected economic benefits. Nevertheless, privatization remains an important part of Ukraine's economic reform efforts. The path of the Ukrainian privatization under the different policy regimes is briefly represented in Table 6.2.

During this period the legal and organizational components were formed.

Table 6.2 Privatization in Ukraine under different policy regimes

Presidency and period	*Characteristics*	*Income from privatization of state property, billion USD*	
President Kravchuk 1991–1994 Legal base formation	The first legislation acts on privatization were adopted Concept of denationalization and privatization of utilities, land, and housing stock. Creation State Property Fund (1992) and Regional Branches State Property Fund (1993) The Law of Ukraine "On the Privatization of the State Housing Fund" (1992) The Land Code of Ukraine (1992) Law of Ukraine "On Privatization of State Property" (1992)		
President Kuchma 1994–2005	1994–1997 In October 1994, the president message "On the basic principles of economic and social policy" focused on the privatization of state and communal property. The issue of privatization certificates Managers of enterprises that were subject to certificate privatization began to buy vouchers for next to nothing in order to become legal owners. Formally, 19 million shareholders appeared in Ukraine, but practically none of them gained access to the property privatized with the help of their certificates. 1997–2005 – Oligarch era formation State Property Fund of Ukraine began to put up for competitive Privatization of large industrial and commercial enterprises, regional energy companies, and transport utilities.	1997	0
		1998	0.1
		1999	0.2
		2000	0.4
		2001	0.4
		2002	1
		2003	4.7
		2004	0.1
		2005	0.5
President Yushchenko 2005–2010	The way of enterprises of state objects practically has not changed. In 2005, a demonstration sale of four subdivisions (including Kryvorizhstal) was carried out at an open tender, but the same number of enterprises were sold at closed tenders. In 2006, one enterprise was sold at an open tender, eight at closed tenders	2006	0.1
		2007	0.1
		2008	0.1
		2009	1.4
		2010	0.8

(*Continued*)

Table 6.2 (*Continued*)

Presidency and period	*Characteristics*	*Income from privatization of state property, billion USD*	
President Yanukovych 2010–2014	According to data at the beginning of 2010, most of the main industrial and production funds still belong to the state (32% – in communal, 21% – in state ownership). However, the share of private enterprises (47% by fixed assets) in the gross domestic product is predominant. This means that privatization remains relevant, despite all the losses that the budget has suffered.	2011 2012 2013 2014	0.2 0 0 0
President Poroshenko	Low of Ukraine "On the privatization of state and communal property" (2018)	2015 2016 2017 2018 2019	0 0 0.1 0 0
President Zelenskii	On February 10, he approved the procedure for using funds from the Fund for Liquidation of the Consequences of Russia's Armed Aggression and the procedure for selling confiscated Russian assets.	2020 2021	0.1 5.1

Source: Own preparation based on: Wilson and Burakovsky (1996), Legal aspects of privatization in Ukraine (1996), Uschapovsky (1999), and Van Zon (2000).

Legal component. It began with the adoption of the first legal act, namely, the Concept of denationalization and privatization of utilities, land, and housing stock, The Law of Ukraine "On the Privatization of the State Housing Fund" (1992), The Land Code of Ukraine (1992), Law of Ukraine "On Privatization of State Property" (1992), and the presidential message "On the basic principles of economic and social policy" (1994). Due to the data of the State Property Fund, 8,348 state companies were privatized in 1992–1994.

Organizational component. During Kravchuk's presidency (1991–1994), the State Property Fund was formed (1992), which is responsible for conducting public auctions for the sale of state-owned assets, as well as for monitoring the implementation of privatization deals. Soon after that, its regional centres were formed, which later became the institutional infrastructure of privatization. Subsequently, the Office of Permanent Investments was also established at the State Property Fund, as the need arose due to a significant increase in the number of projects and their scale. This created risks related to the controllability of the processes. We are talking about an unprecedented number of facilities transferred to the Fund for further privatization, and the challenges associated with the Coronavirus pandemic.

The establishment of a legislative field and an institution capable of implementing privatization became the first step for the subsequent issuance of privatization certificates. At the beginning of 1997, approximately 80% of privatization certificates were issued. A total of 5.3 million citizens never applied for them, and 2.5 million did not use them. There are mixed results as follows: while some privatized enterprises have become successful and profitable, others have been poorly managed, leading to economic losses and social problems. Unfortunately, the privatization process in Ukraine has been marred by corruption, with many assets sold off to insiders and oligarchs at below-market prices. This has led to a concentration of wealth in the hands of a few individuals and has contributed to the country's economic and social problems (Van Zon, 2000).

Moreover, as can be seen from Table 6.1, the deductions from privatization to the budget did increase, but not in the expected amounts. The oligarchs closely connected with the power structures tried to prevent free competition, and the privatization of large enterprises was carried out in non-commercial tenders with great losses for the budget.

A total of 96,500 facilities were privatized in the period of 1992–2004, including state-owned property – 71,400. The privatized facilities were distributed by industry as follows: industry – 8,564, construction – 3,750, wholesale and retail trade, repair and transport, and trade. services – 38,371, hotels and restaurants – 7,085, transport and communications – 1,997, and financial sector – 363 (Dubrovskyi, 2007).

6.4.2 Current situation of state-owned enterprises in Ukraine and their potential for privatization

There were more than 3,293 state-owned enterprises in Ukraine in 2021, which employ about 700,000 people (see Table 6.3). At first glance, this makes the Ukrainian state a real business power. However financial indicators say the opposite: state-owned enterprises consistently perform worse than private ones, regardless of the economic situation or the industry in which they operate.

The afore-mentioned data demonstrates that centrally owned and state-owned enterprises in Ukraine are significant players in the country's economy, contributing to employment figures and economic output. Here is an overview of the sectoral distribution of centrally owned and state-owned enterprises by employment and value. According to the information in the table above, *the number of employees* at the state-owned enterprises is highly engaged in the transport industry (41%), the main sector (mining and quarrying, agriculture, forestry and fisheries), while also production (relatively 13% and 12%). At the same time, the transport industry also has the largest *equity value* ($9.7 billion), while others have an equity value of $15.4 billion, as well as energy and gas – $7.3 billion.

Despite such an impact on the labour market of the state-owned enterprises in Ukraine, their other economic indicators are not comparable with private ones. In each of the last ten years, state-owned enterprises have produced less return on invested capital (ROE). In general, 61.1% of state-owned enterprises are less

Table 6.3 Sectoral distribution of centrally owned state-owned enterprises by employment and value in Ukraine in 2021

	Number of state enterpirses	*%*	*Number of employees*	*%*	*Equity value (thousand UAH)*	*Equity value (thousand USD)*
Main sector (mining and quarrying, agriculture, forestry and fisheries)	818	25%	93673	13%	–11 808 897	–429 102
Production	729	22%	86 599	12%	10 414 625	378 438
Finance	32	1%	353	0%	12 348 187	448 699
Telecommunications	128	4%	12 000	2%	–1 005 874	–36 551
Energy and gas	42	1%	71 342	10%	201 368 730	7 317 178
Transport	113	3%	296 229	41%	267 009 549	9 702 382
Utility entities	28	1%	5 460	1%	1 396 848	50 758
Real estate	50	2%	927	0%	602 793	21 904
Other (professional, scientific, and technical services)	1353	41%	157 001	22%	423 014 211	15 396 461
Total	3293	100%	723584	100%	903 340 172	32 850 167

Source: Own preparation based on OECD (2021).

profitable than private ones (OECD, 2021). This shows a comparison with the median ROE of private companies of the same year and industry. This trend is confirmed for all industries, although to varying degrees. Public companies tend to spend more on labour than their private competitors. On the one hand, such a situation can be related to poor governance, while on the other hand to the essence of the enterprise and the industry where it is operating (e.g. social sphere).

The other indicator that describes the privatization structure in Ukraine is the number of enterprises that have been sold in the recent years in Ukraine. There is a web platform known as privatization.gov.ua where enterprises for the privatization process are offered. According to the data of the web platform privatization.gov.ua, from 2013 to 2023 only 1,375 property units have been sold (see Figure 6.2).

The privatization process was carried out via such ways of privatization as auctions with terms/without terms (546), auction by the method of reduced the starting price and subsequent submission of price positions (401), auction by the method of reducing the starting price (66) and others (63).

These property facilities were located in different oblasts (administrative districts) of Ukraine (see Figure 6.3). Luganska and Donetska oblasts, which are in the minority of facilities (29 and 25 facilities relatively speaking) have been sold via privatization mechanisms. It is related to the occupation of a part of these territories

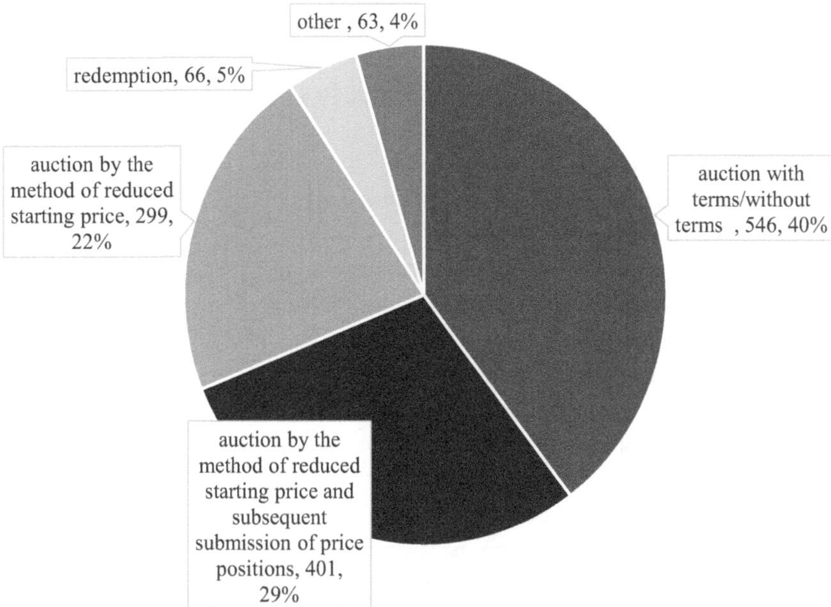

Figure 6.2 Sold property objects, 2013–2023, units and %.

Source: own preparation based on www. privatization.gov.ua

by the Russian Federation since 2014 and the SOE located there have been stolen by them.

It is interesting that traditionally Kyiv and Kyivska oblasts are the leaders in economic indicators, however, in terms of privatization, the leaders are unexpectedly Vinnytska (142), Lvivska (86), and Rivnenska (87) oblasts.

6.4.3 Special programmes of privatization in the war period

Privatization in the war period is extremely significant, because the cost of fighting with the enemy is too high and there is a strong need to increase the budget. At the beginning of 2022, when Russia's aggression was not obvious to many, the state budget was planned to be replenished with UAH 8 billion, thanks to privatization. Privatization during the war looked strange, at least from an ethical point of view, because not all potential clients could take part in it. At such a time, of course, there was no question of foreign investors, who had been lured by the government for many years.

However, in July, the parliament approved draft law No. 7451 relating to the simplification of privatization, including the facilitation of the relocation of enterprises. Large-scale privatization was abandoned, as well as the sale of property in the occupied territories.

On the other hand, the privatization process has been significantly simplified. Audits and appraisals became optional, auction terms were shortened, while new

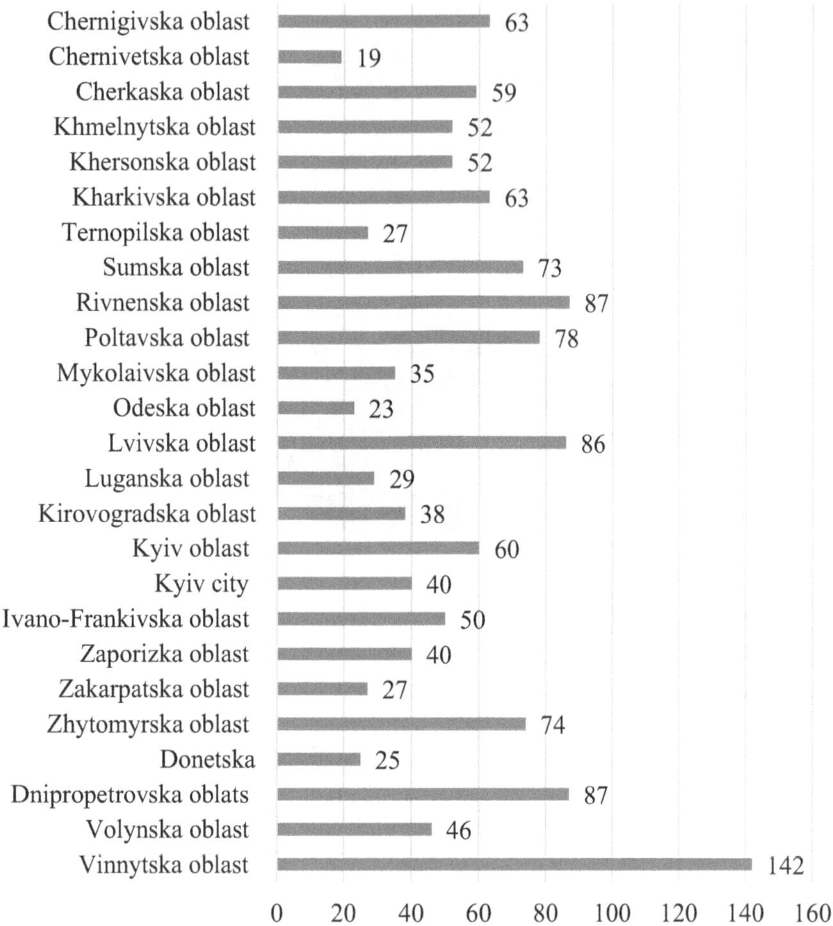

Figure 6.3 Privatization in Ukrainian oblasts, 2013–2022, units.

Source: own preparation based on www. privatization.gov.ua

rules for determining the starting price and the size of the guarantee fee appeared, the process was digitized (submission of documents online, e-signatures), while the terms of redemption and transfer of property were changed.

Since the February invasion by the Russian army in Ukraine, the Ukrainian government has been looking for ways of surviving and since the summer of 2022, the government has been actively searching for ways to cope with the crisis via privatization mechanisms. Due to a new law entitled "On the privatization of state and communal property" (2018)[2] facilities for privatization are divided into facilities of small privatization and facilities of large privatization, the specifics of which are described in Table 6.4.

The State Property Fund specified that for the period from the end of 2022 to the beginning of 2023, the Fund had already accepted about 1,500 enterprises

Table 6.4 Small and large privatization programmes

	Small privatization	*Large privatization*
Book value	Less than 250 million UAH	More than 250 million UAH
Privatization objects	• Single property complexes • Objects of socio-cultural purpose • Objects of unfinished construction, packages of shares • Separate property • Real estate • Movable property	• Single property complexes • Packages of shares

Source: Own preparation based on: https://privatization.gov.ua

under management. Due to the plans of the government, no more than 100 enterprises should remain in state ownership, while most of them will come under the government's control. All these enterprises must be transformed into joint-stock or limited liability companies and the state can be a shareholder. The purpose of such ownership is simple – to make a profit through dividends. To achieve maximum dividends, it is necessary to separate business ownership (shareholder role) and business management (management role). Therefore, in enterprises that will remain in state ownership, a system of corporate governance must be fully implemented when management is controlled not by officials, but by members of the supervisory board, most of whom are independent. This separation of functions is the main idea of corporate reform, which the government is now actively implementing. All funds from this sale will be directed to the restoration of Ukraine, the energy system, people's housing, while also demining.

The Cabinet of Ministers adopted an order on the transfer of about 2,400 state-owned enterprises with a total debt of UAH 200 billion to the sphere of the management of the Fund. A total of 1,300 of them at the time of transfer are subject to liquidation or have signs of bankruptcy, 600 are located in the temporarily occupied territories, and there is no current information about their condition.

What will not be privatized: enterprises that ensure the security of the state, enterprises that are natural monopolies, enterprises that are important to society, or whose services/goods cannot be performed by private business.

6.5 Risks and threats that emerge because of changes of ownership structure in the national economy

6.5.1 Destroying national industry (especially strategic sectors) because of targeted malicious actions of new owners

With the independence of Ukraine after the collapse of the Soviet Union there were changes in the structure of property in the Ukrainian economy. Such changes were mostly caused by the processes of privatization, because deals of

M&A are not so widespread in Ukraine. Moreover, such deals are often made "in silence" without any loud publicity, except the legal limitations (cases when the public is informed about M&A deals and changes of ownership structure are obligatory). Before the Russian aggression against Ukraine there were spread deals of foreign direct investments. For example, FDI in Ukraine in 2021 went from $1,201m to $1,421m ("Foreign direct investments", 2022). At the same time, according to the information of the Fund of the State Property of Ukraine privatization gave to the Ukrainian State Budget 5.1 billion hryvnyas (approx. $188m) ("The income of privatization", 2022). Hence, the processes of changing the ownership structure existed. The considered risks and threats have to be analysed in detail.

Destroying the national industry (especially the strategic sectors of industry) because of the new owners' targeted malicious actions can be persuasively shown in the example of the Russian infiltration into the Ukrainian economy even before the unprovoked Russian aggression in 2022. As already mentioned ("From merging to cutting into scrap metal", 2023), the

> Russian impact on the Ukrainian economy has grown since 1990 until the Revolution of Dignity, but in practice it became clear that in almost every case when the Russians played a pivotal role, plants and factories did not develop. The maximum impact was when they stopped the business activities in the interests of competing companies from Russia, while they were cut into scrap metal.

So, changes in the Ukrainian economy ownership in the interests of Russian capital did not only cause regression of Ukrainian business, but it went totally backwards, while such changes caused a decay of Ukrainian production and destruction of Ukrainian industry despite the initial "foreign investments". These are only some examples of changing ownership of the Ukrainian economy for the benefit of Russian business, yet, not all ("From merging to cutting into scrap metal", 2023; "SBU informed concerning the suspect", 2017).

- The only producer of primary aluminium in Ukraine since 2006 had been destroying the interests of Russian metallurgical enterprises for some time. Russian businessmen became the new owners of this enterprise and the new owners stopped the main production cycle in 2009 and cut all the equipment into scrap metal in 2015 instead of conducting modernization and further economic development of this enterprise.
- In 2010 Russian "Transmashholding" became the new owner of Ukrainian "Luganskteplovoz", which was one of the leaders in building diesel locomotives in the former USSR and the top producer of diesel locomotives in Ukraine. There were fears that after changing the owner, "Luganskteplovoz" would cease its business activities. Unfortunately such a fear was justified, and now Ukrainian "Luganskteplovoz" almost does not work at all.

- Almost all Ukrainian enterprises with new Russian owners did not develop and such a fact is clearly presented in the Ukrainian metallurgical industry. The Ukrainian metallurgical enterprises in the period of 2003–2014 bought new equipment, adopted new technologies, etc., whereas in contrast to such trends in Ukrainian metallurgy, enterprises with Russian owners did not develop at all.

These specified examples show that new owners of enterprises can be extremely toxic and even dangerous for the national economy in some cases, because their infiltration on an absolutely legal basis may cause destruction of national businesses. Hence, it is possible to reach the conclusion that the process of changing the structure of ownership in any national economy is inextricably linked with macroeconomic and even political factors. In fact, not every "foreign direct investment" and "new effective owner", even with primary sufficient investments are positive both for an enterprise and for the national economy.

6.5.2 Forming the dependence of the national economy and/or strategic sectors of the economy on foreign owners of the national business

The other threat that emerges because of changes to the ownership structure in the national economy is that of forming the dependence of the national economy and/or strategic sectors of economy on foreign owners of the national business. The classical example of such a situation in Ukraine is the structure of ownership in the transportation of electric power.

One of the key elements to satisfying all the industrial and household consumption of electrical energy is the aggregate of regional grids that unite the production of electric power and its consumption by the final consumer. According to (Orel, 2022), the Ukrainian government controls approximately 20% of regional grids, whereas 10% of regional grids are owned by VS Energy group (the company with some Russian beneficial owners), approximately 50% of regional grids are controlled by DTEK, one of the largest business groups in Ukraine (F4 according to the Forbes in Ukraine rating). The Ukrainian State (represented by the Cabinet of Ministers of Ukraine and the Fund of the State Property of Ukraine) owns 6 regional grids, VS Energy group owns 5 regional grids, and some Ukrainian businessmen own 14 regional grids in Ukraine. VS Energy group according to various sources (Orel, 2022; Topalov, 2022; Yillyin & Samofalov, 2023) is associated with Russian beneficial owners.

The current structure of property in the energy sector of Ukraine is the result of privatization, because all the regional grids were first of all state enterprises, while after privatization they became private owned. However, it is obvious that the owners of regional grids make a huge impact on almost every Ukrainian enterprise and every Ukrainian household. Such owners influence the socio-economic stability, employment, and the stable functioning of every enterprise in the region forming GDP just because stable and sufficient power supply is obligatory for every enterprise and household nowadays. According to Ukrainian legislation, the providers of power supply cannot define the price for electric power (making the price of electric power within the power of the National Commission for Regulating Energy and Public Utilities). However, the providers of power supply have a lot of options to make a huge impact on every energy consumer by defining the limits of consumption for industrial consumers, influencing the terms, price and specification of making new electricity networks, while also making preventive maintenance, etc.

The fact of the huge impact of privately owned regional grids on the national economy in Ukraine does not mean that their owners *will* harm the national economy, but this fact demonstrates convincingly that they *can* do this. In the conditions of the Russian war against Ukraine, the situation when there are *Russian* beneficial owners of the *Ukrainian* grids who can make a significant impact on the Ukrainian economy becomes absurd and grotesque. Hence, as it may be clearly seen in the example of the Ukrainian energy sector, uncontrollable changes in the structure of the national economy may cause the emergence of the dependence of the national economy and/or strategic sectors of the economy on the foreign owners of some national enterprises. It is obvious that such a dependence can create threats and risks of a different nature.

6.5.3 Underestimation of the value of enterprises during privatization

One of the key issues during the privatization of any state enterprise is the price that a new owner pays to the state for obtaining ownership. The price of shares can be easily defined in the case of a developed stock market as the balance of the buying and selling price in real deals. The primary price of any enterprise in total and/or its shares is not an unequivocally defined measure in the process of privatization. In some cases, as mentioned by Moyseenko (2022), the initial price is the disputed value.

There are a lot of facts when the initial price of state enterprises and/or state property grows 2.5–3 times during the auction in the process of privatization. There are cases when the final price is ten times higher than the initial one. Some cases of the increase in price during privatization in Ukraine are the following: the price of a building in Poltava region in the process of privatization grew from 22,000 hryvnias (approx. \$800) to 6.5 million hryvnias (approx. \$232,000); the price of a building in the Cherkassy region grew from an initial 22,000 hryvnias (approx. \$800) to 5 million hryvnias (approx. \$178,000); the price of a building in Kirovograd region grew from an initial 3,000 hryvnias (approx. \$107) to 1.5 million hryvnias (approx. \$53,500) (Moyseenko, 2022).

The situation in the energy sector is the same: in 2017, 25% of shares of Kyiv Regional Grid were assessed and bought for \$28 million; however, in 2021 the same 25% of shares of Kyiv Regional Grid were assessed at \$110 million, which is approximately four times more, despite the fact that there was no significant economic growth in Ukraine during 2017–2021; in 2017, 25% of shares of Donetsk Regional Grid were sold for only \$5m, however in 2021 these shares were assessed at $80m, which is 16 times more (Kaluzhna, 2021). There are examples when the final price of the privatized facilities is more than the initial one by tens and even hundreds of times (Moyseenko, 2022).

Of course, one would like to consider such facts as evidence of the efficiency of the national economy in Ukraine and the high demand for privatized facilities. However, it is reasonable to assume such facts as proof of underestimating the initial value of facilities that were suggested for privatization. Such undervaluations cause a lot of negative consequences: the shortfall of budgetary funds as a result of privatization, premises of acts of corruption (undervaluation of state property is impossible without actions of some state bodies, and such actions can be the result of mistakes or purposeful actions by some state authorities), the "shady" nature of privatization, while also limited access of market players to the processes of privatization, etc.

6.5.4 Mass layoffs because of privatization, mergers and acquisitions

The next threat that emerges because of the changes of the ownership structure in the national economy is a rise in unemployment. It is often the case that a new owner dismisses some of the "old personnel". Such a situation can be considered as an unfair one, albeit, it is not uncommon: a new owner obtains an enterprise, equipment, markets, and technology, while local authorities witness the problem of a rise in unemployment. The connection between changing the property structure and a rise in unemployment is an "international" one and is relevant not only for the developing countries, but also for the USA, UK, EU, etc. (e.g., Cartwright & Cooper, 1990; Conyon et al., 2002; Gugler & Yurtoglu, 2004; McGuckin & Nguyen, 2001).

The most well-known fact of mass layoffs because of changing the structure of ownership in Ukraine is the case of "Krivorozhstal". In 2005, Mittal Steel became the owner of the state joint-stock company "Krivorozhstal", the biggest producer of steel in Ukraine. In 2007, the new owner began the programme of voluntary redundancies and for the period of 2007–2015 the personnel of "ArcelorMittal Kryvoi Rogh" (the new name of "Krivorozhstal") decreased from 57,900 to 29,100 ("ArcelorMittal Kryvoi Rogh ceased voluntary redundancies", 2016). To be honest, it is necessary to specify that first and foremost, all redundancies were voluntary, second, all the people made redundant were given compensation, which was from 15 to 25 monthly salaries, plus medical insurance for two years (For voluntary redundancy, 2011). However, in fact, for ten years after changing the ownership structure of the only enterprise under analysis, there have only been new job opportunities created, but the number of people made redundant who made additional pressure on labour market was nearly 30,000 ("ArcelorMittal Kryvoi Rogh ceased voluntary redundancies", 2016).

Thus, changing the structure of ownership in the national economy may cause mass layoffs. The negative impact of such changes on the economy of some territory (a town, a city, a region) may exceed the positive changes (increasing tax payments, creating new job opportunities). In addition, often a new owner obtains only positive results because of the changing structure of ownership in the national economy, while the local authorities and local population may have both positive and negative consequences.

6.5.5 Raiding and the vulnerability of investors in conditions of immature institutions and criminal actions

One of the most sensitive threats to changing the structure of ownership in any national economy which is impossible to ignore and which should be analysed is that of raiding.

The issue of the voluntary nature of changing ownership in the national economy causes the phenomenon of raiding in the Ukrainian economy. To be correct, it is necessary to specify such a notion in the Ukrainian economy. According to Kozachenko, Pogorelov and Andrushchenko (2020),

> In world practice, raiding is commonly understood as an absolutely legal and transparent acquisition of the controlling block of shares of the acquired company, however, without any agreement on the owner's side. In Ukraine though, raiding is mostly treated as a solely negative phenomenon and is mostly understood as a range of illegal acts aimed at taking over other property under the cover of seemingly legitimate grounds which are often presented as falsified documents or as an illegitimate court decision… In Ukraine, the difference between "white" [that is totally legal], "grey" and "black" [criminal] raiders is very blurred. In recent years, "grey" raiding has become especially widespread, and counteracting its growth is very hard.

To imagine the scale of raiding in Ukraine, it is useful to consider some statistics: from 2014 until 2021, the profoundness of raiding cases had increased; during 2012–2019, there were approx. 3,200 cases of raiding registered in Ukraine ("Raiding in Ukraine", 2019).

The impact of raiding in Ukraine for the national economy and the international image of Ukraine is obvious: according to the International Property Rights Index (IPRI, by the Property Rights Alliance), in 2022, Ukraine was ranked 105th among 128 countries included in the overall ranking, whereas in 2021 Ukraine was ranked 106th, in 2020 – 105th, in 2019 it was 109th (International Property Rights Index, 2019–2022). Hence, unfortunately Ukraine is not only in the top 25, top 50, or even first 100 countries by indicators of property rights protection, for the last five years Ukraine has been prominent in the *last* quartile by indicators of property rights protection. Such a situation concerning the protection of property rights is correlated with a generalized evaluation of the power of law in Ukraine: according to the World Justice Project (World Justice Project, 2019–2022), during 2015–2022 Ukraine ranked 70–78 by the indicator of Global Ranking of Justice among 102 countries under consideration. Thus, raiding is both a negative consequence and negative factor in the Ukrainian economy. It is obvious that the phenomenon of raiding makes a great impact on changing property rights in Ukraine.

It would be unfair to consider that the Ukrainian authorities and State bodies are doing nothing to fight with raiding and raiders in Ukraine. Over the last few years, there have been organizational actions conducted and legal documents approved to overcome the problem of raiding in Ukraine (Kozachenko, Pogorelov & Andrushchenko, 2020, 2021; Law of Ukraine, 2019; "A new stage of protection, 2019") with the establishment of the Anti-Raiding Chamber in Ukraine, opening the Office for counteraction to raiding, while also approval of the Law of Ukraine "Introduction of changes to several legal acts of Ukraine concerning the protection of property rights" # 159-IX of 3.10.2019, increasing the level of responsibility for violations in state registration, as well as verification of representative credentials prior to their actions with relation to property rights and their encumbrance at the pre-notary stage, while using specific forms of notarized documents for a state registration, etc.

Due to the Law of Ukraine "Introduction of changes to several legal acts of Ukraine concerning protection of property rights", raiders lost some far-reaching approaches and actions to become owners of someone's property in an illegal way (Kozachenko, Pogorelov & Andrushchenko, 2021), and thus, the possibility of seizing some property in the whole territory of Ukraine using one and the same "black" notary since the extraterritorial principles have been revoked; while in order to organize state registration of immovable property using a fabricated court decision that would be "missed" in the Court register (because of making links between the State Register of Property Rights on immovable property and their encumbrances and the Unified State Register of Court Decisions in Ukraine – as soon as a court decision is added to the Court register, the state register has to make the necessary changes in the State Register of Property Rights on immovable property and their encumbrances); in order to make a raiding attack on immovable property without the knowledge of its owner; so as to provide the public register with a fabricated set of documents concerning the transition of corporate rights to unknown third parties (because of the requirement to witness the signatures of a legal person's representatives and the signatures of the head and the secretary of the stakeholders' general meeting on a document with the decision of the stakeholders' general meeting and also on the charter documents. Moreover, the signatures on the act of transfer and on the separation balance sheet must also be witnessed); to involve public registers who conduct registrations, as their responsibility for such illegal actions has seriously increased; to use a computer of a public register illegally in order to get the licence keys, to enter the State register and perform fabricated registration actions, etc.

Despite all the mentioned efforts of the public authorities in Ukraine, unfortunately, the problem of raiding, while changing the ownership structure in Ukrainian economy has not disappeared and continues to thrive.

By analysing ("ArcelorMittal Kryvoi Rogh", 2016; "From merging to cutting into scrap metal", 2023; "The income of privatization", 2022; Kaluzhna, 2021; Kozachenko, Pogorelov & Andrushchenko, 2020; Moyseenko, 2022; Orel, 2022; "Raiding in Ukraine", 2019; "SBU informed concerning the suspect", 2017) and as a result of analysing the risks and threats that emerge because of changes in the

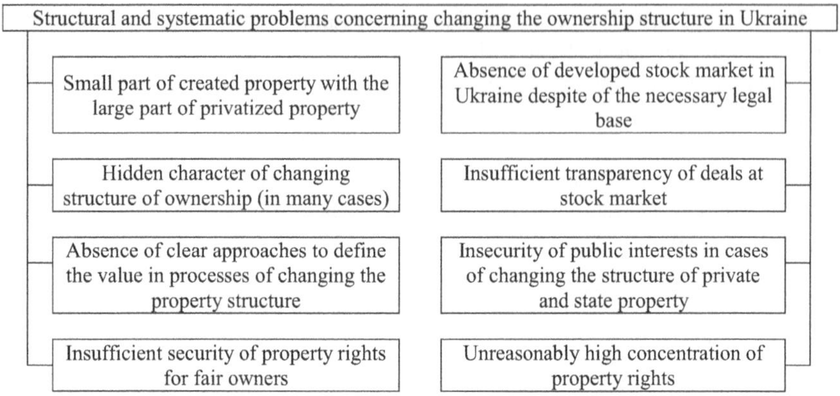

Figure 6.4 Structural and systematic problems concerning changing the ownership structure in Ukraine.

ownership structure in the national economy, one can consider some structural and systematic problems with regard to changing the ownership structure in Ukraine (Figure 6.4).

The public bodies and state authorities should pay attention to solving and overcoming such problems, because it is obvious that such structural and systematic problems limit the development of the national economy in Ukraine, while also decreasing its investment attractiveness, contributing to the "high price" of involved or loaned capital, as well as decreasing the attractiveness of the Ukrainian economy for foreign direct investments and simultaneously contributing to the national capital outflow.

Thus, as has been shown, changing the ownership structure causes not only positive results, such as increasing the effectiveness of property usage because of privatization, involvement of additional funds because of investments, etc. Changing the ownership structure, especially in conditions of immature institutions not only *can* cause, but likely *will* cause specified risks and threats that are considered on the basis of the example of Ukraine. Such risks and threats should be taken into account both by state bodies and participants in the stock market.

6.6 Conclusions

In conclusion, the privatization policy in Ukraine has gone through a significant transformation from the moment of gaining independence to the post-war recovery period. The country started its journey with a command economy, where state ownership dominated, but has made significant strides in transitioning to a market-based economy with a greater role for private enterprise.

Privatization in Ukraine took place within the framework of the development of its two main institutional components: legal and organizational. After the collapse of the USSR and the acquisition of independence, Ukraine chose the right path for the development of transformation from state to private property. Not all political regimes implemented certain changes in Ukrainian legislation for effective privatization. By way of confirmation, we see the low indicators of the sales of state-owned facilities until 2022. Those volumes of funds received from the sale of privatization facilities did not have an economic effect at the national level.

The development of the organizational component is also available. At the same time, the emergence of institutions (the State Property Fund and the Anti-Monopoly Committee, while also the creation of digital tools for moderating the privatization process) has not become a guarantee of effective work in the field of privatization.

We observed a revival in the number of sold facilities in 2022 and associated it rather with the requirement of wartime. More than 50% of budgetary revenues are planned to be spent on the security component in 2023 (fighting the enemy). It was then that the previously created institutions and institutes could be said to have started to work with the introduction of separate state programmes.

The privatization process in Ukraine has faced several challenges, including corruption, inadequate legal frameworks, and insufficient implementation of reforms. The Ukrainian government has taken steps in recent years to reform and modernize these enterprises, including by means of the privatization and implementation of business-friendly reforms.

However, the country has made significant progress in attracting foreign investment, while also modernizing its state-owned enterprises and improving the business environment for private enterprises.

Despite the challenges faced during the war recovery period, Ukraine has continued to pursue a policy of privatization with a focus on small and medium-sized enterprises, as well as modernizing and attracting investments in key sectors of the economy. This approach has contributed to the recovery of the country's economy and has the potential to drive growth and development in the future.

Thus, as it was analysed in the case of examples from Poland, the Czech Republic, Slovakia (Abarbanell & Bonin, 1997; Balfour & Crise, 1993; Bellas et al., 1994; Bochniarz, Jermakowicz &, Meller, 1994; De Fraja & Roberts, 2009; Lipton & Sachs, 1992; Ord, Walker & Hunt, 2016), changing the ownership structure causes some positive results, such as increasing the effectiveness of property usage because of privatization, while also the involvement of additional funds because of investments, etc. However, as it is considered and summarized on the basis of the example of Ukraine (ArcelorMittal KryvoiRogh, 2016; For the voluntary dismissal, 2011; From merging to cutting into scrap metal б 2023; Kaluzhna, 2021; Kozachenko, Pogorelov & Andrushchenko, 2020, 2021; Moyseenko, 2022; Orel, 2022; Raiding in Ukraine, 2019; SBU informed, 2017; Topalov, 2022; Yillyin, A. & Samofalov, 2023, etc.), changing the ownership structure, especially in conditions of immature institutions not only *can* cause, but likely *will* cause specified risks and threats. Such risks and threats should be taken into account both by state bodies and participants in the stock market.

Overall, the privatization policy in Ukraine has been a complex and evolving process, with both successes and challenges. While there is still much work to be done to fully realize the potential of privatization, the country has made significant progress in transitioning to a market-based economy and attracting foreign investment. With continued reforms and a commitment to a transparent and fair privatization process, Ukraine can continue to make progress in its economic development and achieve greater prosperity for its citizens.

Notes

1 Due to the European classification applied by the State Statistics Service in Ukraine (European Commission 2016).
2 https://zakon.rada.gov.ua/laws/show/2269-19#Text.

References

Abarbanell, J. S. & Bonin, J. P. (1997). Bank Privatization in Poland: The Case of Bank Śląski. *Journal of Comparative Economics*, 25(1), 31–61. https://doi.org/10.1006/jcec.1997.1447

A new stage of the protection of ownership rights has triggered in Ukraine (2019, December 18). Communications Department of the Secretariat of the Cabinet of Ministers of Ukraine. Retrieved from https://www.kmu.gov.ua/en/news/v-ukrayini-pochavsya-novij-etap-zahistu-prav-vlasnikiv-oleksij-goncharuk-pid-chas-vidkrittya-ofisu-protidiyi-rejderstvu

Arcelor Mittal Kryvoi Rogh ceased voluntary dismissals ["АрселорМитталКривойРог" завязал с добровольнымиувольнениями]. (2016, March 28). Ukrrudprom. Retrieved from https://ukrrudprom.ua/news/ArselorMittal_Krivoy_Rog_zavyazal_s_uvolneniem_podobromu.html

Balfour, M. & Crise, C. (1993). A Privatization Test: The Czech Republic, Slovakia and Poland. *Fordham International Law Journal*, 17(1), 84–125.

Bellas, C. J., Bochniarz, Z., Jermakowicz, W. W., Meller, M. & Toft, D. (1994). *Foreign Privatization in Poland.* Warsaw: Center for Social & Economic Research.

Beraho, E. K. (2008). A Study of Global Bankruptcy Trends: Examples from USA, UK, Australia, Ukraine, Malaysia and China. *Problems and Perspectives in Management*, 6(3), 4–14.

Beraho, E. K. (2011). A Comparative Review of Bankruptcy Reforms in the USA, the UK, China and Malaysia. *Problems and Perspectives in Management*, 9(3), 9–18.

Berle, A. A., & Means, G. G. C. (2017). *The Modern Corporation and Private Property.* London & New York: Routledge.

Bochniarz, Z., Jermakowicz, W. W. & Meller, M. (1994). *Privatization Through Foreign Direct Investment in Poland.* Minneapolis: University of Minnesota, Hubert H. Humphrey Institute of Public Affairs

Botis, S. (2013). Mergers and Acquisitions in the International Banking Sector. *Bulletin of the Transylvania University of Braşov*, 6(55, 1), 119–126.

Buttwill, K. & Wihlborg, C. (2004). *The Efficiency of the Bankruptcy Process.* An International Comparison. Ratio Working Paper, p. 60.

Cartwright, S. & Cooper, C. L. (1990). The Impact of Mergers and Acquisitions on People at Work: Existing Research and Issues. *British Journal of Management*, 1(2), 65–76. https://doi.org/10.1111/j.1467-8551.1990.tb00163.x

Collett, N. (2015). Mergers and Acquisitions. In C. L. Cooper & K. Paudyal (Eds.) *Wiley Encyclopedia of Management. Finance* (Volume 4, 2nd ed.). New York: John Wiley & Sons, pp. 1–7 https://doi.org/10.1002/9781118785317.weom040085

Conyon, M. J., Girma, S., Thompson, S. & Wright, P. (2002). The Impact of Mergers and Acquisitions on Company Employment in the United Kingdom. *European Economic Review*, 46(1), 31–49. https://doi.org/10.1016/S0014-2921(00)00086-6

De Fraja, G. & Roberts, B. M. (2009). Privatization in Poland. What Was the Government Trying to Achieve? *Economics of Transition and Institutional Change*, 17(3), 531–557. https://doi.org/10.1111/j.1468-0351.2009.00356.x

Demsetz, H. (1967). Toward a Theory of Property Rights. *American Economic Review*, 2(57), 347–359. https://doi.org/10.1057/9780230523210_9.

Dubrovskiy V., Paskhaver A., and Verkhovodova L., and Blaszczyk B. (2007). *Conditions for Completion of Privatization in Ukraine: Analytical Report and Recommendations for the State Privatization Program* [Умови завершення приватизації в Україні: Аналітичний звіт та рекомендації для Державної програми приватизації]. Kyiv: CASE Ukraine. (see: https://case-ukraine.com.ua/content/uploads/2020/09/Conditions-of-resuming-and-completing-privatization-in-Ukraine.pdf)

Eggertsson, T. (1990). *Economic behavior and institutions: Principles of Neoinstitutional Economics.* Cambridge: Cambridge University Press.

Entreprises Activity, State Statistic Service of Ukraine. Retrieved from https://www.ukrstat.gov.ua/

Foreign direct investments from 2022 to 2022 [Прямі іноземні інвестиції з 2002 по 2022 рр.]. (2023, January 15). Bankchart. Retrieved from https://bankchart.com.ua/spravochniki/indikatory_rynka/foreign_direct_investment

For the voluntary redundancy from "ArcelorMittal Kryvoi Rogh" employees are given 70 thousand hryvnias [Задобровольноеувольнение с "ArcelorMittal КривойРог" сотрудникамвыплачивают 70 тыс. грн]. (2011, June 09). Delo.Ua. Retrieved from https://delo.ua/lifestyle/za-dobrovolnoe-uvolnenie-s-158899/

From merging to cutting into scrap metal. How Putin's oligarchs tried to seize Ukrainian industry and what they obtained [Відпоглинаннядорізанинина металобрухт. Як путінські олігархи намагалися захопити українську промисловість і що в них вийшло]. (2023, January 12). *New Voice Business*. Retrieved from https://biz.nv.ua/ukr/economics/rosiyskiy-biznes-v-ukrajini-yak-oligarhi-iz-rf-ruynuvali-ekonomiku-ukrajini-50295840.html

European Commission (2016). *Glossary: Enterprise Size.* Retrieved from https://ec.europa.eu/eurostat/statistics-explained/index.php?title=Glossary:Enterprise_size

Gugler, K., Mueller, D. C., Yurtoglu, B. B. & Zulehner, C. (2003). The Effects of Mergers: An International Comparison. International Journal of Industrial Organization, 21(5), 625–653. https://doi.org/10.1016/S0167-7187(02)00107-8

Gugler, K. & Yurtoglu, B. B. (2004). The Effects of Mergers on Company Employment in the USA and Europe. *International Journal of Industrial Organization*, 22(4), 481–502. https://doi.org/10.1016/j.ijindorg.2003.12.003

Hudson, J. (1997). Company Bankruptcies and Births Matter. *Applied Economics*, 29(5), 647–654. https://doi.org/10.1080/000368497326840

International Property Rights Index. (2019–2022). Retrieved from https://www.internationalpropertyrightsindex.org/

Jackson, G. & Miyajima, H. (2007). Varieties of Capitalism, Varieties of Markets: Mergers and Acquisitions in Japan, Germany, France, the UK and USA (June 2007). RIETI Discussion Paper Series, p. 56. Retrieved from https://ssrn.com/abstract=1012210. https://doi.org/10.2139/ssrn.1012210

Kaluzhna, A. (2021, May 11). Bihus. Info Investigated for what Price Oligarchs Bought Regional Grids from a State [Bihus.Infoз'ясувализаскількиолігархискупили у державиобленерго]. *Bihus.Info.* Retrieved from https://bihus.info/bihus-info-zyasuvaly-za-skilky-oligarhy-skupyly-u-derzhavy-oblenergo/

Kozachenko, G., Pogorelov, Y. & Andrushchenko, I. (2020). Raiding as a Threat to Economic Security of Ukraine: Legal Framework of Counteraction. *Journal of Law and Political Sciences*, 23(2), 297–341. Retrieved from https://drive.google.com/file/d/1-JFztlZq1HNBTUMuis21mPjZGgopaB-Z/view

Kozachenko, G., Pogorelov, Y. & Andrushchenko, I. (2021) Improving Legislation on Counteraction of Raiding as a Direction in Strengthening Ukraine's Economic Security. *Legal, Economic Science and Praxis. Journal of Law and Social Sciences*, no. 1, 51–58.

Land Code of Ukraine. # 562-XII, of 1992, March 13, Verkhovna Rada of Ukraine. Retrieved from https://zakon.rada.gov.ua/laws/show/561-12#Text

Law of Ukraine "On Introduction of Changes to Several Legal Acts of Ukraine Concerning Protection of Property Rights" #159-IX of2019, October 3.Verkhovna Rada of Ukraine. Retrieved from https://zakon.rada.gov.ua/laws/show/159-20

Law of Ukraine "On Privatization of State Property", #2164-XII of 1992, March 4. Verkhovna Rada of Ukraine. Retrieved from https://zakon.rada.gov.ua/laws/show/2163-12#Text

Law of Ukraine "On the Privatization of the State Housing Fund", #2482-XII, of 1992, June 19. Verkhovna Rada of Ukraine. Retrieved from https://zakon.rada.gov.ua/laws/show/2482-12#Text

Law of Ukraine "On the Privatization of State and Communal Property", # 2597-VIII, of 2018, October 2018. Verkhovna Rada of Ukraine. Retrieved from https://zakon.rada.gov.ua/laws/show/2269-19?find=1&text=%D0%B2%D0%B5%D0%BB%D0%B8%D0%BA#Text

Legal aspects of privatization in Ukraine [Правовіаспектиприватизації в Україні], vol. 1–2, K., 1996

Lipton, D. & Sachs, J. (1992). Privatization in Eastern Europe: The Case of Poland. In S. Sharma (Ed.) *Development Policy*. London: Palgrave Macmillan. https://doi.org/10.1007/978-1-349-22385-5_10

Lyvch, D. (2022, August 29). The New Face of Ukrainian Entrepreneurship. How the War Influenced the Small and Medium Sized Enterprises in Different Regions of Ukraine [Новеобличчяукраїнськогопідприємництва. Яквійнавплинуланамалийтасереднійбізнес у різнихрегіонахУкраїни]. *Economichna Pravda*. Retrieved from: https://www.epravda.com.ua/columns/2022/08/29/690937/

McGuckin, R. H. & Nguyen, S. V. (2001). The Impact of Ownership Changes: A View from Labor Markets. *International Journal of Industrial Organization*, 19(5), 739–762. https://doi.org/10.1016/S0167-7187(00)00092-8

Miroshnik, R. O. & Prokopieva, U. O. (2020). Developing Small and Medium-Sized Enterprises in Ukraine: Problems and Perspectives [Розвитокмалоготасередньогобізнесу в Україні: проблемитаперспективи]. *The Herald of the National University "Lviv Polytechnic"*, 4(1), 63–71.

Moyseenko, O. (2022, December 27). Privatization during the War: What, for Whom and What Is the Price [Приватизаціяпідчасвійни: що, кому і заскільки]. *Economichna Pravda*. Retrieved from https://www.epravda.com.ua/columns/2022/12/27/695450/

OECD, Review of the Corporate Governance of State-Owned Enterprises: UKRAINE, 2021. Retrieved from https://www.oecd.org/corporate/SOE-Review-Ukraine.pdf

Ord, K., Walker, D. A. & Hunt, C. R. (2016). Privatization and Fiscal Deficits in European Emerging Markets. *Emerging Markets Finance and Trade,* 52(11), 2585–2594. https://doi.org/10.1080/1540496X.2015.1087788

Orel, I. (2022, September 15) Akhmetov, Kolomoyskiy, Grigorishin, Deputies of OPFL and, Probably, Crimes. Who Owns the Ukrainian Regional Grids that Define if Ukrainian Have Electricity in Winter [Ахметов, Коломойський, Григоришин, депутати ОПЗЖ і, можливо, злодії в законі. Хто володіє українськими обленерго, від яких залежить, чи буде світло взимку]. *Forbes*. Retrieved from https://forbes.ua/company/akhmetov-kolomoyskiy-grigorishin-deputati-opzzh-i-mozhlivo-zlodii-v-zakoni-khto-volodie-ukrainskimi-oblenergo-vid-yakikh-zalezhit-chi-bude-svitlo-vzimku-15092022-8227

Privatization revenues in 2021 are record-breaking over the past decade. (2021). State Property Fund in Ukraine. Retrieved from https://www.spfu.gov.ua/en/news/8524.html

Raiding in Ukraine: Around 400 Attacks Are Happening Annually, Most of them Are in Kyiv [Рейдерство в Украине: ежегоднопроисходитоколо 400 атак, большевсего - в Киеве]. (2019, June 24). Economichna Pravda. Retrieved from https://www.epravda.com.ua/rus/news/2019/06/24/649011/

SBU informed about the Russian suspects who were involved in the destruction of the unique industrial giant in Zaporizhya [СБУ повідомилапропідозруросіянам, причетни мдознищенняунікальногопромисловогогіганта в Запоріжжі]. (2017, August 29). New Voice. Business. Retrieved from https://nv.ua/ukr/ukraine/events/sbu-povidomila-pro-pidozru-rosijanam-prichetnim-do-znishchennja-unikalnogo-promislovogo-giganta-zaporizhzhi-1757950.html

Statistics of External Sector. National Bank of Ukraine. Retrieved from https://bank.gov.ua/ua/statistic/sector-external

The income of privatization in 2021 is a record-setting one for the last decade [Надходження від приватизації у 2021 є рекордними за останнє десятиліття]. (2022, January 10). State Property Fund of Ukraine. Retrieved from https://www.spfu.gov.ua/ua/news/8524.html

The Report of the President of Ukraine. Relating to the Report of the President of Ukraine: "On basic principles of economic and social policy", #216/94-BP, of 1994, October 19.Verkhovna Rada of Ukraine. Retrieved from https://zakon.rada.gov.ua/laws/show/216/94-%D0%B2%D1%80#Text

Tomczak, S. K. (2018). Statistics on bankruptcy of Companies in Poland. *Nauki o Zarządzaniu*, 23(3), 39–50. https://doi.org/10.15611/ms.2018.3.05

Topalov, M. (2022, July 21). VS Energy Case. Why Courts Do Not See Russians and Their Relatives as Figureheads [Справа VS Energy. Чому суди не бачать росіян за підставними особами та родичами]. *Economichna Pravda*. Retrieved from https://www.epravda.com.ua/publications/2022/07/21/689418/

Balina, S. N., Uschapovsky, V. F. (1999). *Legal Basis of Privatization in Ukraine and its Protection against Criminal Encroachments* [Правові Основи Приватизації в Україні Та Захист Від Злочинних Посягань]. Kyiv: Atika.

Van Zon, H. (2000). *The Political Economy of Independent Ukraine*. London: Macmillan.

Wilson, A. & Burakovsky, I. (1996). *The Ukrainian Economy under Kuchma.* London: Royal Institute of International Affairs.

World Justice Project. (2019–2022). Retrieved from https://worldjusticeproject.org/rule-of-law-index/global/2015/

Yillyin, A. & Samofalov, A. (2023, February 1). The Great Story. How Russian Business in Ukraine Becomes a European One and Avoids Sanctions. VS Energy Case. [Великаісторія. Як російськийбізнес в Українístaєєвропейським іуникаєсанкцій — кейс VS Energy]. *New Voice Business*. Retrieved from https://biz.nv.ua/ukr/economics/vs-energy-yak-rosiyskiy-biznes-v-ukrajini-hovayetsya-vid-sankciy-rozsliduvannya-novini-ukrajini-50300865.html

Part III

Framing of policies

7 Stages in the development of competition and consumer protection policy in Poland in 1990–2021 and their contribution to the foundations of Poland's socio-economic order

Katarzyna Kamińska

7.1 Introduction

Free competition is a fundamental mechanism governing the functioning of a market economy. The process of competing for customers, which has become extremely important in modern times, may ultimately lead to lower prices on the market, the provision of better quality products and services by producers, while also increasing their choice. Another role of free competition is to create impulses for companies to increase their creativity, in order to provide pro-innovation incentives. It is noteworthy that the US Supreme Court has referred to competition law as a basic economic law (Magna Carta of free enterprise) (Craine, 2013). The existence of free competition is one of the prerequisite conditions for the very existence of the free-market economy.[1] Therefore, free competition is one of the key features that distinguish a system based on the free market from the command-and-distribution economy system, based on central planning, which functioned in Poland up to the transformation of 1989 (Kamińska, 2021, p. 206).

Nowadays, the role of regulations protecting competition and consumers introduced by states or regional integration agreements such as the European Union is becoming increasingly important. Above all, it is about ensuring that society benefits from their introduction. In particular, it is about eliminating restrictive, illegal, and harmful agreements between companies, as exemplified by cartels, which can take the form of collusion between competitors, which usually involves fixing prices. However, it is equally important to take action against abusive practices by companies with a dominant market position, which may use the following practices: influencing the price (directly and indirectly) in such a way as to put the consumer at a disadvantage, imposing unreasonable transaction conditions apart from prices, limiting production, technical development and markets to the detriment of consumers, applying unequal conditions for trading partners, while also using prohibited clauses, e.g. making the conclusion of contracts subject to other ancillary obligations which are not related to the subject matter of these contracts. They may also set excessive prices for customers who are forced to pay more for products and services because they have no other choice.

Competition policy consists of the actions of states and international organizations whose goal is to create competitive market structures and activities to

DOI: 10.4324/9781003425717-10

stimulate pro-competitive behaviour in entrepreneurs (Błachucki and Stankiewicz, 2010, p. 79). Competition law is an integral part of competition policy. Its task is to ensure market competition between entrepreneurs, e.g. by eliminating behavioural patterns contrary to the order of competition (Włudyka, 2002, p. 121). This goal can be achieved in such a way that the created law prohibits the creation of cartels and abuse of a dominant position on the market, while also introduces control over mergers of enterprises and adopts regulations that enable control of the granting of state aid, which, in turn also requires the creation of the appropriate institutions that will guard the implementation of this law in business practice.

The issue of the development of competition and consumer protection legislation, while also the development of the appropriate policies is particularly important in countries with the experience of a centrally planned economy, such as Poland. It is important to make constant efforts to ensure that the laws created and policies implemented do not restrict competition. It may happen that the state, through its actions, may deprive consumers of the benefits of market competition, if only as a result of harmful lobbying by competitors protecting their interests, or by adopting legal solutions which, in the long term, will restrict free competition on the domestic market. Under the Polish legislation, the highest-ranking legislative act referring to the country's economic system is the Constitution of the Republic of Poland,[2] which defines a Social Market Economy (SME) based on the freedom of economic activity, private property, solidarity, dialogue, and cooperation of social partners. The roots of this doctrine can be traced back to ordoliberalism, for which competition policy is a central aspect of the state's activity in shaping economic governance. A leading representative of ordoliberalism, Walter Eucken, together with other ordoliberals, advocated an active state policy to counter attempts to restrict free competition (Rogall, 2006, p. 233).

In Poland, since the beginning of the systemic transformation, competition and consumer protection policy has undergone systematic changes. In 1990, the Anti-Monopoly Office (currently *Urząd Ochrony Konkurencji i Konsumentów* – UOKiK) was established. This office operates under the Act on Competition and Consumer Protection.[3] The task of this institution with German roots (the equivalent of the German *Bundeskartellamt*) is to protect free competition and consumers on the market (Kamińska and Trybuchowicz, 2018, p. 66). It uses its legal instruments in the public interest to solve current market problems, and thus counteract competition-restricting practices or prevent concentrations that may lead to its limitation, and since 2014 this institution has also taken care of consumer welfare and the creation of economic conditions in which effective competition means fair relations between entrepreneurs and consumers.

Before 2004, Poland adjusted the anti-monopoly law and the state aid regulations to the EU standards, and this process was continued after 2004. As a consequence of Poland's membership of the EU, there are new opportunities for using the Community's economic freedoms and reducing the antitrust risk for Polish enterprises in the large common market (Fornalczyk, 2019, p. 83). The concern for the proper functioning of free competition is one of the European Union's priorities. It reflects the main premise of German ordoliberalism and the SME, which in the unfettered operation of free competition sees the way to a properly functioning economic order and social welfare (Erhard, 2012, p. 19). The idea of protecting free competition and measures taken to combat monopolies in the European Union may be counted among the values of social relations. They ensure the effectiveness of the market mechanisms by regulating equal access to information, credit, labour resources, and other economic assets, as well as equal opportunities for distribution and sales (Kowalski, Golinowska, and Błaszczyk, 2019, p. 19).

The aim of this chapter is to present the stages of development of competition and consumer protection policy in Poland from 1990 to 2021 and the assessment of its place in shaping the Polish economic model. As this policy evolved significantly during this period due to Poland's accession to the European Union in 2004, the work will be divided into two periods describing its development from 1990 to 2003 and from 2004 to 2021. To solve this research problem, the method of economic law analysis in the field of competition and consumer protection law was applied, as well as elements of institutional analysis. The empirical analysis was based on data from UOKiK reports.

7.2 Development of competition in Poland until accession into the European Union

The first competition regulations were adopted in Poland in the 1930s.[4] The overriding objective of this regulation was to protect consumers against the unfair use of market power by cartels. Interestingly, at that time, cartelization was considered a natural stage of development and, in principle, cartel agreements were valid. The 1933 Act lasted until the late 1980s, because in the post-war period, the socialist economic system, which was based on central planning, led to the concentration of the state economy, while at the same time denied antitrust law (Filipowski, 2011, pp. 227–228).

The first contemporary regulations were adopted in 1987 (Act of 28 January 1987 on counteracting monopolistic practices in the national economy, Journal of Laws of 1987, No. 3, item 18), even before the transformation of the political system. This act can be described as the first post-war and relatively comprehensive "Antitrust law"; it included the definition of monopolistic practices, designated the group of entities to which it applied (the economic units), and defined the anti-monopoly authority (the Minister of Finance). The introduction of this act could have been one of the elements supporting the implementation of economic changes in Poland in the years 1982–1987, the aim of which was to bring the socialist economy out of a deep crisis. The reform programme assumed the replacement of the central control system with a system of many autonomous enterprises controlled by economic tools, while retaining the dominant role of state ownership of the means of production (Grala, 2005). The fundamental change was brought on only by the Act of December 23, 1988 in terms of economic activity, constituting in Article 1 that undertaking and running a business was free and permissible for every person on equal terms subject to the conditions specified by law.[5]

It was not until the political decisions taken in 1989 on the commencement of the political transformation in Poland that the adoption of a package of legal acts introducing market reform became possible; one of them being the Act on Counteracting Monopolistic Practices of 1990.[6]

One of the vital problems that Poland had to face during the transformation period was the ineffective production system, which was utterly inadequate to the requirements of the modern economy, as it was inefficient, dominated by state ownership, while also unable to develop in conditions of external openness. From the beginning of the 1980s, the average rate of monopolization was 71.9%. The highest degree of monopolization prevailed in the metals industry (98.1%), fuels (96.7%), precious ceramics (95%), chemicals (93.9%), and means of transport (91.3%). In 1989, small enterprises (up to 200 employees) employed only 6% of the total workforce, while in Western Europe this ratio was five and six times higher. The largest enterprises, manufacturing half of the value of the production in the economy, employed over one-third of the total workforce employed in the industry (Misiąg, 1990, pp. 19–20).

One of the most evident problems was the conspicuous lack of competitive markets. Open markets constitute an element that is necessary for enabling long-term, effective economic development (Orłowski, 2005, p. 38). Only competition is able to eliminate entities from the market that do not operate efficiently and therefore enable a more rational use of resources available to the public and cause production to adapt to the market needs, while prices do not deviate from reasonable production costs that are increased by the commonly accepted profit rate. Thus, a competitive market is a prerequisite for high economic efficiency, which is possible thanks to the smoothly functioning price signals, while also the pressure to eliminate the wasting of resources and taking care of the customer (Orłowski, 2005, p. 38).

In Poland and other post-communist countries, it was very important that state-owned companies were not favoured at the expense of other entities and consequently consumers. It was also important to ensure that the laws created and policies implemented do not restrict competition. Indeed, there is a danger that the state itself may deprive consumers of the benefits of market competition, e.g. as a result of harmful lobbying by competitors protecting their interests, or as a result of adopting solutions that may in effect protect incumbent layers from competition by means of various legal barriers.

The beginning of the political transformation resulted in the adoption of the Act of February 24, 1990, on counteracting monopolistic practices. Under this law, *Urząd Antymonopolowy, UA* (The Antitrust Authority), was established as the fundamental body of state administration regarding matters of counteracting monopolistic practices, headed by a president who was to be appointed and potentially dismissed by the Prime Minister. UA was subordinate to the Council of Ministers. The President of the Authority could establish its delegations and specify their headquarters together with territorial and material competence.

The prototype for UA was the German Cartel Office (*Bundeskartellamt*).[7] The idea of a cartel office is an original and globally innovative German idea, which was advocated by the German economist and leading representative of ordoliberalism, Walter Eucken. The office was established in the German Federal Republic in

1958 by *Gesetz gegen Wettbewerbschränkungen* (GWB), a law against the restriction of competition. What was peculiar was that it was guaranteed political independence in terms of its decision-making and actions, although the law explicitly stated that decisions of the office's individual decision-making departments could be taken if they received the approval of the Minister of Economic Affairs or, if they received the acceptance of the Minister of the Economy or, with the minister's permission they could be approved by the presidential office. However, it is interesting to note that in some cases where the public interest was at stake, the Minister of the Economy was able to challenge decisions taken by the authority (Kamińska, 2018, p. 238).

Of all the post-communist countries, Poland was the first one to establish an anti-monopoly office to protect fair competition. In order to strengthen the activities of this office in local markets, between 1990 and 1991, at the request of the President of the Office, seven delegations were established in cities such as Gdańsk, Lublin, Łódź, Katowice, Kraków, Poznań and Wrocław.

An important role of the office was the participation in creating a new system of economic law adapted to the needs of the market economy. The competition rules were introduced by UA via three methods: the preparation of bills and executive acts; the development of regulations promoting competition within legal regulations; and administrative acts concerning various spheres of economic activity, while also issuing opinions on bills and executive acts prepared by other central government administration bodies. An equally important area of the Office's activities was the opinion on draft bills prepared by the government (Fornalczyk, 2005, p. 33).

Since its establishment, the office has been involved in the process of the restructuring and privatization of state-owned enterprises, as well as entire sectors. One of the ways of doing this was through the statutory control of ownership transformations of state-owned enterprises (until 1998), as well as through the participation of its representatives in the work of government teams preparing sectoral restructuring and privatization programmes (coal, fuel, steel, petrochemicals, heavy chemicals, electricity, heat, armaments, automotive, and the sugar industry). The Authority's representatives were careful to prevent excessive restriction of competition in the proposed solutions and to ensure that the burden of restructuring was not passed on to consumers by price increases assumed in the programme or implemented by the companies themselves (Fornalczyk, 2005, p. 31).

Thanks to the introduction of the Anti-Monopoly Act, the office has gained the opportunity to influence the organizational structure of the economy (control of ownership transformations of enterprises, while also concentration and the right to split enterprises – demonopolization). The most effective at that time was the elimination or reduction of the causes of monopolistic practices (Fornalczyk, 2019, p. 84). In 1996, the name of the office was changed to *The Office of Competition and Consumer Protection* (*Urząd Ochrony Konkurencji i Konsumentów, UOKiK*), which indicated that the activity of the office would also include protection of the customers. UOKiK's mission has become to promote the highest possible level of consumer welfare through the effective protection of competition and consumer interests and rights, while respecting the principles of procedural fairness in relations with entrepreneurs (UOKiK, 2018).

While Poland was planning to join the European Union, it had to adapt its antitrust legislation to EU requirements. This process started on January 1, 1992 and can be assessed as a significant help in building a modern system of antitrust law. As a consequence of the measures taken, further changes and new regulations on competition and consumer protection have emerged. We can list the following legislative acts here: the Act of December 15, 2000 (Journal of Laws No. 122, position 139) that replaced the Act of 1990; the Act of May 1, 2004 on the implementation of the rules of competition laid down in Articles 81 and 82 of the Treaty and the Act of February 16, 2007 on competition and consumer protection, Journal of Laws of 2007 No. 50, item 331.

If we compare the Polish antitrust authority with its German prototype, the question of the political independence of the authorities of this institution arises. The effectiveness of its activities may largely depend on whether its decisions are free from political pressure and dependence on the state administration. The 2000 Act stipulated the requirement of the tenure of the President of UOKiK in Article 24, but already in 2007 the new Act in Article 29 revoked this requirement (Fornalczyk, 2019, p. 85). The activities of the President of the UOKiK were supervised by the Prime Minister and these standards were maintained in the 2007 Act. The guarantees of independence of the UOKiK were lost in 2006 when the Act on State Personnel Resources and High State Positions came into force. They were restored with the coming into force of the current Act on the Protection of Competition and Consumers of February 16, 2007, but already in April 2007 the legislator decided to return to the state of affairs prior to the enactment of the new Act, i.e. the absence of any guarantees of independence. As a result, the President of the Office of Competition and Consumer Protection can be dismissed by the Prime Minister at virtually any time and for no specific reason. Currently, the Head of the Office is appointed by the Prime Minister from a group of people belonging to the state personnel resources[8] (Kamińska, 2021, p. 212).

7.3 Development of consumer protection policy in Poland from the beginning of the systemic transformation to 2004

In the initial period of the system transformation, consumer protection policy in Poland developed relatively slowly. Arguably, this may have had its roots in the experience of the socialist system, in which the consumer and his or her rights were of little importance, as his or her preferences did not influence the volume and quality of production, as opposed to the capitalist system. The constant scarcity of goods on the market, often combined with the poor quality of products characteristic of socialism, while also the monopolistic structure of the market was not conducive to the development of either free competition or consumer care. Furthermore, consumer rights continued to be violated due to information asymmetry, widespread ignorance, the abuse of financial advantage and, finally, common fraud. The process of limiting these phenomena was gradual, and UOKiK's activities played an important educational role. Furthermore, the process of liberalization and deregulation of the services market has had a significant role in the process of consumer protection (Orłowski, 2005, p. 42). The following years saw an increase in the UOKiK's competence in the field of consumer protection and in 1996 it was officially included in the scope of statutory tasks. Accordingly, the Department of Consumer Policy was established in the office. In practice and in legal terms, this meant that consumer protection acquired the status of an independent state policy with a status equal to that of competition policy. Furthermore, this opened up the possibility that the two policies could play complementary roles with relation to each other.

However, it is important to bear in mind that combining both functions within one office can raise various issues. Competition cases tend to be legally and factually complex and resource-intensive, and thus it is essential to have adequate human resources and time, while they also require dealing with influential interest groups, of which large state-owned companies are a sizable one. By contrast, consumer protection cases tend to be less complicated, do not consume as many financial resources as competition protection, and tend to be more favoured by the media and the wider office environment. Hence, there is a real risk that it is the latter function that will absorb more of the institution's activity (Martyniszyn, 2019). In Germany, competition protection and consumer protection are dealt with by two separate institutions. Consumer affairs are dealt with by an institution set up by consumers themselves, namely, the Federation of Consumer Organisations VZBV.[9]

In the same year, the Trade Inspection, which was tasked with controlling turnover in consumer markets and with providing public information on actions taken in the interest of consumers, was subjected to the President of UOKiK. Four years later, in 2000, the definition of consumer was also introduced into the Civil Code.[10] The same year also saw the enactment of one of the first laws in the set of laws on the special protection of consumer rights.

The issue of competition and consumer protection has gained prominence in Poland as a result of the adoption of the SME as an economic system in the 1997 Constitution of the Republic of Poland: *A social market economy, based on the freedom of economic activity, private ownership and solidarity, dialogue and cooperation between social partners, shall be the basis of the economic system of the Republic of Poland.*[11]

The SME is associated with the ordoliberal doctrine, which has developed from German economic and legal thought from the early 1930s onwards and which must be defined in particular by its adaptability with relation to the accompanying social, cultural, and economic framework (Müller, 2019, p. 47). On the other hand, the concept of the SME is primarily associated in economic literature with Alfred Müller-Armack and Ludwig Erhard. According to the former, this doctrine is an attempt to form a social idea that unites different worldviews and captures the social dimension of the economic order. Within this model, the assumption is made that within the framework of a free-market economy, the recognition of freedom and social justice as fundamental values can be guaranteed (Müller, 2019, pp. 47–48).

First of all, it is the freedom to compete, understood as the freedom of companies from the anti-competitive behaviour of other entrepreneurs, such as collusion or abuse of a dominant market position. Second, it is freedom from intervention, which is understood as freedom from unjustified wider public interest distortions of competition by the state. Finally, it is fair competition, understood as dealing with other market participants (competitors, customers, consumers) while only with methods that are consistent with good practices (UOKiK, 2015, p. 9). The SME concept not only combines the principles of economic liberalism and the market economy but also exposes social objectives. Ludwig Erhard believed that the goal of the economy should be widespread social prosperity (*Wohlstand für alle*) and that the road to it should be a well-functioning system of free competition (*Wohlstand durch Wettbewerb*). The economy in the light of this doctrine should be efficient, which, through a well-functioning system of competition, should ensure the achievement of social justice. It is therefore the task of the state to protect competition and to control compliance with its rules using various institutions from a well-functioning legal system to an antitrust authority. The role of the state is also to act as the main moderator, intending to bring together social and public interests and to resolve the various conflicts that often arise in the functioning of society and the economy (Kundera, 2015, pp. 86–87).

Likewise, the consumer protection policy is grounded in the Constitution. The consumer law implements Article 76 of the Constitution, which states the following: “the public authorities shall protect consumers, users and tenants from acts that endanger their health, privacy and safety and from unfair market practices”.[12]

In 2002, an amendment to the Act on Competition and Consumer Protection entered into force; which allowed the office to conduct proceedings in the field of practices infringing collective consumer interests. At the same time, this institution was able to publicize information on actions taken in the interests of consumers (Kamińska, 2021, p. 213).

From 1996 to 2018, UOKiK gradually started conducting the following tasks:

- prevention and elimination of disturbances in the functioning and development of competition,
- M&A control,
- protection of the collective interests of consumers,
- monitoring of public aid,
- taking care of product safety and supervision over the market of non-food products and agri-food products in terms of commercial quality,
- participating in the legislative process to create the legal environment stimulating competition and effectively protecting the interests of consumers (UOKiK, 2018).

The period 1990–2003 is the first stage of building the foundations of a market economy and its institutions in Poland, as well as the development of competition and consumer protection policy, while also adapting this law to EU requirements.

At this stage, it was clear that the competition policy was influenced by the idea of an SME. It is about the shape of the implemented legislation and the institution of the anti-monopoly office which would guard free competition. An anti-monopoly office was established, which was modelled on the German Bundeskartellamt, whose task until 1996 was solely to protect fair competition. Since 1996, it has received its first competition protection tasks. Over time, it has become one of the key institutions from the perspective of the functioning of competition, and thus the economy itself.

7.4 Competition and consumer protection policy in Poland after 2004

On May 1, 2004, when the European Union was enlarged by ten of the new Member States, regulations of art. 101 and 102 TFEU came into force on its enlarged base territory (the Treaty on the Functioning of the European Union).

They concerned the prohibition of agreements between enterprises, both horizontal and vertical, restricting unfair competition on the market. The agreements that are insignificant for the market and which involve the abuse of the dominant position of enterprises on the market by imposing prices or other adverse conditions on contractors and consumers, while also discriminating against trading partners and limiting production, technical progress, or sales to restrict competition on the market are excluded from this prohibition.[13]

EU competition law has been heavily influenced by German legislation from the very beginning. The German Antitrust Act has had a major impact on EU antitrust legislation. Its basic assumptions underpinned the EU prohibition of abuse of a dominant position, namely, Articles 81 and 82 of the Treaties of Rome. Ordoliberal assumptions not only influenced the content of the prohibition but also above all the law-shaping jurisprudence of the EU courts and the decision-making practice of the European Commission (EC) itself. This was reflected in individual legal rules (institutions) that concerned the application of Article 102 TFEU. Indeed, many of these rules are still in force today, which include the following: the criteria for establishing dominance attaching fundamental importance to the size of market shares, the doctrine of "special responsibility" incumbent on dominant undertakings, the formal approach to certain market practices of dominant undertakings and the relatively wide range of abusive practices of an unfair nature (Kamińska, 2013, p. 240).

The Treaty on the European Union of 2004, subsequently supplemented by the Treaty of Lisbon of 2009, states in Article 3, paragraph 3, that the SME model is the economic model for the European Union, namely,

> The European Union shall establish an internal market. It shall work for the sustainable development of Europe based on balanced economic growth and price stability, a highly competitive social market economy, aiming at full employment and social progress, and a high level of protection and improvement of the quality of the environment.

It also means that the competition policy in the new Member States should undergo changes, elements of which can be traced back to the German model.

Furthermore, under Regulation 1/2003 (The Council of the European Union, 2003[14]), the following solutions were introduced into the EU competition policy:

- the right to fully apply to national competition authorities Articles 101 and 102 of the TFEU.
- This meant strengthening the position of these institutions in the EU competition policy, which resulted from the need to guarantee the smooth functioning of this policy after the accession of ten Member States and providing them with the power to adjudicate under EU law in matters of competition (McGovan, 2010, pp. 153–155).
- the lifting of the notification of agreements between enterprises for self-assessment, which in fact can be seen as replacing the hitherto penalty with the enterprise's self-evaluation of its actions and withdrawal from use. This change was dictated by the increasing number of applications for individual exemptions from the ban on cartels.
- the rules for close cooperation between the EC and national competition authorities within the European Competition Network (ECN). In this way, an innovative management model was built based on the dynamic arrangement of discussion forums and working groups, which brings together national competition authorities and the European Commission (Jóźwiak, 2011).

The new regulations imposed an obligation on national competition authorities to apply the EU law in a situation whereby, after using the domestic law, it turned out that trade between the Member States was affected by the consequences of anti-competitive practices (UOKiK, 2017).

The leniency programme imposed on the enterprises participating in an anti-competitive collusion was a significant change introduced to Polish competition law in 2004. It consisted of a possible reduction of the penalty imposed by UOKiK for the participants of collusion who provide the office with information to facilitate its detection and liquidation.[15] Their main goal was to undermine the stability of the functioning of illegal cartels; increase the effectiveness of combating agreements by breaking the solidarity of their participants; while destabilizing the agreements, encouraging the companies to cooperate with the antitrust authority, and overcoming evidentiary difficulties. In practice, it consisted of the fact that the participants of an illegal cartel who voluntarily cooperated with the office in the area of assistance in discovering other illegal cartels could apply for a fine reduction or total leniency. The latter would take place when a given cartel is the first to submit an application to UOKiK for coverage under this programme (Kamińska, 2021, p. 216).

Poland passed a new Act on Competition and Consumer Protection on February 16, 2007. In order to improve the actions taken by UOKiK, the discontinuation of the proceedings on the application of competition-restricting practices and on practices that violate collective consumer interests was established.[16] It also introduced the possibility of imposing fines by the President of UOKiK on the entrepreneurs who violated collective consumer interests. As regards the protection of competition, this law prohibits all practices restrictive of competition, i.e. such behaviour of entrepreneurs that leads to the disruption of the mechanisms of the free market. It divides the anti-competitive activities of entrepreneurs into two categories: restrictive agreements and the abuse of a dominant position (UOKiK, 2018).

The result of the aforesaid changes in the years 2004–2021 was a clear reduction in the number of proceedings conducted by UOKiK, which is illustrated by Table 7.1.

The data comprised in the table above shows that the most significant changes in the amount of case actions of UOKiK conducted took place in the field of explanatory antitrust proceedings. Their number decreased from 559 in 2004 to 12 in both 2018 and 2021. Such a significant reduction in the number of investigations was due to the replacement of requests by market abuse reports. The change was that since 2007, any person has had the possibility to file a written report regarding suspected restrictive practices. This report may include an indication of information that further specifies the alleged prohibited practices. Previously, the following entities could apply for the initiation of antitrust proceedings on suspicion of violation of the provisions of the previous Act[17]: an entrepreneur or an association of entrepreneurs who demonstrate their legal interest, a local government body, a state control body, a consumer ombudsman, and a consumer organization. The lack of restrictions on who can submit a notification to UOKiK relating to an infringement of competition rules may have led to fears that if someone submits such a notification, they themselves may also be subject to

Table 7.1 Explanatory antitrust proceedings and decisions regarding concentration of control of UOKiK in years 2004–2021

Areas of UOKiK's activities	*2004*	*2018*	*2021*
The number of cases and decisions of the President of UOKiK regarding concentration control:	**256**	**252**	**300**
– Consent to concentration	175	228	295
– Conditional consent	1	0	4
– Prohibition of concentration	2	0	1
– Discontinuance of the proceedings	10	1	3
– Return of the application	19	10	10
The number of decisions issued by the President of UOKiK-statement of practice:	8	3	7
– Horizontal agreements	6	0	4
– Vertical agreements	45	5	1
– Abuse of a dominant position			
Antitrust investigations:	**559**	**12**	**12**
– Horizontal	32	9	7
– Vertical	27	3	2
– Abuse of market position	296	1	2

Source: Own preparation based on: UOKiK (2005), UOKiK (2018), and UOKiK (2021).

inspection later. In addition, availing of the EU's experience, regulatory bodies were established in Poland in sectors such as telecommunications, railways, energy, water and sewage, and waste processing. Polish companies that wanted to compete on the EU market had to make an effort to modernize their technology and products (Fornalczyk, 2019, p. 87).

As for the decisions of the President of UOKiK concerning the control of concentrations, the number of cases consented in 2004 was 256, which decreased to 252 in 2018 and increased to 300 in 2021. In the first year under review, 68% of the entities seeking concentration consent were granted, while in 2021 almost 98%. This apparent upward trend in the number of concentration-related cases and decisions by the President of the Office of Competition and Consumer Protection reflects the trend of the increasing concentration of businesses observed in Europe and the nature of this concentration. Pursuant to the Competition and Consumer Protection Act 2007, entrepreneurs planning, for example, a merger or acquisition, are required to notify the President of UOKiK of such an intention. The transaction is subject to notification if it involves entities whose combined turnover in the preceding year exceeded EUR 1 billion worldwide or EUR 50 million in Poland. In light of the research conducted by CompNet (The Competitiveness Research Network) in 2020, it appears that the increasing market concentration in Europe should not necessarily be seen as a cause for concern regarding a weaker competitive environment, as it appears to primarily reflect the effects of a reallocation of revenue shares from less productive to more productive companies. Increasing concentration is partly a reflection of more efficient market processes with more technologically advanced production methods benefiting large and highly efficient companies. This situation has important implications for antitrust policy, but also for industrial policy, which must be based on a careful assessment of the costs and benefits of increasing market concentration. In particular, assessments of the detrimental effects of excessive market power must be based on more direct measures of that market power and its associated rents, rather than on the observed increase in concentration (CompNet, 2020, pp. 55–56).

The largest number of concentration control decisions issued in 2021 concerned real estate (e.g. industrial property rental, office space rental, development services, and residential sales), commerce, and energy (UOKiK, 2021, p. 27).

One of the significant changes that took place in 2021 is that UOKiK took control of the concentration from the EC, which means, in practice, that participants in a concentration that has a Community dimension, may apply to the EC to have its effects examined by a member state, if it is likely to have a significant impact on competition in that state. This was the case in the transaction involving the acquisition of control by Orlen group (Polski Koncern Naftowy Orlen S.A.) over PGNiG (Polskie Górnictwo Naftowe i Gazownictwo S.A.). Thus, in March 2021, the EC forwarded an assessment of its impact to the President of UOKiK for consideration. According to the EC, the Office has adequate experience in assessing the characteristics of markets in the energy sector, as reflected in the decisions issued to date regarding this area of the economy (UOKiK, 2021, p. 30). The decision on this merger provoked a great deal of commentary and criticism in Poland, which exposed its primarily political nature.[18] However, it should be remembered that every merger has its supporters and opponents, and the consolidation of Orlen, PGNiG, Lotos, and Energia is by far the largest merger in the history of the Polish economy to date. Development on local markets, as well as international expansion, new business areas, or competitive advantages are all associated with consolidation processes. In this context, the decision to merge in this group can be seen as the beginning of a longer road aimed at creating a business-complementary organism whose main commodity is energy. In the current situation of the ongoing war in Ukraine, such a move is justified by the need to ensure the security and independence of energy in Central and Eastern Europe. However, in order to assess the economic consequences of this merger, it would be necessary to undertake an in-depth analysis of this market and the consequences of its impact on energy prices in the Polish market. The ambiguity about the possible political nature of the decisions taken does not only apply to UOKiK but appears in the experience of other countries, such as Germany.

These situations arise from the complexity of the issues that these bodies have to deal with, as well as from the interconnection of these issues with the national interests of individual states. In 2015, the *Bundeskartellamt*, famous for its political independence, authorized the establishment of the Nord Stream 2 consortium, which would be responsible for the project of the same name. The project envisaged the expansion of the Nord Stream pipeline by a third and fourth line. The consortium, comprising Gazprom, Wintershall, Shell, E.on, Engie, and OMV, was formed in July of the same year. Gazprom was left with a 50% stake. The European partners each received 10% of the shares. A situation was created in which, on the one hand, the Germans and the Dutch have consistently supported the implementation of the project, with the probable support of France and even the UK, yet on the other hand, ten countries, including Eastern European countries and Italy, strongly oppose the project. In October 2020, UOKiK imposed financial penalties of more than PLN 29 billion on Gazprom and more than PLN 234 million on the other entities involved in the Nord Stream 2 pipeline project (including a PLN 172 million penalty on Engie Energy for failing to provide information on Nord Stream-2). According to UOKiK, in 2018 Gazprom entered into an agreement with the afore-mentioned companies without the prior consent of the Polish regulator, which may have led to a restriction of competition in the market. Representatives of the UOKiK also believe that the joint venturers started financing the project without forming a joint venture and through loans, which is a violation of antitrust laws. Both Gazprom and the other penalized companies appealed the ruling. On November 21, 2022, the Court of Competition and Consumer Protection (SOKiK) overturned the decision (Rzeczpospolita, 2022b).

Among the examples of concentration approvals issued in the UOKiK's 2021 annual report, we can find the following cases:

- concentration approval in the market for the provision of passive telecommunications infrastructure was obtained by Cellnex Poland, an operator of infrastructure used to provide, among other things, mobile telephony services, which obtained approval from the President of UOKiK to acquire control over Polkomtel Infrastruktura (UOKiK, 2021, p. 28);

- in the pharmaceuticals market, UOKiK approved DOZ's acquisition of control over Euro-Apteka, Super Zdrowie, and MLV18 (UOKiK, 2021, p. 29);
- the approval of PKN Orlen's acquisition of control over Polska Press. The Orlen group includes Ruch, which distributes newspapers and also sells them in retail chains, mainly through a network of kiosks. Polska Press, on the other hand, heads a capital group, which operates mainly on local markets, including the publication of 20 regional dailies, nearly 120 local weeklies, as well as free press. The President of the Office analysed the effects of the planned transaction based on information and data provided by the parties and entities competing with Ruch and contractors of Polska Press. In addition, it analysed the materials sent, among others, by the Helsinki Foundation for Human Rights, the Journalist Association or the Ombudsman. Ultimately, the President of UOKiK concluded that the planned transaction would not affect competition on the local press publishing market where Polska Press is present, while PKN Orlen has not been present so far. Only the owner of Polska Press will change, while the market shares of its individual participants remain unchanged. This is a so-called vertical concentration occurring between entities operating at different levels of press circulation (UOKiK, 2021, p. 28).

There was also one concentration ban in 2021. The case concerned a ban on the acquisition of Eurozet by Agora. According to the President of UOKiK, the merger would have resulted in a strong radio group that could have limited competition in the local and national radio advertising market. Agora heads a capital group primarily engaged in the press business, while also publishing and radio activities (examples include TOK FM, Radio Zlote Przeboje (Golden Hits), Radio Pogoda, Rock Radio), as well as advertising sales. Eurozet's business domain is the production and broadcasting of radio programmes (its main stations are Radio ZET, Meloradio, Antyradio, Radio Plus, Chili ZET), the sale of advertising time, as well as the management of Internet services. For both groups, their activities overlap primarily in radio broadcasting, the sale of advertising time, and the intermediation in the sale of radio advertising time. In UOKiK's view, the transaction could have led to the creation of a duopoly and marginalization of the other groups and radio stations – the two leading radio groups (Eurozet and RMF FM) would have held a combined market share of around 70% (UOKiK, 2021, p. 30).

One of the most effective means to gather evidence of an unlawful restrictive practice is through a search. The office may carry out such a search as part of its investigation, where it suspects that an entity has relevant information which may constitute evidence in the case. In 2018, UOKiK conducted 9 searches of 28 entrepreneurs (UOKiK, 2019) and in 2021 – 7 searches of 18 entrepreneurs (UOKiK, 2021).

Other important areas of UOKiK's activity in terms of quantity was preventive concentration control, which, on the one hand, was a sign of changes in the structure of the entity's economy, yet on the other hand showed the emergence of certain distortions in the functioning of free competition (Fornalczyk, 2019, p. 87). As far as concentration control decisions are concerned, in 2018 they most often concerned the financial and insurance market, followed by real estate, automotive, and food industries, and in 2021, concentration control decisions that included the energy sector.

With the emergence of the pandemic caused by the SARS-CoV-2 virus in 2020, the authority has taken steps to monitor the market for new breaches and to launch a new channel of communication with traders. Proceedings were conducted on the markets for products that were important for preventing the spread of the coronavirus, including in particular tests, laboratory reagents, components of medical supplies medical supplies (masks), and alcohols for disinfection (UOKiK, 2021).

In July 2020, the investment control law, which is part of the government's Anti-Crisis Shield 4.0, entered into force.[19] Since that moment, the President of UOKiK has had the ability to block the acquisition of Polish companies of strategic importance for public order, safety, or health by entities outside the EU, EEA, and OECD. The protection applies to those entrepreneurs who are based in Poland, but whose revenue from sales and services in Poland exceeded the equivalent of EUR 10 million in one of two years prior to the notification of the intention to make acquisitions. In this situation, the entity carrying out the transaction must report it to the office.

Investment control proceedings, as in concentration cases, consist of two phases. In the first phase, after receiving notification of the planned transaction, the President of UOKiK decides to initiate the proceedings check. Its purpose is to separate matters that are less complex from the more complicated ones. If the transaction does not raise the objections of the authority, it issues a refusal decision initiation of control proceedings and no objections to the transaction. Phase II deals with cases that may pose a serious threat to public policy, public security, or public health (UOKiK, 2021, pp. 30–31). In 2021, the President of UOKiK initiated eight proceedings in this case investment control and issued three decisions. The first of them is the proceedings, which went to the second phase, concerning the takeover of Odlewnia Zawiercie (Zawiercie Foundry) by the Chinese company Meide Group. However, the Office's analysis showed that the planned investment does not pose a threat to public safety and order. The remaining two cases ended at the stage of verification proceedings (UOKiK, 2021, p. 31).

The European Union allows the possibility of granting support from public funds as an exception to general prohibition. This implies state interference in business processes and selective state aid to certain undertakings. State aid, however, is subject to many legal regulations to protect the internal market, and the EC itself has exclusive competence for deciding on the eligibility of support from public funds (Kamińska, 2021, p. 218).

As a rule, the EC must be notified of projects providing grants or changing public aid. The President of the UOKiK plays a key role in this process, as it is he/she who notifies the EC of any intention to grant support to an entrepreneur by a Polish administrative body and any other private or public entity that acts under the authority of the state. The principle is that a Member State cannot implement measures that are designed until a final decision is obtained from the EC on the compatibility of support with Community law (UOKiK, 2018).

With the accession of Poland into the EU, a market surveillance system was created, based on the laws on general product safety and the conformity assessment system. Other consumer regulations followed, setting the rules of the game in the most important areas and defining the framework of UOKiK's activities. An important role is played by the Act of June 10, 2014 amending the Act on Competition and Consumer Protection.[20] This law has introduced solutions to further strengthen the position of consumers and safeguard their collective interests in the most serious and harmful practices by traders. Furthermore, the amendment of the Civil Code and the Act on Consumer Rights of May 30, 2014 should be mentioned.[21] The Act sets out the obligations of an entrepreneur concluding a contract with a consumer, while also the rules and procedures for concluding distance and off-premises contracts with a consumer, as well as the rules and procedures for exercising the consumer's right of withdrawal from a distance or off-premises contract and the rules and procedures for concluding distance contracts with a consumer on financial services (Kancelaria Senatu. Biuro Analiz, Dokumentacji i Korespondencji, 2017, pp. 7–8).

In the field of consumer protection policy, UOKiK also takes action in cases of significant importance to the collective interests of consumers. We can distinguish the basic tasks performed in this area as follows:

- elimination of practices infringing the collective interests of consumers;
- control of contractual patterns;
- ensuring product safety and service quality (UOKiK, 2015, p. 13).

In order to eliminate anti-consumer practices, UOKiK continuously monitors the behaviour of entrepreneurs. Moreover, it analyses signals coming from market participants themselves. Of particular importance in this respect are the complaints of consumers who can make written notification of the suspected use of illegal practices (Kamińska, 2021, p. 219).

UOKiK maintains a register of abusive clauses and makes it available on their website, which contains contractual terms that are considered to be not permissible by a final judgement of the Court of Competition and Consumers (SOKiK). In the following years, the number of proceedings for practices infringing the collective interests of consumers is decreasing. In 2016, there were 98 proceedings, 62 in the following year, while 65 in 2018. In 2021, this number was 45. As regards the data on cases concerning recognition of the provisions of the model agreement as prohibited, in 2016 there were 10 such proceedings, whereas in 2017, there were 13, while in 2018 their number was 26 and in 2021 only 4. This trend is caused by a change in the attitude of entrepreneurs who adapt to UOKiK's soft calls, as well as by their elimination of infringements identified by the authority within the framework of its investigations and the elimination of their negative effects. This means that there is ultimately no need to initiate proceedings that are appropriate in these matters (UOKiK, 2019, p. 46, 2021, pp. 48–49).

The proceedings result in decisions in which UOKiK may order an entrepreneur to refrain from unlawful actions. Moreover, it may also impose a financial penalty of up to 10% of turnover. The entrepreneur may also voluntarily undertake to change his/her behaviour towards the customers and submit a proposal of actions to UOKiK aimed at eliminating the infringement and its effects on the market (UOKiK, 2019, p. 49).

To sum up, the second stage of the development of competition and consumer policy began from the moment of Poland's accession into the European Union in 2004. This meant that EU regulations in the field of competition and consumer protection, and in particular regulations of art. 101 and 102 of the Treaty on the functioning of the European Union are beginning to play a dominant role in shaping this policy. The new regulations imposed the obligation to apply EU law on the National Competition Protection authorities in a situation whereby, after applying national law, it turned out that trade between Member States was affected by the effects of anti-competitive practices. An important change introduced to Polish competition law was the programme to relieve penalties imposed on enterprises participating in anti-competitive collisions or monitoring issues related to public aid. As a consequence, legal changes occurred in terms of, among others, a significant decrease which was noted in the number of matters conducted by UOKiK in the scope of explaining antitrust proceedings. In the field of the development of consumer policy, there has also been an air of caution. With Poland's accession into the EU, a market supervision system was created based on laws on the general product safety and compliance assessment system, UOKiK monitors the behaviour of entrepreneurs on an ongoing basis, while also conducting and providing a register of abusive clauses on their website, which includes contractual provisions recognized by a final judgement by the Court of Competition and Consumer Protection (SOKiK) relating to what is not permissible.

7.5 Summary

The development of competition policy and consumer protection played a significant role in shaping the market economy in Poland and the development of an SME model in the field of competition protection policy, which in this model plays a key role. In the subsequent pre-establishment development of both policies, an antitrust authority was established with similar functions to the German *Bundeskartellamt,* which over time, in addition to upholding competition, also upheld consumer protection.

Poland may be considered to be an example, while at the same time the precursor of a solution combining competencies in the field of competition and consumer protection within a single administrative body *Urząd Ochrony Konkurencji i Konsumentów.* The competition and consumer protection policy implements the principles of the SME in terms of building competitive order.

The development of policies of competition and consumer protection supported the process of the transformation of the Polish economy, while also the process of ownership change and the demonopolization of state-owned enterprises. Since both types of policy played a mutual role, this caused a situation in which funds supporting effective competition were also consumer-protecting funds and *vice versa*. It could have been important for a country that had a centrally planned economy experience, where both types of policies practically did not exist. The informed consumer stimulates competition and innovation, which increases the added value and prosperity.

Poland is an example of a country testing "competition and consumer protection networks" to improve the process of faster detection of cartel practices, offer rigging and abuse of consumer rights.[22]

On 1 May 2004, Poland joined the European Union and, as a consequence of this fact, Articles 101 and 102 of the Treaty on the Functioning of the European Union came into force on its territory. They relate to the ban on agreements between entrepreneurs, both horizontal and vertical, while also limiting competition on the market. These regulations began to play a key role in shaping the competition policy in Poland. Likewise, there is an official statement in art. 3 paragraph 3 of the Treaty on the functioning of the European Union, which stipulates that the SME is a model of economic order for the entire European Union, which was particularly evident in the scope of the foundations of the competition policy. It can therefore be considered that the development of competition policy in Poland referred to the principles of the SME.

Poland's accession into the EU made it possible to improve competition law and the application of EU legislation has allowed for more effective prevention of monopolies. Poland's participation in the common market and regulatory mechanisms for certain sectors of the economy have enabled UOKiK to increasingly address consumer protection issues (Fornalczyk, 2019, p. 92).

In addition, a number of solutions have been introduced that improved the shaping of the policy of contention and consumer protection, such as the programme to mitigate the penalties imposed on enterprises participating in an anti-competitive collapse. Monitoring of public aid has also become an important issue. As a result, there were positive changes in the functioning of the competitive market in Poland, which illustrates a significant decrease in the number of cases carried out by UOKiK regarding the clarification of antitrust proceedings.

One important and problematic issue in UOKiK's operation is the lack of the political independence of the President of UOKiK, who, since 2007, can be dismissed by the Prime Minister at any time, without a valid reason. The danger here is that the chairman of this body may come under pressure if he is about to take a decision contrary to the government's expectations. Reintroducing the term of office of the President of UOKiK and the possibility to dismiss him/her only for important reasons could increase the political independence of this institution. The current situation is not in line with the ECN+ Directive (Directive (EU), 2019/1). Its purpose is to empower the competition authorities of the Member States to enforce the law more effectively and to ensure the proper functioning of the internal market. It stipulates that people in charge of a competition authority may only be removed from office if they no longer fulfil the conditions required for the performance of their duties, or if they are found guilty of serious misconduct under national law. The conditions required for the performance of their duties and the definition of serious misconduct must be laid down in advance in national law, while taking into account the need to ensure effective enforcement (Directive (EU), 2019/1).

From 2021, there was a further extension of the UOKiK's competence, which was the assumption of the control of concentration by UOKiK from the EC. In practice, this will mean that participants in a concentration that has a Community dimension can apply to the EC to have its effects examined by a Member State, particularly if it is likely to have a significant impact on competition in that State. However, this extension of powers may increase political pressure on these institutions in EU countries.

When it comes to the development of consumer protection policy, we can also optimize a number of new solutions, such as the creation of a market supervision system, monitoring the behaviour of entrepreneurs, whereby UOKiK conducts and provides a register of abusive clauses on its website.

Notes

1 The English equivalent of the term competition is derived from the Latin phrase cum petere, meaning "to seek together". Competition is a phenomenon in which participants compete with each other in pursuit of analogous goals, meaning that actions taken by some to achieve certain goals make it difficult (or may even prevent) others from achieving the same goals [Nickels, 2000, p. 18].

2 The Constitution of the Republic of Poland, Journal of Laws 1997, No. 78, item 483.

3 The Act of February 16, 2007 on competition and consumer protection (Journal of Laws of 2007 No. 50, item 33, as amended).

4 It was, e.g. the Cartel Act of 1933, Journal of Law RP 83, item 651.

5 Journal of Laws No.41, item 324, as amended.

6 The Act of February 24, 1990 on counteracting monopolistic practices (Journal of Laws No. 14, item 88).

7 In Poland, during the market transformation period, some German institutional solutions were implemented, such as the idea of an anti-monopoly office, the independence of the central bank and the export support system. Analysis of Polish institutions shows some elements of similarity with German institutions which were established earlier than their Polish counterparts. Moreover, the Treaty of a Good Neighbourship between Poland and the Federal Republic of Germany contained a provision in Article 9 stating that the Federal Republic of Germany is ready to act, both bilaterally and multilaterally, to promote Poland's economic development within a fully developed SME. Thus, as we read in Article 9, conditions should also be created for a significant reduction of developmental differences [Treaty of Good Neighbourship between Poland and the Federal Republic of Germany, 1991]. With regard to the similarities between the Polish and German export support systems, see Kamińska and Kulińska-Sadłocha (2019, pp. 195–216].

8 The state personnel resources – the existing collection of candidates for high state positions in 2006–2009. The high state positions were those referred to in Article 4 of the Act of August 24, 2006 on the state personnel resources and high state positions [Journal of Laws of 2006, No. 170, item 1217]. The purpose of the establishment of the state personnel resources was to create conditions to ensure the professional, impartial and reliable performance of tasks in high state positions.

9 Note by Poland, Roundtable on Changes in Institutional design of Competition Authorities,
OECD, December 10, 2014, DAF/COMP/WD(2014)135, available at http://www.oecd.org/daf/competition/changes-in-competition-institutional-design.htm.
10 According to the new definition, a consumer is a natural person who performs a legal act with the entrepreneur not directly related to his business or professional activity. Journal of Laws 2019.0.1145 Act of April 23, 1966 Civil Code, article 22, paragraph 1.
11 The Constitution of the Republic of Poland, Journal of Laws 1997, No. 78, item 483.
12 The Constitution of the Republic of Poland, Journal of Laws 1997, No. 76.
13 The control of the concentration of enterprises has also been harmonized with the EU regulations.
14 Council Regulation (EC) 1/2003 of December 16, 2002 on the implementation of the competition rules laid down in Articles 81 and 82 of the EU Treaty.
15 Regulation of the Council of Ministers of December 23, 2014 on the manner and procedure for dealing with an application for waiving or reducing a fine.
16 A practice which prejudices the collective interests of consumers by detracting from the trader's conduct contrary to law or morality, in particular: breach of the obligation to give consumers a fair deal, or the provision of true and informative communication; unfair market practices or acts of unfairness of the competition; offering consumers the purchase of financial services which do not meet their established needs while taking into account the information available to the trader on the characteristics of these consumers or proposing to purchase these services in a way that is not appropriate to their nature [Kancelaria Senatu. Biuro Analiz, Dokumentacji i Korespondencji, 2017, p. 7].
17 The Act of December 15, 2000 [Journal of Laws No. 122, position 139].
18 At least two applications have been made to invalidate the resolution of the Extraordinary General Meeting of PGNiG on the merger of the two companies, [Rzeczpospolita, 2022a].
19 Act of July 24, 2015 on the control of certain investments [Journal of Laws of 2020, item 2145].
20 The changes introduced by this act entered into force on January 18, 2015.
21 Journal of Laws, item 847. The Act came into force on December 25, 2014.
22 Note by Poland, Roundtable on Changes in Institutional design of Competition Authorities, OECD, December 10, 2014, DAF/COMP/WD(2014)135, available at http://www.oecd.org/daf/competition/changes-in-competition-institutional-design.htm.

References

Błachucki, M., and Stankiewicz, R. (2010), Polityka konkurencji w dobie kryzysu gospodarczego – prawne aspekty problematyki, "Equilibrium", 2010, nr 1(4), UMK, Toruń.

CompNet. (2020), *Firm Productivity Report*, May 2020. https://www.comp-net.org/fileadmin/_compnet/user_upload/Documents/Productivity_Report_FINAL-.pdf (accessed: 01/04/2023).

Craine, D. (2013), The Magna Carta of Free Enterprise "Really?" https://repository.law.umich.edu/articles/1172. (accessed: 20/01/2023).

Directive (EU) 2019/1 of the European Parliament and of the Council of December 11, 2018 to empower the competition authorities of the Member States to be more effective enforcers and to ensure the proper functioning of the internal market. https://eur-lex.europa.eu/legal-content/EN/TXT/?uri=CELEX%3A32019L0001 (accessed: 24/04/2023).

Erhard, L. (2012), *Dobrobyt dla wszystkich*, Polskie Towarzystwo Ekonomiczne, Warszawa.

Filipowski, O. (2011), Rozwój ochrony konsumenta, "Przegląd Prawa i Administracji", nr 85, Wydawnictwo Uniwersytetu Wrocławskiego.

Fornalczyk, A. (2005), *Pierwsze doświadczenia urzędu antymonopolowego*, ed. Banasiński, C., *Ochrona konkurencji i konsumentów w Polsce i Unii Europejskiej* (studia prawno-ekonomiczne), Urząd Ochrony Konkurencji i Konsumentów, Warszawa.

Fornalczyk, A. (2019), *Konkurencja i pomoc państwa,* eds. Kowalski, P., Golinowska, S. and Błaszczyk, B., w: *Nasza Europa: 15 lat Polski w Unii Europejskiej. Wartości, instytucje, swobody, polityki sektorowe, problemy i kluczowe wyzwania,* Raport CASE, Warszawa.

Grala, D. T. (2005), *Reformy gospodarcze w PRL (1982–1989) Próba ratowania socjalizmu,* Wydawnictwo Trio, Warszawa.

Jóźwiak, S. (2011), *Europejska Sieć Konkurencji – model: struktura i współpraca oraz kompetencje decyzyjne członków,* UOKIK, Warszawa.

Kamińska, K. (2013), *Wpływ ordoliberalizmu na rozwój polityki konkurencji w RFN I Unii Europejskiej,* "Ekonomia i Prawo", Polszakiewicz, B., and Boehlke, J. (red.), Tom XII, nr 2/2013.

Kamińska, K. (2018), *Polish and German cartel office against challenges facing European competition policy,* ed. Bielig, A., *Polsko-niemieckie stosunki gospodarcze między intergracją a brexitem,* Oficyna Wydawnicza SGH, Warszawa.

Kamińska, K. (2021), *Rozwój polityki ochrony konkurencji i konsumnetów w Polsce po 1989 roku,* eds. Kaleta, M., Laska, M. and Żuchowska, D., *Współczesne uwarunkowania i dylematy polityki gospodarczej,* AKSIM, Toruń.

Kamińska, K., and Kulińska-Sadłocha, E. (2019), *Polityka wspierania eksportu w Polsce na tle rozwiązań niemieckich,* eds. Wandel, J. and Kamińska, K., *Polityka gospodarcza Niemiec i Polski w kontekście europejskim: aktualne tendencje i implikacje dla współpracy bilateralnej,* Oficyna Wydawnicza SGH, Warszawa.

Kamińska, K., and Trybuchowicz, M. (2018), *Instytyucja urzędu kartelowego jako strażnika konkurencyjnego ładu gospodarczego,* Biuletyn PTE nr 2 (81), Czerwiec.

Kancelaria Senatu. Biuro Analiz, Dokumentacji i Korespondencji. (2017), *Ochrona praw konsumentów w Polsce i w wybranych krajach,* Warszawa.

Kowalski, P., Golinowska, S., and Błaszczyk, B. (2019), in: *Nasza Europa: 15 lat Polski w Unii Europejskiej. Wartości, instytucje, swobody, polityki sektorowe, problemy i kluczowe wyzwania,* Raport CASE, Warszawa.

Kundera, E. (2015), *Koncepcje Społecznej Gospodarki Rynkowej,* "Acta Universitatis Wratislaviensis" No 3695 –"Przegląd Prawa i Administracji", Wrocław.

Martyniszyn, M. (2019), *Urząd Ochrony Konkurencji i Konsumentów czyli urząd od wszystkiego. Pora na zmiany,* "Dziennik Gazeta Prawna", December 6, 2019. https://prawo.gazetaprawna.pl/artykuly/1443208,martyniszyn-o-odlaczeniu-ochrony-konkurencji-od-spraw-konsumenckich.html (accessed: 20/02/2023).

McGovan, L. (2010), *The Antitrust Revolution in Europe,* Edward Elgar Publishing, Northampton.

Misiąg, P. (1990), *Demonopolizacja rynku,* Instytut Rynku Wewnętrznego i Konsumpcji, Warszawa.

Müller, M. H-P. (2019), *Neo-Ordoliberalismus. Ein Zukunftsmodell für die Soziale Marktwirtschaft,* Springer-Gabler, Wiesbaden.

Nickels, W. G. (2000), *Zrozumieć biznes,* Dom Wydawniczy Bellonna, Oficyna Wydawnicza Rytm, Warszawa.

Note by Poland, Roundtable on Changes in Institutional design of Competition Authorities.

OECD, December 10, 2014, DAF/COMP/WD(2014)135. http://www.oecd.org/daf/competition/changes-in-competition-institutional-design.htm.

Orłowski, W. (2005), *Piętnaście lat walki z monopolem – kilka uwag z perspektywy makroekonomicznej praktyki monopolistyczne w polskiej gospodarce 1990–2005,* ed. Banasiński, C., *Ochrona konkurencji i konsumentów w Polsce i Unii Europejskiej* (studia prawno-ekonomiczne), Urząd Ochrony Konkurencji i Konsumentów, Warszawa.

Rogall, H. (2006), *Volkswirtschaftslehre für Sozialwissenschaftler*, VS Verlag, Wiesbaden.

Rzeczpospolita. (2022a), *Jest kolejny wniosek o unieważnienie fuzji Orlenu z PGNiG.* https://energia.rp.pl/surowce-i-paliwa/art37596841-jest-kolejny-wniosek-o-uniewaznienie-fuzji-orlenu-z-pgnig (accessed: 24/04/2023).

Rzeczpospolita. (2022b), *Gazprom wygrał w Polsce z UOKiK. Urząd zaskoczony, będzie odwołanie.* https://energia.rp.pl/gaz/art37456661-gazprom-wygral-w-polsce-z-uokik-urzad-zaskoczony-bedzie-odwolanie (accessed: 24/04/2023).

The Act of February 24, 1990 on counteracting monopolistic practices (Journal of Laws No. 14, item 88).The Act of February 16, 2007, on competition and consumer protection (Journal of Laws of 2007 No. 50, item 33, as amended).

The Act of December 15, 2000 (Journal of Laws No. 122, position 139).

The Act of July 24, 2015 on the Control of Certain Investments (Journal of Laws of 2020, item 2145).

The Act on Consumer Rights of May 30, 2014 (Journal of Laws, item 847).The Constitution of the Republic of Poland, Journal of Laws 1997.

The Council of the European Union (2003). *Council Regulation (EC) 1/2003 of December 16, 2002 on the implementation of the competition rules laid down in Articles 81 and 82 of the EU Treaty.* Brussels: The European Union.

The Treaty of Good Neighbourship and Friendly Cooperation between the Republic of Poland and the Federal Republic of Germany signed in Bonn on June 17, 1991.

UOKiK. (2005), *Sprawozdania z działalności UOKiK – rok 2004*, Warszawa.

UOKiK. (2015), *Polityka ochrony konkurencji i konsumentów*, Warszawa.

UOKiK. (2017), *Klauzule abuzywne*, Warszawa.

UOKiK. (2018), *Sprawozdania z działalności UOKiK – rok 2017*, Warszawa.

UOKiK. (2019), *Sprawozdania z działalności UOKiK – rok 2018*, Warszawa.

Włudyka, T. (2002), *Model społecznej gospodarki rynkowej a transformacja ustrojowa polskiej gospodarki. Analiza prawno-gospodarcza*, Wydawnictwo UJ, Kraków.

8 Economic policies and entrepreneurial activity in transition economies from the institutional perspective as evidenced by Kosovo and North Macedonia

Fadil Sahiti

8.1 Introduction

In many countries of the world, governments try to create policies aimed at increasing the level of entrepreneurial activity. The rationale for these efforts is based on the belief that a high level of entrepreneurial activity is vital to economic growth (Carree & Thurik, 2003; Acs & Szerb, 2007). Expectations are that new firms bring added value to the economy through increased fiscal revenue, increased employment (Fritsch & Mueller, 2004; Storey & Greene, 2010), and especially in bringing innovations to the country's market (Audretsch & Beckman, 2007). More importantly, new firms are the vital ingredient for creating a dynamic and vibrant business sector that forms the core of today's most competitive economies in the world (Disney et al., 2003; Bartelsman et al., 2013).

The focus of the analysis is that of the economic policies, both macro- and microeconomic, relating to the two countries in transition, namely, Kosovo and North Macedonia, which have an impact on the performance of entrepreneurship. Macroeconomic policies include policies that affect the general economic aspects of a country, such as fiscal and monetary policies, tax policies, business regulations, while also mechanisms aimed at regulating market competition, etc. Meanwhile, microeconomic policies include those policies that aim to improve the culture of entrepreneurship in society, facilitate financial access for entrepreneurs, support technology and innovation, advisory and assistance policies, etc. The process of economic policy research is conducted from an institutional perspective.

Although the focus of analysis is on two transition economies, the findings are reviewed in a comparative context with a group of former socialist economies that are now developed and members of the European Union, namely, Estonia, Latvia, and Slovenia. A vital component of the analysis is that of entrepreneurial policies that can underlie differences at the levels of entrepreneurship and consequently to underlie the different levels of economic development. This topic is motivated by the growing amount of empirical evidence pertaining to the reduced level of entrepreneurship in less developed economies (Bento & Restuccia, 2021).

Our findings suggest that after the fall of the socialist system, the transition economies have experienced an intense transformation, especially in terms of the design

DOI: 10.4324/9781003425717-11

and implementation of economic policies aimed at promoting entrepreneurial activities. Many economic policies (both at macro and micro level) from these economies are largely consistent with those in developed countries, but there are others that remain idiosyncratic to these economies. For example, some micro-scale policies lack coherence in providing education that strengthens the culture of entrepreneurship among the new generation; or the design and especially the implementation of these policies lack coordination between the local and central government, as well as the private sector in entrepreneurship policymaking; or the lack of policies and institutions that financially support new businesses and small entrepreneurs.

Databases relating to economic policies have ranged from official sources of the respective countries to sources from international organizations such as the World Bank, World Economic Forum (WEF), International Bank for Reconstruction and Development (IBRD), Global Entrepreneurship Monitor (GEM), etc. When examining the entrepreneurial performance of transition countries, we used data released by the relevant official statistical agencies, while Eurostat data was used for the same indicators for European Union (EU) countries.

In entrepreneurship-related literature, there are various studies that have focused on investigating the impact of economic policies on entrepreneurial activities. In many of them, the investigation process was carried out either from the perspective of a country, or from the perspective of the quality of an institution (Amorós, 2009; Cole et al., 2016). Empirical studies that aim to study the relationship between economic policies and entrepreneurial activities in transition economies, from an institutional perspective, have been relatively less present (Sobel, 2008; Dorado & Ventresca, 2013). This chapter aims to provide an important contribution by shedding more light on the impact of macro and microeconomic policies on entrepreneurial activities in economies that have not yet completed the transition process. Finally, our results should provide a basis for further research on these important aspects, namely, the relationship between macro and micro-scale policies and entrepreneurial activity.

This chapter is organized as follows: Section 8.2 discusses the reasons why governments aim to provide support for entrepreneurs, whereas Section 8.3 discusses the theoretical concepts this study is based upon. In Section 8.4, we provide an overview of the economies in transition and the reference countries. Section 8.5 summarizes the main findings related to macro and microeconomic policies and presents the findings on entrepreneurship performance. Section 8.6 provides some concluding remarks.

8.2 Why is it essential for governments to provide support for entrepreneurs?

There is a wide range of policies open to governments seeking to enhance entrepreneurship. These policies have been the subject of investigation of many empirical studies. Their purpose was to understand the link between the quality of economic policies and higher entrepreneurship level and hence higher economic growth. While there is comparatively greater evidence that supports this link in advanced economies, less evidence is available for less advanced economies (Hsieh & Klenow, 2014).

While endeavouring to explain the link between economic policies, institutional conditions, and entrepreneurship levels, scholars have used various theories, such as the ones developed by Schumpeter (1950) and Kirzner (1973). Researchers have used a range of indicators including those related to institutional quality, financial indicators, and indicators related to the quality of human capital. In general, the findings suggest that in almost all stages of entrepreneurship, from the moment of entry into the market, the process of the expansion or decline of a firm, while also exit from the market, effective and transparent policies, as well as an institutional and regulatory environment are crucial (OECD, 2017). As the findings in this chapter will show, some combinations and similarities of these policies exist in almost all economies, both advanced and less advanced ones. However, just because these similarities exist does not diminish the need to consider the rationale for designing policies that aim to boost entrepreneurial activities, in particular in the economic context. Basically, the question that may arise in this case is: Why is it important to have these specific policies?

To answer this question, however, requires some sort of historical context. As Audretsch and Thurik (2000) argue, until the 1980s governments designed and implemented entrepreneurial policies primarily to satisfy the needs and interests of large firms. They give two reasons for this. First, the aim of large firms was to produce standardized products, and this was carried out by applying economies of scale and mass production. In this way, they managed to meet the needs of the majority of their customers. Secondly, during that period there was closer cooperation between unions, governments, and firms, and therefore employees were given the opportunity to have lifelong employment (Galbraith, 1957). In other words, until the late 1970s employees believed that their entire working life could be tied to one firm, and this required them to be union members. In contrast, small firms were considered old-fashioned and backward, which contribute little to the level of employment, while also pay less and offer poor employment conditions compared to large firms; as well as having lower efficiencies than large firms, and finally, they were viewed as entities without any significant impact on the field of innovation (Schumpeter, 1950; Baswell, 1973; Audretsch, 2002; Robson & Haigh, 2008). Audretsch and Thurik (2000) note that the period before the 1980s was the period, as they call it, of the "managed economy", in which business ownership was concentrated. The main preoccupation of firms was how to produce mass products; it was a period in which governments, unions, and firms sought the best ways to work together.

According to the same authors, from the 1980s onwards, the world's economy in general, but in developed countries in particular, changed as it had moved from a "managed" economy to an "entrepreneurial" economy. Thus, in the 1980s governments in various countries began to see entrepreneurship as an important factor influencing economic and social development (Baumol, 1990). Since then, policymakers have sought to find the best ways to promote entrepreneurial activities. According to Storey and Greene (2010), there may be various reasons why policymakers endeavour to create policies that promote entrepreneurship. First, with the shift in belief that small firms contribute little to employment growth, the engagement of policymakers in creating favourable economic policies that foster greater entrepreneurial activities began to change as well. The influence of smaller firms on employment growth began to be supported both theoretically and empirically, especially from the empirical studies published by Birch in 1981 and 1987.

Second, other studies began to emerge, offering empirical evidence and suggesting the valuable contribution of small firms to the economic development of countries (Romer 1990; Audretsch et al., 2006). Findings suggested that by increasing market competition, small firms influence a country's economic growth (Autio et al., 1999; Disney et al., 2003). The third reason emphasizes other sustainable benefits. For example, the products and services of small firms have the capacity to offer consumers a wider range of solutions and variations for their needs; small firms enable people to have their own businesses when they may not be able to work for others; small firms can also act as agents of social change by integrating environmental and social concerns into their business operations, etc. (Tracey & Jarvis, 2007). Another reason why governments seek to design and implement favourable entrepreneurial policies has to do with what is called "market failure".[1] If there is evidence of a lack of fair competition in the market; when customers and suppliers are not properly informed about market conditions; or when we have the presence of externalities, the need for government intervention is necessary. However, according to the political economy approach, there may be more reasons why policymakers formulate policies, including government elections, power relations, bureaucracy, equal and distribution issues, and so on (Coen & Dannreuther, 2002).

8.3 Economic perspectives, concepts, and theoretical framework

In this section, we review the economic perspectives, concepts, and the theoretical perspective on which the analysis of this chapter is based upon. First, we review the economic perspectives, then we continue with a review of the concepts (economies in transition, entrepreneurship, and entrepreneurship policies) and finally, the theoretical framework used in the study will be examined.

Theoretically, this study is based on two economic perspectives that are fundamentally related to each other: development economics and neo-institutional economics. Both theories argue that regardless of the level of development of an economy, the influence of the institutional factor on entrepreneurship is essential. For example, according to the former view, in economies with less stable institutions, the entrepreneurial process continues despite the lack of effective property protection provided by the government (see, e.g., Nenova, 2004; Powell et al., 2008). The latter perspective assumes that laws, rules, and social norms have a fundamental influence on the development of entrepreneurship and thus on the economic development of a country (see, e.g., North, 1990; Alston, 1996; Furubotn & Richter, 2005; Keefer & Shirley, 2000; Rodrik et al., 2002). Proponents of the neo-institutional economic perspective believe that institutions are an important driver of the distribution of entrepreneurial talent in any society.

The notion of an economy in transition in this study refers to countries that are in the process of macroeconomic reform, or, more precisely, countries that are in a process of change from a state-driven economy to a more market-driven economy (Svejnar, 2002). This transition process is comprehensive, as it covers the main aspects of the society, such as market liberalization, macroeconomic stabilization, privatization of state economic assets, and legal and institutional reforms (Berend, 2003; Kornai, 2008).

As Edith Penrose noted over six decades ago (1959, p. 77), entrepreneurship can be a very slippery concept to handle. Prominent economists have offered different definitions related to the topic of entrepreneurship (see, e.g., Baumol, 1990, Davidson, 2004; Storey & Greene, 2010). In this study, we adopt the concept offered by Lundström and Stevenson. They define entrepreneurship

> ... as a process whereby individuals become aware of business ownership as an option or viable alternative, develop ideas for businesses, learn the processes of becoming an entrepreneur, and undertake the initiation and development of a business.... Entrepreneurship can be found in both the initiation and growth of businesses.
>
> (Lundström & Stevenson, 2005, p. 42)

Given that entrepreneurial activity is considered healthy for the economic development, the question that can be raised is what are the policies that lead to a higher level of entrepreneurial activities? It is worth noting that the focus of this study is policies affecting entrepreneurial activities, and not SME policies. Although there are similarities between the two concepts, as stated by Stevenson and Lundström (2007), there are also some important differences between them. Entrepreneurship policies deal with issues such as motivation, opportunities, and skills, with the aim of creating an encouraging institutional basis for people to start their own businesses. Furthermore, entrepreneurship policies are designed to influence a wide range of areas, including education at three levels (primary, secondary, and tertiary), as well as the promotion of entrepreneurship in media and society, reduction of administrative, legislative barriers and regulations for establishing a firm, while also financial support for new entrepreneurs, etc. (Stevenson & Lundström, 2007, p. 105).

On the other hand, the purpose of SME or business policies is to support firms after they enter the market, especially during their survival and growth process. In particular, the objective of these policies is to create a level playing field for small firms, so that they can more easily overcome their market disadvantages resulting from their "smallness liability" and "poverty of resources", thus improving their competitiveness with other firms (Stevenson & Lundström, 2007, p. 105).

There are various theoretical frameworks that can be used to investigate policies that stimulate entrepreneurship. Amongst them, perhaps the two most prominent are those provided by OECD (2008) and UNCTAD (2012). In this study, we have used and combined variables from these two organizations. More specifically, the theoretical framework used in this study includes the main policy variables that are currently used to promote entrepreneurial activities. In addition, in our

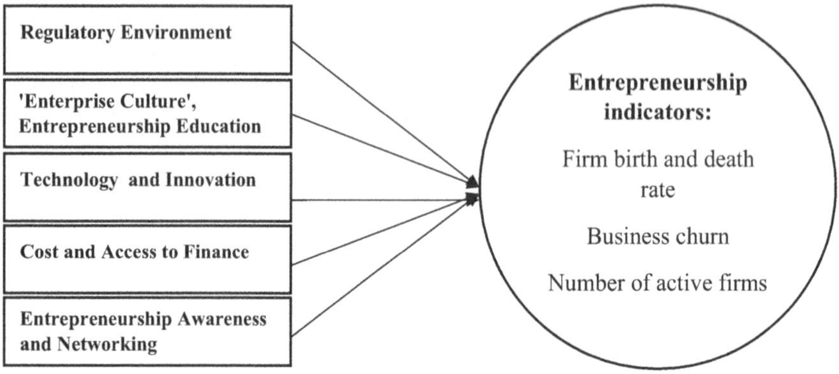

Figure 8.1 Entrepreneurship policy and performance framework.

framework, we have also included empirical indicators of entrepreneurial performance (see Figure 8.1). This framework assumes that the more advanced and contextual the entrepreneurship policies of a country, especially the more efficient their institutionalization in practice, the higher the level of entrepreneurial activities is expected to be.

8.4 Economic context of transition countries and reference countries

The economies of the two countries in transition, Kosovo, and North Macedonia, have emerged from the breakup of the former Yugoslavia, which means that in the past their economies were centrally planned economies (Estrin & Uvalic, 2008). The economies of both countries are still undergoing the process of transition from a socialist economy to a free market capitalist economy. Due to the war during the post-Yugoslav period, compared to other former socialist countries, this process has not been easy (Bartlett, 2008; Uvalic, 2012). According to the World Bank, Kosovo and North Macedonia are middle-income economies (Table 8.1). The economies of both countries are small and considered open and dominated mainly by the services sector.[2]

Numerous national and international reports suggest that the governments of both countries have made significant progress in transforming the economy and society in general from a centralized economy to one governed by market rules. Despite this transformation, the economies of both countries still suffer from various problems inherited from the past economic system (Uvalic, 2012). They are characterized by relatively weak productivity and with slower growth prospects. Compared to EU countries, labour productivity in both economies is lower than nearly a quarter of the average of EU member countries (Makstat, 2019; ILO, 2021; World Bank, 2021). Due to the limited functioning of market mechanisms, the reallocation of resources from less productive sectors and firms to more productive ones has slowed down (European Commission, 2021).

Table 8.1 Economic indicators – 2019

	EST	*LVA*	*SVN*	*MKD*	*KOS*
Size of population in million	1,326	1,913	2,088	2,076	1,788
GNI per capita (US$)	23,250	17,790	25,950	5,890	4,640
GDP in $ – billion	31.04	34.09	54.18	12.60	7.90
Profit tax (% of commercial profits)	7.7	7.8	12.7	11.0	9.3
Rate of unemployment	4.5	6.31	4.45	17.2	26.2
Informal economy	18.2	22	–	17	31.0
GDP growth (annual %)	4.1	2.5	3.2	3.9	4.7
Lending interest rates	3.85	4	2.48	5.6	6.3
Number of active firms – thousands	94.9	112.6	149.7	58.5	35.2

Source: Own preparation based on data of World Bank, EUROSTAT, and statistical state agencies for Kosovo and N. Macedonia.

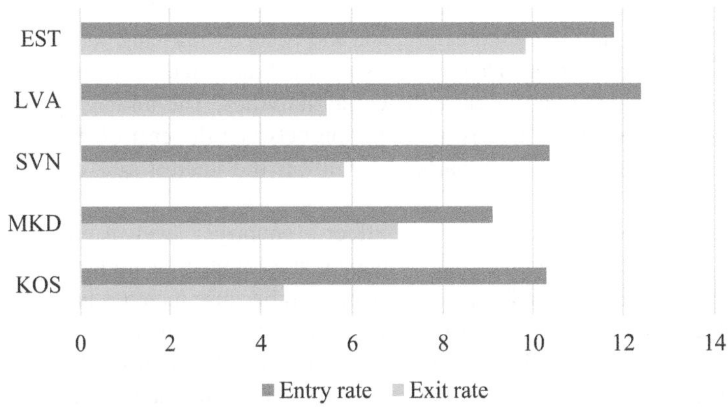

Figure 8.2 Enterprise entry and exit rates in business economy, 2019.

Note: Birth rate and death rate are defined as the number of new firms created and the number of firms that cease to exist over a given year, respectively, each scaled by the number of active firms at the beginning of the year.

Source: EUROSTAT for EU countries, and statistical agencies for Kosovo and N. Macedonia

This shows the importance of market mechanisms in allocating investments through the reallocation of capital and other inputs from unproductive sectors and firms to more productive sectors and firms (World Bank, 2020). Moreover, the findings presented in this chapter show that the entrepreneurship level in the transition countries is significantly lower than in the reference countries. The entry rate in Kosovo and North Macedonia is lower (see Figure 8.2). In particular, the stock of active firms, namely, those that manage to survive and grow, is significantly low when compared to EU countries. The lack of strong dynamism in the economy is due to numerous structural challenges and problems, including insufficient access to finance, significant gaps in infrastructure, insufficient competition, a large informal economic sector, high levels of corruption, etc. (Sahiti & Lawton Smith, 2017).

8.5 Analysing economic policies in transition countries

The following section contains two parts. In the first part, we analyse macroeconomic policies, while in the second part, we analyse microeconomic policies that have an impact on entrepreneurs. To identify the similarities and differences between transition countries and reference countries, the whole analysis is placed in a comparative context. The set of macro-scale policies includes policies aimed at managing aggregate demand through fiscal and monetary policies, as well as other high-impact public policies such as business regulations, infrastructure, and regulations related to business taxes.

8.5.1 Macroeconomic policies

There are several macroeconomic factors that can influence the decision of entrepreneurs whether to start their own private business or not. Findings from previous studies (e.g., Shane, 1996) suggest that a more accommodative monetary policy means more availability of financial funds and cheaper financing costs for those in need of external financing. Therefore, favourable financial conditions are expected to have a positive effect on entrepreneurial activities. The findings presented in Figure 8.3 suggest that there is a correlation between the cost of financial funds and entrepreneurial activities, namely, the lower the interest rate, the higher the entry rates.

Other macroeconomic factors can affect a country's level of entrepreneurial activity, that is, the higher the level of income in a country, the higher the entrepreneurial activity is expected to be. This happened because incomes have an impact on the increase in total demand for goods and services and, in this way, the increase in demand also affects the increase in the number of new firms (Parker, 1996; Stiglitz, 2000). This correlation between income and entrepreneurial activity can also be seen in our findings, where countries with higher incomes report a significantly higher number of new firms compared to economies in transition (see: Figure 8.4). The quality of institutional and governance factors is another factor likely to influence the level of entrepreneurial activities. According to the World Bank, which measures the quality of institutions and governance, in some basic indicators Kosovo and North Macedonia perform significantly worse than Estonia, Slovenia, and Latvia, especially in indicators relating to the rule of law, political stability and violence, as well as corruption (World Bank, 2020).

The quality of infrastructure, e.g. roads, telecommunication, energy, and water supply, affects the level of entrepreneurial activity too. Where these services are lacking or are unreliable, firms are forced to produce or provide their own energy, transport, or communication services. The findings suggest that despite some progress, countries in transition still lack some key infrastructure services. This is particularly evident for Kosovo, which still faces an unreliable electricity supply. In a World Bank survey (BEEPS), 63% of all firms and 78% of manufacturing firms consider electricity supply to be an essential problem (World Bank, 2020). Although significant progress has been made in infrastructure, deficiencies in this area continue to undermine Kosovo's attractiveness as an investment destination.

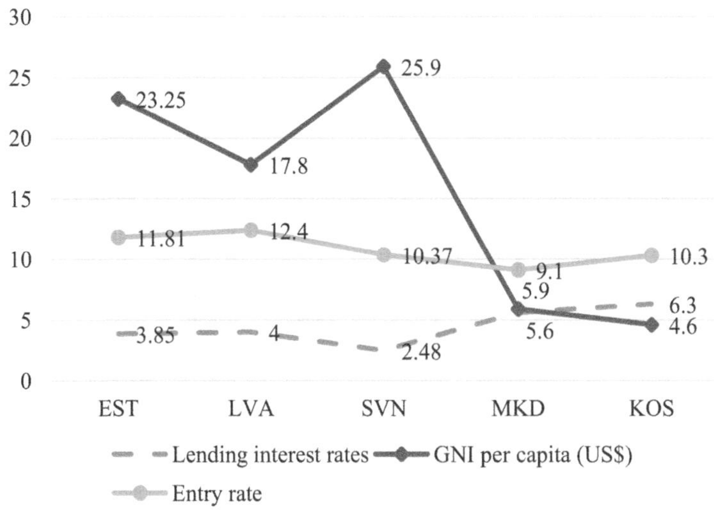

Figure 8.3 Macroeconomic indicators and entry rates.

Source: own preparation based on KSA, MAKSTAT, World Bank, EUROSTAT data.

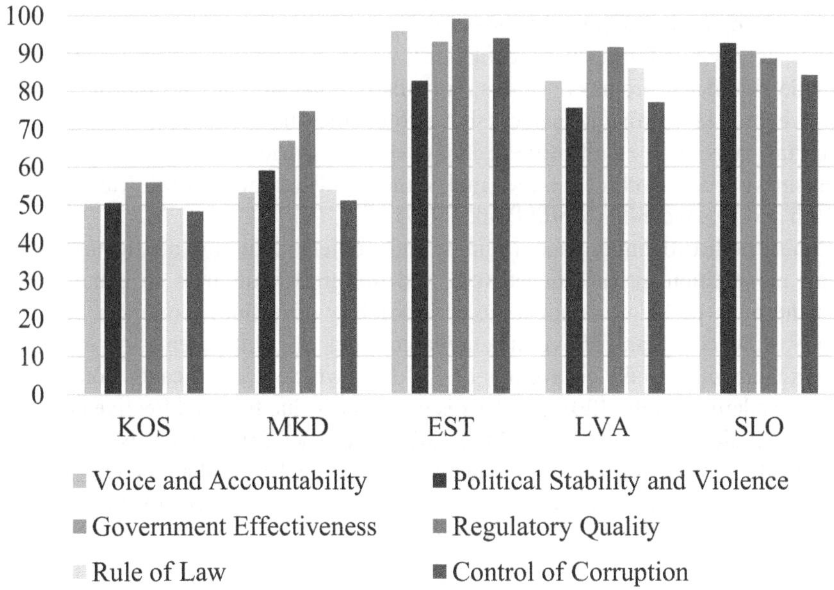

Figure 8.4 Institutional and governance indicators 2019.

Source: own preparation based on World Bank data.

Rail transport remains a major problem, especially in Kosovo, which lags behind its counterparts in terms of the network size and transported goods, especially compared to economies with similar output-sized sectors such as North Macedonia (Eurostat, 2018; European Commission, 2019).

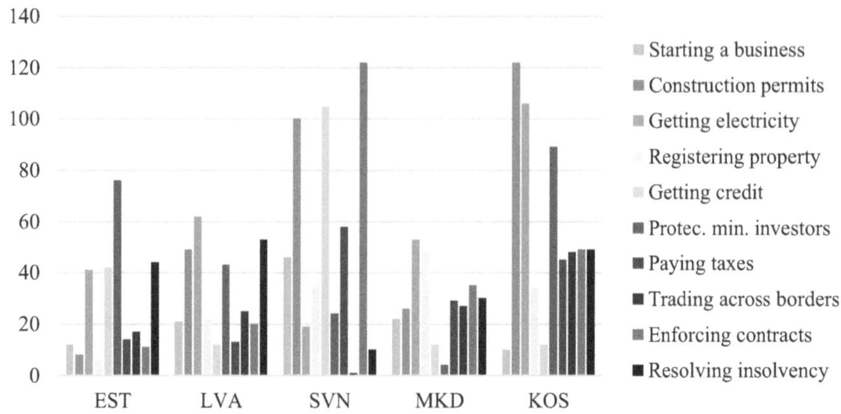

Figure 8.5 Doing business indicators 2019.

Note: the lower the number the better the economy rank.

Source: own preparation based on World Bank data.

Other macroeconomic factors such as tax policies and business regulations also have an important impact on the level of entrepreneurial activities. In both components, countries in transition do not differ much from developed countries. This is especially true for business regulations, where in the last two decades they have made significant progress. This is particularly noticeable in the improvement of procedures for starting a business, but also in other indicators, too, such as lowering tax rates. As a result of these improvements, in the 2019 World Bank Doing Business Index, both economies rank quite highly, namely, North Macedonia is 10th and Kosovo 44th (World Bank, 2019).

Yet, both economies face a number of problems that continue to undermine fair competition, private investment, and the growth of firms in general. One of the main problems remains the enforceability of business contracts, which is very slow, costly and above all unreliable. Thus, the implementation of a business contract can take an average of 330 days, which is significantly longer than the standard, namely, 120 days. This is particularly due to an ineffective and inefficient judicial system (World Bank, 2020). Contract enforcement is also costly, typically at 34.4% of the claim value, which is much higher than the OECD average of 21.5% (OECD, 2021). In the recent BEEPS survey, 43% of firms identified courts as a major barrier to doing business (World Bank, 2020). Another important problem has to do with unfair competition in the market, especially with business informality. In the World Bank survey (BEEPS), 63.4% and 54.5%, respectively, of the managers interviewed in both countries see economic informality as a major obstacle to the growth of their business (World Bank, n/a) (Figure 8.5).

8.5.2 Microeconomic policies

In this section, the focus of the analysis is on those policies that specifically aim to support entrepreneurs. The analysed variables correspond to the theoretical framework given in Figure 8.1. The analysis begins by describing the rationale for creating each policy, so that the findings for each policy are then examined in light of the impact they have on entrepreneurship performance.

8.5.2.1 Developing an "entrepreneurial culture" through education and skills development

The rationale for designing policies that promote "entrepreneurial culture" is based on the premise that the more developed the entrepreneurial mindset in a society, the greater the likelihood that people will one day start their own businesses (European Commission, 2003). Meanwhile, the creation of new firms potentially brings economic benefits to the rest of society, especially through employment and tax collection, as well as bringing innovative activities to the market. In this part, three institutional mechanisms aimed at building an entrepreneurial mindset among people are examined: the inclusion of entrepreneurship teaching and learning in the formal educational system, while also the development of Vocational Education and Training (VET) education, as well as the provision of entrepreneurship training.

The most traditional way to develop entrepreneurial "culture" in a society is to institutionalize entrepreneurial education in the formal educational system. Governments around the world are making efforts to include educational materials in educational programmes that encourage the creation of an entrepreneurial culture. This is done through the inclusion of entrepreneurship education at all levels of the educational system (European Commission, 2004; Athayde, 2009).

Various international organizations provide empirical data that underline the fact that transition economies lag behind developing countries in the inclusion of entrepreneurship in educational programmes at all three educational levels. According to the GEM report, the inclusion of entrepreneurship education in primary or secondary school curricula in transition economies is significantly lower than in developed economies. In the case of Kosovo, out of a maximum score of 5, Kosovo has a score of 1.8 and North Macedonia has 2.06, while the score for Estonia and Latvia is 2.96 and 2.62, respectively (see Table 8.2). Entrepreneurship education at the tertiary level is necessary and more useful for the new generations, since at this level of education students learn more practical things, such as writing business plans, simulation of practical situations to do business, etc. According to the report issued by the OECD (2019), despite the formal inclusion of entrepreneurship programmes, there is not enough evidence to clearly suggest that teaching and learning entrepreneurship in schools leads students to start their own businesses. Another important and highly emphasized problem in this report underlines the lack of a coherent policy that coordinates activities between different government agencies, specifically between municipalities, higher education institutions, and the private sector.

In particular, countries in transition have not yet created functional mechanisms that monitor the implementation of plans and strategies for the development of entrepreneurship culture, or mechanisms that measure the impact of these programmes in practice. None of the countries in transition offer any systematic

Table 8.2 Entrepreneurship education and training indicators

	KOS	*MKD*	*EST*	*LAT*	*SLO*
Entrepreneurship education at basic school (1–5)*1	1.8	2.06	2.96	2.62	2.07
Entrepreneurship education at post-secondary levels (1– 5)*1	2.87	2.51	3.39	2.86	2.66
VET (% of total secondary education enrolment)	53	60.2	39.8	38.9	70.8
Tertiary education (aged 30–34) (%)*2	20.8	35.7	44.01	45.7	44.9
Knowledge Economy Index (total score out of 10)*3	3.22	4.5	6.82	5.88	6.65
Staff training 1– 7 (best)*4	2.7	3.2	4.7	4.4	4.5
Business entries 2019 in thousands	9.8	7.8	11.1	13.1	15.5

*1 *Source:* GEM for Kosovo (2014), World Bank for N. Macedonia & EU countries
*2 *Source:* for Kosovo European training foundation, for other countries Eurostat
*3 *Source*: EBRD Knowledge Economy Index
*4 *Source:* for Kosovo European training foundation, for other countries WEF

training for those who want to start a private business, as is the case with Slovenia, whose government finances a specific programme called SPOT Point (OECD, 2019). Other organizations, such as IBRD, provide other empirical data that underline the fact that economies in transition lag behind developed countries in other aspects, such as the knowledge economy index. This indicator suggests the country's ability to benefit from scientific discoveries and applied research is the knowledge economy index. The score of the transition economies is much lower than in the reference countries (see: Table 8.2).

VET is seen as an facilitator of entrepreneurial competence development. Theoretically, in both transition economies, VET has been integrated into the education system, especially at the level of upper-secondary education. About 53% in Kosovo and 60.2% in North Macedonia of secondary school students choose vocational education – which is above the EU average of 47.8% (EUROSTAT, n.n.). However, the VET system in both countries suffers from numerous problems, such as the mismatch of curricula with market needs, the poor quality of teaching and learning, the lack of practical teaching materials, while especially the lack of practical work (internship) (European Commission, 2019; OECD, 2019). Unlike countries in transition, practical work is a legal obligation in developed countries. For example, Slovenian law defines the status of students attending vocational schools, according to which, each student is obliged to spend 50% of the time at school and the rest of the time in practical work (SBA Fact Sheet, 2019). In the reference countries, the employability of VET graduates is very high – Slovenia 84.5% and Latvia 78.8%, although no data is available for Kosovo and North Macedonia.

8.5.2.2 Access and provision of finance

Financial capacity is often the main drawback to starting a business activity. Therefore, governments mobilize funds and create institutional mechanisms to help potential entrepreneurs to start their business. This section examines three micro-institutional approaches that aim to bridge this "gap" by availing of: loan guarantee schemes, business grants, and the provision of equity financing for new firms.

The findings from this study suggest that for entrepreneurs in transition countries, debt remains the main external source of financing business activities. Yet, accessing bank funds is not easy at all for startups and small firms. Banks require large amounts of collateral from them to secure the requested loans. In trying to alleviate this obstacle, governments in transition have built guarantee schemes through which they share the responsibility of loan repayments with small loan borrowers. These loan guarantee schemes are financed by public funds, but also by other donor organizations such as USAID, KFW, and others. However, according to the OECD (2019), the magnitude of these schemes does not even approximately meet the requirements and needs of startup businesses. In contrast, the number and magnitude of these loan guarantee schemes in the reference countries is significantly larger (see Table 8.3).

Business grants can also support startups to invest in equipment, workforce training and consultancy for managers and employees. As shown in Table 8.3, the size of business grants for startups and young firms in transition economies are significantly limited compared to reference countries. In most cases, grants to transition economies come from donor organizations and in very small amounts (3,000–5,000 dollars). This is different in EU countries, where governments have established multiple agencies, the main purpose of which is to provide grants to startups and young firms.

Table 8.3 Access to finance indicators, 2019

	KOS	*MKD*	*SVN*	*LVA*	*EST*
Loan-guarantee schemes	The Kosovo Credit Guarantee Fund (KCGF)	Development Bank of North Macedonia	SEF - Slovene Enterprise Fund	Portfolio Guarantee Instrument (PGI)	KredEx/Estonia
Business grants	Millennium Foundation Kosovo (MFK), EU, USAID. KFW, etc	Fund of Innovation and Technological Development (FITD)	Slovenian Enterprise Fund, Employment Service of Slovenia, SPIRIT Slovenia	The EEA and Norway Grants	Enterprise Estonia, Kredix
Equity financing from business angles	Gjirafa Lab	IFI - Supported Enterprise Innovation Fund (ENIF)	Slovenian Regional Development Fund, SID Bank, Business Angles of Slovenia	BuildIT Latvia, The Commercialisation Reactor Fund, Overkill Ventures	European Structural and Investment Funds, (Baltic Innovation Fund, The EstFund, the SuperAngel

Source: Own preparation based on National Banks, *World Bank, ** S&P data.

The source of financing through equity continues to be one of the main obstacles for transition countries. These economies have not yet succeeded in creating institutional mechanisms that provide equity financing. Some venture capital programmes exist, but they are in their infancy, and those that are operational are negligible in number and magnitude (OECD, 2019). As Table 8.3 shows, in developed economies, the number of agencies offering equity financing to young entrepreneurs is significantly higher, especially in Slovenia and Estonia. In Slovenia, for example, the government has established the Slovenian Enterprise Fund, whose purpose is to connect business angels with entrepreneurs.

8.5.3 Supporting technology and innovation

Entrepreneurship is often associated with technology and innovation. Therefore, policymakers see the benefits of supporting the innovative skills of potential entrepreneurs. A specific benefit has to do with the spillover effects, as new businesses diffuse their ideas to other businesses and customers. Governments therefore have a role to play in facilitating the development of these "spillovers". In this section, we examine two examples of institutional interventions, namely, business incubators and R&D funding.

The creation of business incubators is seen as one of the main mechanisms for offering various facilities, conditions, and services to startups and small firms. In Kosovo, there is a good institutional framework that stimulates the development of business incubators.[3] However, despite this favourable framework, apart from the small number of incubators operating in the country, their level of development leaves much to be desired. The two most important of them, the Innovation Centre Kosova (ICK) and Gjirafa Lab, do not have stable and long-term funding as both are mainly financed by donor grants. There are several other similar incubators, but their activity has been significantly reduced (OECD, 2019). There is no data available to measure their productivity - the number of startups they have supported, as is, for example, the case with incubators in Estonia.

Similarly, North Macedonia has established the innovation policy framework, which was adopted in the Innovation Strategy 2012–2020. In 2013, the government established the so-called Fund for Innovation and Technology Development (FITD), as an agency that aims to implement innovation policies. There are several incubators that are active in North Macedonia. One of them is the business incubator of the YES Foundation in Skopje, aiming to provide services, training, mentoring, and networking opportunities to firms operating in the field of information and communication technology. Another business incubator is TechPark which operates within the Southeast European University in Tetovo. CEED Hub in Skopje also offers cooperation to young entrepreneurs and offers opportunities for education and mentoring programmes. Finally, at the Faculty of Electrical Engineering in Skopje, an incubator called the Centre for Technology Transfer and Innovation is in operation, which mostly functions as an office for technology transfer, but also offers limited space and cooperation services for startup businesses.

Another useful indicator that enables the measurement of the government's institutional commitment to innovative and scientific research projects is the allocation

Table 8.4 Business incubators and R&D financing

	Business incubators	*Share of budget in % in total national R&D expenses*
KOS	Innovation Center Kosovo (ICK), Gjirafa Lab, The Jakova Innovation Center, Innovation and Training Park (ITP).	0.1
MKD	YES Foundation, TechPark which operates within the South East European University, CEED Hub in Skopje, Center for Technology Transfer and Innovation.	0.36
EST	BuildIt – Incubating Promising Hardware Startups (26 startups), Startup Wise Guys – B2B Experts Ready to Accelerate Your Startup (53 startups), Tehnopol Startup Incubator – Work Next to the Best Tech Talents in Estonia (40 startups), Tallinn Business Incubators – Long Commitment for Long-term Goals (170 startups), GameFounders – Take Your Video Game Startup to the Next Level (10 startups per batch), VUNK Labs and Accelerator – Scale Your Ideas with a Telecommunication Leader (7 startups), etc.	1.3
LAT	Commercialization Reactor, Buildit, EIT Urban Mobility Incubator, UL Student Business Incubator, etc.	0.53
SLO	ABC Accelerator (200 startups in six years), Reveris, Kovačnica - business incubator Kranj, Hekovnik Startup School, Incubator Sežana, Ljubljana University Incubator, SAŠA Incubator,	1.86

Source: Government agencies for transition economies, and Eurostat for EU countries.

of the budget for this purpose. The available data suggests that the amounts allocated by the governments of transition countries for innovative activities and R&D purposes are significantly lower than in developed countries (see: Table 8.4). When we consider the size of the budget in transition economies compared to the developed economies (Kosovo's national budget in 2019 was 7.9 billion dollars and for North Macedonia 12.5 billion dollars, while, for instance, Latvia this year had a budget of 34.3 billion dollars), we can form a clearer opinion that the differences between the economies in spending on R&D are substantial.

8.5.3.1 Promoting entrepreneurship and business networking

Negative socio-cultural perceptions for entrepreneurship can be a major obstacle to entrepreneurship development for all countries, especially for post-socialist countries such as Kosovo and North Macedonia. The promotion of entrepreneurship can be performed through different forms, such as organizing awareness campaigns for entrepreneurship at the national and local levels, using the media to communicate support for entrepreneurship, organizing networking activities through which different models of entrepreneurs are promoted, while also involving entrepreneurs in political dialogue processes to sensitize government officials, etc.

Both transition countries are in the initial stages of creating policies and institutions that promote entrepreneurial culture, as well as policies and other institutional mechanisms in providing business advice to young entrepreneurs. Although North Macedonia seems more advanced in this regard, Kosovo lacks clear policies aimed at promoting entrepreneurship. Agencies involved in promoting entrepreneurship are mainly financed by donations (USAID, EU, GIZ, etc.), and less by state institutions (OECD, 2019). The main agency that tries to promote entrepreneurship is the Kosovo Investment and Enterprise Support Agency (KIESA), whose task is to identify the needs for training and other assistance for startups and young entrepreneurs (KIESA, 2018).

The Government of North Macedonia has established the "Program for Self-Employment", through the Employment Agency, which is in close cooperation with the Agency for the Promotion of Entrepreneurship (APPRM). This programme has been operational since 2007, through which every year around 500 unemployed people register their startup companies. In cases where an unemployed person joins this agency, he/she can avail of 100% free counselling services through voucher schemes. Services introduce various elements of business development, from developing a business plan to support for a startup registration. In addition, successful candidates receive a grant of €3000 to start a business.

8.6 Conclusions

The purpose of this chapter has been to examine economic policies at two levels – macro- and microeconomic – and how they affect entrepreneurial activity in two transition economies. The analysis was carried out from an institutional perspective using empirical data from Kosovo and North Macedonia. The findings from these two economies were benchmarked with the findings of three developed economies – Estonia, Latvia, and Slovenia. The notion of entrepreneurship in this study is conceived as an activity that leads to the creation of new firms.

From the results presented in this chapter, it can be inferred that there is a correlation between the macroeconomic factors and levels of entrepreneurial activity. As a result of better macroeconomic conditions, the level of entrepreneurial activities in developed economies is significantly higher than in transition economies. Similarities in policies and institutions have been observed in the field of business regulations, where in recent years transition economies have made significant progress, having drafted regulations and created institutions that stimulate a higher level of entrepreneurship. However, despite this, their influence is still modest. In particular, the findings suggest that factors related to political and economic stability, and especially the quality of institutional and governance factors have a strong impact on the level of entrepreneurial activity. This is not surprising given that entrepreneurs are more sensitive to external environmental uncertainties. Albeit not directly, our findings suggest that the quality, continuity, and direction of a country's public institutions often influence the business investment decisions of entrepreneurs. Faced with these difficulties, the level of entrepreneurial activity in transition economies is significantly lower compared to reference countries.

In terms of microeconomic policies, the findings suggest that although the governments of countries in transition have made efforts to include entrepreneurship education within the education system, many students still leave their schools and universities with limited knowledge and skills of how to start a business. This has made the impact of the educational system on creating an entrepreneurial culture lower than in developed countries. Despite significant improvements, entrepreneurs in transition economies do not have the comprehensive financial support that their counterparts in developed countries have. The main source of financing for business projects remains mainly bank loans, as equity financing remains undeveloped. Our findings also show that policymakers in transition countries understand the importance of promoting innovations. To this end, they have developed a policy framework that supports the creation of business incubators, the purpose of which, among other things, is the promotion of technology and innovation. However, despite the progress made, the contribution of incubators is limited in some key respects, especially in terms of human capacities and financial stability. Visible progress has also been made in the field of promoting entrepreneurship. However, policies and programmes designed for this purpose often suffer from a lack of clear objectives.

To summarize, our findings suggest that countries in transition have managed to design entrepreneurship policies and create institutions that are, to a large extent, similar to those of developed countries. However, despite this, their influence in practice is not so pronounced. The design of entrepreneurial policies in transition economies seems to be based on a "me too" approach rather than any rigorous analysis of their practical impact. This fact suggests that a country may design "sound" entrepreneurship policies, yet find that these do not have sufficient impact due to failures in other areas. It seems that entrepreneurship policies, no matter how good they are, are not enough to have higher levels of entrepreneurship. Other macroeconomic factors such as the political and economic stability of a country, and especially the political regime, have a strong influence on regulating the investment climate for many entrepreneurs. Therefore, entrepreneurial activities are not exclusively a matter of macro or micro-scale policies but are based on the interaction they have between them. In particular, the creation of stable and effective institutions helps a lot in creating conditions that support higher entrepreneurial activities in transition economies and on a wider scale.

Finally, public policymakers can put entrepreneurs at the core of their area of interest, but this may not be enough, as the entrepreneurial community is heterogeneous and has different interests. Our modest recommendation is that when designing entrepreneurship policies, policymakers in transition countries should avoid the "me too" approach. This is because policies that have been successful in one country will not necessarily be successful in another country. The aim of the policymakers should be to design policies that address the specific and real problems of entrepreneurs in countries in transition. The best approach is to create common forums where different business issues and perspectives can be discussed and incorporated. This approach would enable more integrated choices of entrepreneurial policies.

Notes

1 Market failure occurs when economic agents are encouraged to favour a riskier outcome by not having to incur full "downside losses" (Storey & Greene, 2010).

2 In the case of Kosovo, the sector of services contributes about 47.5% to gross domestic product (GDP), while in the case of North Macedonia, this contribution is about 54.5% (Makstat, 2019; Kosovo Agency of Statistics, 2021).
3 Kosovo's government has adopted the Strategy for Supporting Innovation and Entrepreneurship (2019–2023) and the Law on Innovation.

References

Acs, Z. J., & Szerb, L. (2007). Entrepreneurship, economic growth and public policy. *Small Business Economics*, 28, 109–122. https://doi.org/10.1007/s11187-006-9012-3

Alston, L. (1996). Empirical work in institutional economics: An overview. In L. Alston, T. Eggertsson, & D. North (Eds.), *Empirical Studies in Institutional Change* (Political Economy of Institutions and Decisions, pp. 25–30). Cambridge: Cambridge University Press. https://doi.org/10.1017/CBO9781139174633.004

Amorós, J. E. (2009). *Entrepreneurship and Quality of Institutions: A Developing-Country Approach* (No. 2009.07. Research paper/UNU-WIDER) (Online). http://hdl.handle.net/10419/45174

Athayde, R. (2009). Measuring enterprise potential in young people. Entrepreneurship Theory and Practice, 33(2), 481–500.

Audretsch, D. B., Keilbach, M. C., & Lehmann, E. E. (2006). *Entrepreneurship and Economic Growth*. New York: Oxford University Press.

Audretsch, D., & Thurik, A. (2000). Capitalism and democracy in the 21st century: From the managed to the entrepreneurial economy. *Journal of Evolutionary Economics*, 10, 17–34. https://doi.org/10.1007/s001910050003

Audretsch, D. B. (2002). *Entrepreneurship: A Survey of Literature*. Brussels: European Commission.

Audretsch, D., & Beckman, I. (2007). From small business to entrepreneurship policy. In D. Audretsch, I. Grilo, & R. Thurik (Eds.), *Handbook of Entrepreneurship Policy* (pp. 3653). Cheltenham, MA: Edward Elgar Publishing.

Autio, E., Wallenius, H., & Arenius, P. (1999). *Finish Gazelles: Origins and Impacts*. Paper presented at the ICSB conference, Naples, 20–23 June.

Bartelsman, E., Haltiwanger, J., & Scarpetta, S. (2013). Cross-country differences in productivity: The role of allocation and selection. *The American Economic Review*, 103, 305–334.

Bartlett, W. (2008). *Europe's Troubled Region. Economic Development, Institutional Reform and Social Welfare in the Western Balkans*. London and New York: Routledge.

Baswell, J. (1973). *The Rise and Decline of Small Firms*. London. George Allen and Unwin.

Baumol, W. J. (1990). Entrepreneurship: Productive, unproductive, and destructive. *Journal of Political Economy*, 98(5), 893–921. http://www.jstor.org/stable/2937617

Berend, I. T. (2003). *In History Derailed: Central and Eastern Europe in the Long Nineteenth Century* (1st ed., pp. i–iv). Berkeley, Los Angeles & London: University of California Press.

Birch, D. L. (1981). Who creates jobs? *The Public Interest*, 65, 3–14.

Birch, D. L. (1987). *Job Creation in America: How Our Smallest Companies Put the Most People to Work*. New York: Free Press.

Bento, P., & Restuccia, D. (2021). On average establishment size across sectors and countries. *Journal of Monetary Economics*, 117, 220–242. https://doi.org/10.1016/j.jmoneco.2020.01.001

Carree, M. A., & Thurik, A. R. (2003). The impact of entrepreneurship on economic growth. In Z. J. Acs & D. B. Audretsch (Eds.), *Handbook of Entrepreneurship Research*. International

Handbook Series on Entrepreneurship, vol. 1, pp 437–471, Boston, MA: Springer. https://doi.org/10.1007/0-387-24519-7_17

Coen, D., & Dannreuther, C. (2002). When size matters: Europeanization of large and SME business government relations. *Politique européenne*, 7, 116–137. https://doi.org/10.3917/poeu.007.0116

Cole, R., Cumming, D., & Li, D. (2016). Do banks or VCs spur small firm growth? *Journal of International Financial Markets, Institutions and Money*, 41, 60–72. https://doi.org/10.2139/ssrn.2517291

Davidson, P. (2004). *Researching Entrepreneurship*. New York: Springer.

Disney, R., Haskel, J., & Heden, Y. (2003). Restructuring and productivity growth in UK manufacturing. *The Economic Journal*, 113(489), 666–694. http://www.jstor.org/stable/3590194

Dorado, S., & Ventresca, M. J. (2013). Crescive entrepreneurship in complex social problems: Institutional conditions for entrepreneurial engagement. *Journal of Business Venturing*, 28(1), 69–82. https://doi.org/10.1016/j.jbusvent.2012.02.002

Estrin, S., & Uvalic M. (2008). From Illyria towards capitalism: Did labour-management theory teach us anything about Yugoslavia and transition in its successor states? *Comparative Economic Studies, 50th Anniversary Essay*, 50, 663–696.

European Commission. (2003). *Entrepreneurship in Europe: Green Paper*. Brussels: Enterprise Publications.

European Commission. (2004). *Helping to Create an Entrepreneurial Culture: A Guide on Good Practices in Promoting Entrepreneurial Attitudes and Skills through Education.* Brussels: Enterprise Publications.

European Commission. (2019). *Kosovo 2019 Report*. Commission Staff Working Document. Strasbourg. Available at: https://ec.europa.eu/neighbourhood-enlargement/sites/near/files/20190529-kosovo-report.pdf

European Commission. (2021). *Kosovo Factograph*. Brussels: European Commission. Available at: https://ec.europa.eu/neighbourhood-enlargement/sites/near/files/near_factograph_kosovo.pdf

Eurostat. (2018). *Length of Transport Networks, 2008, 2013 and 2018* (km). Available at: https://ec.europa.eu/eurostat/statisticsexplained/index.php?title=File:Length_of_transport_networks,_2008,_2013_and_2018_(km)_CPC20.png

Fritsch, M., & Mueller, P. (2004). The effects of new business formation on regional development over time. *Regional Studies*, 38, 961–975.

Furubotn, E. G., & Richter, R. (2005). *Institutions and Economic Theory: The Contribution of the New Institutional Economics*. Ann Arbor: University of Michigan Press. https://doi.org/10.3998/mpub.6715

Galbraith, J. K. (1957). *American Capitalism, the Concept of Countervailing Power*. London. H. Hamilton.

Hsieh, T., & Klenow, P. J. (2014). The life cycle of plants in India and Mexico. *Quarterly Journal of Economics*, 129(3), 1035–1084. https://doi.org/10.1093/qje/qjs044

ILO. (2021). *Strengthening Social Dialogue in North Macedonia*. International Labour Organization. Available at: https://www.ilo.org/budapest/what-we-do/projects/WCMS_679543/lang--en/index.htm

Keefer, P., & Shirley, M. (2000). Formal versus informal institutions in economic development. In Claude Ménard (Ed.), *Institutions, Contracts and Organizations* (Chapter 10, pp. 88–107). Location: Cheltenham, UK: Edward Elgar Publishing.

KIESA. (2018). *KIESA Services*. Available at: https://kiesa.rks-gov.net/page.aspx?id=2,3 (accessed on 2 June 2022).

Kirzner, I. M. (1973). *Competition and Entrepreneurship*. Chicago, IL: The University of Chicago Press.

Kornai, J. (2008). The great transformation of Central Eastern Europe: Success and disappointment. In J. Kornai, L. Mátyás, & G. Roland (Eds.), *Institutional Change and Economic Behaviour*. International Economic Association Series. London: Palgrave Macmillan. https://doi.org/10.1057/9780230583429_1

Kosovo Agency of Statistics. (2021). *Statistical Business Register: The Number of New and Reregistered Enterprises by Sections of Economic Activities, 2012–2020*. Available at: https://askdata.rksgov.net/PXWeb/pxweb/en/askdata/askdata__Statistical%20business%20register__Statistical%20repertoire/enterprises01.px/table/tableViewLayout1/?rxid=849047f5-19f1-46f0-81f5-019778e93dad

Lundström, A., & Stevenson, L. (2005). *Entrepreneurship Policy – Theory and Practice*. New York: Springer.

MAKStat. (2019). *MAKStat Database: Basic Structural Business Indicators, by Activity Sector*, by NKD REV 2, State Statistical Office. Available at: http://makstat.stat.gov.mk/PXWeb/pxweb/en/MakStat/MakStat__StrukturniStat/225_StrDel_Mk_03byactivity_en.px/table/tableViewLayout2/?rxid=3a369496-b1a4-4809-bede-5f896f540e79

Nenova, T. (2004). *Private Sector Response to the Absence of Government Institutions in Somalia*. Washington, DC: World Bank.

North, D. C. (1990). *Institutions, Institutional Change and Economic Performance*. Cambridge: Cambridge University Press.

OECD. (2008). *Measuring Entrepreneurship*. Paris: Statistics Directorate.

OECD. (2017). *Financing SMEs and Entrepreneurs 2017: An OECD Scoreboard*. Paris: OECD.

OECD. (2021). *Competitiveness in Southeast Europe 2021: A Policy Outlook, Competitiveness and Private Sector Development*. Paris: OECD Publishing. https://doi.org/10.1787/dcbc2ea9-en

OECD, ETF, EU, & EBRD. (2019). *SME Policy Index: Western Balkans and Turkey 2019: Assessing the Implementation of the Small Business Act for Europe*, SME Policy Index. Paris: OECD Publishing. https://doi.org/10.1787/g2g9fa9a-en

Parker, S. C. (1996). A time series model of self-employment under uncertainty. *Economica*, 63(251), 459–475. https://doi.org/10.2307/2555017

Penrose, E. T. (1959). *The Theory of the Growth of the Firm*. New York: John Wiley & Sons.

Powell, B., Ford, R., & Nowrasteh, A. (2008). Somalia after collapse: Chaos or improvement? *Journal of Economic Behaviour and Organization*, 67, 657–670.

Robson, S., & Haigh, G. (2008). First findings from the UK Innovation Survey 2007. *Economic & Labour Market Review*, 2, 47–53. https://doi.org/10.1057/elmr.2008.58

Rodrik, D., Subramanian, A., & Trebbi, F. (2002). *Institutions Rule: The Primacy of Institutions over Geography and Integration in Economic Development*. CID Working Paper No. 97, Center for International Development, Harvard University, Cambridge, MA.

Romer, P. M. (1990). Endogenous technological change. *Journal of Political Economy*, 98(5), S71–S102. http://www.jstor.org/stable/2937632

Sahiti, F., & Smith, H. L. (2017). An application of growth diagnostics on the growth of firms: With evidence from Kosovo firms. *Journal of Innovation and Entrepreneurship*, 6(16), 1–24. https://doi.org/10.1186/s13731-017-0078-8

SBA. (2019). *Enterprise and Industry European Commission*. Brussels. Available at: https://ec.europa.eu/docsroom/documents/32581/attachments/26/translations/en/renditions/native (accessed 7 May 2022).

Schumpeter, J. A. (1950). *Capitalism, Socialism and Democracy*. New York: Harper and Row.

Shane, S. (1996). Explaining variation in rates of entrepreneurship in the United States: 1899–1988. *Journal of Management*, 22(5), 747–781. https://doi.org/10.1016/S0149-2063(96)90021-5

Sobel, R. S. (2008). Testing Baumol: Institutional quality and the productivity of entrepreneurship. *Journal of Business Venturing*, 23(6), 641–655. https://doi.org/10.1016/j.jbusvent.2008.01.004

Stevenson, L., & Lundström, A. (2007). Dressing the emperor: The fabric of entrepreneurship policy, chapters. In David B. Audretsch, Isabel Grilo & A. Roy Thurik (Eds.), *Handbook of Research on Entrepreneurship Policy* (Chapter 6, pp. 94 – 129). Cheltenham, UK & Northampton, USA: Edward Elgar Publishing.

Stiglitz, J. (2000). Unravelling of the Washington consensus. *Multinational Monitor*, 21(4), 13–17.

Storey, D. J., & Greene, F. J. (2010). *Small Business and Entrepreneurship*. London: Pearson Education Limited.

Svejnar, J. (2002). Transition economies: Performance and challenges. *Journal of Economic Perspectives*, 16(1), 3–28. https://doi.org/10.1257/0895330027058

Tracey, P., & Jarvis, O. (2007). Toward a theory of social venture franchising. *Entrepreneurship Theory and Practice*, 31(5), 667–685. https://doi.org/10.1111/j.1540-6520.2007.00194.x

UNCTAD. (2012). *Entrepreneurship Policy Framework and Implementation Guidance*. Geneva.

Uvalic, M. (2012). Transition in Southeast Europe: Understanding economic development and institutional change. In: G. Roland (ed.) *Economies in transition: The long-run view* (pp. 364–399). *London: Palgrave Macmillan UK.*

World Bank. (2019). *Doing Business Report*. Washington, DC: World Bank. Available at: https://www.doingbusiness.org/content/dam/doingBusiness/media/Annual-Reports/English/DB2019-report_web-version.pdf

World Bank. (2020). *World Development Indicators*. World Bank Databank Website. Available at: https://databank.worldbank.org/source/world-development-indicators

World Bank. (2021). *Macro Poverty Outlook – Kosovo*. Washington, DC: World Bank. Available at: https://pubdocs.worldbank.org/en/993701492011106034/mpo-ksv.pdf

World Bank. (n.d.a). Current account balance (% of GDP) - North Macedonia. *World Bank DataBank* website. Available at: https://data.worldbank.org/indicator/BN.CAB.XOKA.GD.ZS?locations=MK

World Bank. (n.d.b). Unemployment, youth total (% of total labour force aged 15–24) (modelled ILO estimate). *World Bank DataBank* website. Available at: https://data.worldbank.org/indicator/SL.UEM.1524.ZS

9 Evolution of institutional determinants of innovation policy in Poland

Karolina Trzaska and Ewa Gruszewska

9.1 Introduction

The innovation policy in Poland has been developing since the 1990s. However, prior to joining the European Union, there was a problem with identifying the right tools to influence the innovation activity of firms. Accession to the EU caused the need to adjust to the Lisbon Strategy and had an impact on the inclusion of innovation in the long-term plans of the state (Stanisławski 2011). In 2016, the Innovation Council was established, which became the key interdepartmental coordinator of innovation policy executed by the government in Poland.

The formulation of innovation policy facilitates the understanding of the evolutionary changes in the system of institutions, which is reflected in the creation of the concept of national innovation systems (Freeman 1987; Lundvall 1992; Nelson 1993). They can be defined as a network of public and private sector institutions whose activities and interactions favour the creation, import, modification, and dissemination of new technologies. The narrow understanding of national innovation systems (Lundvall 1992) should be indicated, which is identified with the set of institutions that purposefully promote the acquisition and dissemination of knowledge. Indeed, they can be regarded as the main sources of innovation. It is also possible to look more broadly and outline the setting of the first group of institutions in the socio-cultural, economic, or political environment. The economic policy also affects the size, dynamics, and direction of innovative activity and may also determine the effectiveness of these activities (Freeman 2002). The process of implementing a new paradigm based on a systemic approach to innovation, which has been taking place since the 1990s, emphasized the role of relations and feedback between system elements, and gradually included social and cultural conditions in the analysis of innovation sources.

The aim of this chapter is to identify changes in the innovation policy in the context of transformations in the institutional structure of the Polish economy. The analysis of the impact of institutional factors in the regulatory sphere has a particular significance in explaining the dynamics of innovation processes. The starting point for the analysis of the objectives and tools of the innovation policy in this article is the low level of innovativeness of the Polish economy. The conducted innovation policy is ineffective in increasing the dynamics of creating new technologies.

DOI: 10.4324/9781003425717-12

Despite the evolution of the applied tools and regulations, these activities do not lead to a clear reduction in the innovation gap that Poland suffers from. The chapter presents changes in the institutional conditions for innovation in the Polish economy and puts forward a hypothesis on the low efficiency of innovation policy, which is the reason for the persistently low level of innovation in various aspects.

9.2 Assessment of innovation level in Poland

Innovativeness is the ability to create and implement innovations, which is determined by a variety of factors, including institutions[1]. Institutions strongly influence the innovation process, inherently determining its success or failure. Innovation processes are not autonomous and depend on investments in knowledge, education, and R&D activities (Ciborowski 2012). Institutional efficiency is one of the key factors in innovation growth. Thus, the level of innovativeness of a country is a derivative of the effectiveness of the innovation policy.

In the Innovation Union Scoreboard 2021, Poland belongs to the group of "emerging innovators", which means that the country's innovation rate does not exceed 70% of the EU average. The low level of innovativeness is a result of weaknesses in the areas of, i.a. knowledge, education, investments, and innovative activity of the SME sector, while also the impact of innovations on sales and employment. Over the analysed period, Poland's aggregate innovation indicator has been increasing, but both the development and innovation gap have not decreased with relation to the EU (Figure 9.1).

Sub-indicators distinguishing Poland from other countries in 2021 are as follows: digitalization, the percentage of the population with tertiary education, broadband penetration, HRST mobility between workplaces, and design applications. On the other hand, Poland is consistently one of the lowest-rated countries in terms of: internationalization, SMEs introducing business process innovations, PCT patent applications, employment in innovative enterprises (EIS… 2021).

R&D expenditures are not an expression of the level of innovation, albeit, the level of commitment of funds provides crucial information on the importance and

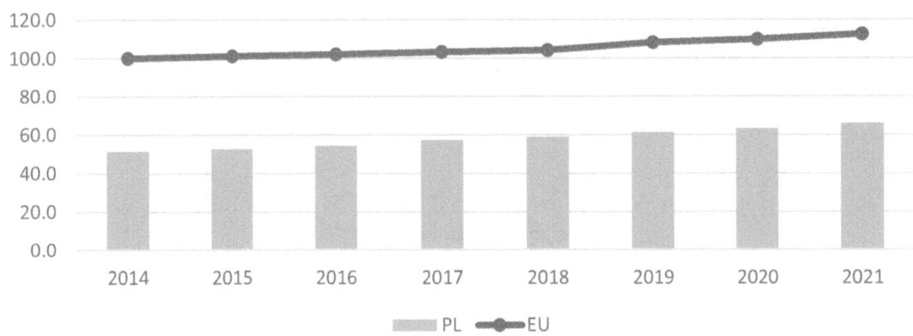

Figure 9.1 European Innovation Scoreboard in Poland and the EU (relative to the EU in 2014).

Source: self-analysis based on data from OECD (2021).

scale of support for scientific activity in the country. GERD increased significantly from the 1990s to 2020. Business expenditure (BERD) accounts for the largest share of GERD components, while higher education expenditure accounted for just over 30% of total R&D expenditure. Private non-profit expenditure represents the lowest share of funds. During the period under review, the share of total R&D expenditure by the government sector was small. Moreover, there was an almost tenfold decrease in the value of GOVERD in 2016 (Figure 9.2).

One of the primary goals of the Europe 2020 strategy is investment in R&D, which should be allocated to the tune of 3% of GDP. This target highlights the importance of public and private investment in R&D. In the period under review in Poland, despite the growth of R&D, this target has not been achieved. According to Statistics Poland (pl. *GUS*), in 2020, GERD was 1.39% with relation to GDP.

Poland performs below the high-income group average and the European average in all Global Innovation Index (GII) pillars. In 2021, Poland ranked 40th in the overall GII ranking (out of 132 countries) and improved its position compared to 2013. The problem is low performance in market sophistication (ranked 60th), i.e. efficiency in translating innovation inputs into outputs. On the other hand, the best performance is achieved in knowledge and technology outputs (ranked 36th). In terms of the seven innovation pillars of the GII, institutions stand out in terms of their impact on the innovation index (Figure 9.3). However, countries with a poor institutional environment score can have a high (competitive) level of innovation, as long as this is compensated by the other indicators, in particular knowledge and technology outputs. This regularity is exemplified by the results of Switzerland, Sweden, China, Israel, the Czech Republic, and Italy (WIPO 2021b).

Based on the GII ranks between 2013 and 2016, the political environment in Poland and especially the political and operational stability was rated very highly.

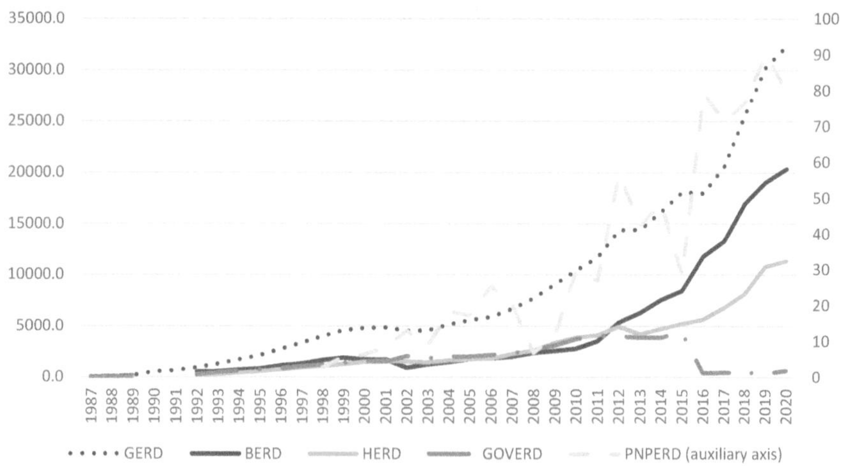

Figure 9.2 Gross expenditures on R&D in various sectors of the economy.

Note: GERD - Gross domestic R&D expenditures (totals all expenditures in a given territory), GOVERD - all expenditure on R&D executed by the Government sector, in a given territory (GERD component), PNPERD - Private non-profit R&D expenditures (GERD component), BERD - Business R&D expenditures, HERD - Higher Education R&D expenditures.

Source: self-analysis based on data from STI. Scoreboard platform (2021).

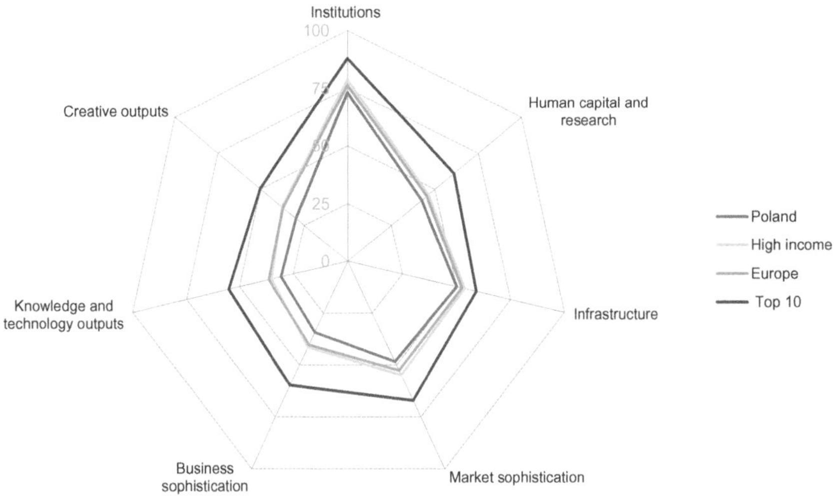

Figure 9.3 The seven GII pillar scores for Poland.

Source: WIPO (2021): https://www.wipo.int/edocs/pubdocs/en/wipo_pub_gii_2021/pl.pdf. License CC BY 4.0 DEED

As of 2017, the strongest aspect of the institutional pillar is the ease of resolving insolvency, and the weakest is the ease of starting a business. Since 2018, the regulatory environment has deteriorated, which is influenced by the low rating of the rule of law (Table 9.1). The rule of law index *reflects perceptions of the extent to which agents have confidence in and abide by the rules of society, and in particular the quality of contract enforcement, property rights, the police, and the courts* (WIPO 2021b). The rule of law index reflects perceptions of the extent to which agents have confidence in and adhere to social rules (e.g., quality of enforcement of contracts, property rights, police, and courts) (Table 9.1). A major weakness of the institutional environment is the procedures officially required when setting up and running a business, as well as the time and cost of completing these procedures and the requirement for paid-in minimum capital (WIPO 2021a).

In conclusion, the intensive growth of R&D spending does not translate into an increased level of innovation in Poland, unless there are solid institutional pillars supporting enterprises to create and commercialize innovations. The efficiency of the institutional set-up in Poland remains low, which is directly reflected in the heavily averaged Innovation Input in the Global Innovation Index.

9.3 Evolution of innovation policy in Poland

The concept and the main trends of innovation policy have evolved, along with the changing perceptions of innovation in the economy. *Innovation policy* and *science and technology policy* are terms used interchangeably by many authors. Furthermore, terms such as *science policy, industrial policy, research and development policy, and technology policy* are also used, but they in a more limited sense.

Table 9.1 The innovation level and assessment of Poland's institutional environment in the ranking of the global innovation index

Indicator (rank)	*2013*	*2014*	*2015*	*2016*	*2017*	*2018*	*2019*	*2020*	*2021*
Global innovation index	49	45	46	39	38	39	39	38	40
Innovation input sub-index	39	40	39	39	37	38	37	38	37
Innovation output sub-index	64	48	56	46	41	40	41	40	42
Institutions (rank)	35	35	34	32	33	36	37	39	38
1 Political environment	27**	27**	35	33	33	41	39	40	43
1.1 Political and operational stability	16**	18**	20**	26**	26	38	35	38	37
1.2 Government effectiveness	42	42	40	39	40	40	40	39	42
2 Regulatory environment	43	42	42	41	41	37	42	47	47
2.1 Regulatory quality	31	34	28	30	33	35	36	36	31
2.2 Rule of law	39	38	36	36	35	38	42	46	47
2.3 Cost of redundancy dismissal, salary weeks	89	88	85	79	78	72*	77*	77*	78*
3 Business environment	48	42	39	34	30	33	34	35	35
3.1 Ease of starting a business	75	66	71	66	82*	92*	93*	99*	99*
3.2 Ease of resolving insolvency	34	33	30	30	25**	20**	23**	23**	23**
3.3 Ease of paying taxes	74	72	69	49	40	–	–	–	–

*Note: *Indicates a weakness; **Indicates a strength.*

Source: Self-analysis based on WIPO (2021b) & Cornell University, INSEAD, and WIPO (2013, 2014, 2015, 2016, 2017, 2018, 2019, and 2020).

Innovation policy occupies a special place in the process of regulation, support, and participation in financing the environment in which innovations are created (Ciborowski 2016). There are three main groups of instruments of influence on innovation that may be identified. They include regulatory institutions (laws), tools affecting economic transactions (mainly financial), and soft ones from the group of informal institutions (Borrás & Edquist 2013). In the group of tools in the regulatory sphere, we should mention intellectual property regulations (e.g., patent regulations); regulations of research funds from public sources, including higher education; competition; ethics; and others concerning the functioning of the production sector. Tools affecting business transactions are, e.g., public aid to universities and other research organizations; tax incentives for running R&D; grants for scientific research; support for risk capital and seed capital, as well as instruments supporting technology transfer. The group of soft instruments includes, e.g., codes of conduct for universities, research institutions, firms; voluntary technical standards; regulation of public–private partnership relations, while also management contracts in public research institutions (Weresa 2014).

In terms of the analysis of the motives for undertaking innovative activity by firms, it should be stated that the innovation policy should not be limited to science and technology policy (Lundvall & Borrás 2005), but should also include the formation of rules of operation of markets, the tax sphere and infrastructure development (Hadjimanolis & Dickson 2001). Designing innovation policy instruments should include the diagnosis of the current situation and identification of the causes of the problem (Edquist 2001; Borrás & Edquist 2013).

Statistical reports (GUS, OECD) have been using the term *science, technology and innovation (STI) policy* for some time to emphasize the importance of science and technology. The term STI policy aligns with the concept of innovation systems and has been used in OECD nomenclature since the 1990s (OECD 1998). In this chapter, the terms innovation policy and STI policy shall be used interchangeably. Innovation policy is part of the state's economic policy, which is intended to lead to the improved competitiveness of economies, enhanced business innovation, and socio-economic development (Rothwell & Zegveld 1982).

The beginning of the 1980s was a period recognized as the popularization of the concept of innovation policy and the creation of a framework for innovation strategy. There was a more intense focus on the issue of science and technology development. However, the history of innovation policy is based on the policies of the 1940s–1960s, when industrialization was an essential element of development (Figure 9.4). This gave rise to the need for an industrial policy that ensured the protection of emerging industries, as well as state coordination and ownership. The period of Technology Push dominance was based on science policy and basic research that was not geared towards commercialization (Dodgson & Rothwell 1994). From the 1970s, there was a recognition that the failure of government-led industrial policy was more acute than the failure of the market. To address this, policy practices and instruments were changed to include greater liberalization, structural adjustment programmes, attracting foreign direct investment (FDI), privatization, and macroeconomic stability. The 1980s marked a watershed in the development of innovation policy principles. Two important issues were recognized during this period. First, the formal importance of the innovation function in economic development was identified. Second, universities were acknowledged as significant in the process of knowledge transfer and networking. Models of non-linear, coupled innovation, including the dependencies and interactions of the innovation process built a policy paradigm of Complex Adaptive Innovation Systems (Weresa 2014), which was based on three aspects as follows: (1) stimulating educational institutions and economic actors; (2) developing integrated and coordinated objectives

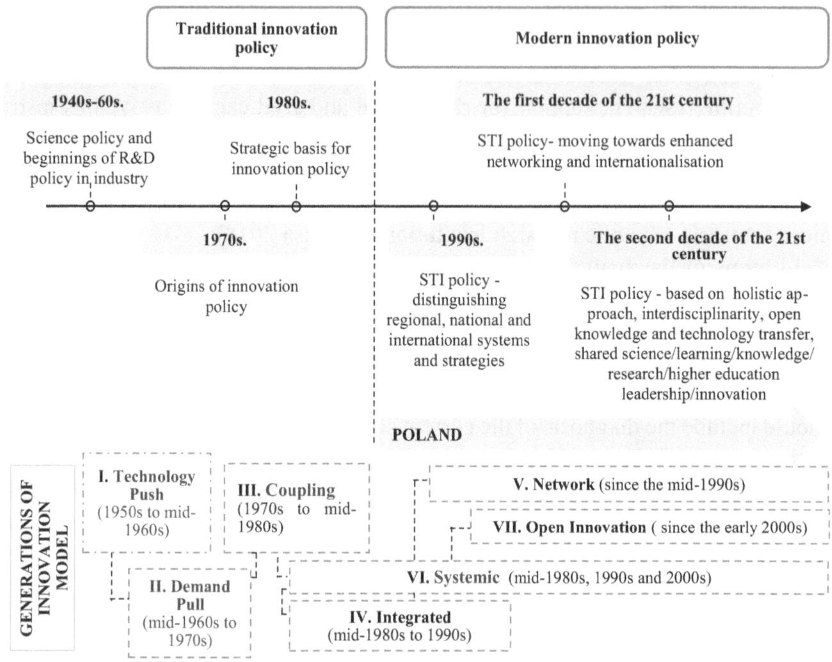

Figure 9.4 Transformation of innovation policy over generations of innovation models.

Source: Self-analysis

and instruments to enhance innovation; and (3) shaping a policy that continuously adapts to the demands of the economy and evolves through a process of continuous improvement (Lundvall & Borrás 2005).

The early 1990s marked the boundary between the traditional and contemporary trends of innovation policy (Figure 9.4). It is also regarded as the beginning of innovation policy in the European Union and Poland. The approach for the emerging policy was conditioned by the need for flexibility, resulting from technological modernization, as well as successive generations of innovation (networks and innovation systems). The new paradigm, based on a systemic approach to innovation, emphasized the role of relationships and feedbacks between system elements. Social and cultural conditions were gradually incorporated into the analysis of the sources of innovation (in the process of implementing innovation systems). Hence, innovation policy stems from innovation strategies from the national, regional, and local levels. Innovation strategy, in the most general sense, implies a programme for the functioning of the country or region in the future and includes possible ways of responding to changes in the environment (Stoner, Freeman, & Gilbert 1997).

In 1995, the *Green Paper on Innovation* was the basis for the development of European innovation policy. Its aim was to identify the factors (positive and negative) that affect Europe's innovation performance and to formulate actions leading to an increase in the Union's innovation capacity. Another important EU document from 1996 was *The First Action Plan for Innovation in Europe*. This plan emphasized that an effort at national, regional, and local levels was needed to implement innovation activities. Moreover, it covered three areas as follows (The First…, 1995):

1 fostering a genuine culture of innovation (a culture defined as creativity, entrepreneurship, good organization and responsibility for deadlines and costs, willingness to take risks, ability to anticipate needs, and acceptance of geographical, social, and/or professional social mobility). The means of fostering an innovation culture were neither legislative, nor short-term measures, but activities in terms of national and international initiatives. The aim was to create pan-European networks/systems to promote good innovation practices (e.g., the benchmarking system, the continued implementation of the White Paper on education and training, as well as instruments in the form of framework programmes and structural funds);
2 setting up frameworks conducive to innovation (regulatory, legal, and financial);
3 linking research and innovation more closely (both at national and regional level).

After the end of the Lisbon Strategy implementation period, the continuation of its functions became the Europe 2020 strategy. Innovation policy regulations have been evolving in Poland since 1993; however, there is a perception that prior to accession to the European Union, there was a problem with defining the right tools for influencing the innovative activity of firms. EU membership had a significant impact on the inclusion of innovation in the long-term plans of the state, as it made it necessary to adapt to the Lisbon Strategy, while further development of innovation was stimulated by the Europe 2020, including EU programmes and funds (Table 9.2). Since accession to the EU, reform programmes for pro-innovation activities in Poland have gained economies of scale and necessitated closer cooperation between institutions and decentralization of management.

The formulation of innovation policy in the 1990s and in the following decade influenced a change in institutional structures. Innovation policy has gained prominence due to the following (OECD 2006):

- Policymakers who paid more attention to innovation. Formal STI policy strategies and plans were supported by increased funding and changes in institutional structures.
- Reforms of universities and public research institutions to improve their ability to respond to socio-economic needs.
- Consolidation and streamlining of public support for business R&D. The government has recognized the role of small businesses in innovation. Support occurring either directly (e.g., grants, loans) or indirectly (through R&D tax incentives, start-up capital funds).
- Focus on collaboration and regional dimension. Growing interest in strengthening the link between science and industry has prompted actions to expand public–private partnership programmes for innovation.

Table 9.2 Pro-innovation government documents and programmes from 1993 to 2003

Responsible authority	*Title and date of receipt of document*
State committee for scientific research	Assumptions Regarding the State Science Policy and Technology Policy in Poland (20.07.1993) Assumptions of state pro-innovation policy (22.11.1994) Bases of the Scientific and Scientific-Technological Policy. Preferable Directions of the Scientific Research and Development Projects helpful in the Innovation Growth of the Polish Economy (16.01.1996) Supplement to the Assumptions of the state's scientific, science and technology (16.01.1996) State Innovation Policy Assumptions up to 2002 (06.12.1999) Polish Optical Internet PIONIER (29.06.2000)
Ministry of industry and trade	International Competitiveness of the Polish Industry (16.05.1995)
Ministry of economy	Programme to support the development of regional institutions for technology transfer activities in the SME sector (04.03.1997)
Ministry of economy, department of economic strategy	Increasing Economy Innovativeness in Poland up to 2006 (11.07.2000)
Government centre for strategic studies	Concept of the National Spatial Development Policy (26.07.2001)
Ministry of economy, labour and social policy	Pro-Growth Action Plan 2003-2004 - Entrepreneurship-Development-Work II (01.07.2003)

Source: Self-analysis based on Committee for Scientific Research (1993, 1994, 1999), NIK (1999), Pro-Growth … (2003).

- New challenges, notably the growing role of services and rapid globalization. Innovation policy makes it possible to understand the main forces changing the economy, attract foreign R&D investment and innovation, and foster international partnerships.

In summary, the changes in STI policy institutional structures had two main causes. First, they resulted from attempts to integrate responsibility for associated areas of innovation policy priorities under a single institutional umbrella, and hence a desire to improve the coordination of activities. On the other hand, they resulted from a reshuffling of responsibilities and changes in government.

Poland's STI policy is a continuation of the strategy initiated in the 1990s. The main trends expanding the regulatory sphere are as follows (Table 9.3):

- Development towards a Knowledge Economy;
- Digital transformation, providing a new standard for information processing and exchange, allowing science and innovation to be considered in terms of "openness";
- The concept of a *common space* in: science, knowledge, R&D, higher education, innovation, and industry;

Table 9.3 Poland's main STI plans and/or strategies (after EU accession up to 2020)

Title	*Period covered*	*Main objectives*
National Plan of Growth 2004–2006	2004–2006	• Supporting cooperation between research and development institutions and industry • Strengthening innovation in the regions, including the preparation of projects for implementing regional innovation strategies
Assumptions of the state's scientific, science and technology, and innovation policy until 2020	2005–2020	• Modernizing the selection of priorities for the development of science and technology • Increasing the efficiency of public spending on R&D • Expanding international cooperation and increasing participation in the European Research Area • Supporting private initiatives (spending) on R&D activities through systemic, organizational, and legislative changes
Operational Programme Innovative Economy 2007–2013	2007–2013	The main objective was the development of the Polish economy based on innovative enterprises. In addition, implementation was based on: • Development of human resources towards building a knowledge-based economy • Mobilization of private capital to create and develop innovative companies • Linking public R&D activities to the needs of enterprises • Improving intellectual property rights and building innovation infrastructure • Support for the creation of cooperation networks and development of clusters
Strategy for Increasing the Innovativeness of the Economy (taking into account the National Development Strategy 2007–2015)	2007–2015	• Selection of appropriate priorities and research programmes • Reforming the management and restructuring of the HEI (e.g., creation of the Council for Science and Innovation to prepare strategic directions of development) • Raising the level, potential, and efficiency of science in Poland, as well as increasing its influence in the world • Stimulating growth of innovativeness of the Polish economy • Integration activities within the European Research Area • Promoting drivers of the knowledge-based economy (e.g., nanotechnology, biotechnology, information technology) • Increasing competitive funding relative to statutory funding and revising performance evaluation criteria. The quantitative targets by 2015 are: • To increase science and technology spending to 1.7% of GDP • To increase investment in science to 1% of GDP

(*Continued*)

Table 9.3 (*Continued*)

Title	*Period covered*	*Main objectives*
Strategy for an Innovative and Efficient Economy–*Dynamic Poland 2020*	2013–20	• Adapting the financial and regulatory environment to the needs of innovation • Equipping the economy with adequate knowledge and human resources • To ensure the sustainable use of resources • Increasing the internationalization of the Polish economy Quantitative targets by 2020 are as follows: • Increasing outlays on R&D to 1.7% of GDP • Increasing resource productivity (GDP/DMC) to 0.5, raising the rank of the Global Competitiveness Report innovation index among EU countries to 15 • Raising the rank of the Summary Innovation Index (SII) among EU countries to "Innovation Followers"
National Foresight Programme – Poland 2020	2020	• Identification of development challenges that outline the potential paths of Poland's development vision up to 2020 as the basis for Poland's Long-Term Development Strategy • Adjustment of the principles of the Polish scientific policy to the EU requirements • Shaping scientific and innovation policy towards a knowledge economy
Intelligent Development Operational Programme 2014–2020	2014–2020	The main objective of the Programme is to support the innovativeness and competitiveness of the Polish economy by increasing private expenditure on research and development activities, in particular by means of: • Assistance to enterprises in R&D and innovation activities • Increasing interdisciplinarity and quality of scientific research by supporting research cooperation in the scope of scientific and scientific-industrial networks of national and international character, while also development of research and development personnel • Generating mechanisms of cooperation with foreign researchers by financing international programmes involving Polish research teams (e.g., Horizon 2020)

Source: Self-analysis based on OECD (2004, 2006, 2010, 2014).

- Working towards increased competitiveness and innovation through the implementation of sustainable development goals.

Unfortunately, the current level of openness of science in Poland is still relatively low and constitutes a limitation to the development of science (Gruszewska 2019).

Innovation policy has evolved with an increased research focus on competitiveness, as well as social and environmental challenges. This has resulted in strong links (between public and private actors) in intellectual property and incubation beyond the traditional links. Contemporary innovation strategy is based on collaboration, internationalization, and interdisciplinarity, thus enabling the exploitation of potential cross-sectoral synergies. Based on an analysis of the first formal innovation policy documents in Poland with the current ones (Table 9.2), it is worth noting that the objectives presented are not new. In fact, the biggest change over the years has been to increase the potential and scale of their implementation.

Poland's innovation policy was developed in short-term cross sections (Jasiński 2018):

- In the late 1980s and early 1990s, there was a relatively broad set of financial incentives as legal solutions for stimulating research and innovation activities, especially for small businesses.
- In 1991–1994, as part of the Balcerowicz Plan and the reliance on the role of the *invisible market force*, much of the existing stimuli were eliminated.
- In 1995–1999, some of the previous incentives for R&D and innovation activities were restored.
- Since 2000, the number of incentives has been reduced due to budgetary problems.
- In 2005, in connection with accession to the European Union, several important and new instruments were introduced, while some of the previous tax tools were restored.
- 2007–2013 and 2014–2020 were periods of implementing new instruments based largely on EU funds.

The ripple effect of Poland's innovation policy was caused by the lack of a long-term strategy for the development of science and technology for the period of systemic transformation. During this period, the policy was characterized by insufficient coordination of activities between government agencies, while also a relative decline in budgetary outlays on R&D. In addition, after 1990, the relatively strong centralization of policy (especially in the area of research funding) and greater emphasis on support for science rather than innovation per se had a negative impact. Added to this factor, there was insufficient support for applied research, a lack of a regional approach, and no policy for the technology transfer/diffusion of innovations (Jasiński 2018).

9.4 Institutional environment of innovation policy in Poland

The institutional environment contains political, economic, social, and legal structures and conditions that underlie business activities (Oxley 1999). It is an open, multi-level structure that is continuously undergoing restructuring, transformation, and diversification processes.

Institutions comprise formal rules, informal constraints, and their enforcement characteristics (North 1990). The choice of innovation policy (objectives, tools) is typically made in a complex process. The policy formulation process takes into account the results of parliamentary committee deliberations, the position of government and local government agencies, while also the interests of political parties. Public consultation and the voices of civil society are also essential. Ineffective institutions are believed to be the cause of economic failure in many countries. Economic development requires that the appropriate country-specific formal institutions are implemented. However, formal rules will only be effective if they are embedded appropriately in informal institutions. Informal institutions also influence the final shape of a given solution. Tradition, namely, the previous ways of solving similar issues and social attitudes (the propensity for risk-taking, openness to change, acceptance of difference, short- and long-term orientation) are all taken into account. There is no doubt that there may be influences that arise from pressure from interest groups seeking to increase their own benefits. Ultimately, the formal institutions implemented are the product of conflicts between the interests of different groups or communities. It is worth emphasizing the fact that any institutional change depends on the solutions that have been applied in the area to date. They are shaped by the so-called path dependence.

The broader scope of STI policy has resulted in STI policy matters being decentralized to different ministries and departments responsible for economic policy, employment, competitiveness, or global challenges (social and environmental issues). Innovation policy has become more complex and requires a holistic institutional approach.

In 1993, the State Committee for Scientific Research developed the assumptions of the state's scientific, science, and technology policy and defined the directions of state innovation policy. Today, responsibility for STI policy decisions lies with the relevant ministries and inter-ministerial teams. The Innovation Council was established in 2016 and since then has become the key inter-ministerial coordinator of innovation policy implemented by the Polish government. The current structure of the system responsible for research and innovation can be divided into three spheres that are responsible for the creation and coordination of innovation policy (Figure 9.5):

1. Political level (including government and local government institutions, international organizations);
2. Structure of organizations responsible for innovativeness in the country (divided into: subordinate ministries and units covered by R&D financing);
3. Network of R&D and innovation centres (Higher Education Institutions, Polish Academy of Sciences, research institutes, innovation incubators, and others).

The indicated levels form a network of institutions within the National Innovation System. Decentralization of the organization favours greater integration at the level of Regional Innovation Systems. It is worth emphasizing that the largest part of innovations (especially at the microeconomic level) is created through bottom-up

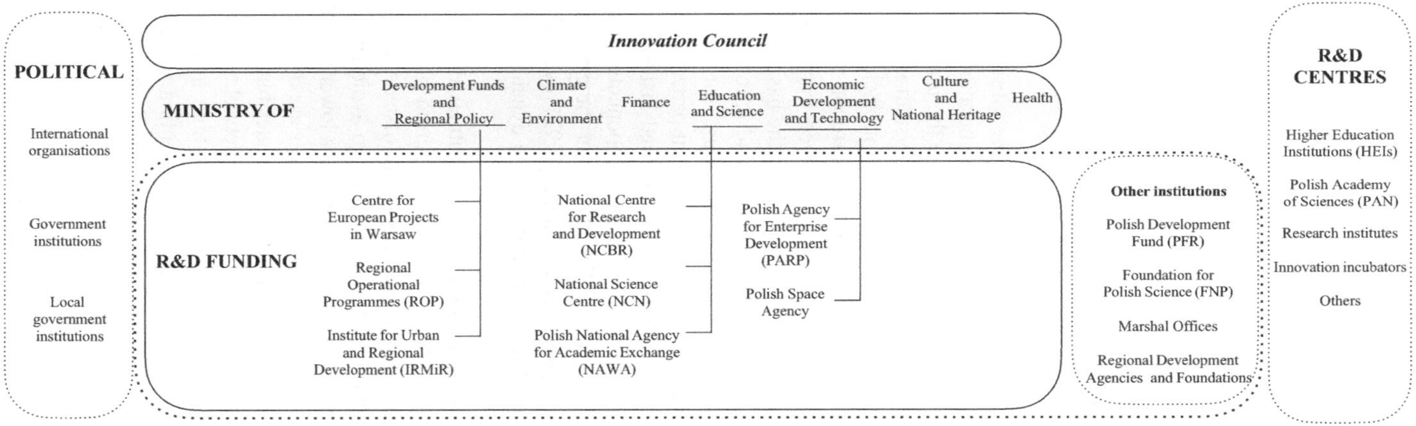

Figure 9.5 Key elements of the research and innovation system structure in Poland.

Note: Structure updated as at 30.07.2021.

The Innovation Council is composed of ministers responsible for the economic departments mostly related to innovation and a representative of the Chancellery of the Prime Minister. The ministries presented refer to members of the Inter-Ministerial Innovation Team which carries out the Council's tasks. At the time of its creation in 2016, the membership included the Undersecretary of State at the Ministry of Digitalization, but this ministry was abolished in 2020 (Zarządzenie, 2016, art. 3, ust. 1).

Source: Self-analysis

initiatives, hence building a network of relations with institutions in the region is a great advantage for individual enterprises and clusters.

Innovation systems are built on the quadruple-helix model, which is a form of collaboration in R&D between: research institutes, government, industry, and the public (Carayannis & Campbell 2009, 2012; Andrews & Entwistle 2010; Brink & Madsen 2016). The project RiConfigure reaffirmed that for QH collaborations to be successful, the processes of building a structure are key (Schroth et al. 2019). Furthermore, a more accurate depiction of the structure of the institutional environment of contemporary innovation policy is the Quintuple Helix. In the model, the process of knowledge circulation involves institutions pursuing sustainable development goals. This process contributes to the improvement of the country by providing instruments for creating innovation and solving socio-economic problems (Trzaska 2021).

Each element of the helix is equally important. However, it seems that too often the final element, namely, society, is overlooked in deliberations. This is largely due to the fact that it is much more difficult to measure the impact of social attitudes and their changes on policy. Every institutional system is based on family, ethnic, or religious connections. Institutional determinants include values formed into moral and ethical codes of conduct. Social attitudes are formed under the influence of social norms, traditions, and conventions derived from cultural heritage and are deeply rooted in the core of society. They form the basis on which formal institutions are established and reinforce the impact and enforcement of formal rules and regulations. Informal institutions such as culture, trust, social relations, norms, or values have a strong effect on the development patterns of countries, in which their role is enhanced in those states where formal institutions are poorly regulated. The inertia of the subsystem of informal components (informal institutions change very slowly) becomes a peculiar barrier for the effectiveness of the institutional system. For example, research by Shane (1993) revealed that increasing public R&D spending is insufficient to improve the dynamism of innovation when informal institutions are weak.

The set of formal and informal norms formed constitutes the so-called entrepreneurial culture. The system evolving over a long period of time can be presented according to G. Hofstede's cultural dimensions (Hofstede Insight 2022). For example, Poles are characterized by a high propensity to avoid risk, while also a significant power distance, a short-term orientation, and a lower rate of individualism than in highly developed countries. These differences are revealed not only in comparison with countries with the highest innovation rates but also with relation to countries with a similar level of development. A society characterized by high uncertainty avoidance, a short-term orientation, and a high level of distance to authority may face a number of difficulties in implementing regulatory changes in the economic sphere. The area of innovative activity is particularly sensitive to social acceptance. Studies on the influence of Hofstede variables on economic activity in many countries indicate that a high degree of individualism, a low power distance, a long-term orientation, and a low propensity to avoid uncertainty are desirable in terms of creating entrepreneurship and innovativeness. Strengthening cultural change in this direction in Poland would influence the formation of a positive entrepreneurial environment. The creation of a business-friendly environment is a crucial element in the pursuit of prosperity.

The changes in the value systems of Poles observed over the long term reveal an increase in expansiveness. Research indicates an increasing propensity for self-realization and concentration on one's own goals. There is a gradual shift away from conservative values towards rational and secular values. However, Poles are still more conservative than the inhabitants of highly developed countries. Rational and secular values are much less important than in highly developed countries. This hinders the expansion of companies into wider areas of activity and ties them to traditional, established paths of activity. This makes activities undertaken within the framework of innovation policy hit a difficult ground, namely, a traditional society that is resistant to change. Recent results of research on value systems (Inglehart-Welzel 2022) indicate that Poles are characterized by similar values to societies in Latin America (Uruguay) and Asia (Vietnam). This is associated with low trust in other members of society and uncertainty. An increase in the scale of acceptance of rational and secular values would mean greater individualism and independence in actions taken, as well as greater openness to change and new stimuli, while also a greater willingness to take risks. An increase in individualism as a socially acceptable trait (especially amongst entrepreneurs) renders it possible to accelerate economic growth even under conditions of weak formal institutions. The experience of many European countries indicates these processes.

The indicated features of Polish society are accompanied by a low level of trust. Many sociological studies show the so-called short "radius" of trust. Only one in five Poles (19%) believe that most people can be trusted, while the remaining 77% are of the opinion that one should be very cautious in relations with others. Such attitudes have persisted for more than 20 years, and over the past 12 years, the percentage of people trusting others has fallen by 7% pp (*Zaufanie*... 2022).

It is considered necessary to be very vigilant in order not to be cheated (73% of Poles) (Fazlagić 2016). Thus, social norms advocating suspicion and caution prevail. Rules that accept exploitation and cheating of others are widespread and recommend distrust, suspicion, while also caution. In the Polish language, distrust is more strongly expressed than attitudes based on openness and trust. The lack of trust hinders the creation of a favourable environment for the diffusion or exchange of information, while also the synergy of ideas for motivating employees. It therefore hinders innovation processes and productivity growth (Kaasa 2016). Recent research has found that social attitudes of uncertainty avoidance or risk aversion may not be the most important in terms of undertaking economic activity. Indeed, they may be constrained by the appropriate actions of the state or various institutions, e.g., through the means of insurance. It is pointed out that creativity and security are much more important in terms of enhancing entrepreneurship and innovativeness (Mickiewicz & Kaasa 2020).

The analysis of informal institutions also renders it possible to identify positive manifestations of the attitudes of Poles that indicate favourable prospects for change. Poles are open to change. More often than the citizens of other European countries, they express an expectation of institutional change. It seems that Poles are more likely to value openness than the citizens of other European countries. This is indicated by the results of Eurobarometer. Openness to change values comprise indexes of the desires of self-direction-making one's own decisions and views independently, as well as an openness or desire to acquire new experiences. New experiences are very important among the social values of Poles and are in second place in Europe in terms of such expectations (58% Poland, 47% Europe). However, worse results are recorded in other areas of openness. On average, 78% of EU respondents indicate placing a high degree of importance on the value of self-direction. In the case of the Poles, this amounts to only 69% (5th from last). A total of 73% of EU respondents consider it important to form their own opinions independently, while only 63% of Poles feel this way (7th from last) (*Values and…* 2021).

The characteristics of the informal institutions presented and the values behind their formation in Polish society indicate the constraints faced by innovators. On the one hand, the inefficiencies of innovation policy associated with the volatility of this policy and the tools used, as well as the modest funding schemes should be mentioned. On the other hand, high transaction costs of the introduced changes resulting from the "resistance" of traditional informal institutions are evident. The lack of compatibility between formal and informal institutions creates an environment that cannot be described as conducive to innovation (Godlewska 2021).

9.5 Conclusions

The policy landscape (see Figure 9.5) creates a broad set of STI policy instruments and actors involved in innovation policy development and implementation. Increased complexity creates the need to optimize the policy mix, as well as multi-level governance. The traditional "silo" approach underpinning STI policy development (thematic, vertical segmentation) has changed to the approach of "integrating" policies at different levels (regional, national, and international) and across disciplines. The search for greater efficiency is driving the change in innovation policy, which is succeeding through, among other things, new governance arrangements (public–private partnerships) and the consolidation of STI policy programmes (OECD 2014).

Due to the lack of a long-term strategy for the development of science and technology for the period of systemic transformation, Poland's innovation policy went through various stages of development. The period of policy centralization, the emphasis on the wrong areas of development (science rather than innovation per se), and the volatility of instruments to stimulate innovation have negatively affected the process of forming innovation policy in Poland. The result is the lack of autonomy in the innovation policy and the reliance of the current direction of development on EU funds.

Based on the analysis carried out, it may be concluded that the low level of innovativeness of the Polish economy is strongly linked to the institutional environment. Innovation policy has evolved in line with the development of socio-economic needs towards a holistic approach. However, the effectiveness of innovation policy is insufficient to increase the country's innovativeness. Poland's innovativeness is the result of a relatively low level of the main innovation pillars identified in the GII: SMEs introducing business process innovations, PCT patent applications, while also employment in innovative enterprises. From an institutional perspective, the reasons for the low level of innovativeness of the Polish economy include the following:

1 In terms of regulatory instruments – regulations not conducive to starting a business, regulatory environment, especially in the rule of law and cost of redundancy dismissal;
2 In terms of tools affecting business transactions – insufficient level of financing of R&D and pro-innovative activities (from private, as well as public funds), ease of paying taxes, volatility of the tax system;
3 In terms of informal institutions – low trust, high power distance, low acceptance of uncertainty, short-time orientation.

An increase in the innovativeness in Poland requires not only changes at the level of innovation policy, or an increase in the scale of R&D financing. Social attitudes must change. Societies with a high level of entrepreneurship and innovativeness are characterized by specific value systems including a high level of individualism, low power distance, acceptance of uncertainty, and long-term orientation. Openness to change and trust in others should also be mentioned.

The question is whether action can be taken to accelerate change in informal institutions? They would certainly have to include education in terms of entrepreneurship. It would be worthwhile for such programmes to be implemented from the first years of educating young people, who are potentially the future entrepreneurs and innovators. Additionally, it is also worth creating a positive image of the entrepreneur through the media.

Note

1 Institutions – systems of established and prevalent social rules that structure social interactions. There are two main groups of institutions: formal and informal. Formal institutions include the property rights system, laws and regulations. Informal institutions are defined as socially shared rules that are usually unwritten, which emerge evolutionarily and are transmitted and enforced outside official channels.

References

Andrews, R., and Entwistle, T. (2010). Does Cross-Sectoral Partnership Deliver? An Empirical Exploration of Public Service Effectiveness, Efficiency, and Equity. *Journal of Public Administration Research and Theory*, 20(3), 679–701. https://doi.org/10.1093/jopart/mup045.

Borrás, S., and Edquist, C. (2013). The Choice of Innovation Policy Instruments. *Technological Forecasting and Social Change*, 80(8), 1513–1522. https://doi.org/10.1016/j.techfore.2013.03.002.

Brink, T., and Madsen, S. O. (2016). The Triple Helix Frame for Small- and Medium-Sized Enterprises for Innovation and Development of Offshore Wind Energy. *Triple Helix*, 3(1), 4. https://doi.org/10.1186/s40604-016-0035-8.

Carayannis, E.G., and Campbell, D.F.J. (2009). 'Mode 3'and'Quadruple Helix': Toward a 21st Century Fractal Innovation Ecosystem. *International Journal of Technology Management*, 46(3/4), 201–234. https://doi.org/10.1504/IJTM.2009.023374.

Carayannis, E.G., and Campbell, D.F.J. (2012). *Mode 3 Knowledge Production in Quadruple Helix Innovation Systems. 21st-Century Democracy, Innovation, and Entrepreneurship for Development*, New York: Springer. https://doi.org/10.1007/978-1-4614-2062-0.

Ciborowski, R. (2012). *Region jako źródło wiedzy i innowacji.* In R. I. Dziemianowicz, A. Kargol-Wasiluk, J. Wilkin, & M. Zalesko (Eds.), *Między Ekonomią a Historią. Studia Oferowane Profesorowi Czesławowi Noniewiczowi z okazji 75 urodzin* (pp. 464–476). Białystok: Wydawnictwo Uniwersytetu w Białymstoku. Retrieved from http://hdl.handle.net/11320/13068.

Ciborowski, R. (2016). *Międzynarodowy transfer technologii a innowacyjność krajów Europy Środkowo-Wschodniej*. Białystok: PTE.

Committee for Scientific Research. (1993). *Założenia polityki naukowej i naukowo-technicznej państwa. Cele, priorytety, finansowanie* [Assumptions Regarding the State Science Policy and Technology Policy in Poland]. Dokument rządowy przyjęty przez Radę Ministrów na posiedzeniu w dniu 20 lipca 1993 r. Warszawa.

Committee for Scientific Research. (1994). *Założenia polityki proinnowacyjnej państwa* [Assumptions of State Pro-Innovation Policy]. Dokument rządowy przyjęty przez Radę Ministrów 22 listopada 1994 roku. Warszawa.

Committee for Scientific Research. (1999). *Założenia polityki innowacyjnej państwa do 2002 roku* [State Innovation Policy Assumptions to 2002]. Dokument rządowy przyjęty przez Radę Ministrów 6 grudnia 1999 roku. Warszawa.

Cornell University, INSEAD, and WIPO. (2013). *The Global Innovation Index 2013: The Local Dynamics of Innovation.* Geneva, Ithaca, and Fontainebleau.

Cornell University, INSEAD, and WIPO. (2014). *The Global Innovation Index 2014: The Human Factor in Innovation, second printing*. Fontainebleau, Ithaca, and Geneva.

Cornell University, INSEAD, and WIPO. (2015). *The Global Innovation Index 2015: Effective Innovation Policies for Development*. Fontainebleau, Ithaca, and Geneva.

Cornell University, INSEAD, and WIPO. (2016). *The Global Innovation Index 2016: Winning with Global Innovation*. Ithaca, Fontainebleau, and Geneva.

Cornell University, INSEAD, and WIPO. (2017). *The Global Innovation Index 2017: Innovation Feeding the World.* Ithaca, Fontainebleau, and Geneva.

Cornell University, INSEAD, and WIPO. (2018). *The Global Innovation Index 2018: Energizing the World with Innovation.* Ithaca, Fontainebleau, and Geneva.

Cornell University, INSEAD, and WIPO. (2019). *The Global Innovation Index 2019: Creating Healthy Lives—The Future of Medical Innovation.* Ithaca, Fontainebleau, and Geneva.

Cornell University, INSEAD, and WIPO. (2020). *The Global Innovation Index 2020: Who Will Finance Innovation?* Ithaca, Fontainebleau, and Geneva.

Dodgson, M., and Rothwell, R. (1994). *The Handbook of Industrial Innovation.* Aldershot; Brookfield, VT: E. Elgar.

Edquist, C. (2001). Innovation Policy – A Systemic Approach. In B. Å. Lundvall & D. Archibugi (Eds.), *Major Socio-Economic Trends and European Innovation Policy* (pp. 219–238). Oxford: Oxford University Press.

EIS interactive tool. (2021). *European Innovation Scoreboard.* Retrieved from https://ec.europa.eu/research-and-innovation/en/statistics/performance-indicators/european-innovation-scoreboard/eis.

Fazlagić, J. (2016). Przez brak zaufania przedsiębiorców polska gospodarka traci 280 mld zł rocznie. *Forbes*. Retrieved from https://www.forbes.pl/opinie/przez-brak-zaufania-przedsiebiorcow-polska-gospodarka-traci-280-mld-zl-rocznie/rm1s09g.

Freeman, C. (1987). *Technology Policy and Economic Performance*. London: Pinter.

Freeman, C. (2002). Continental, National and Sub-National Innovation Systems—Complementarity and Economic Growth. *Research Policy*, 31 (2), 191–211. https://doi.org/10.1016/S0048-7333(01)00136-6.

Godlewska, M. (2021). The Impact of Interplay between Formal and Informal Institutions on Innovation Performance: Evidence from CEECs. *Inzinerine Ekonomika-Engineering Economics*, 32(1), 15–26. https://doi.org/10.5755/j01.ee.32.1.27390.

Gruszewska, E. (2019). Open Science. Reality or Fiction. In P. Chomik, H. Kościuch, & J. Żochowska (Eds.), *Konferencja jubileuszowa z okazji 50-lecia Biblioteki Uniwersyteckiej im. Jerzego Giedroycia "Biblioteki Podlasia i Polski północno-wschodniej. Prze szłość – teraźniejszość – przyszłość", 15–16 listopada 2018 r.* (pp. 183–198). Białystok: Wydawnictwo Uniwersytetu w Białymstoku.

Hadjimanolis, A., and Dickson, K. (2001). Development of National Innovation Policy in Small Developing Countries: The Case of Cyprus. *Research Policy*, 30(5), 805–817.

Hofstede Insights. (2022). *Compare Countries*. Retrieved from https://www.hofstede-insights.com/product/compare-countries/.

Jasiński, A. H. (2018). Innovation Policy in the Transformation Process: Was it Effective? *Optimum. Economic Studies*, 3(93), 221–239. https://doi.org/10.15290/oes.2018.03.93.18.

Kaasa, A. (2016). Social Capital, Institutional Quality and Productivity: Evidence from European Regions. *Economics and Sociology*, 9(4), 11–26. https://doi.org/10.14254/2071-789X.2016/9-4/1.

Lundvall, B. Å. (Ed.) (1992). *National Systems of Innovation: Towards a Theory of Innovation and Interactive Learning*. London: Pinter.

Lundvall, B. Å., and Borrás, S. (2005). Science, Technology, and Innovation Policy. In J. Fagerberg, D. C. Mowery, & R. R. Nelson (Eds.), *The Oxford Handbook of Innovation* (pp. 599–631) Oxford: Oxford University Press. https://doi.org/10.1093/oxfordhb/9780199286805.003.0022.

Mickiewicz, T., and Kaasa, A. (2020). Creativity and Security as a Cultural Recipe for Entrepreneurship. *Journal of Institutional Economics*, 18(1), 119–137. https://doi.org/10.1017/S1744137420000533.

Nelson, R. R. (Ed.) (1993). *National Innovation Systems: A Comparative Analysis*. Oxford: Oxford University Press.

NIK. (1999). *Informacja o wynikach kontroli realizacji Harmonogramu działań implementacyjnych Narodowej Strategii Integracji* [Information on the Results of the Audit of the Implementation Schedule of the National Integration Strategy]. Department of Economy and European Integration, Warsaw.

North, D. C. (1990). *Institutions, Institutional Change and Economic Performance*. New York: Cambridge University Press.

OECD. (1998). *Science, Technology and Industry Outlook 1998*. Paris: OECD Publishing. https://doi.org/10.1787/sti_outlook-1998-en.

OECD. (2004). *OECD Science, Technology and Industry Outlook 2004*. Paris: OECD Publishing. https://doi.org/10.1787/sti_outlook-2004-en.

OECD. (2006). *OECD Science, Technology and Industry Outlook 2006*. Paris: OECD Publishing. https://doi.org/10.1787/sti_outlook-2006-en.

OECD. (2010). *OECD Science, Technology and Industry Outlook 2010*. Paris: OECD Publishing. https://prima.uwb.edu.pl:2060/10.1787/sti_outlook-2010-en.

OECD. (2014). *OECD Science, Technology and Industry Outlook 2014*. OECD Publishing, Paris, https://doi.org/10.1787/sti_outlook-2014-en.

Oxley, J. E. (1999). Institutional Environment and the Mechanisms of Governance: The Impact of Intellectual Property Protection on the Structure of Inter-Firm Alliances. *Journal of Economic Behavior & Organization*, 38(3), 283–309. https://doi.org/10.1016/S0167-2681(99)00011-6.

Pro-Growth Action Plan 2003–2004: Entrepreneurship-Development-Work II. (2003). *Przegląd Rządowy*, 7, 87–114.

Rothwell, R., and Zegveld, W. (1982). *Industrial Innovation and Public Policy: Preparing for the 1980s and the 1990s*. London: Printer.

Schroth, F., Häußermann, J., Ruhrmann, H., Kaiser, S., Nielsen, R., and Degnbol, D. (2019). *RiConfigure D1.1: Analytical Framework. v4.0.0*. Retrieved from http://riconfigure.eu/wp-content/uploads/2019/10/D01.1_Analytical-Framework_v3.0.3-1.pdf.

Shane, S. (1993). Cultural Influences on National Rates on Innovation. *Journal of Business Venturing*, 8(1), 59–73. https://doi.org/10.1016/0883-9026(93)90011-S.

Stanisławski, R. (2011). Założenia polityki innowacyjnej państwa. *Zeszyty Naukowe Uniwersytetu Szczecińskiego. Ekonomiczne Problemy Usług*, 654 (70), 13–35. Retrieved from http://www.wzieu.pl/zn/654/ZN_654.pdf.

Stoner, J. A. F., Freeman, R. E., and Gilbert, D. R., Jr. (1997). *Kierowanie*. Warszawa: PWE.

The First Action Plan for Innovation in Europe, COM (1995) 589. Retrieved from https://eur-lex.europa.eu/legal-content/EN/TXT/PDF/?uri=CELEX:51996DC0589&from=nl.

The Inglehart-Welzel World Cultural Map – World Values Survey 7 (2022). Retrieved from http://www.worldvaluessurvey.org/.

Trzaska, K. (2021). Instytucje szkolnictwa wyższego jako instrument walki z kryzysem (perspektywa Unii Europejskiej). *UR Journal of Humanities and Social Sciences*, 4(21), 82–99. https://doi.org/10.15584/johass.2021.4.6.

Values and Identities of EU citizens. (2021). Special Eurobarometer 504, European Union. Retrieved from https://europa.eu/eurobarometer/api/deliverable/download/file?deliverableId=78557.

Weresa, M. (2014). *Polityka innowacyjna*. Warszawa: Wydawnictwo Naukowe PWN.

WIPO. (2021a). *Global Innovation Index 2021: Poland*. Geneva: World Intellectual Property Organization. Retrieved from https://www.wipo.int/edocs/pubdocs/en/wipo_pub_gii_2021/pl.pdf.

WIPO. (2021b). *Global Innovation Index 2021: Tracking Innovation through the COVID-19 Crisis*. Geneva: World Intellectual Property Organization. https://doi.org/10.34667/tind.44315. Retrieved from https://tind.wipo.int/record/44315.

Zarządzenie nr 4 Prezesa Rady Ministrów z dnia 18 stycznia 2016 r. w sprawie utworzenia Rady do spraw Innowacyjności (M.P. 2016 poz. 63). Retrieved from https://isap.sejm.gov.pl/isap.nsf/DocDetails.xsp?id=WMP20160000063.

Zaufanie społeczne. (2022). Komunikat z badań CBOS (37). Warszawa: Fundacja CBOS. Retrieved from https://www.cbos.pl/SPISKOM.POL/2022/K_037_22.PDF.

Part IV

Sectoral case studies

10 Intangible investment and governance quality in the new and old member states of the European Union[1]

Črt Kostevc and Tjaša Redek

10.1 Introduction

(Public) Governance as a process encompasses the processes, the nature/characteristics of systems, while also structures through which public decisions are made and implemented. In the context of the state or in the context of public governance, this refers to how the exercise of political power is done, while also the processes of policy formulation, decision-making, as well as the processes of the implementation and enforcement of policies and laws (Kaufmann, Kraay, and Mastruzzi 2010; The World Bank 1992). The quality of governance is evaluated by looking at elements such as political stability, voice and accountability, government effectiveness, regulatory quality, the rule of law, and control of corruption (Kaufmann, Kraay, and Mastruzzi 2010; Kaufmann and Kraay 2020). Subject-related literature has also long recognized the importance of the quality of governance. The World Development Report (1997) in particular stressed the importance of good governance for development and examined various aspects of governance, including public sector management, accountability, and institutional quality.

The concept of governance is also closely related to the concept of institutions, although the two are not the same. Institutions in general are defined as all rules and norms that guide our behaviour, or in the words of North (1991, 112), "*Institutions are the humanly devised constraints that structure political, economic and social interaction*". When discussing public institutions, the concept of institutional quality or the quality of public institutions is a bit narrower and closer to public governance and refers to the efficiency, transparency, accountability, and integrity of the various institutions within a country's public sector (Kaufmann, Kraay, and Mastruzzi 2010; Kaufmann and Kraay 2020; The World Bank 1997). Public institutions can include government ministries, agencies, regulatory bodies, law enforcement, judiciary, public service organizations, and others (Pratt 2006; The World Bank 1997). The quality of public institutions is measured by factors such as the rule of law, bureaucratic effectiveness, and absence of corruption (Kaufmann and Kraay 2020), as well as elements such as public financial management, and service delivery (World Bank 2020). The quality of institutions has also long been recognized as one of the key factors of the long-term development performance of countries

DOI: 10.4324/9781003425717-14

(Acemoglu and Johnson 2005) that impacts the long-term development, as well as the behaviour and investments of private companies (Blejer and Khan 1984).

Institutional/governance quality is important both for the developed and in particular developing countries (Acemoglu and Robinson 2008; Aysan, NABLI, and Veganzones 2007; Barrios and Schaechter 2008), with both the size of the government and quality of governance being important (Su Dinh and Bui 2017). Institutional and governance quality affects economic growth and development in the long term by affecting the size, structure, and dynamics of different investments by impacting company behaviour, while also the behaviour of individuals, efficiency of markets, nature and structure of trade, and other developmental perspectives (Acemoglu 2010; Barro 1996; Dawson 1998; Kafouros and Aliyev 2016; Xi 2017).

The recent literature on productivity growth in particular focuses on the role of knowledge capital or intangible capital for growth and development. Corrado, Hulten, and Sichel (2006) proposed the currently prevailing classification of intangible capital consisting of three main types: computerized information, innovative property, while also economic competencies. Each of these types is further subdivided into specific subcategories. Computerized information is categorized into software and databases, while innovative property is divided into five subcategories, covering areas such as research and development (R&D) and design. Economic competencies are classified into subcategories including brand equity, company-specific human capital, and organizational structure. Knowledge capital is a very closely related category, which is defined by the OECD (OECD 2013). Intangible capital has been shown to significantly contribute to company/sectoral and aggregate performance. The studies, either those examining just the contribution of selected categories or those investigating the contribution of all combined categories, have been unanimous in confirming the relationship (Carol Corrado, Hulten, and Sichel 2009; Fukao et al. 2009; Piekkola 2018; Piekkola et al. 2011, 2021; Roth 2022b, 2022a; van Ark et al. 2009).

While analysis of the impact of the intangible capital on growth and the impact of governance or institutions on growth have been widely discussed, the relationship between intangible investment and governance or institutional quality still largely remains insufficiently analysed (e.g. Roth 2022b).

This chapter focuses on the relationship between the governance quality and private sector investment in intangible assets in new EU member states in comparison to old EU members. In this context, governance quality is investigated as an outside element that could contribute to the differences between countries. The analysis relies on two separate data sources: the EU Klems data on intangible capital and Worldwide Governance Indicators that focus on the period between 2000 and 2018.

Following the introduction, we first present the literature on the relationship between governance, institutions, and intangible capital. Secondly, the data and methodology are presented, followed by the results. This chapter concludes with a summary of the main findings and challenges for future analysis.

10.2 Institutions, governance, intangible investments, and growth in economic literature

10.2.1 Institutions, governance, and economic growth

According to Douglas North (1991, 112), "institutions are the rules of the game" or "*humanly devised constraints that structure political, economic and social interaction*". The interactions in question also refer to the structure, dynamics, and nature of all investments. Governance at the level of the "public sector" is, as previously mentioned, closely related to the problem of institutions, therefore, our discussion is ongoing, which aims to show the link between economic performance and institutions and will also rely on the link between institutions and growth. Knowing that growth is closely linked to investments, this literature review will also provide a link to investments.

Acemoglu et al. (2005) divide institutions between economic and political institutions. Economic institutions stimulate economic growth and development, while political institutions create more or less efficient constraints according to Acemoglu et al. (2005):

> Economic institutions determine the incentives of and the constraints on economic actors, and shape economic outcomes. (…) Political institutions allocate de jure political power, while groups with greater economic might typically possess greater de facto political power. (…) Economic institutions encouraging economic growth emerge when political institutions allocate power to groups with interests in broad-based property rights enforcement, when they create effective constraints on power-holders, and when there are relatively few rents to be captured by power-holders.
>
> (Acemoglu, Johnson, and Robinson 2005, 387)

Since Adam Smith announced his Wealth of Nations (Smith 1776), the central question in economics has been why some countries are developed and rich and others lag behind. Acemoglu (2010) argues that there are two groups of factors that can be related to long-term economic performance, or in other words, there are two types of growth causes, (1) proximate, which are human and physical capital and technology, while also (2) fundamental. The first group, the proximate causes, in their opinion are only proximate because they immediately lead to the next question, namely, why some countries have more human, physical capital, and better technology. Acemoglu (2010) claims that institutions are in fact a fundamental cause of growth, apart from geographical and cultural factors, as well as luck. This theory is also well supported in subject-related literature empirically. Different authors examine different aspects of institutions and growth, while also confirm a significant and strong relationship between different institutions (components of institutions) and economic performance at a national level. While Smith already recognized the importance of institutions (in 1776, as well as older theories, for example mercantilist) and the state for economic performance, the institutional tradition became strong with North in the 1990s and the literature widely supports the statement of Acemoglu (2010). Among others, for example, the idea of the impact of institutions and institutional change on economic performance had already been discussed extensively by North (1990), while a number of other studies also did so by focusing on very different aspects or transmission channels of institutions on economic performance at an aggregate or company level (Acemoglu, Johnson, and Robinson 2005; Ahlers and Nellis 2016; Aralica, Svilokos, and Bacic 2018; Barro 1996; Borghi, Del Bo, and Florio 2016; Breton 2004; Dawson 1998; del Pilar Baquero Forero, Ida, and Kuroda 2015; Diwan, Keefer, and Schiffbauer 2018; Driffield, Mickiewicz, and Temouri 2014; Foss and Garzarelli 2007; Giannetti 2003; Holland 2001; Knack and Keefer 1995; Mauro 1995; Rizov 2008; Shapiro and Nugent 2012; D. T. Wang et al. 2013).

Abundant sources of literature link governance or institutional quality to economic performance, investment, and firm productivity and performance, among them most notably, Acemoglu et al. (2010), who refer to institutions as the fundamental cause of growth or development differences in the world. The literature has provided numerous investigations of the relationship between the institutions, governance, growth, and investment (Acemoglu 2010; Acemoglu, Johnson, and Robinson 2005; Dawson 1998; Hall and Ahmad 2014; North 1987; Rizov 2008; Smith 1776; Spruk and Kovac 2018; Xi 2017; Zhang 2010). First of all, the quality of institutions has been widely linked to economic growth, productivity growth, and investment and has been referred to as one of the fundamental causes of cross-country differences in terms of performance or GDP, impacting the levels of investment, the structure of investment, foreign direct investment (FDI), labour markets, company efficiency, corruption, and others (Bergeaud, Cette, and Lecat 2018; Khanna and Sharma 2018; Młynarzewska-Borowiec 2018; Tons and Serrasqueiro 2020; Xi 2017), which also includes the EU economies (Rodríguez-Pose and Ganau 2022). The subject-related literature often focuses on the nature of property rights and their impact on investments, as well as on innovation and investments in knowledge or intangible capital, where improved governance positively impacts the investment and innovation and consequently contributes to economic growth (Kukharskyy 2020; Martins 2018; Papageorgiadis, Wang, and Magkonis 2019; Piekkola et al. 2011; Spulber 2015).

The legal system, its nature, and efficiency have also been shown to be statistically significant for growth with a robust positive impact on economic growth through similar channels as the aforesaid, stimulating investment, innovation, as well as employment, in particular related to employment laws and labour market rigidity (Rodríguez-Pose and Ganau 2022; Roth 2022b, 2022a; Schwartz 2013). Strongly protected property rights also stimulate FDI and increase the intensity of cross-national cooperation (Kukharskyy 2020), while patent enforcement, for example, positively impacts the number of patent and trademark applications (Papageorgiadis, Wang, and Magkonis 2019). Private property has long been recognized as the key driver of company efficiency, where in particular former transition economies have been lagging, in which privatization has been one of the core factors of the transformation process (Estrin et al. 2009; Ghulam 2017; Sgard 2001; Tichá 2012; Vukšić 2016; Yilmaz and Koyuncu 2018). Likewise, the development of the financial markets, which also relies on legal aspects and other institutional aspects is a significant matter. As stressed in Redek et al. (2019), according to (Heil 2017) (1) financial development positively affects productivity; (2) financial frictions can mitigate the positive effects; and (3) the productivity costs of financial frictions are generally small in financially developed economies, yet are considerably larger in developing economies. Other institutional factors matter as well.

It is also important to clearly note at this point that institutional quality, characteristics of (formal) institutions, and quality of governance are closely related to the state and its institutional structure in the broadest sense. Therefore, the discussion of the quality of governance and the impact of this governance on the intangible capital accumulation should consider general governance quality, but also consider that general governance quality is in fact a reflection of the (intangible) investments in the public sector as well.

10.2.2 Intangible capital and growth

Intangible capital encompasses three primary categories of factors that can enhance productivity growth: (1) computerized information, which includes computer software and computerized databases; (2) innovative capital, comprising primarily research and development (R&D) but also other innovative expenditures; and (3) economic competencies, encompassing brand equity, company-specific human capital, while also organizational structure. This concept was defined by Corrado, Hulten, and Sichel (2006) and has since been extensively studied in relation to both company and aggregate performance.

In terms of investment, estimates suggest that certain countries allocate a similar proportion of their investment to intangible capital as they do to tangible assets (e.g., the US). In other countries, the share of intangible investment in GDP ranges from approximately 5% to 13%, varying by country and year (Carol Corrado, Hulten, and Sichel 2009; "CoInvest Project" 2012; Fukao et al. 2009; Innodrive 2008; van Ark et al. 2009). On average, between 2000 and 2013, intangible investment accounted for 9.2% of GDP in the EU14 (Jona-Lasinio and Meliciani 2018).

Early estimations regarding the impact of intangible capital on overall productivity growth indicate that intangible assets contributed up to one-third of the total growth. For instance, in the US, between 1995 and 2006, total labour productivity growth was 2.96%, with intangibles contributing 0.83 percentage points of this growth. Similar significant contributions were observed in other countries, ranging from approximately one-quarter to one-third of total labour productivity growth (Corrado, Hulten, and Sichel 2009; Fukao et al. 2009; van Ark et al. 2009). Recent estimates by Jona-Lasinio and Meliciani (2018) indicate that intangibles accounted for 14% to 30% of the total factor of productivity growth between 2000 and 2013, with Denmark at 14% and the Netherlands at 30%, while slightly higher percentages were noted in Spain, Finland, and the UK (e.g. 33%). The authors argue that the overall decline in labour productivity growth primarily resulted from a slowdown in total factor productivity (TFP), rather than tangible and intangible capital.

Piekkola (2011) summarized the key findings from the Innodrive study, which examined the impact of intangibles on European performance. First, when intangibles are considered as investments rather than costs, GDP experiences a 5.5% increase. Albeit there are significant differences among European countries studied between 1995 and 2006/2008, convergence is observed. High-income countries with a relatively lower share of intangible capital have been increasing their investments, thus indicating a move towards a knowledge economy and convergence. The authors also identified a link between FDI and the growth of intangible capital, particularly in terms of increased research and development (R&D) and organizational capital. This supports the notion that FDI has a positive impact on company performance. Jona-Lasinio and Meliciani (2018) also found a significant and positive relationship between participation in global value chains (GVC) and intangible capital. This relationship is attributed to the specialization in productive activities, technology transfer, knowledge spill-over, and competition.

Roth and Thum (2013) discovered a robust and positive relationship between intangible investment and labour productivity growth. They also found that intangibles explain a substantial portion of the unexplained variance in labour productivity growth, with the unexplained variance decreasing by up to 51%. This relationship was stronger between 1995 and 2000 compared to the period between 2000 and 2005. During the economic crisis, Corrado et al. (2018) observed that intangible investments were relatively resilient, while tangible investment experienced a decline. Furthermore, intangible investment recovered relatively quickly.

Empirical research indicates that all components of intangible capital are positively related to productivity growth. However, the contribution and size of investments in each component depend on the structure and development of the economy. Innovative property and economic competencies represent the largest shares of intangible capital. For example, in Japan, investments in innovative property alone accounted for 6% of GDP between 2000 and 2005, reaching 11% in the manufacturing sector. Similarly high investments in innovative property were recorded in Canada (5%) and the US (5.5%) (Miyagawa 2010). Innovative property contributes significantly to total productivity growth in many countries. In Germany, for instance, between 1995 and 2006, innovative property contributed 0.23 percentage points out of the total 0.38 percentage points contributed by intangibles to labour productivity growth, thus accounting for approximately 60%. In Austria, the Czech Republic, Slovakia, and Denmark, the contribution was around half of the total contribution of intangibles, reflecting the relatively prominent role of manufacturing (van Ark et al. 2009).

The investment and contribution of economic competencies to labour productivity growth are also significant in certain economies, depending on their structure and development. For example, according to van Ark et al. (2009), in 2006, intangible investment in economic competencies accounted for 5.5% and 5.8% of GDP in the UK and the US, respectively. In France, Germany, Italy, and Spain, the percentage ranged between 1.9% and 3.3%, significantly lower than in the UK and the US. The contribution of competencies to labour productivity growth varied as well, accounting for approximately half of the total contribution of intangibles in the UK (total labour productivity growth was estimated at 3.06%, while intangibles contributed 0.69 and competencies 0.36 percentage points).

Due to the clear importance of intangible capital for economic growth, it is important to understand whether investment in intangible capital also depends on institutional quality or governance quality as one of the conditions. If so, then lags in institutional improvements, or even possible (relative or absolute) deterioration can spur changes in long-term development patterns.

10.3 Governance and intangible investment in the EU

10.3.1 Research goals, data, and methodology

In continuing these deliberations, this chapter therefore addresses the following research questions: (1) What are the general characteristics of governance in the EU economies where we are particularly interested in the differences between the old and new EU members? (2) What are the characteristics of intangible capital in the private sector in the European Union? and (3) Is intangible investment in the private sector related to governance quality?

The analysis relies on two data sources: (1) EU Klems data (Adarov and Stehrer 2019; The Vienna Institute for International Economic Studies 2019; Vienna Institute for International Economic Studies 2019) and (2) Worldwide governance indicators (Kaufmann and Kraay, 2020). **EUKlems** dataset provides an abundance of variables that present economic growth in detail, while also productivity, employment, tangible and intangible capital formation with data on the components, as well as on the contributions to growth and the role of technological change at the industry level (NACE level 1 and level 2 in some cases) for all European Union member states, but also for Japan, and the US between 1995 and 2017. The data provides the details on the standard variables needed for growth accounting, which are value added, inputs of capital and labour, but from the perspective of this analysis, it is more important that the database also provides detailed insight into the intangible and tangible investment. Tangible investments and capital comprise the following categories: Computing equipment, Communications equipment, Computer software and databases, Transport equipment, Other machinery and equipment, Total non-residential investment, Residential structures, Cultivated assets, Research and development and Other IPP assets. Intangible investments and capital data in the database comprise the following categories: Intangible Software and databases capital services, Advertising, market research and branding, Design and other product developments, Purchased organizational capital, Vocational training, and Own-account organizational capital.

Worldwide governance indicators (Kaufmann and Kraay 2020) provide data on institutional quality, for which we investigate the link to investments in intangible capital in the private sector. Data for governance quality is provided for more than 200 countries between 1996 and 2019. This chapter only focuses on the period between 1996 and 2017, as EU Klems was not available at the time of the analysis after 2017. The indicators in the World governance quality analysis are based on over 30 different data sources, among which are different institutes, responses and data from companies, international organization, and others. Governance quality is a multidimensional construct that measures the following (Kaufmann and Kraay 2020): Voice and Accountability, Political Stability and Absence of Violence, Government Effectiveness, Regulatory Quality, Rule of Law, and Control of Corruption.

10.3.2 Results

10.3.2.1 Stylized facts on governance quality in the European Union

To investigate the differences in the governance/institutional quality between different countries in the EU, the WGI indicators are used. They provide an evaluation of regulatory quality by availing of six different criteria (Table 10.1), where for each category different estimates are provided: from the value of the indicator to ranks, standard deviations, etc. (for details, consult (Kaufmann and Kraay 2020)). In order to present the differences in the quality of institutional environment for each of the investigated categories, as well as the overall mean rank, we calculated a simple average of the individual ranks. Table 10.1 presents the details.

Governance quality in the EU27 significantly differs (Table 10.1) between countries, with new member countries on average ranked below the EU27 average. Among the investigated EU countries (UK is still included), Finland ranked highest with an overall mean percentile rank of 96.5. Finland has the highest rank among the investigated countries in four out of six subcategories. Luxemburg ranked among the top two in only one category, albeit, it was consistently very high and above 93 in all subcategories, which led the country to take second place in the overall mean ranking. Sweden was third with two categories among the top two, while the Netherlands was fourth. Even high-ranking countries had on average the lowest scores in political stability and the absence of violence category. Interestingly, France was even in the bottom two among all of the investigated countries in this category.

The new members of the EU were on average in the bottom half of the ranking, with the exception of Malta which was above average, together with Estonia. The average percentile rank of all investigated countries was 80.8 and most of the countries which were below the average were new member states of the EU. In the bottom part of the panel were also Greece, Italy, and Spain, which are old members of the EU. A more detailed look at the subcategories reveals that apart from Greece, which was at the bottom of all of the EU economies and performed among the worst two in five out of six indicators (Political Stability Absence of Violence, Government Effectiveness, Regulatory Quality, Rule of Law, Control of Corruption), Bulgaria was also a country with four indicators ranking it among the lowest in the EU (Voice and Accountability, Government Effectiveness, Rule of Law, Control of Corruption).

Table 10.1 Governance quality in 2017 in selected countries (EU, Japan, US)

	Percentile rank						
	*Overall rank *(mean rank)*	*Voice and accountability*	*Political stability, absence of violence*	*Government effectiveness*	*Regulatory quality*	*Rule of law*	*Control of corruption*
FI	96.5	97.5	87.6	98.1	96.6	100.0	99.0
LU	95.2	97.0	95.2	93.8	93.8	95.2	96.2
SE	95.1	99.5	81.9	96.2	95.7	99.0	98.1
NL	94.5	99.0	80.5	96.6	98.6	97.1	95.2
DK	92.8	96.6	76.2	95.7	92.3	97.6	98.6
AT	91.7	93.6	86.7	91.8	90.9	96.2	90.9
DE	89.4	95.6	65.7	94.2	95.2	91.3	94.2
IE	89.2	90.6	85.2	87.0	91.8	88.9	91.3
UK	87.4	93.1	59.0	90.4	94.2	92.8	94.7
MT	85.3	87.2	93.8	80.8	88.0	85.1	76.9
PT	85.0	88.7	89.5	87.5	79.3	84.1	80.8
EE	84.7	89.7	69.0	82.7	93.3	86.5	87.0
BE	84.3	94.6	62.4	85.1	86.5	87.5	89.9
FR	81.7	85.7	55.7	88.0	83.7	89.4	87.5
Average	80.8	83.7	71.5	83.4	84.4	82.5	79.5
CZ	80.4	77.3	83.3	81.3	86.1	83.7	70.7
SI	79.3	80.3	76.7	84.6	72.1	82.7	79.3
CY	78.0	83.3	65.2	79.8	81.3	79.8	78.4
LT	77.6	78.3	72.9	80.3	83.2	80.8	70.2
ES	74.8	81.3	56.2	81.7	79.8	81.3	68.3
LV	74.7	73.9	62.9	78.8	82.7	80.3	69.7
SK	73.6	75.9	80.0	75.0	76.4	71.6	62.5
PL	72.4	72.9	64.3	74.0	78.8	68.3	76.0
IT	68.1	82.8	57.1	69.7	75.0	62.5	61.5
HU	67.6	58.1	74.8	70.2	73.1	70.2	59.1
HR	66.6	64.0	70.0	72.1	68.8	63.5	61.1
BG	59.5	58.6	59.5	63.5	72.6	51.9	51.0
EL	58.6	70.9	41.9	66.3	63.0	56.7	52.9

* *Mean rank was calculated by the authors as a simple average of all sub-rankings. Sub-rankings are original data.*

Note: Dark grey – top 2 with the highest ranking in a category, light grey – bottom 2 with the lowest ranking in a category (ranking among 214 countries).

Source: Kaufmann and Kraay (2020).

Figure 10.1 depicts the mean rank of a country in 1996 and 2017 among all the investigated economies of the world in WGI, as well as the change in the percentile rank between 1996 and 2017. A negative value signifies decline in the global positioning. The data reveals that there is quite a lot of stability in terms of global positioning of countries according to the calculated mean rank, mainly among the old members of the EU. The more significant differences only appeared among

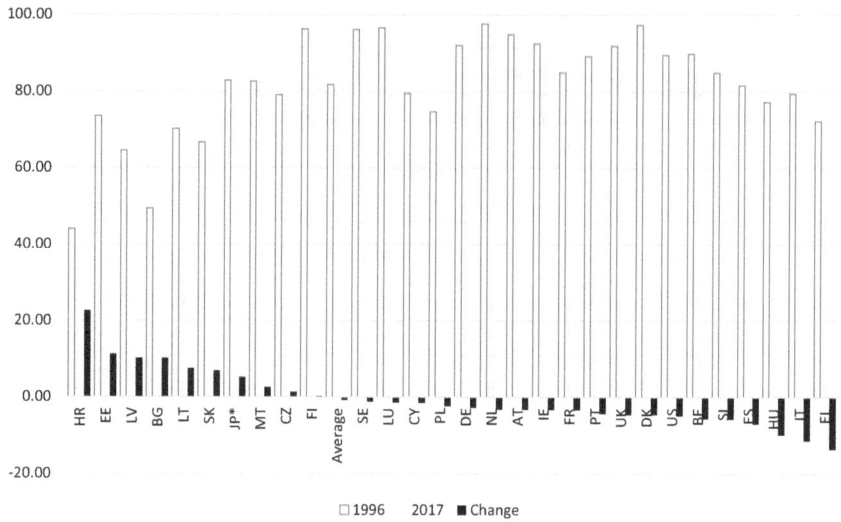

Figure 10.1 Governance quality in 1996 and 2017 in selected countries (EU, Japan, US): mean rank.

Data: (Kaufmann and Kraay 2020).

*Mean rank was calculated as a simple average of all sub-rankings. Japan and US are not part of the EU, thus the data is provided for comparison.

former transition economies. Bulgaria, Croatia (HR), Latvia, Lithuania and Slovakia significantly improved their mean rank, while most notably Croatia, where the change in percentile rank was from 44 to 66 in the investigated period. Yet, the situation has not improved in all transition countries. In Hungary, it deteriorated quite a bit, namely, by 10 percentiles, which was the most among the transition countries. Interestingly, Slovenia was also one of these countries where relative governance quality significantly declined. Among the new members, Poland and Cyprus also recorded very modest declines. Albeit, on average, modest deterioration was found primarily among the old members of the EU. But there were few exceptions where the governance quality decreased more significantly. The deterioration was particularly pronounced in Greece and in Italy.

Overall, the data shows that governance quality varies significantly across the EU (Table 10.1, Figure 10.1). While on average governance quality in the EU is better than global figures, significant differences exist. Generally, Scandinavian economies had the best governance, followed by a number of EU15 members, while the new members were mostly below the average. On average, countries also scored better in terms of the rule of law (among those selected that are presented in Figure 10.2) than on government effectiveness and in particular in regulatory quality. On average, however, the governance quality estimates were lower in terms of the Political Stability and Absence of Violence and Control of Corruption. On average, as in the first three indicators, the governance quality estimates were a bit lower with regard to the new members and the Mediterranean countries.

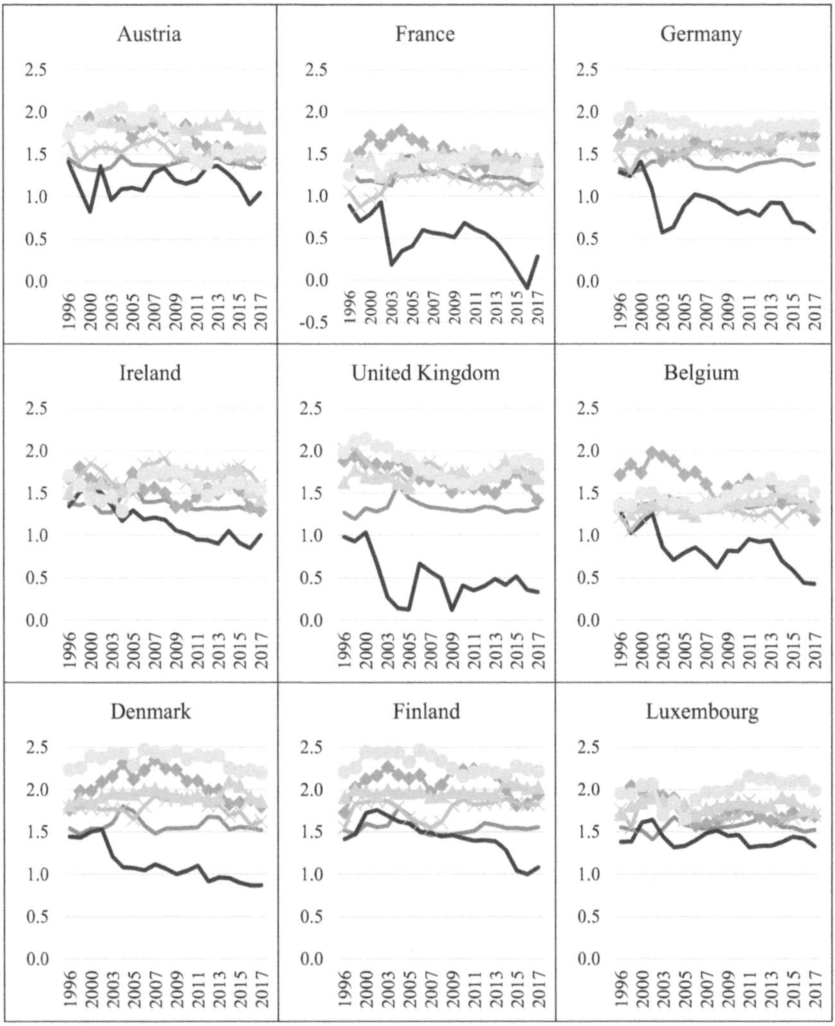

Figure 10.2 Governance quality estimates in European economies (EU28, including UK) between 1996 and 2017.

Data: Online interactive Worldwide governance indicators (Kaufmann and Kraay 2020), own estimates.

A closer look at the indicators and their development by mean rank reveals further interesting observations. Countries are grouped into four groups for the purpose of this analysis as follows: the "old" EU, divided into "central" (Germany, Austria, France, Ireland, UK), old "northern" EU members (Belgium[2], Denmark, Finland, Luxemburg, Netherlands, Sweden), the Mediterranean group (Cyprus, Greece, Italy, Malta, Portugal, Spain), and the Eastern EU consisting of predominantly new members (Bulgaria, Croatia, Czechia, Estonia, Hungary, Latvia, Lithuania, Poland, Romania, Slovakia, Slovenia).

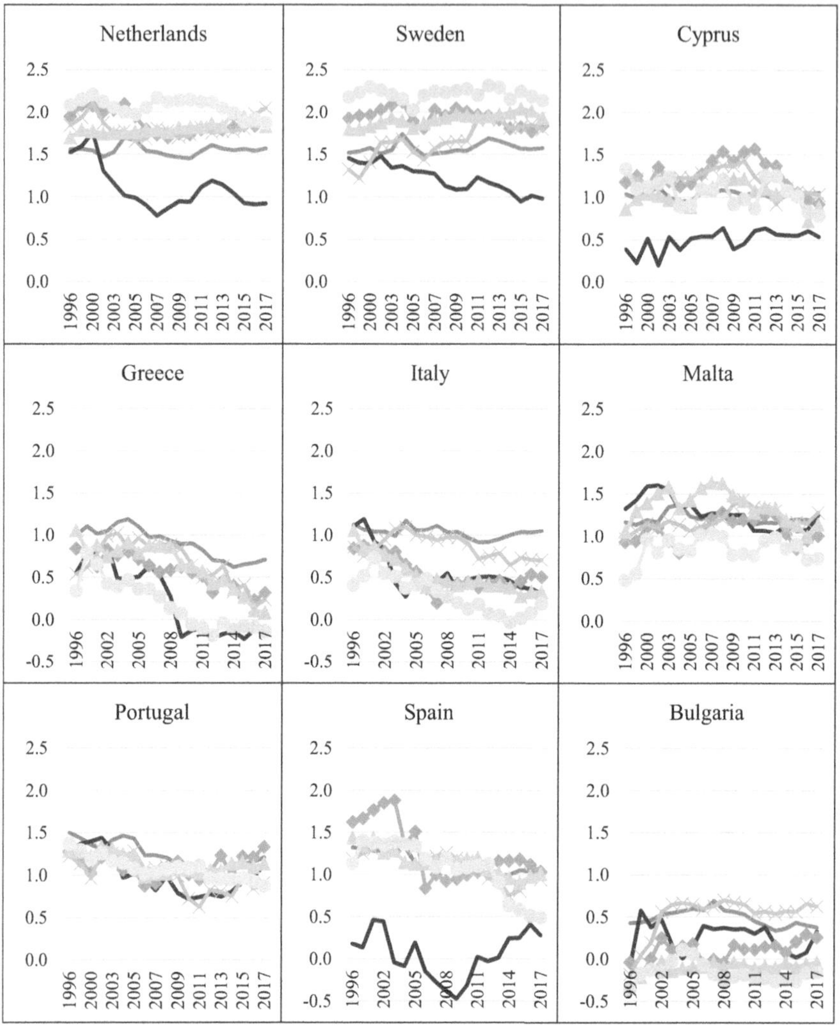

Figure 10.2 Continued

When considering changes in rankings and estimated values of indicators, the transition countries displayed the most significant improvement despite their overall positioning in 2017, which was still below the EU average. This progress may be attributed to the gradual completion of transition reforms, the pre-accession period to the European Union, while also the impact of EU membership. Interestingly, some countries demonstrated improvements across all indicators, e.g. Latvia, Lithuania, and Croatia. Poland and Portugal also made significant progress in all but one indicator. On the other hand, the Mediterranean countries experienced the most pronounced decline in regulatory quality. Spain, Greece, Italy, and

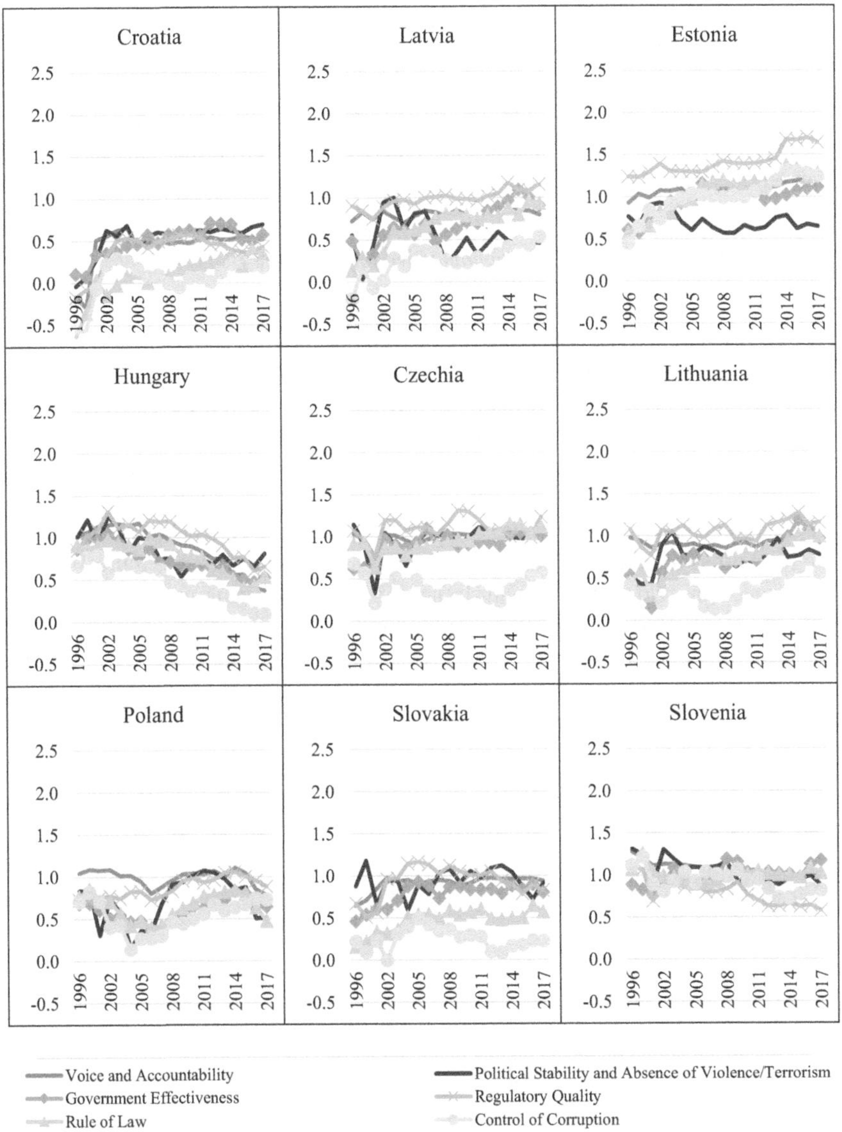

Figure 10.2 Continued

Hungary all displayed declines across all indicators, potentially influenced by the profound impact of the financial and economic crisis that struck the Mediterranean region much more than the rest of the EU comparatively speaking. The two new members shown in Figure 10.2 maintained a higher level of stability, although Malta experienced a notable decline in the control of corruption. Among the transition countries, Hungary experienced a striking downward trend, while Latvia,

Lithuania, Estonia, and Croatia showcased improvements. Other countries within this group remained relatively stable or lacked a clear directional change. The old EU15 members (upper two panels), excluding those from the Mediterranean, generally exhibited relatively stable situations, with Political Stability and Absence of Violence being the only indicator that experienced deterioration and consistently ranked the poorest.

10.3.3 The characteristics of intangible investments in the EU

The intensity of intangible investment and capital accumulation varies significantly among EU countries, as was found by a number of studies (Corrado et al. 2013; Corrado, Haskel, and Jona-Lasinio 2016; Corrado et al. 2018; Roth 2020; van Ark et al. 2009). To investigate the nature of intangible capital in the EU, the EU Klems database was used. In order to calculate intangible capital, the real data on R&D, other IPP, design, purchased organizational capital, vocational training, while also own organizational capital, advertising, market research and branding, and software and databases (2010 priced) were all used. Share is calculated as the share of the total gross fixed capital formation. As EU Klems data shows (Figure 10.3), the differences are wide-ranging, with Ireland, Sweden, UK among the countries that on average invested the most in intangible capital between 1996 and 2017. The data for three transitional countries (Bulgaria, Croatia, and Malta) was not available.

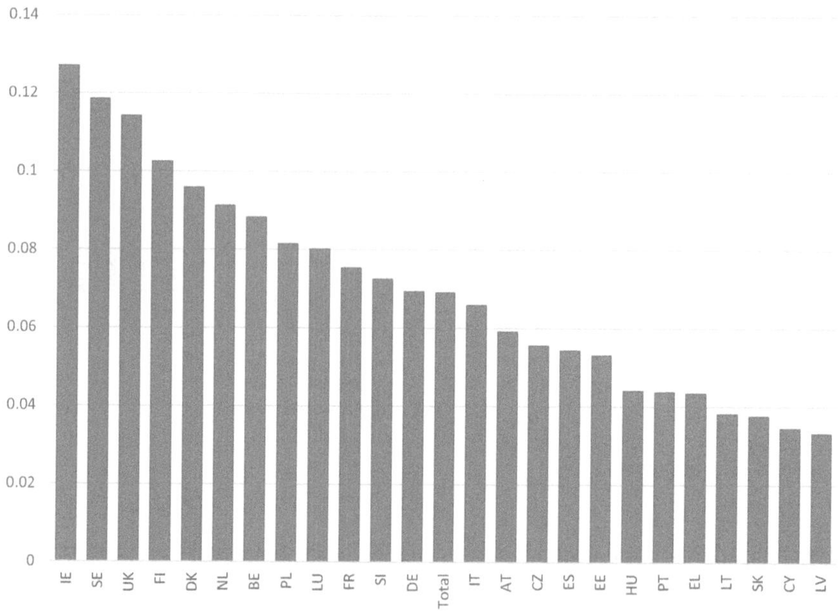

Figure 10.3 Average share of intangible capital in gross fixed capital formation in the period 1996–2017, in %.

Data: (The Vienna Institute for International Economic Studies 2019).

Among the investigated economies in the period of 1996–2017, with the exception of Slovenia and Poland, other transition economies were below the average. Of course, the intangible capital and tangible capital structure also depend on industry structure, as well as investment cycles (here the impact of the crisis is also important). However, new members of the EU generally invested less in intangibles.

Countries, regardless of development and industrial structure, invested most on average in R&D in the investigated period, so total R&D capital reached even 7.2% of gross fixed formation in Sweden and around 5% in Finland. Among the new members (where data was available), Slovenia invested most in R&D, accumulating a total of 2.3% of R&D capital in total gross fixed capital formation, followed by Czechia with 1.8%. Design capital was most important in Luxemburg with 3.6% of gross fixed capital formation, whereas software and databases were most important in Sweden, while interestingly, vocational training reached the highest levels in the Netherlands and Hungary (Table 10.2).

Table 10.2 Average share of intangible capital by category in gross fixed capital formation in the period 1996–2017

	R&D	*Other IPP*	*Design*	*Purchased organizational capital*	*Vocational training*	*Own organizational capital*	*Advertising, market research and branding*	*Software and databases*
AT	3.0%	0.1%	0.8%	0.6%	0.1%	.	0.5%	1.1%
BE	3.7%	0.2%	1.7%	2.4%	0.2%	.	0.6%	0.7%
CY	0.7%	.	0.5%	1.3%	0.2%	0.3%	0.5%	0.4%
CZ	1.8%	0.3%	1.8%	0.4%	0.1%	0.3%	0.7%	0.6%
DE	3.9%	0.2%	1.1%	0.6%	0.1%	0.2%	0.3%	0.6%
DK	5.6%	0.6%	1.7%	0.5%	0.2%	.	0.4%	1.2%
EE	1.0%	0.1%	1.4%	0.9%	0.3%	0.7%	0.6%	0.4%
EL	0.8%	0.8%	1.1%	1.2%	0.0%	.	0.4%	0.4%
ES	2.0%	0.3%	1.4%	0.3%	0.2%	0.3%	0.6%	1.2%
FI	5.2%	0.3%	1.9%	1.2%	0.3%	0.3%	0.8%	0.8%
FR	3.6%	0.1%	1.4%	1.0%	0.4%	.	0.3%	1.8%
HU	1.3%	0.2%	1.0%	0.9%	0.5%	0.6%	0.3%	0.6%
IE	4.8%	0.2%	2.0%	1.2%	0.4%	0.5%	2.2%	0.4%
IT	1.8%	0.2%	2.5%	0.8%	0.1%	.	0.6%	1.3%
LT	0.4%	0.7%	0.6%	0.5%	0.1%	0.7%	0.4%	0.4%
LU	1.7%	0.1%	3.6%	0.6%	0.4%	.	1.1%	0.9%
LV	0.5%	0.3%	1.0%	0.4%	0.0%	0.6%	0.7%	0.2%
NL	3.5%	0.4%	0.7%	2.0%	0.5%	0.5%	0.7%	1.8%
PL	1.2%	0.3%	1.5%	1.4%	0.4%	0.9%	2.1%	0.7%
PT	1.3%	0.1%	1.2%	0.9%	0.1%	.	0.7%	0.4%
SE	7.2%	0.1%	2.0%	1.2%	0.4%	.	0.4%	2.1%
SI	2.3%	0.6%	2.1%	1.0%	0.2%	0.4%	0.7%	0.6%
SK	0.9%	0.3%	0.9%	0.6%	0.1%	0.2%	0.4%	0.5%
UK	2.0%	1.eah6%	2.1%	1.7%	1.1%	1.6%	0.8%	1.8%

Source: The Vienna Institute for International Economic Studies (2019).

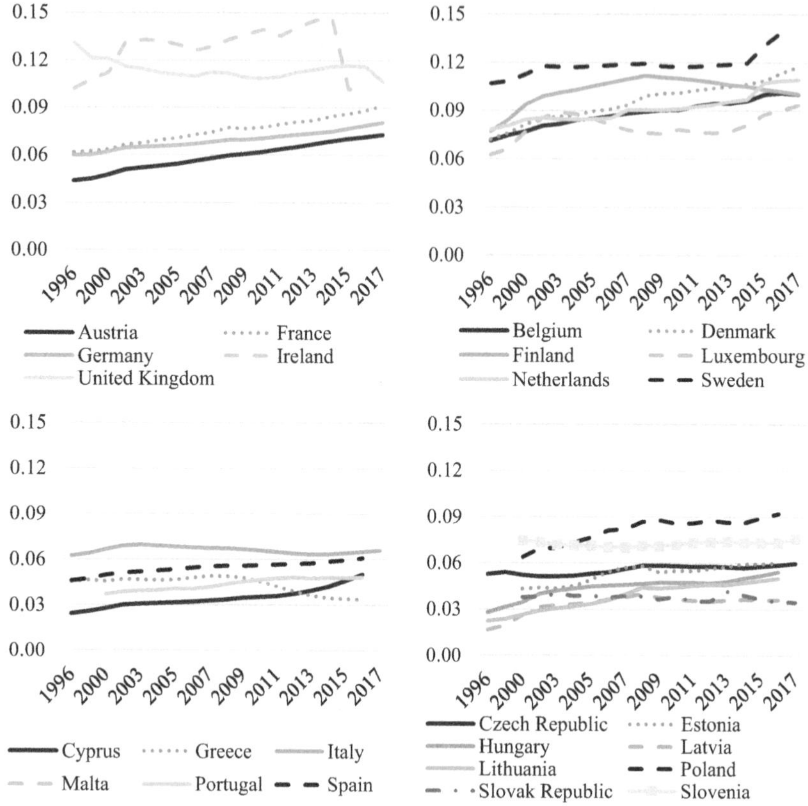

Figure 10.4 The share of intangible capital by category in gross fixed capital formation in the period 1996–2017.

* Scale on axis y runs from 0-0.15 (i.e.15%) in all charts.

Data: Own calculations using data by The Vienna Institute for International Economic Studies (2019).

Figure 10.4 depicts the dynamics of intangible capital in the analysed economies between 1996 and 2017. Overall, intangible capital grew systematically in the majority of countries, despite significant variations in some countries. In some countries, the impact of the 2009 crisis is more pronounced, especially in Lithuania, as well as in Finland, where the investments have been strongly influenced by the Nokia example as well. The new EU member states have on average recorded an increase, but Slovenia and also Slovakia have observed the most volatile pattern.

The differences between countries in terms of the intensity of intangible investments are significant, as is evident from the data (Figure 3.4) both in terms of intangible investments as the share of gross fixed capital formation, as well as in governance quality. The data also shows that on average, old EU members (EU15) were above average, while the majority of new members had a lower share than

5%. The question is whether there is also a relationship between governance quality and intangible investment.

10.3.4 Governance quality and intangible investments

So far, subject-related literature has not provided direct evidence of the link between intangible investments and governance quality. Figure 10.5 shows that there is an evident link between the total share of intangible capital in the total gross fixed capital formation (calculated based on EU Klems database) if related to the measures of governance quality of the WGI dataset. The relationship is most evident between the share of intangible capital and the control of corruption, the rule of law and government effectiveness. These factors are part of the quality of the institutional environment that matters most according to subject-related literature (Everhart, Vazquez, and McNab 2009; Rodrik, Subramanian, and Trebbi 2004; Roth 2022a, 2022b; Sala-i-Martin 2002).

A closer look at intangible investments and indicators of governance quality (Figure 10.6) reveals that intangible investments (as the share of total capital) is

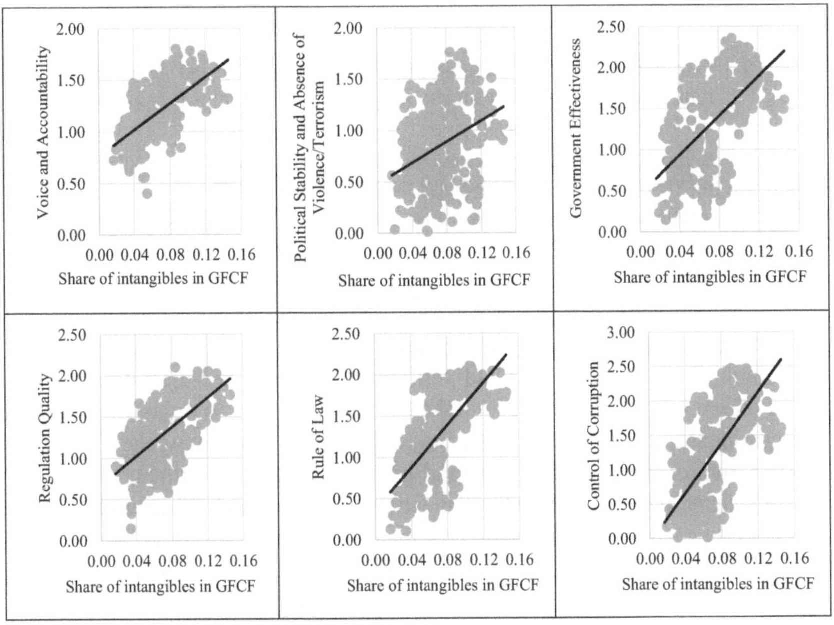

Figure 10.5 Governance quality estimates and intangible investments in European economies (EU27) between 1996 and 2017.

* Causality not implied by positioning on axes, only the relationship is depicted. Romania not included due to the lack of data on intangibles.

Data: Online interactive Worldwide governance indicators (Kaufmann and Kraay 2020) and Globalinto country and (The Vienna Institute for International Economic Studies 2019), own estimates.

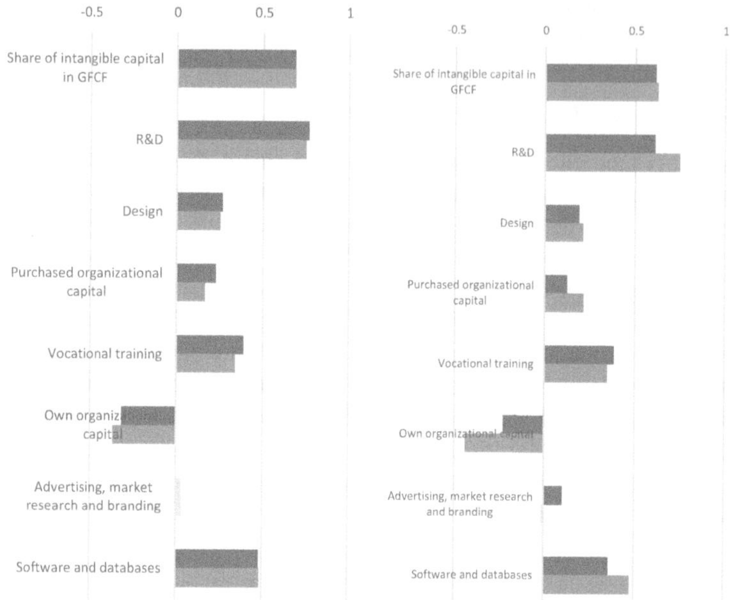

Figure 10.6 Correlation coefficients between governance quality and governance quality rank and intangible investment in European economies (EU27, without UK) between 1996 and 2017.

Data: Online interactive Worldwide governance indicators (Kaufmann and Kraay 2020) and Globalinto country and (The Vienna Institute for International Economic Studies 2019)

* The Pearson coefficients that were not significant, namely, at least p=0.05, are displayed with light grey shade.

in most cases also statistically significantly correlated to governance indicators. The relationships are strongest and significant primarily for the total intangible capital (share of total intangibles in GFCF), R&D, purchased organizational capital, vocational training, and software and databases. Interestingly, the relationship between own organizational capital and governance quality estimates is negative and significant, while purchased organizational capital is in a positive relationship with governance quality. This indicates that these two types could be substitutes and that in a more uncertain environment, companies are more inclined to invest their own resources instead of seeking external support.

To further confirm the importance of regulatory quality for economic performance, two sets of regression analyses were conducted. The first evaluates the impact of governance quality in a standard growth setting for economic performance, while the second links intangible investments to investment determinants, primarily change in GDP dynamics and tangible capital, as well as governance quality.

The impact of governance quality on aggregate performance is evaluated in a standard production function setting with $Q = f\left(K_{\text{tangible}}, L, K_{\text{itangible}}, \text{Governance quality}\right)$, where K is capital (tangible and intangible), L is labour and Governance quality represents different layers of institutional quality. The empirical function that was evaluated is the following:

$$lnY_{it} = b_0 + b_L lnL_{it} + b_K lnK_{it} + b_{INT} lnK_{INTit} + b_{Gov} lnG_{it} + + lne_{it} \quad (1)$$

where a double logarithmic form is used, and Y represents aggregate value added, L represents the number of employees, K represents standard capital, K_{INT} represents intangible capital and G refers to a measure of governance quality in a specific year (t) and country (i). Panel data estimation was used, while fixed effects were availed of to control country-specific effects (Hausman test significant at p=.000). The estimates include 26 out of 27 EU27 (2020) economies (Romania not included due to the lack of data) in the period between 1996 and 2017. Table 10.3 summarizes the descriptive statistics.

Table 10.4 depicts the regression results. The results show that regulatory quality has a statistically significant impact on economic performance, regardless of whether the rank as the aggregate measure is used or if particular subcomponents

Table 10.3 Descriptive statistics

	Mean	*p50*	*p25*	*p75*	*SD*	*N*
Value added	1798092	276074	39682	1577412	4705316	1798092
Number of employees	6679	3356	1175	7135	8995	6679
Intangible capital	427993	71489	8957	432304	1013264	427993
Tangible capital	7340822	995195	117810	5317803	21600000	7340822
Governance (overall rank)	83.54	82.08	75.64	93.41	10.01	83.54
Control of corruption	1.18	1.16	0.45	1.85	0.74	1.18
Rule of law	1.24	1.19	0.84	1.78	0.52	1.24
Regulatory quality	1.27	1.23	0.98	1.62	0.38	1.27
Government effectiveness	1.27	1.19	0.84	1.73	0.54	1.27
Political stability absence of violence	0.86	0.91	0.59	1.11	0.41	0.86
Voice and accountability	1.21	1.16	1.00	1.45	0.27	1.21

Source: Online interactive Worldwide governance indicators (Kaufmann and Kraay 2020) and (The Vienna Institute for International Economic Studies 2019).

of governance quality are used as a measure of regulatory quality. The rule of law had the strongest partial impact, followed by voice and accountability and the absence of corruption. With regard to other explanatory variables, the coefficients display the expected positive impact and are statistically significant.

To further examine the importance of regulatory quality, the possible impact on intangible investment was also estimated. The investment in theory depends on a number of different factors, from economic, to financial as well as other institutional ones. Due to the nature of data, a simplified model is used, where investment in intangible capital is assessed as a function of the change in GDP (value added) and investment in tangible capital (because intangible and tangible capital are related, e.g. Marčič and Redek 2022), as well as the variables of governance quality. The following model is empirically evaluated using panel data estimation, while also fixed effects with country and time controls:

$$lnINV\_INT_{it} = b_0 + b_{GDP} lndGDP_{it} + b_K lnINV\_TANG_{it} + b_{Gov} lnG_{it} + + lne_{it} \quad (2)$$

where INV_INT represents intangible investments, GDP is summarized by aggregate value added, INV_Tang are tangible investments, and G is a measure of governance quality in a specific year (t) and country (i).

If the determinants of intangible investments are studied (panel, random effects), the results again show that regulatory quality elements are important and all are significant, but not all types are equally important (as was also indicated before with a simple analysis). The rule of law, regulatory quality, and government efficiency have the most impact. As expected, intangible investments also have a strong and significant impact on economic performance (Table 10.4). Table 10.5 shows that the intangible investments calculated as the change in the level of intangible capital on the one hand significantly depend on economic dynamics, while governance quality indicators also matter, particularly in terms of the rule of law and political stability.

The empirical analysis shows that the regulatory quality as measured by the Worldwide governance indicators differs significantly across the EU countries and that in general, former transition economies lag behind in terms of the governance quality indicators, where these countries are in fact in the lower half of the distribution in the EU, albeit, the Mediterranean countries also lag behind the other more developed EU countries. This is in line with a number of transition studies, stressing the problems of corruption, lack of regulatory change, while also political problems (Beca and Barabaş 2016; Domadenik, Koman, and Prasnikar 2018; Iwasaki, Mizobata, and Muravyev 2018; Mahran 2022; H. Wang et al. 2019). The regression estimates also confirm the relationship between the intangible investments and economic performance, which is in line with the findings of a number of papers, focusing on the key contribution of intangible capital (Fukao et al. 2009; Piekkola et al. 2021; Roth 2022b, 2022a; van Ark et al. 2009). In addition, the results are also in line with the findings of Roth (2022b), who links the rule of law with intangible investments.

Table 10.4 Regression results (value added as dependent variable)

Value added	*Reg1*	*Reg2*	*Reg3*	*Reg4*	*Reg5*	*Reg6*	*Reg7*
	b/se	*b/se*	*b/se*	*b/se*	*b/se*	*b/se*	*b/se*
Ln(number of employees)	0.308***	0.301***	0.378***	0.269***	0.417***	0.310***	0.297***
	0.054	0.056	0.054	0.056	0.056	0.057	0.057
Ln(intangible capital)	0.470***	0.493***	0.415***	0.475***	0.473***	0.498***	0.499***
	0.027	0.027	0.028	0.027	0.027	0.028	0.028
Ln(tangible capital)	0.053	0.008	0.052	0.032	0.002	0.003	0
	0.043	0.043	0.042	0.043	0.041	0.044	0.044
Governance rank	0.008***						
	0.001						
Control of corruption		0.091***					
		0.02					
Rule of law			0.197***				
			0.024				
Regulatory quality				0.135***			
				0.023			
Government efficiency					0.136***		
					0.018		
Political Stab., Abs. of violence						0.040**	
						0.015	

(*Continued*)

Table 10.4 (Continued)

Value added	*Reg1*	*Reg2*	*Reg3*	*Reg4*	*Reg5*	*Reg6*	*Reg7*
	b/se	*b/se*	*b/se*	*b/se*	*b/se*	*b/se*	*b/se*
Voice and accountability							0.107**
							0.035
_cons	3.560***	4.518***	4.007***	4.577***	3.825***	4.532***	4.572***
	0.449	0.434	0.418	0.424	0.433	0.449	0.442
N							
r2_w	418	418	418	418	418	418	418
r2_b	0.84	0.827	0.845	0.834	0.841	0.821	0.823
r2_o	0.958	0.955	0.94	0.964	0.937	0.96	0.959
sigma_e	0.956	0.953	0.938	0.962	0.935	0.958	0.957
sigma_u	0.061	0.064	0.06	0.062	0.061	0.065	0.064
rho	0.663	0.705	0.726	0.715	0.692	0.697	0.708

** significance at the 0.01 level, *** significance at the 0.001 level.

Source: Online interactive Worldwide governance indicators (Kaufmann and Kraay 2020) and (The Vienna Institute for International Economic Studies 2019), own estimates.

Table 10.5 Regression results (intangible investment as dependent variable)*

Intangible investment	*Reg1*	*Reg2*	*Reg3*	*Reg4*	*Reg5*	*Reg6*	*Reg7*
	b/se	*b/se*	*b/se*	*b/se*	*b/se*	*b/se*	*b/se*
Ln(Change in value added)	0.63740*** 0.04915	0.62612*** 0.04956	0.62362*** 0.04949	0.64228*** 0.04898	0.62725*** 0.04973	0.65656*** 0.05088	0.63391*** 0.05029
Ln(Tangible investment)	0.39124*** 0.04839	0.40245*** 0.04852	0.40153*** 0.04857	0.38982*** 0.04873	0.40130*** 0.04861	0.37784*** 0.04911	0.39347*** 0.04882
Governance rank	0.01737** 0.00631						
Control of corruption		0.24507** 0.08468					
Rule of law			0.32550** 0.11879				
Regulatory quality				0.24186 0.15907			
Government efficiency					0.30050** 0.11319		
Political Stab., Abs. of Violence						0.34262* 0.14513	
Voice and accountability							0.40044 0.2379

(*Continued*)

Table 10.5 (Continued)

Intangible investment	*Reg1*	*Reg2*	*Reg3*	*Reg4*	*Reg5*	*Reg6*	*Reg7*
_cons	–5.55050***	–4.35538***	–4.42771***	–4.44853***	–4.44564***	–4.49869***	–4.55363***
	0.63872	0.3925	0.39273	0.42354	0.40435	0.43427	0.46807
N							
r2_w	322	322	322	322	322	322	322
r2_b	0.14725	0.1499	0.14607	0.13613	0.14767	0.15879	0.14167
r2_o	0.98048	0.98067	0.98094	0.97935	0.98032	0.97531	0.97827
sigma_e	0.85428	0.85467	0.85424	0.85111	0.85393	0.85163	0.85172
sigma_u	0.80195	0.80153	0.80191	0.79425	0.802	0.79765	0.79974
rho	0.18495	0.19034	0.1811	0.16748	0.19228	0.21283	0.20163

Source: Online interactive Worldwide governance indicators (Kaufmann and Kraay 2020) and (The Vienna Institute for International Economic Studies 2019), own estimates.

*The Random effects model was used, while the Hausman test was insignificant (p=0.233).
** significance at the 0.01 level, *** significance at the 0.001 level.

10.4 Conclusions

The connection between intangible capital and productivity has been extensively explored in subject-related literature. However, the examination of the relationship between intangibles and governance quality has received limited attention. This research aims to initiate the discussion on the connection between governance and intangible investments more broadly.

The existing subject-related literature has so far insufficiently investigated the relationship between intangible investments and governance or institutional quality, apart from certain partial analyses that primarily focus on innovation and human capital. While the institutional literature covers a wide range of development topics, the exploration of the relationship between intangibles and governance or institutions, specifically regarding public sector intangibles, remains inadequately explored.

The analysis, which is based on Worldwide governance indicators (Kaufmann and Kraay 2020) and EU Klems data, reveals that there is a significant link between the variables in question and those in terms of governance indicators, particularly with regard to the control of corruption, the rule of law and regulatory quality. Apart from identifying large cross-country differences, the paper stresses that there are statistically significant links between the variables, which require further exploration.

In the future, the subject-related literature should focus more on the quality of the institutional environment and the nature of the intangible investment in the public sector. First, the components of intangible capital within the public sector have a direct influence on its own efficiency. For instance, the adoption of information technology enables quicker and more efficient operations, thereby suggesting a relationship between intangible investments and governance indicators that serve as proxies for the "productivity of the public sector or administration". Indirectly, public intangibles also have an impact on the performance of the private sector by facilitating faster and improved services. Administrative procedures and bureaucratic hurdles are frequently identified as major obstacles to business operations (World Bank 2020). Enhancing the quality of the business environment in general can be achieved by means of the development of public sector intangible capital. Furthermore, the intangible capital of the public sector can directly benefit the private sector by providing tailored services that address specific needs. This, in turn, may lower the transaction costs for businesses.

Notes

1 This analysis partially relies on the work done within the Globalinto project, which was financed by the European Union's Horizon 2020. The mechanisms to promote smart, sustainable and inclusive growth under grant agreement No. 822259. The work is also financed by the following projects: P5-0096, P5-0128, J5-4575 financed by the Slovenian Research and Innovation Agency and Ministry of Digital Transformation.

2 The Benelux countries were grouped together.

References

Acemoglu, D. (2010). Growth and Institutions. In S.N. Durlauf and L.E. Blume (Eds.) *Economic Growth* (pp. 107–115). The New Palgrave Economics Collection. London: Palgrave Macmillan UK. https://doi.org/10.1057/9780230280823_16.

Acemoglu, D., and S. Johnson. (2005). Unbundling Institutions. *Journal of Political Economy,* 113(5), 949–995. https://doi.org/10.1086/432166.

Acemoglu, D., S. Johnson, and J.A. Robinson. (2005). Institutions as a Fundamental Cause of Long-Run Growth. In Ph. Aghion, and S.N. Durlauf (Eds.) *Handbook of Economic Growth* (pp. 385–472). North Holland: Elsevier. https://doi.org/10.1016/S1574-0684(05)01006-3.

Acemoglu, D., and J. Robinson. (2008). *The Role of Institutions in Growth and Development.* Working Paper. Washington, DC: World Bank. https://openknowledge.worldbank.org/handle/10986/28045.

Adarov, A., and R. Stehrer. (2019). *Tangible and Intangible Assets in the Growth Performance of the EU, Japan and the US (Publication).* WIIW Research Report No. 442. Vienna Institute for International Economic Studies (wiiw). https://wiiw.ac.at/p-5058.html.

Ahlers, T., and J. Nellis. (2016). Building Effective Institutions—The Biggest Challenge. *Global Journal of Emerging Market Economies,* 8(2), 247–270. https://doi.org/10.1177/0974910116634471.

Aralica, Z., T. Svilokos, and K. Bacic. (2018). Institutions and Firms' Performance in Transition Countries: The Case of Selected Cesee Countries. *South East European Journal of Economics and Business,* 13(1), 68–80. https://doi.org/10.2478/jeb-2018-0005.

Ark, B. van, J.X. Hao, C. Corrado, and Ch. Hulten. (2009). *Measuring Intangible Capital and Its Contribution to Economic Growth in Europe.* EIB Paper 3/2009. European Investment Bank, Economics Department. http://econpapers.repec.org/paper/riseibpap/2009_5f003.htm.

Aysan, A., M. NABLI, and M.A. Veganzones. (2007). Governance Institutions and Private Investment: An Application to the Middle East and North Africa. *The Developing Economies,* 45(September), 339–377. https://doi.org/10.1111/j.1746-1049.2007.00042.x.

Barrios, S., and A. Schaechter. (2008). The Quality of Public Finances and Economic Growth. *European Economy Economic Papers* 337, Directorate General Economic and Financial Affairs (DG ECFIN), European Commission.

Barro, R.J. (1996). Institutions and Growth, an Introductory Essay. *Journal of Economic Growth,* 1(2), 145–148.

Beca, M.P., and C.S. Barabaş. (2016). The Effects of Gaps and Disparities on Economic Growth. A Study of 10 Former Socialist Countries from Central Eastern Europe, Members of the EU. *Amfiteatru Economic,* 18(43), 592–610.

Bergeaud, A., G. Cette, and R. Lecat. (2018). Long-Term Growth and Productivity Trends: Secular Stagnation or Temporary Slowdown? *Revue de l'OFCE,* 157(3), 37–54. https://doi.org/10.3917/reof.157.0037.

Blejer, M.I., and M.S. Khan. (1984). Government Policy and Private Investment in Developing Countries (Politique Des Pouvoirs Publics et Investissement Privé Dans Les Pays En Développement) (Política Estatal e Inversión Privada En Los Países En Desarrollo). *Staff Papers (International Monetary Fund),* 31(2), 379–403. https://doi.org/10.2307/3866797.

Borghi, E., C. Del Bo, and M. Florio. (2016). Institutions and Firms' Productivity: Evidence from Electricity Distribution in the EU. *Oxford Bulletin of Economics and Statistics,* 78(2), 170–196. https://doi.org/10.1111/obes.12087.

Breton, T.R. (2004). Can Institutions or Education Explain World Poverty? An Augmented Solow Model Provides Some Insights. *Journal of Socio-Economics,* 33(1), 45–69. https://doi.org/10.1016/j.socec.2003.12.004.

"CoInvest Project." 2012. (2012). http://www.coinvest.org.uk/bin/view/CoInvest.

Corrado, C., J. Haskel, C. Jona-Lasinio, and M. Iommi. (2013). Innovation and Intangible Investment in Europe, Japan, and the United States. *Oxford Review of Economic Policy,* 29(2), 261–286. https://doi.org/10.1093/oxrep/grt017.

Corrado, C., J. Haskel, and C. Jona-Lasinio. (2016). *Intangibles, ICT and Industry Productivity Growth: Evidence from the EU. The World Economy: Growth or Stagnation?* Cambridge, UK: Cambridge University Press. https://doi.org/10.1017/9781316534502.009.

Corrado, C., J. Haskel, C. Jona-Lasinio, and M. Iommi. (2018). Intangible Investment in the EU and US before and since the Great Recession and its Contribution to Productivity Growth. *Journal of Infrastructure, Policy and Development,* 2(1), 11–36. https://doi.org/10.24294/jipd.v2i1.205.

Corrado, C., Ch. Hulten, and D. Sichel. (2006). *Intangible Capital and Economic Growth. 2006–24.* Finance and Economics Discussion Series Divisions of Research & Statistics and Monetary Affairs Federal Reserve Board, Washington, D.C. https://www.federalreserve.gov/pubs/feds/2006/200624/200624pap.pdf.

———. (2009). Intangible Capital and U.S. Economic Growth. *Review of Income and Wealth,* 55(3), 661–685. https://doi.org/10.1111/j.1475-4991.2009.00343.x.

Dawson, J.W. (1998). Institutions, Investment, and Growth: New Cross-Country and Panel Data Evidence. *Economic Inquiry,* 36(4), 603–619. https://doi.org/10.1111/j.1465-7295.1998.tb01739.x.

Diwan, I., P. Keefer, and M. Schiffbauer. (2018). Pyramid Capitalism: Cronyism, Regulation, and Company Productivity in Egypt. *Review of International Organizations*, 15, 211–246. https://doi.org/10.1007/s11558-018-9327-2.

Domadenik, P., M. Koman, and J. Prasnikar. (2018). Do Governmental Subsidies Increase Productivity of Firms? Evidence from a Panel of Slovenian Firms. *Društvena Istraživanja,* 27(2), 199–220.

Driffield, N., T. Mickiewicz, and Y. Temouri. (2014). Institutions and Equity Structure of Foreign Affiliates. *Corporate Governance: An International Review,* 22(3), 216–229. https://doi.org/10.1111/corg.12054.

Estrin, S., J. Hanousek, E. Kočenda, and J. Svejnar. (2009). The Effects of Privatization and Ownership in Transition Economies. *Journal of Economic Literature,* 47(3), 699–728. https://doi.org/10.1257/jel.47.3.699.

Everhart, S.S., J. Martinez-Vazquez, and R.M. McNab. (2009). Corruption, Governance, Investment and Growth in Emerging Markets. *Applied Economics,* 41(13), 1579–1594. https://doi.org/10.1080/00036840701439363.

Foss, N.J., and G. Garzarelli. (2007). Institutions as Knowledge Capital: Ludwig M. Lachmann's Interpretative Institutionalism. *Cambridge Journal of Economics,* 31(5), 789–804. https://doi.org/10.1093/cje/bem003.

Fukao, K., T. Miyagawa, K. Mukai, Y. Shinoda, and K. Tonogi. (2009). Intangible investment in Japan: measurement and contribution to economic growth. *Review of Income and Wealth,* 55(3), 717–736. https://doi.org/10.1111/j.1475-4991.2009.00345.x.

Ghulam, Y. (2017). Long-Term Performance of an Industry after Broader Reforms Including Privatization. *Research in International Business and Finance,* 42, 745–768. https://doi.org/10.1016/j.ribaf.2017.07.014.

Giannetti, M. (2003). Do Better Institutions Mitigate Agency Problems? Evidence from Corporate Finance Choices. *Journal of Financial and Quantitative Analysis,* 38(1), 185–212. https://doi.org/10.2307/4126769.

Hall, S.G., and M. Ahmad. (2014). Revisiting the Institutions–Growth Nexus in Developing Countries: The New Evidence. *New Zealand Economic Papers,* 48(3), 301–312. https://doi.org/10.1080/00779954.2013.867795.

Heil, M. (2017). *Finance and Productivity*. OECD Economics Department Working Papers. March. https://doi.org/10.1787/41194fea-en.

Holland, J. (2001). Financial Institutions, Intangibles and Corporate Governance. *Accounting, Auditing & Accountability Journal,* 14(4), 497–529. https://doi.org/10.1108/EUM0000000005871.

Innodrive. (2008). Innodrive Project. www.innodrive.org.

Iwasaki, I., S. Mizobata, and A. Muravyev. (2018). Ownership Dynamics and Company Performance in an Emerging Economy: A Meta-Analysis of the Russian Literature. *Post-Communist Economies,* 30(3), 290–333. https://doi.org/10.1080/14631377.2018.1442036.

Jona-Lasinio, C., and V. Meliciani. (2018). Productivity Growth and International Competitiveness: Does Intangible Capital Matter? *Intereconomics - Review of European Economic Policy,* 2018(2), 58–62.

Kafouros, M., and M. Aliyev. (2016). Institutions and Foreign Subsidiary Growth in Transition Economies: The Role of Intangible Assets and Capabilities. *Journal of Management Studies,* 53(4), 580–607. https://doi.org/10.1111/joms.12169.

Kaufmann, D., A. Kraay, and M. Mastruzzi. (2010). *The Worldwide Governance Indicators: Methodology and Analytical Issues*. SSRN Scholarly Paper. Rochester, NY. https://papers.ssrn.com/abstract=1682130.

Kaufmann, D., and A. Kraay. (2020). *Worldwide Governance Indicators.* https://info.worldbank.org/governance/wgi/.

Khanna, R., and C. Sharma. (2018). Do Infrastructure and Quality of Governance Matter for Manufacturing Productivity? Empirical Evidence from the Indian States. *Journal of Economic Studies,* 45(4), 829–854. https://doi.org/10.1108/JES-04-2017-0100.

Knack, S., and Ph. Keefer. (1995). Institutions and Economic Performance: Cross-Country Tests Using Alternative Institutional Measures. *Economics & Politics,* 7(3), 207–227. https://doi.org/10.1111/j.1468-0343.1995.tb00111.x.

Kukharskyy, B. (2020). A Tale of Two Property Rights: Knowledge, Physical Assets, and Multinational Firm Boundaries. *Journal of International Economics,* 122, 1–19. https://doi.org/10.1016/j.jinteco.2019.103262.

Mahran, H. A. (2022). The Impact of Governance on Economic Growth: Spatial Econometric Approach. *Review of Economics and Political Science,* 8(1), 37–53. https://doi.org/10.1108/REPS-06-2021-0058.

Marčič, E., and T. Redek. (2022). *SMEs »Growing Smart«: The Complementarity of Intangible and Digital Investment in Small Firms and Their Contribution to Company Performance*. Ljubljana: Mimeo. University of Ljubljana, School of Economics and Business.

Martins, A. (2018). The Portuguese Intellectual Property Box: Issues in Designing Investment Incentives. *Journal of International Trade Law and Policy,* 17(3), 86–102. https://doi.org/10.1108/JITLP-11-2017-0044.

Mauro, P. (1995). Corruption and Growth*. *The Quarterly Journal of Economics,* 110(3), 681–712. https://doi.org/10.2307/2946696.

Miyagawa. (2010). *Intangible Capital*. Presented at the Presentation at University of Ljubljana, FELU, Ljubljana.

Młynarzewska-Borowiec, I. (2018). Determinants of the Real Convergence Process in the European Union – A Panel Analysis for 2004–2015. *Argumenta Oeconomica,* 40(1), 345–363. https://doi.org/10.15611/aoe.2018.1.15.

North, D. C. (1987). Institutions, Transaction Costs and Economic Growth. *Economic Inquiry,* 25(3), 419–428. https://doi.org/10.1111/j.1465-7295.1987.tb00750.x.

———. (1990). *Institutions, Institutional Change and Economic Performance*. Political Economy of Institutions and Decisions. Cambridge: Cambridge University Press. https://doi.org/10.1017/CBO9780511808678.

———. (1991). Institutions. *Journal of Economic Perspectives,* 5(1), 97–112. https://doi.org/10.1257/jep.5.1.97.

OECD. (2013). *New Sources of Growth: Knowledge-Based Capital - OECD*. http://www.oecd.org/sti/inno/newsourcesofgrowthknowledge-basedcapital.htm.

Papageorgiadis, N., C. Wang, and G. Magkonis. (2019). Factors Contributing to the Strength of National Patent Protection and Enforcement after TRIPS. *Transnational Corporations* 26(1), 87–108. https://doi.org/10.18356/96de74c3-en.

Piekkola, H. (2011). Intangible Capital: The Key to Growth in Europe. *Intereconomics,* 46(July/August 2011). https://archive.intereconomics.eu/year/2011/4/intangible-capital-the-key-to-growth-in-europe/search/intangible+capital/0/.

Piekkola, H. (2018). Broad-Based Intangibles as Generators of Growth in Europe. *Economics of Innovation and New Technology,* 27(4), 377–400. https://doi.org/10.1080/10438599.2017.1376170.

Piekkola, H., C. Bloch, M. Rybalka, and T. Redek. (2021). *Intangibles from Innovative Work – Their Valuation and Technological Change*. Deliverable 5.3. H2020 Globalinto Project Report. University of Vaasa.

Piekkola, H., M. Lintamo, K. Geppert, B. Görzig, A. Neumann, M. Henningsen, T. Skjerpen, S. Jurajda, J. Stancik, and M. Verbič. (2011). Company-Level Intangible Capital in Six Countries: Finland, Norway, the UK, Germany, the Czech Republic and Slovenia. In Hanna Piekkola (Ed.) *Intangible Capital – Driver of Growth in Europe* (pp. 63–95). Vaasa: University of Vaasa. https://www.niesr.ac.uk/publications/firm-level-intangible-capital-six-countries-finland-norway-uk-germany-czech-republic-0.

Pilar Baquero Forero, M. del, T. Ida, and T. Kuroda. (2015). Institutions and Cultural Heterogeneity as Determinants of National Income: A Random-Coefficients Stochastic Frontier Model. *Review of Development Economics,* 19(3), 710–724. https://doi.org/10.1111/rode.12153.

Pratt, D. (2006). "Fairness, Globalization, and Public Institutions." In Jim Dator, Richard C. Pratt, and Yongseok Seo (Eds.) *East Asia and Beyond* (pp. 35–46). Honolulu: University of Hawaii Press. https://doi.org/10.1515/9780824841966-005.

Redek, T., P. Domadenik, D. Farčnik, T. Istenič, M. Koman, Č. Kostevc, J. Sambt, R. Spruk, and V. Žabkar. (2019). *A Survey on Challenges to Growth: The Productivity Puzzle in the Context of (New) Growth Determinants*. H2020 GLOBALINTO WP1 Report. Foresight on growth, methodologies and data for measuring intangible assets. Ljubljana: FELU - Faculty of Economics University of Ljubljana.

Rizov, M. (2008). Institutions, Reform Policies and Productivity Growth in Agriculture: Evidence from Former Communist Countries. *NJAS - Wageningen Journal of Life Sciences,* 55(4), 307–323. https://doi.org/10.1016/S1573-5214(08)80023-1.

Rodríguez-Pose, A., and R. Ganau. (2022). Institutions and the Productivity Challenge for European Regions. *Journal of Economic Geography,* 22(1), 1–25. https://doi.org/10.1093/jeg/lbab003.

Rodrik, D., A. Subramanian, and F. Trebbi. (2004). Institutions Rule: The Primacy of Institutions Over Geography and Integration in Economic Development. *Journal of Economic Growth,* 9(2), 131–165. https://doi.org/10.1023/B:JOEG.0000031425.72248.85.

Roth, F. (2020). Revisiting Intangible Capital and Labour Productivity Growth, 2000–2015 : Accounting for the Crisis and Economic Recovery in the EU. *Journal of Intellectual Capital,* 21(5), 671–690. https://doi.org/10.1108/JIC-05-2019-0119.

———. (2022a). *Intangible Capital and Growth: Essays on Labour Productivity, Monetary Economics, and Political Economy, Vol. 1.* Cham, Switzerland: Springer Nature. https://doi.org/10.1007/978-3-030-86186-5.

———. (2022b). *The Rule of Law and Investment in Intangible Capital: Evidence for the EU-16, 1996–2017.* Working Paper 12. Hamburg Discussion Papers in International Economics. https://www.econstor.eu/handle/10419/253363.

Roth, F., and A.-E. Thum. (2013). Intangible Capital and Labour Productivity Growth: Panel Evidence for the EU from 1998–2005. *Review of Income and Wealth,* 59(3), 486–508. https://doi.org/10.1111/roiw.12009.

Sala-i-Martin, X. (2002). *15 Years of New Growth Economics: What Have We Learnt*? Columbia University, Department of Economics Discussion Paper Series, Discussion Paper #:0102-47, Columbia University, New York. https://doi.org/10.7916/D8K93KSW.

Schwartz, P. (2013). Capitalism, International Investment Law and the Development Conundrum. *Law and Development Review,* 6(2), S217–253. https://doi.org/10.1515/ldr-2013-0025.

Sgard, J. (2001). *Direct Foreign Investments and Productivity Growth in Hungarian Firms, 1992–1999.* 2001–2019. Sciences Po Publications. Sciences Po. https://ideas.repec.org/p/spo/wpmain/infohdl2441-6926.html.

Shapiro, M.A., and J.B. Nugent. (2012). Institutions and the Sources of Innovation: The Determinants and Effects of International R&D Collaboration. *International Journal of Public Policy,* 8(4–6), 230–250. https://doi.org/10.1504/IJPP.2012.048715.

Smith, A. (1776). *An Inquiry into the Nature and Causes of the Wealth of Nations*. Reprint: Create Space Independent Publishing Platform. https://www.econlib.org/library/Smith/smWN.html.

Spruk, R., and M. Kovac. (2018). Inefficient Growth. *Review of Economics and Institutions,* 9(2), 59. https://doi.org/10.5202/rei.v9i2.268.

Spulber, D.F. (2015). How Patents Provide the Foundation of the Market for Inventions. *Journal of Competition Law and Economics,* 11(2), 271–316. https://doi.org/10.1093/joclec/nhv006.

Su Dinh, T., and T.M.H. Bui. (2017). Government Size, Public Governance and Private Investment: The Case of Vietnamese Provinces. *Economic Systems*, 41(4), 651–666. https://doi.org/10.1016/j.ecosys.2017.01.002

The Vienna Institute for International Economic Studies. (2019). EU Klems Documentation. EU KLEMS Release 2019 (blog). https://euklems.eu/documentation/.

Tichá, M. (2012). State or Private Ownership? A Survey of Empirical Studies. *Review of Economic Perspectives,* 12(2), 120–144. https://doi.org/10.2478/v10135-012-0006-6.

Tons, Y., and Z. Serrasqueiro. (2020). The Influential Factors on Capital Structure: A Study on Portuguese High Technology and Medium-High Technology Small and Medium-Sized Enterprises. *International Journal of Financial Research,* 11(4), 23–35. https://doi.org/10.5430/ijfr.v11n4p23.

Vukšić, G. (2016). Effects of Private Ownership, Trade, and Foreign Direct Investment on Labour Productivity Growth in Transition Economies: Evidence from the Croatian Manufacturing Industry. *Emerging Markets Finance and Trade,* 52(2), 322–335. https://doi.org/10.1080/1540496X.2015.1011540.

Wang, D.T., F.F. Gu, D.K. Tse, and C.K.B. Yim. (2013). When Does FDI Matter? The Roles of Local Institutions and Ethnic Origins of FDI. *International Business Review,* 22(2), 450–465. https://doi.org/10.1016/j.ibusrev.2012.06.003.

Wang, H., Y. Liu, W. Xiong, and J. Song. (2019). The Moderating Role of Governance Environment on the Relationship between Risk Allocation and Private Investment in PPP Markets: Evidence from Developing Countries. *International Journal of Project Management,* 37(1), 117–130. https://doi.org/10.1016/j.ijproman.2018.10.008.

World Bank. (1992). *Governance and Development.* Washington: The World Bank. https://doi.org/10.1596/0-8213-2094-7.

———. (1997). *World Development Report 1997: The State in a Changing World: Overview.* New York: Oxford University Press. https://onlinelibrary.wiley.com/doi/abs/10.1111/j.1759-5436.1998.mp29002003.x.

———. (2020). *Doing Business.* World Bank. https://www.doingbusiness.org/en/doingbusiness.

Xi, T. (2017). Inclusive Institutions and Economic Growth: Comparative Perspective and Policy Implications for China. *China Economic Journal,* 10(2), 108–127. https://doi.org/10.1080/17538963.2017.1321212.

Yilmaz, R., and J.Y. Koyuncu. (2018). The Impact of Privatization on Labour Productivity in Transition Economies and the Turkic Republics [Geçiş Ekonomilerinde ve Türki Cumhuriyetlerde Özelleştirmenin Emek Verimliliği Üzerindeki Etkisi]. *Bilig,* 85, 257–281.

Zhang, J. (2010). *China's Economic Growth: Trajectories and Evolving Institutions.* New York: Oxford University Press. https://doi.org/10.1093/acprof:oso/9780199580606.003.0004.

11 Regulatory governance in the telecommunications industry in Poland

Renata Śliwa

11.1 Introduction

In the absence of a level playing field,[1] regulation that was meant to be a sort of rule enforcer (as opposed to regulation as a detailed intervention) (Ricketts, 2006) was missing in post-communist market economies, which was most evident at the first stages of transition. Additionally, it was not just about the abuse of market power that the incumbent held (the core of the regulatory problems within neoclassical reasoning approached by the combinations of antitrust provisions), as it referred to a less obvious regulatory problem, namely, the problem of restraining government opportunism[2] from expropriating the firms' quasi-rent (temporary rent).

The key regulatory problem that arose was curbing the motivation of the politicians-regulator to expropriate once the investments were made, which is the issue of regulatory governance. The main area of the assessment of the effectiveness of regulatory processes in a utility is that of investment. The purpose of regulatory governance is to increase critical areas of performance for sectoral development, such as investments, which is an especially sensitive issue when it comes to sunk investments, as in the case of infrastructure-based industries. By setting prices, quality standards, or other impositions, the government may limit the ability of firms to invest or when invested, to recover the investment (even if variable operating costs are covered). The structure and processes of regulation determine the political risk and cost of capital for investors. Usually the state monopoly, subsequently privatized, or vertically integrated, which had dominated the telecommunications[3] markets from the dawn of economic transformation was simultaneously marked by special features such as operating on huge sunk infrastructure, exploiting significant economies of scale and scope, servicing massive consumption (that seriously coincided with a pool of voters), while also a significant threat of opportunistic behaviour from many participants of regulatory processes. All of these elements made the issue of telecommunications regulation entrenched as much in technology-driven processing, as in the endemic structures of political processes.

The optics of new institutional economics in sectoral regulation is applied herein through the notion of regulatory governance which places particular emphasis on the dependence of the sectoral performance on the institutional environment, while

DOI: 10.4324/9781003425717-15

at the same time implicitly meaning the (evolutionary) development of institutional conditions under which incentive regulation becomes feasible.[4]

What is claimed here is that Poland's economic transition economy lacked the regulation in the sense of its conductive nature in the early stages of its transformational implementation. The institutionalization in an advanced phase of maturing (noticeably since 2006) was aimed at balancing between stimulating competition, resulting in expropriating the incumbent's quasi-rent (the use of regulatory tools forcing service competition), while also the stimulation of investments. What was the overall picture of the regulatory governance for infrastructure sectors in Poland in 2004–2021? What are the main phases in the evolution of regulatory governance for infrastructure sectors in Poland at that time? These questions emerge as the main issues of this chapter.

11.2 Regulatory frameworks in telecommunications industry in a country under economic and institutional transformation

11.2.1 Regulatory governance

Regulatory governance is perceived as a framework of regulatory structures and processes to achieve and sustain the desired regulatory outcomes. It is an essential element of a regulation process. Besides regulatory objectives (the problems the regulation is addressed to), it concerns the instruments used to solve a regulatory problem. To optimize the regulatory outcomes, internal control mechanisms need to codify and institutionalize the regulatory processes, whose aim is to regulate the regulator.

Examples of regulatory governance in sectoral regulation can be found in formal administrative procedures (delegation to bureaucracy), judicial review (delegation to the judiciary), participation of multiple interest groups (preferably with conflicting interests) in the administrative process (regulatory transparency) (Spiller and Tomassi, 2008, 530).

The structure and processes of regulation involve regulatory governance as the core of analysis. Regulatory governance is meant to constrain regulatory discretion (Levy and Spiller, 1996, 1–35) with calls for checks and balances among market, state, and civil society, while also making it of pivotal importance for designing socio-economic frameworks. Accountability, independence, and transparency are the features that stimulate the openness, flexibility, and efficiency of the regulatory ecosystem (Śliwa, 2019, 77, 80), while also the advanced results of the sectoral performance. Regulatory governance concerns the tools that are or could be at the disposal of societies to keep the governmental opportunism in check and to deal with the problems that can arise from it. The substance of the regulatory frameworks focuses on the determinants of restraining the excessive power of industrial regulators, not specifically on the outcomes of the market players within an industry (Spiller and Tomassi, 2008, 515, 517). Institutionalists discern the sources of regulatory problems not through the opportunism of a regulator *per se*, or exercise of market power or pure efficiency incentives as such, but through the emphasis on the institutional aspects of regulatory frameworks, while also the importance of contracting schemes towards the second-best incentives, as well as the significance of the shift of the analysis from the regulatory policy to regulatory governance strictly linked to the institutional environment.

Regulation in the institutional sense is a product of the political and legislative processes, an implicit contract out of exchanges of a political nature, where the binding agreement between the regulator (government) and the firm is less exposed (unlike in incentive regulation literature).

Regulatory governance requires the flexibility and adaptation to the changing environment, as well as learning from mistakes (Vass, 2006, 188). Likewise, it delivers a different scope of the limits of government opportunism and conducts a specific level of incentive power. Where the motivation for governmental opportunism is high, more low-power incentive regulation is applicable (such as assurances on the rate-of-return, exclusivity licences) in order to grant investors enough incentives (motivation and stimulation) to invest. For relatively efficient regulatory schemes (high-power incentive schemes), to be effectively implemented, substantial regulatory flexibility and granting of discretion to the regulators are required. The weaker the institutional ecosystem, the more inflexible (rigid; *ad hoc*) the regulatory structures are (Laffont and Tirole, 2001).[5] Otherwise, in order to provide operators with powerful incentives to reduce costs, while also to make the operator more accountable for the costs in monopolistic markets, while at the same time provide the operator with a guarantee not to seize the operator's extra profits, the regulator needs to restrain from grabbing the quasi-rents (temporary) – the more systemically, the better.[6]

Sectoral regulatory frameworks that are geared towards limiting the potential for governmental opportunism are expected to stimulate investment, while also "credibly enhance the political restraint over operators' opportunism" (Spiller and Tommasi, 2005, 523).

The type of regulatory institutions determines "the extent of commitment the polity can provide to enterprises and thus the potential for the sectoral performance" (Spiller and Tommasi, 2005, 523). The key is to find a balance between the stability and flexibility of the regulation in order to provide the optimal power of the incentive to invest. Regulatory institutions are the products of a game among politicians with conflicting interests (e.g. those preferring to stimulate long-term investments vs those opting for short-term redistributive gains – lower prices for consumers). Their aim is to provide limitations on political behaviour that would occur unexpectedly to block sectoral investors. This way, policy becomes more predictable and conducive to long-term investments, although at the same time the limitation means less power to adjust to the unexpected economic and technological shocks, including positive ones.[7]

For the regulatory governance to thrive in terms of regulatory transparency and arranging interest group participation, a set of endogenously built institutions is required, namely, interest groups (regulated firms, consumer groups, unions, environmental groups, and so on) that have their say within administrative procedures, including that of regulatory agencies. Interest groups are provided with the procedural path to manifest their interests and in that manner contribute to gathering information in a systematic and schematic way.[8] The participation of multiple interest groups, preferably with conflicting interests, is a way to limit the information power of (dominant) interest groups (at the cost of delays in the decision-making process or blocking regulatory adoption).

11.2.2 Telecommunications industry

The specificity of industries based on strategic infrastructure rests on the features of public services being as much the outcomes of production processes in public utilities as the reflections of social and political considerations. As public utilities are featured by the simultaneous occurrence of the combination of technologies that are driven by large, specific, and sunk investments by technologies that generate important economies of scale and scope (Laffont and Tirole, 2001), while also by the production of services massively consumed across societies, in which they are extremely prone to political turbulence and become the subject of significant pressures of an opportunistic nature. The economics of the regulation that therefore emerges is deeply rooted in the political economy of public utilities (Goldberg, 1976, 426–452; Williamson, 1988, 65–93; North, 1990; Joskow, 1991, 253–283; Spiller and Cezley, 1993; Levy and Spiller, 1996, 1–35).

The extensive consumption of utility services, specific sunk investments, and economies of scale constitute favourable conditions for the government to behave opportunistically towards an investor, which involves such tactics as imposing rigid pricing, additional investments, movement of capital, purchasing, or employment patterns.

Under the conditions of the post-socialist economy, the initial phase of the regulatory transformation of the telecommunications sector was marked by a sequence of sectoral transformation from liberalization to privatization. This significantly determined the monopolistic role of the incumbent and its dominant share in the investment activities of the sector and the process of shaping the prices of telecommunications services determining their availability to consumers, thus influencing the subsequent shape of the development of the telecommunications services sector in Poland.[9] Telekomunikacja Polska SA(TP) displayed monopolistic behaviour, in addition to the high cost of entering markets and the often-ambiguous nature of the law, which helped to prevent the realization of the possibilities introduced by laws to increase competition against TP.[10]

Prior to this, it was more liberalization than privatization which allowed TP to strengthen its monopoly position. The delayed privatization of the monopoly in the liberalized service markets, which was intended, among other things, to drive up the company's selling price (as the legal maintenance of a strong monopoly in a lucrative market for international calls can clearly indicate), but above all, the transition of this state monopoly into a private monopoly in markets where alternative operators initially had no chance to exist defined for many years the scale of consumer access to important telecommunications services. As a result of this liberalization-privatization transition, 12,544,700 active fixed telephone lines were reported in 2004, with TP's share of subscriber lines at 91.2% (after a period of investment expansion in 1992–2000 when network modernization and construction was financed with funds from the World Bank and the European Investment Bank[11]), whereas the total access to telephone lines in 2004 in Poland was 26.7% of those in Germany and 32% of those in the UK (OECD.Stat).[12] International call charges were up to four times higher than in the EU on average, and the ratio of long-distance and local call charges was the highest in Europe, twice as much as in the EU on average (IBM, 2003; Kubasik, 2004).

Thus, the entrenchment of the incumbent's monopoly had resulted in both socially unsatisfactory access to telecommunications services and insufficient investment until at least 2009.

11.2.3 Institutional transformation

The post-socialist economic transition brought with it the liberalization, privatization, demonopolization, while also reregulation of public utilities (services of general economic interest). The need to redesign the interrelationship between strategic enterprises and the domain of public organization resounded even more than ever before. In addition, the fact of technological dynamics and the need for economic dynamics to follow have more vividly illuminated such problems as the relationship between the legal owners and those who control the daily performance of the enterprise.[13] Moreover, the proper relationship between the management of the enterprise and the institutions of the democratic state (how far the regulator's interventions in the enterprise's internal decisions can go[14]) (more on the UK case, Moran, 2003, 98) emerged as a key issue.

Economies in transition, such as that in Poland, were often marked by the search for the answers to favourable solutions in each of these areas in the face of the widespread lack of public accountability and control of political decisions, within which certain clubs in the business sphere operated.

The institutional environment in which privatization was embedded in the first stages of transition was dominated by the theoretical glorification of the autonomy of private enterprises and the concomitant prevalence of the practices of policymakers that marginalized accountability and public transparency. As a result, the regulatory system regarding privatized industries often brought more stringent public service expectations imposed on private enterprises than those previously in place for public enterprises.

Lowering the costs generated by the opportunism of a regulator was of particular importance in the countries under economic and juridical transition where there were "high costs of public funds, low transaction costs of collusion and less efficient technologies" (Laffont, 2005, 242). Reducing the burdens was the core of the institutional transition. To minimize the load, there were essential measures under consideration such as the following: lower costs of public funds (to induce lower price levels of services created by the natural monopoly segments of industry and to make sectoral operators subject to regulation and become more accountable for costs), apply unbiased accounting and auditing of performance evaluation (not to pad costs in order to increase the regulated operator's cost reimbursement from a regulator), use more advanced technology such as software systems to detect cost-padding (inflating and falsifying costs) and evaluate real costs, while also having more capacity to impose high penalties for those running documented malpractice, more efficient credit markets (not to make borrowing highly costly or impossible for effective competition policy while activated and threatening to dismantle the operator rents that are indispensable for an operator to invest), higher constitutional control such as supreme courts, government auditing bodies, independent media, NGOs (not to allow the regulator to be too exposed to interest pressure and to encourage long-term contracts of private enterprises), as well as greater power of the law to enforce contracts. Institutional deficiencies in enforcement, commitment, and auditing called for the separation of powers, and country and sector-tailored regulatory governance (Laffont, 2005, 1–28, 226–242).

11.3 Methodology

Spiller and Tommasi (2005, 515–543), Levy and Spiller (1996, 1–35), and Laffont (2005) stated that understanding regulatory performance requires a grasp of the institutional determinants of regulatory governance.

The institutional approach is useful for answering the question not of the nature of why entrepreneurs of the post-communist generation monopolized certain areas of the economy (an immanent feature of any profit-maximizing entrepreneur), but of what conditions allowed them to achieve the goals they set out (based on: Polanyi, 2010, 183). The concept of regulatory governance focuses on the analysis of the institutional conditions that channel the investment incentives (Levy and Spiller, 1996, 4) of telecommunications entrepreneurs.

Investment is a critical area of performance of an infrastructure operator, while also a vulnerable issue in the process of infrastructure building. At the same time, investment is an economic measure that is easy to undermine by such regulatory decisions as setting prices, quality standards, or any other impositions at the levels that could threaten the recovery of the planned or existing asset building.

Against the backdrop of the activities, there is a search for the right regulatory solution for securing allocative and distributive goals. The regulatory governance concept brings analysis into the area of political and institutional conditions that enable long-term stabilization/maturing of the constraints of government opportunism.

Three perspectives resound throughout the text, permeating theoretical considerations about regulatory governance in a transition economy, namely, market power, incentives to invest, and regulatory governance for making the incentives feasible, in which the last one is the pivotal concept of the analysis.

Market power involves the market incumbent (national operator) whose sectoral operating conditions are characterized by significant sunk investments, economies of scale and scope, massive consumption, and opportunistic behaviour, which have all led to abusive market power.

Channelling incentives through sector regulation balances those that promote service competition (distributional aspects) by capturing the regulated operator's profits through competition enhancement, regulatory downward pressure on prices (lowering wholesale prices for alternative operators), while also those that enhance the investment opportunities of operators by means of infrastructure competition (allocative aspects).

The regulatory governance perspective shows the sector's regulatory policy from the side of limiting the regulator's opportunism in order to seize the operator's temporary profits, i.e. those earned by investing earlier and achieving lower costs. This is illustrated in Table 11.1.

In the transformational conditions of the telecommunications sector regulation, the three outlined perspectives can be characterized by such images of the sector reality in Poland as follows:

Market power perspective: the dominant market position of TP SA, especially in the initial phases of the regulatory transformation of the sector.

Incentives to investment perspective: adopting the direction of stimulating service competition, which ended up neglecting sector investment as a response to TP SA's strong market position and EU directives promoting asymmetric regulation (service competition).

Regulatory governance perspective: giving an institutionally rigid political and institutional impetus towards the growth of sectoral investments (the breakthrough period leading to the TP-UKE Agreement, Mega Law); a successful attempt to shift the responsibility for investments to the largest operator; significantly intensified pressure from a wider range of stakeholders (apart from TP SA) to put pressure

Table 11.1 The presentation of the main research axis

Market power perspective (incumbent operator, abusive market power). Restricting market power		
Incentives to invest perspective (low-powered incentives versus high-powered incentives).	How to secure access to telecommunications services by means of lower prices (distributional aspect) and not to hinder investment and innovation (allocative aspect).	
Regulatory governance to make incentives feasible (regulating regulator)		Restraining regulator from expropriating the operator's temporary rents.
Emanating from the three perspectives: How to boost investment and at the same time secure consumers' access to a wide spectrum of innovative services; how to enhance responsiveness of operators to economic shocks and technological disruptiveness; how to reduce sensitivity of regulator to political demands.		

Source: Self-analysis.

on the regulator to safeguard their economic interests, closely monitor regulatory decisions, participate in public consultations, etc. (this trend resounds in the European Commission's (EC) attempts to create a European digital market).

Therefore, the evolutionary dimension of contracting schemes was developed, namely, the transition of regulatory frameworks in terms of advancement in constraining governmental opportunism to channel the pro-investment incentives. Each stage of the advancement (transition) is depicted by the elements of the regulatory system discerned by the maturity of regulatory governance.

To get an insight into the structure and processes of the regulatory system, the following need to be taken into consideration (Vass, 2006, 190) (the scheme of regulatory governance perspective):

1 Legal framework (codification);
2 Separation of roles and responsibilities (independent regulator rather than from the state);
3 Principles of good regulation (codified principles essential to creating the climate of expectations about regulatory conduct that provides discipline for regulators to operate in the "public interest", while also develop and reform regulatory framework as a means to that end);
4 Forming a "whole-of-government view" (broad programmes of regulatory reforms - adopted at the highest political levels);
5 Provision of relevant information.

Additionally, transparency and accountability are the main principles of regulatory framework i.e.:

1 Reasons for a decision (public consultations, preparation of impact assessment);
2 Exposure to scrutiny (effective consultation processes, independent legal audit of regulatory activities by parliamentary committees, as well as other authoritative bodies such as national audit offices);
3 The possibility of independent review (court and other tribunals having the power to overturn regulatory decisions that are beyond the legal power or authority of the person performing an action that is inequitable, or unreasonable).

11.4 Results and discussion

11.4.1 Regulatory governance perspective

Initially, the environment in Poland's telecommunications sector as an example of regulatory governance in post-communist countries was designed to facilitate the exposure of the regulatory processes to political and then private capture.[15] Such a regulatory construct created an alternative to incumbent operators, namely, private investors, who showed fear and caution in terms of long-term investments, thus focusing more on short-term gains (based on the regulated costs of the lease of the incumbent's infrastructure). The constructive cooperation among policymakers was infeasible, therefore, rigid rules, procedures, and erratic policies arose that were poorly responsive to the economic and technological shocks, as well as being extremely sensitive to political demands.

The regulation was predominantly featured by low-powered incentive regulatory schemes (low accountability of operators for their cost savings, while also low incentives to invest).

Therefore, if the regulatory goal had been to implement the institutional constraint to limit the potential for governmental opportunism, the abusive market power of TP SA had to be curbed. However, for quite a few years after the beginning of the economic transition in Poland[16] politicians did not find it necessary to institutionally limit their discretion over the monopolistically and politically driven power of the main market operator. As Poland's economy was adapting to the institutional and legislative rules of the European Community, while also the technological shocks taking place, the regulatory policies started to emerge as being more "*insensitive to the randomness of politics*" with more predictability and conductivity. In spite of all that, rigid rules featured the state of equilibrium as the divergence in the interests of politicians relating to a particular issue that was more intensive than the volatility of the economic and technological shocks that took place simultaneously, as Spiller and Tommasi (2003) observed in the case of Argentina.

The repeated nature of the game that the regulatory arrangement was gaining over time made the institutional restraints more endogenously designed, namely, regulatory decision-making became more open to sectoral participants.[17] The cooperation which was endogenously driven needed to be founded on the capacity to self-enforce cooperative agreements.[18]

The post-communist institutional endowment of Poland restrained the list of regulatory incentive designs available. For example, the implementation of regulatory schemes to provide strong incentives to reduce costs by investment (and possibly generate high profits) was impossible as there was a significant monopoly power over the main markets held by TP SA and institutions conducive to that formula of regulation were non-existent, such as mature administrative procedure (at least up to 2006), as well as resilient and efficient legislature and judiciary systems, while also transparency in decision-making. In that time, regulatory governance as a choice was limited to the list of institutions acquired through the provisions of the EU law and institutions, which took the form of a complex of formal administrative procedures, as well as regulatory structures. The EU-imposed regulatory schemes promoted service competition with the dominant asymmetric regulation (it lowered the motivation of the largest operator to invest). Additionally, the regulated operators were not made accountable for their costs savings (the operator's costs were to be reimbursed; low-powered incentives).

To put the telecommunications sector problems in more details, Table 11.2 illustrates information on the regulatory governance transformation as depicted in the methodological part of the paper.

Since 2004, when the Telecommunications Law was adopted,[19] while implementations of sector regulations have been subject to EU directives and the Telecommunications Law has been amended several dozen times. This phase of the

Table 11.2 The elements of regulatory governance in telecommunications industry in Poland, 2004–2021

Legal framework	In 2004, two legal regimes were in effect; the 2004 law imposing on the President of the Regulatory Office the goal of promoting equal and effective competition in telecommunications markets and, consequently, ensuring universal access to telecommunications services; over 70 amendments of the Law of July 16, 2004; new electronic communication law implementing European Electronic Communications Code under preparation (2021)
Separation of roles and responsibilities	The Minister and the President of the regulatory authority are the communications administration authorities (art. 189); the President of the Regulatory Authority is a regulatory authority in the field of the market for telecommunications and postal services and a central government administration body appointed by the Prime Minister at the request of the Minister responsible for information technology and potentially dismissed by the Prime Minister; the President of the Regulatory Authority is appointed for a term of five years by the Sejm at the request of the Prime Minister of the Council of Ministers (until 2020, the competence to consent to the appointment and dismissal of the President was also in the hands of the Senate); the Minister responsible for Communications/Information Technology, by means of an ordinance, grants the regulator's statute and determines its organizational units; the Minister responsible for communications shall supervise the President of the Regulator's Office and may also entrust him/her with the performance of controlling activities over the type and scope of investment expenditures carried out by an operator or affiliate to the President of UKE (2005); the President, with the assistance of UKE, shall perform tasks, while also carry out financial management on the principles set out for budgetary entities; the President of the Regulatory Authority shall submit a report on its regulatory activities and the implementation of the telecommunications policy to the appropriate Minister annually (and upon request under Article 190(2c)) for his/her opinion, which shall then go through the Minister to the Prime Minister (2021).
Principles of good regulation	Sectoral directives in electronic communications in the provisions of the 2004 law provide the principles of good governance (the principle of good administration, while also the principle of participation and transparency and the principle of accountability, according to which regulators should undertake regulatory activities); the obligation of the President of UKE to consult before issuing a decision; the obligation of the President of UKE to conduct consultation, consolidation and mediation proceedings in disputes between consumers and telecommunications service providers and entrepreneurs; since 2008, the cyclical publication of indicators monitoring the incumbent's actions in terms of discrimination against alternative operators has been in place.

(*Continued*)

Table 11.2 (Continued)

Forming a "whole-of-government view"	Shaping the model of the functioning of the electronic services market under competitive conditions, while also the development of electronic communications infrastructure aimed at the dissemination, improvement of quality, and reduction of prices of telecommunications services within the framework of promotion of the European Union policy in the area of telecommunications for the information society; as well as regular reviews of relevant markets by the President of UKE to monitor the existence of effective competition and possible response when it turns out that it is lacking, so that the final beneficiary is to be the consumer.
Provision of relevant information	From 2005, publication of a report on the state of the telecommunications market, which was based on information obtained directly from telecommunications companies and on the basis of publicly available reports and studies commissioned by the regulator; draft laws subjected to public consultation and discussions with industry representatives (for example, the National Chamber of Ethernet Communications conferences).
Giving reasons for a decision	In order for regulations to exist and actually make the telecommunication markets more competitive, a mechanism was introduced in the legislation of EU countries, including Poland, for the cyclical review of relevant markets, while ensuring the adequacy of the applied regulations to the changing environment, conditions, and needs; while undertaking some regulatory impact assessments.
Exposure to scrutiny	Annual information from the Supreme Audit Office (NIK) on the results of the UKE's budget execution audit; reporting to the EC and other NRAs of the NRA's findings on market definition, SMP assessment, and possible proposed remedies; the EC, in cooperation with BEREC, examines the NRA's draft regulations, which, if BEREC confirms the EC's serious doubts, may even be subject to a demand for withdrawal.
Possibility of independent review	From 2004 to 2018, there were permanent arbitration consumer courts at the Presidency of the UKE, which dealt with property cases arising from contracts for the provision of telecommunications and postal services; in 2018, which was replaced by the previously functioning alternative consumer dispute resolution (ADR); Proceedings with the President of the Office of the Telecommunications Regulatory Authority (URTiP) are held under the Administrative Procedure Code, and decisions in cases involving the establishment of market dominance, while also the imposition of regulatory obligations, imposition of penalties, decisions in disputed cases can be appealed to the District Court in Warsaw – the Court of Competition and Consumer Protection; appeal proceedings are held in accordance with the provisions of the Civil Procedure Code on proceedings in cases involving the regulation of telecommunications and postal services (art. 206).

Source: Self-analysis based on the reports on the state of the telecommunications market in 2004 – 2021 (UKE); reports on the activities of the President of UKE for the years 2004–2021 (UKE), the Law of July 16, 2004. – Journal of Laws 2004 No. 171, item 1800.

development of regulatory governance mainly called for lower costs of implementing safeguards against government opportunism and private capture. However, under the law, the authorities with the competence to regulate the telecommunications sector were, and still are, the Minister and the President of the Regulatory Authority. The minister remains empowered to grant the regulator's statute and determines its organizational units (Art. 193, p. 3 Telecommunication Law). In 2005, the minister supervised the President of the Regulatory Office in terms of controlling activities over the type and scope of investment expenditures carried out by an operator or affiliate and in 2006, the Deputy Minister and President of the Regulatory Office was the same person for some time.[20] The task and budgetary management have been performed on the principles set out for budget entities.[21]

The principles of good regulation are now based on Directive 2018/1972 establishing the European Electronic Communications Code, which point to the principles of good governance – the principle of good administration, the principle of participation and transparency, the principle of accountability, according to which regulators should undertake regulatory activities. Moreover, the obligation of the President of the Regulatory Office to consult before issuing a decision (for further information, see: Kawka, 2011, 179), by conducting consultation, as well as consolidation and mediation proceedings in disputes between consumers and telecommunications service providers and entrepreneurs made the regulatory environment more conducive and safeguarded against political demands.

As of the end of 2008, the incumbent operator – Telekomunikacja Polska S.A. – began to publish key performance indicators (KPI) in order to be more transparent in order to fend off allegations of discrimination against alternative operators in terms of non-price discrimination, and in that way protected itself against a possible regulatory decision on the incumbent operator's functional separation,[22] albeit, it became clear that institutional drivers emerged to shape the regulatory capacity to self-enforce cooperative agreements. Furthermore, the players of the market by virtue of the law provided more information to be incorporated in the process of regulatory decision-making (from 2004, reports on the state of the telecommunications market were based directly on information from telecommunications operators). Other stakeholders of the telecommunications service markets were included in the process of regulation by means of public consultations, some impact assessments, or regular conferences in industry chambers for example.

The attempts to limit the potential of governmental opportunism and credibly enhance the political restraint over the operator's opportunism were reflected in the regulatory decision-making process that has been exposed to scrutiny within the EU norms – the European Commission and Body of European Regulators for Electronic Communications (BEREC) interventions in case of serious doubts.[23] The possibility of an independent review of the proceedings for the President of Regulatory Office was provided under the Administrative Procedure Code. Appeals in selected cases have been applied to the District Court in Warsaw – the Court of Competition and Consumer Protection decided in accordance with the provisions of the Civil Procedure Code on proceedings in cases involving the regulation of telecommunications and postal services (art. 206), while also decisions in cases involving the establishment of market dominance, the imposition of regulatory obligations, imposition of penalties, while also decisions in disputed cases. Property cases arising from contracts for the provision of telecommunications and postal services were dealt with by constant arbitration consumer courts at the President of the Regulatory Office and since 2018, they have also been dealt with in the previously functioning alternative consumer dispute resolution (ADR). All this meant that the capacity of the regulator to behave opportunistically was more in check. Likewise, the cost of potential opportunism of a regulator got more significant as the procedural and judicial control made it more difficult for the regulator to disregard important market players.

In view of the search for the balance between the distributional aspects and adaptations to technological shocks, forming a whole-of-government view (integrated vision) was reflected in the continued struggle to model the conditions of regulation and development of electronic communications infrastructure so that lower prices, better quality, widespread access to telecommunications services and more investment initiatives made the industry more absorbing for the technological disruption of the sector (allocative aspects), and made the objectives of the European Union's telecommunications policy for the information society more attainable[24] (distributional aspects) (Figure 11.1).

At the outset of the sectoral regulatory transition period, as the indirect institutional costs were low (no checks and balances within regulatory decision-making, administratively centralized regulatory policy, neither strong power nor tradition of judiciary to review administrative decisions), direct costs were low (technology-driven programmes required), and government acted within relatively short deadlines, the regulatory frameworks were featured by relatively high

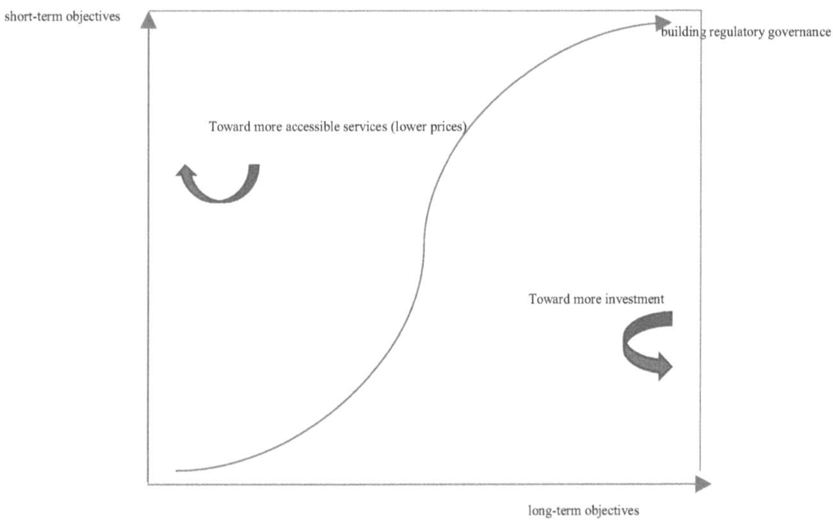

Figure 11.1 Milestones towards sustainable regulatory governance – stages of the transition.

incentives for the expropriation of sunk assets. The environment was conducive to the decisions of the public utilities not to invest, and for the government to intervene. Likewise, assuring the credibility of the government's attitude towards the security of investment was especially required in the face of the urgent need to absorb continuous technological shocks. The inability of a regulatory governance to limit governmental opportunism resulted in inefficiencies and poor sectoral performance, which could be then easily translated into poor service quality, lack of sufficient investment, while also high prices. Regulatory governance was prone to private captures, at least up to 2006, while EU regulation-driven regulatory promotion of service competition forced private investors to abstain from long-term investments and focus more on short-term yield. Continuously low quality, underinvestment, and high prices created a fertile ground for open conflict between operators and the government in the first decade of the 21st century[25] (Office of Electronic Communications, 2005). Aside from this, after the legal adjustments to the EU rules, there was a subsequent breakthrough in the process of shaping institutionally driven regulatory schemes. Currently, regulatory governance adjustment processes are dominated by adjustments of regulatory governance structures to strengthen long-term investment.

The maturity process of regulatory governance as the milestones towards a more stable legal framework, separation of roles and responsibilities, principles of good regulation, forming a "whole-of-government view", provision of relevant information, providing reasons for decisions, exposure to scrutiny, the possibility of independent review are all portrayed through stages of advancement that are presented in Table 11.3.

The key motive of regulatory governance in the initial transition stages was to regulate the behaviour of a powerful player, not to hold back competition in the existing and emerging markets, while also to safeguard user rights in situations where ceding the provision of telecommunications services to market forces led to a lack of access to services in the areas that were not economically viable. This process was filled with the gradual creation of legal norms, the establishment of independent regulatory bodies to guard the proper development of telecommunications markets (anticipatory public influence on the economy), progressive withdrawal of the state from monopolizing the provision of telecommunications services, while increasing the expansion of markets.

Regulatory policy favouring lower retail prices and competition was implemented, yet insufficient promotion of investment[26] was evident. Against the backdrop of the special role of key equipment in the sectoral and ex-ante nature of regulatory law (Skoczny, 2002, 245), the aggravation of the UKE-TP SA conflict in 2006 resounded when the incumbent challenged the legality of the appointment and regulatory decisions of the President of the Regulatory Authority. In 2009, the Agreement between TP SA and the President of UKE emerged, under which Telekomunikacja Polska S.A. pledged to take concrete steps to improve cooperation between TP SA and alternative operators and to properly perform all regulatory obligations imposed on the company. In addition, TP SA undertook to separate the wholesale services section from its structure and to reduce the discriminatory flow

Table 11.3 Stages of the regulatory governance development

2004–2006	*2007–2009*	*2010–2018*	*2019–2021*
Legal frameworks	*TP SA – UKE institutional adjustments/ battles*	*Pro-investment endeavours*	*The EU search for more effective institutional framework for market regulation*
The institutional endowment of Poland's regulatory capacity restrained the list of regulatory governance designs available; additionally, the choice of designs was limited to the list acquired through the EU *acquis communautaire*; The creation of legal norms, while also subjecting the Polish telecommunications regulatory system to the regulation of a specialized regulatory body, intending to protect competition in telecommunications markets under conditions of liberalization of the electronic communications sector.	The costs of implementing safeguards became lower through further acquisition of the EU regulatory rules, but the environment was still not conducive to cooperation so the regulatory policy was implemented with the support of safeguards such as ex-ante, institutionally inflexible regulatory rules to enforce longer-term private investment and restraining incumbent operator's opportunism.	The institutional environment got more and more open to cooperation and regulatory policy was becoming more mature, while the role of costly safeguards was diminishing, as was the responsiveness to political shocks; Attempts were made to find the right regulatory reaction to the lack of high-risk and long-term investment. More intensive presence of industry representatives within public consultations, discussions emerged.	The challenge was to make private investors more open and have less fear of long-term investments in very high-capacity networks, including fixed, mobile, and wireless; leverage the digital inclusiveness of the EU societies; Expectations towards more responsiveness to the economic and technological shocks and less to political demands were viewed critically amid BEREC's and national regulatory agencies' substantial discretion power in areas such as co-investment, symmetric regulation, network neutrality.
Telecommunications Law of July 16, 2004. – Journal of Laws 2004 No. 171, item 1800.	2009 TP SA – UKE Agreement.	The Law on Support for the Development of Telecommunications Networks and Services of May 7, 2010 – Journal of Laws 2010, Journal of Laws 2010 no. 106 pos. 675.	Directive 2018/1972 establishing the European Electronic Communications Code.

Source: Self-analysis based on resources from Tables 11.1 and 11.2.

of unauthorized information both within the company itself and between TP Group entities. One of the most important provisions of the Agreement (institutionally rigid regulatory measure) was a commitment to build or upgrade at least 1.2 million broadband lines, which was part of the regulator's efforts to strengthen the expansion of telecommunications infrastructure in Poland. At the same time, work was underway on a draft law to support the development of telecommunications networks and services, culminating in its passing by the Sejm on May 7, 2010 (Broadband Act). The primary objective of the law was to ensure the development of access to telecommunications services and networks, with particular emphasis on the development of broadband Internet access and the elimination of geographic digital exclusion.

The search for more flexibility of the regulatory ecosystem in terms of institutional patterns in order to make regulatory systems more adaptable to shocks, and the need for more technological responsiveness have led to the new EU regulatory frameworks (European Electronic Communications Code). Within these legal arrangements, more regulatory discretion was granted to the Body of European Regulators for Electronic Communications (BEREC). Moreover, the National Regulatory Agencies (NRAs) are expected to be used to reinforce the policies aiming to boost very high-capacity connectivity and sustainable competition (Vogelsang, 2019, 1–10).

The transposition of the European Electronic Communications Code, which is being implemented in Poland to meet the need to guarantee universal access to fast and reliable Internet for European workers, citizens, and tourists, strengthens the consumer's position vis-à-vis service providers.[27] The expectations relating to the law are all the more realistic because of more check-and-balance properties in existing and emerging institutions (public consultations of draft law, regulatory impact assessment procedures). The delays associated with the transposition of the European Electronic Communications Code into Polish law are explained by officials as the extent of the public consultations carried out (847 comments from consultations on the draft law taken into account). This confirms the strengthening of the participatory pattern – the provision of relevant information, providing reasons for decisions within the framework of regulatory governance, based on the participation of market players, i.e. chambers of commerce, for example, in the regulatory design process.

The pillars of the Digital Single Market Strategy (2015)[28] or the Directive (EU) 2018/1972 establishing the European Electronic Communications Code[29] confirm the EC's efforts to intensify the investment activities of players in the sector throughout all the member countries. The balance between the need to provide the public with full access to telecommunications services and the search for ways to strengthen sector investment continues. This trend has recently resounded with the EC's strong emphasis on favouring the integration of the mobile telecommunications market (building a single telecommunications market), as confirmed in statements by the commissioner responsible for the development of electronic communications in the EU.[30] It is accompanied by constant efforts to adjust the regulatory governance for building a pro-competitive regime for digital markets to balance anti-competitive effects of lower competition with potential efficiencies - the announcement of the Digital Market Unit, as an example.[31]

11.5 Conclusions

Taking a searching perspective in pursuit of the goal of regulatory adjustment in the telecommunications sector into account, which remains the development of regulatory governance that efficiently safeguards socio-economic goals, it is useful to specifically highlight the never-ending evolution of the electronic communications market which is technologically, economically, and politically driven. A crucial element against the background is the distribution of the burden of financing investment. The process of building the regulatory governance of the telecommunications sector in Poland came across a decision corridor defined by, on the one hand, the pursuit of low prices, better availability, and quality of service, while on the other hand, the absorption of technology shocks and increased investment (see: Scheme 1). Over time, as the nature of regulatory governance in the sector took on more intense check-and-balance properties and more advanced telecommunications technology was adopted, the regulatory relations were stronger in terms of the legally secured role of consumers in the markets for the broad perception of telecommunications services. Moreover, they also stabilized more intensive participation of other market participants through consultations on draft legislation in the shape of sectoral regulation, including those related to investments.

The regulatory governance in the telecommunications sector regulation in Poland has been shaped in the dimension of administrative procedures, mainly through a set of administrative obligations resulting from EU law. The regulation of the telecommunications sector which has been in place since 2004 is a serious subject in EU regulations which has made Polish transformation arrangements more open, flexible, and effective. In the judicial review dimension, the shape of regulatory governance in the telecommunications sector in Poland has been influenced by the existence of permanent arbitration consumer courts at the Presidency of the UKE (then, alternative consumer dispute resolution), the Administrative Procedure Code as a basis for resolving proceedings at the Presidency of the Office of the Telecommunications Regulatory Authority, appeals to the Court of Competition and Consumer Protection, the provisions of the Civil Procedure Code (in appeal proceedings concerning the regulation of telecommunications and postal services). At the level of building the platform for the advancement of participation of multiple interest groups in order to enhance regulatory transparency, regulatory governance has been shaped by the obligation of the President of UKE to consult before issuing a decision, while also the obligation of the President of UKE to conduct consultation, consolidation and mediation proceedings in disputes between consumers and telecommunications service providers and entrepreneurs, as well as the cyclical publication of indicators monitoring the incumbent's actions in terms of discrimination against alternative operators, publication of a report on the state of the telecommunications market, while also subjecting draft laws to public consultation and discussions with industry representatives.

Notes

1 According to the Report on the State of the Telecommunications Market in 2004, Telekomunikacja Polska (TP SA) – the incumbent of the telecommunications sector in Poland, dominated the fixed telephony market by holding 65% of the Internet access market, while also owning 91.2% of telephone lines and was a major player in the inter-operator cooperation market with a 90% share; while as a result of the inspection activities of the sector regulator (President of the Telecommunications and Postal Regulatory Authority, URTiP) in resolving inter-operator disputes, it was indicated that in almost all cases the decisions of the President of URTIP regarding the terms of interconnection of the incumbent's network with other operators' networks encountered serious problems during their implementation, in which the main problem was that the regulator's decisions were implemented too slowly.

2 Restraining government opportunism is meant to limit political support for the government-regulator to lower prices at the expense of diminishing an operator's abilities and incentives to invest in longer-term (promoting service competition versus infrastructure competition).

3 The telecommunications industry is meant to be the provision of communications and data services, empowering people in their daily lives to communicate, have access to information, facilitate trade and financial transactions, provide services (entertainment, digital learning, telemedicine), while also to support disruptive new business models technologically. The telecommunication sector sets the basis for ICT development and appears to be the sector that is mostly prone to disruptive technology developments calling for dynamism of regulatory governance adjustment.

4 High-powered incentives provide operators with powerful incentives to reduce costs (a substantial percentage of costs at a margin is borne by a firm; the firm is fully accountable for its cost savings), while at the same time requiring stable and mature institutions to exist and for the high-powered incentives not to be suppressed; low-powered incentives provide operators with no incentives to reduce costs as the firm is not made accountable for its cost savings (the firm's costs are fully reimbursed); J. J. Laffont, J. Tirole, Competition in telecommunications. Munich Lectures in Economics, The MIT Press, 2002, p. 39.

5 Regulatory inflexibility under conditions of institutional immaturity in post-socialist Poland manifested in direct agreements between the regulator and TP SA on the amount of investment, which, for example, must be made by the operator under threat of functional separation (TP-UP Agreement, 2009).

6 In Poland, a period of intensive regulation stimulating service competition (regulatory reduction of wholesale access prices to the incumbent's infrastructure for alternative operators) has shaped a very unfavourable investment environment for operators with the greatest investment potential, i.e. the incumbent. The regulator's forcing of certain actions on the incumbent took the form of issuing a threat to apply a regulatory tool in the form of functional separation of the incumbent, TP SA. This element of the picture of sector regulation in the telecommunications markets (2009) showed the institutional weakness (systemic weakness, shaky stability) of the sector regulatory process and exemplified the use of rigid regulation against incumbents in the markets.

7 For example, the ideological foundation of the regulatory model, whose authorship is attributed to Prof. Littlechild (1983, UK); the model that popularized the concept of incentive regulation with the greatest recognition and widest application; the core of its regulatory design is based on a price system. At the same time, its original concept was aimed at minimizing the regulator's discretion, including deference to interest groups. The proposed price cap regulatory formula was intended to provide the operator with pro-efficiency incentives (shifting responsibility for bearing costs to the operator), while leaving the operator free to use the windfall surplus earned through efficiency gains. Under this formula, there was to be an emphasis on increasing the operator's flexibility

and moving away from the regulator's discretionary power; M. Moran, The British Regulatory State, Oxford University Press 2003, p. 105.

8 In transition economies, i.e. Poland, associations of operators were formed as competition provided by law and problems emerged, especially for alternative operators, in the markets where TP SA dominated. The chambers of commerce in particular had their role in influencing UKE's decisions: the Polish Chamber of Electronic Communications (PIKE), the Polish Chamber of Commerce for Electronics and Telecommunications (KIGEiT), the Polish Chamber of Information Technology and Telecommunications (PIIT), the National Chamber of Ethernet Communications (KIKE), Association (cluster) e-Południe.

9 The liberalization of the telecommunications services sector in post-socialist Poland since the early 1990s manifested itself in the successive adoption and amendment of laws regulating telecommunications activities in the country, i.e. the Communications Act of November 23, 1990 (the establishment of TP SA, the slow liberalization of local and long-distance fixed-line services, the maintenance of TP's monopoly on international services), its amendment in 1995 (allowing the issuance of permits for the establishment and use of telecommunications networks and for the realization of telecommunications activities – in local markets the duopoly principle), the Telecommunications Act of July 21, 2000 (facilitating the activities of operators newly entering markets by abolishing licences, obliging the incumbent to lease lines, while also gradually liberalizing long-distance and international calls), its 2003 amendment (harmonization of Polish law with EU directives and introduction of further liberalization), the Telecommunications Law of July 16, 2004 (expanding consumer rights, introducing more regulatory tools serves to control markets to support equal competition).

The privatization of Telekomunikacja Polska came relatively late at the end of 1998 (compared to, for example, the Czech Republic's Cesky Telekom in 1995, or Hungary's Matav 1993), when the company went public on the Warsaw Stock Exchange (the largest privatization in the Polish market at the time) with 15% of the company's capital, and later on the London Stock Exchange. Subsequently, following a decision of the Council of Ministers in July 2000, the company entered the next phase of privatization and 35% of TP SA shares were sold to a consortium of France Telecom and Kulczyk Holding. In 2001, the consortium bought another 12.5% of shares from the Treasury. In 2005, Kulczyk Holding withdrew from the consortium, and also until 2010 FT made small purchases of TP SA shares from the State Treasury (the last one in 2010 – 4.15%), and as a result FT took a 50.67% stake in TP in 2013; Parkiet, Prywatyzacja Telekomunikacji Polskiej do tej pory budzi kontrowersje, 28.11.2013, https://www.parkiet.com/technologie/art23093681-prywatyzacja-telekomunikacji-polskiej-do-tej-pory-budzi-kontrowersje

10 Examples include TP's monopolistic behaviour triggered by the 1995 amendment to the Communications Act of November 23, 1990, where the announced increase in competition in the markets for local services was not realized, as well as many subsequent behavioural patterns revealed by, for example, the Office of Competition and Consumer Protection (see the decisions of the President of UOKiK against TP SA or later Orange https://decyzje.uokik.gov.pl/bp/dec_prez.nsf).

11 Office of Electronic Communications. (2008). *Analiza funkcjonalnej separacji Telekomunikacji Polskiej S.A.*, KPMG Advisory, Kancelaria Grynhoff, Woźny, Maliński, Instytut Łączności, Warszawa, p. 303-317.

12 OECD. Stat, Telecommunications database; https://stats.oecd.org/#; 2004: POL 10 034 134, GER 39 081 000, UK: 31 331 354 (retrieved 20.02.2023)

13 For example, in Poland, France Telecom (now Orange), on the one hand, is a French public company (50.67% of shares), while on the other hand, it is an important company with a strategic infrastructure for Poland, serving large parts of Polish society with services of particular social and economic importance.

14 For example, the consideration of functional separation as a very interventionist regulatory tool (supported by the European Commission, according to the then UKE President – Anna Streżyńska, a great advocate of this regulatory solution).

15 The Supreme Chamber of Control (Najwyższa Izba Kontroli), Informacja o wynikach kontroli prywatyzacji Telekomunikacji Polskiej SA, Warsaw October 2000; Parkiet, Prywatyzacja Telekomunikacji Polskiej do tej pory ... op. cit. revealed numerous irregularities around the privatization of the national operator in a strategic economic sector; the takeover of TP SA shares by the France Telecom - Kulczyk Holding consortium was marked by staying out of the liberalization of the lucrative market for international fixed-line services for a relatively long period of time, the non-disclosure of the content of the privatization agreement, suspicions of numerous corruptions; Moreover, the presidents of the sector regulatory authority prior to 2006 held positions in oligopolistic telecommunications companies, and so: Stanislaw Szuder (Chief Inspector of the State Telecommunications Inspectorate, 1991–1995), from 1993 in the private sector: Director of AT&T Telfa (Lucent Technologies Poland), 2001–2007 Vice President of the EMEA region of this concern, from 2007 Vice-President, and since 2012 President of the telecommunications company Energo-Tel; Vice-President of the section in the National Chamber of Commerce for Electronics and Telecommunications; Marek Zdrojewski (President of the Telecommunications Regulatory Authority, 2000–2001) appointed to the management and supervisory bodies of, among others, telecommunications companies; Kazimierz Ferenc (President of the Telecommunications Regulatory Authority, 2001–2002) served as President of the Board of Directors of the Centre for Trust and Certification CENTRAST S.A from 2002 to 2005, while also held the position of Vice-President of the Board of Directors of Polskie Sieci Elektroenergetyczne until 2007; Witold Graboś (President of the Telecommunications and Postal Regulatory Authority, 2002–2006) held the position of advisor to the President of Emitel (former branch of TP SA) just before becoming the President of the Regulatory Authority and prior to becoming a member of the National Broadcasting Council in 2010, as well as just after leaving the Council in 2016 (in 1995–2001, while in 2010–2016 he served in the National Broadcasting Council).

16 The cesura that was approved in 1990 when the Balcerowicz Plan was adopted; reforms perceived as a method for rapid transition to a capitalist market economy (also termed "shock therapy").

17 Faced with the threat of UKE's implementation of a regulatory tool in the form of functional separation intensified particularly in 2008, TP SA proposed to the regulator to introduce better monitoring of service quality as part of self-monitoring (TP SA's internal control) in exchange for waiving the use of this instrument. As a result, the content of the TP-UKE Agreement was worked out by October 2009, in which TP SA pledged to build and modernize 1.2 million broadband Internet access lines and improve relations with alternative operators in exchange for maintaining wholesale rates for alternative operators in favour of TP SA until 2012 and suspending the decision to split TP SA into wholesale and retail parts. Despite expressing some reservations about the implementation of the Arrangement, it was assessed in positive terms overall. In 2012, UKE did not decide to split TP SA.

18 In addition to the clear example of the market effects generated as a result of the TP-UKE Agreement, there were numerous entities in the sector in the form of the chambers of commerce, which, bringing together companies operating in the telecommunications area that represented their interests and lobbied for legal solutions that were favourable to them, while also acting as their spokespeople before the legislative, executive or regulatory authorities, as well as working for the equal realization of business by all entities under conditions of the unambiguous interpretation of laws. Examples of such entities are the Polish Chamber of Electronic Communications (founded in 2005), the Polish Chamber of Commerce for Electronics and Telecommunications (founded in 1992),

the Polish Chamber of Information Technology and Telecommunications (founded in 1993), as well as the National Chamber of Ethernet Communications (founded in 2008).

19 Two legal regimes – the Law of July 21, 2000, and the Law of July 16, 2004. – Journal of Laws, 2004 No. 171, item 1800, implemented the so-called regulatory package of Directives of the European Parliament and the Council of 2002, while constituting legal relations in the field of telecommunications within the framework of the Telecommunications Law.

20 For around four months in 2006 the acting President of UKE, Anna Streżyńska, was at the same time Deputy Minister responsible for communications; a fact which was exploited by the incumbent operator (TP SA) that questioned the legality of the appointment of the President of UKE, and apart from this, the legality of her regulatory decisions.

21 The expenses and revenues of the Office of Electronic Communications are realized in part 76 of the state budget. Around 90% of the Authority's main source of income are incomes from fees such as frequency, numbering, etc.

22 Recent KPI analysis indicated no discriminatory phenomena, although the continued need for monitoring in subsequent reporting periods prevails; TP zaczyna publikację KPI, żeby uchronić się przed podziałem, Telepolis 05.11.2008, https://www.telepolis.pl/wiadomosci/wydarzenia/tp-zaczyna-publikacje-kpi-zeby-uchronic-sie-przed-podzialem

23 The EC may require the NRA to withdraw its draft regulatory decision (while attaching a detailed analysis and specific proposals for change) within the new procedure under the EECC which applies only to the symmetric access beyond the first distribution point (art 61.3) and co-investment offers in VHCN (*very high capacity network elements*) (art. 76).

24 In 2004, TP SA remained the largest operator and provider of telecommunications services in the fixed-line market. In terms of Internet access services in Poland, the largest providers held about 82% of the total market share, of which 65% was held by TP SA (Report on the State of the Telecommunications Market in 2004, Office of Telecommunications and Postal Regulation, Warsaw 2005, p. 58). In 2008–2009, TP SA continued to dominate the fixed and mobile Internet access market in terms of the number of users, with a share of 36.4% (2008) and 26.9% (2009). In 2009, the penetration of broadband services provided by fixed networks was 13.5% in Poland (the lowest in the EU, alongside Bulgaria and Romania at 13%, and with an EU-27 average of 24.8%), while in terms of access to broadband services via modems in mobile networks in 2009 at 5.5%, with an EU average of 6% (Report on the State of the Telecommunications Market in Poland in 2009, Office of Electronic Communications, p. 17). Penetration with fixed Internet services (calculated by the number of users per population) in Poland in 2021 increased, but still remained the lowest among EU countries (22.4% with the EU average at 35.4%). The penetration of mobile internet services remained the highest in Poland among the EU countries, in July 2021 – 199.8%, with the EU average at 111% (Report on the State of the Telecommunications Market in Poland in 2021, Office of Electronic Communications, Warsaw 2022, pp. 20, 21, 26, 28; Digital Agenda Scoreboard, July 2021). The cost of fixed Internet access service in Poland in 2021 was at one of the lowest levels among EU countries (Poland was, along with Hungary and Lithuania, the country with the cheapest Internet access). Prices for fixed broadband Internet access in Poland were at a level lower than the EU average, with Netia providing all the least expensive offers (the operator who was the first to obtain a binding agreement with TP SA in 2007 to unbundle access to the local access loop, enabling it to offer its own differentiated broadband services on the basis of TP's access network). Prices for mobile broadband in Poland are much lower than those in the EU on average, with Orange Poland providing the majority of the least expensive offers, and P4 the remainder (Mobile and Fixed Broadband Prices in Europe 2021, European Commission

2022, p. 278, 282). However, the share of 4G in mobile access in Poland in 2021 was the lowest in the EU – with the EU average at 80.6%, whereas 67.2% in Poland (Report on the state of the telecommunications market in Poland in 2021, Office of Electronic Communications, Warsaw 2022, p.29).

25 Concluded with the signing of the TP-UKE Agreement in October 2009.

26 Reports on the state of the telecommunications market in Poland reported that the state of Poland's telecommunications infrastructure, as well as its availability and coverage, were at a very low level, especially compared to other EU member states. Thus, the need for legislative interference was justified.

27 The regulation includes the presentation of pre-contractual information on price, summary of contract terms, the right to compensation, so as to increase the comparability of offers from multiple providers. The regulations cover broader electronic communication services than before, i.e. also interpersonal communication services that do not use numbers (e.g. email, instant messaging). The regulations also introduce a number of legal improvements related to access to property and use of technical infrastructure for public communications (telecommunications networks and related resources for the provision of publicly available telecommunications services).

28 *Better access for consumers and businesses to digital goods and services across the EU; Creating the right conditions and a level playing field for digital networks and innovative service to flourish; Maximizing the growth potential of the digital economy*; Communication from the Commission to the European Parliament, the European Council, the European Economic and Social Committee and the Committee of the Regions. A Digital Single Market Strategy for Europe, COM(2015) 192 final, Brussels, 6.5.2015.

29 Inter alia: *to increase competition and predictability for investment; to reduce regulation for co-investment of rival operators in very high-capacity networks*; Electronic communications sector directives Directive 2002/21/EC of the European Parliament and of the Council of March 7, 2002 on a common regulatory framework for electronic communications networks and services (Framework Directive), in 2018 this was replaced and repealed by the Directive 2018/1972 establishing the European Electronic Communications Code.

30 Margrethe Vestager, the Executive Vice President of the European Commission for a Europe fir for the Digital Age and Commissioner for Competition; S. Bicheno, EU confirms *single telecoms market* policy, Telecoms.com, February 03, 2023, https://telecoms.com/519735/eu-confirms-single-telecoms-market-policy/; As an example of a trans-European operator, one points to the French operator Orange, the same one that was taking over the Polish national operator TP SA since 2000.

31 Regulation (EU) 2022/1925 of the European Parliament and of the Council of 14 September 2022 on contestable and fair markets in the digital sector and amending Directives (EU) 2019/1937 and (EU) 2020/1828 (Digital Markets Act).

References

Decisions of the President of UOKiK against TP SA or later Orange https://decyzje.uokik.gov.pl/bp/dec_prez.nsf.

Directive 2002/21/EC of the European Parliament and of the Council of March 7, 2002 on a common regulatory framework for electronic communications networks and services (Framework Directive).

Directive 2018/1972 establishing the European Electronic Communications Code.

Directive 2018/1972 establishing the European Electronic Communications Code.

Directives of the European Parliament and the Council of 2002, constituting legal relations in the field of telecommunications within the framework of the Telecommunications Law.

Electronic communications sector Directive 2002/21/EC of the European Parliament and of the Council of March 7, 2002 on a common regulatory framework for electronic communications networks and services (Framework Directive).

European Commission. (2022). Mobile and Fixed Broadband Prices in Europe 2021.

European Commission, Digital Agenda Scoreboard, July 2021.

Goldberg, V. (1976). Regulation and administered contracts. *Bell Journal of Economics,* 7 (2), 426–452. https://doi.org/10.2307/3003265

IBM. (2003). *4th Report on Monitoring of EU Candidate Countries* (Telecommunication Services Sector).

Joskow, P. (1991) The role of transaction cost economics in antitrust and public utility regulatory policies. *Journal of Law, Economics and Organization*, 7, 253–283. https://doi.org/10.1093/jleo/7.special_issue.53

Kawka, I. (2011). *Zasady dobrego rządzenia w prawie Unii Europejskiej. Sektory infrastrukturalne*, Wydawnictwo Naukowe Uniwersytetu Pedagogicznego w Krakowie.

Kubasik, J. (2004). Telecommunications tariffs in Poland and new EU member countries: Current status and perspectives. *ITU Seminar*, Vilnius October 5–7.

Laffont, J. J. (2005). *Regulation and Development*, Cambridge: Cambridge University Press.

Laffont, J. J., and Tirole, J. (2001). *Competition in Telecommunications*, Cambridge & London: MIT Press.

Levy, B., and Spiller, P. T. (1996). A framework for resolving the regulatory problem. In Levy, B. and Spiller, P. T. (eds.), *Regulation, Institutions, and Commitment in Telecommunications. A Comparative Analysis of Five Country Studies*, Cambridge: Cambridge University Press.

Moran, M. (2003). *The British Regulatory State*, Oxford: Oxford University Press.

North, D. C. (1990). *Institutions, Institutional Change and Economic Performance*, Cambridge: Cambridge University Press.

OECD (2020). Stat, Telecommunications Database. https://stats.oecd.org/#

Office of Electronic Communications. (2005). *Report on the State of the Telecommunications Market in 2004*, Warsaw.

Office of Electronic Communications. (2008). *Analiza funkcjonalnej separacji Telekomunikacji Polskiej S.A.*, KPMG Advisory, Kancelaria Grynhoff, Woźny, Maliński, Instytut Łączności, Warszawa.

Office of Electronic Communications. (2010). *Report on the State of the Telecommunications Market in Poland in 2009*, Warsaw.

Office of Electronic Communications (2022). *Report on the State of the Telecommunications Market in Poland in 2021*, Warsaw.

Parkiet. (2013). *Prywatyzacja Telekomunikacji Polskiej do tej pory budzi kontrowersje*, 28.11.2013, https://www.parkiet.com/technologie/art23093681-prywatyzacja-telekomunikacji-polskiej-do-tej-pory-budzi-kontrowersje

Polanyi, K. (2010). *Wielka Transformacja. Polityczne i ekonomiczne źródła naszych czasów*, Wydawnictwo PWN, Warszawa K. Polanyi. (1944). *The Great Transformation. The Political and Economic Origins of Our Times*, Boston, MA: Beacon Press.

Ricketts, M. (2006). Economic regulation: Principles, history, and methods. In Crew, M. and Parker, D. (eds.), *International Handbook on Economic Regulation*, Cheltenham, UK and Northampton, USA: Edward Elgar.

Skoczny, T. (2002) Wspólnotowe prawo regulacji „in statu nescendi". In Mika, C. (ed.), *Prawo gospodarcze Wspólnoty Europejskiej na progu XXI wieku*, Toruń.

Śliwa, R. (2019). Towards the maturity of ICT regulation – integrated regulation. *Economic Review,* 48, 2. https://doi.org/10.53465/ER.2644-7185

Spiller, Pablo T., and Sampson, Cezley I. (1993). Regulation, institutions and commitment: The Jamaican telecommunications sector. *Policy Research Working Paper Series* 1362, The World Bank. https://doi.org/10.1017/cbo9781139174589.005

Spiller, P. T., and Tommasi, M. (2003). The institutional foundations of public policy: Theory and an application to Argentina. *Journal of Law, Economics and Organization,* 19(2), 281–306. https://doi.org/10.1017/cbo9780511818219.003

Spiller, P. T., and Tommasi, M. (2005). The institutions of regulation: An application to public utilities. In Menard, C. and Shirley, M. (eds.), *Handbook of New Institutional Economics* , (pp. 515–543), Berlin, Heidelberg: Springer.

Statistics Poland, Telekomunikacja. https://stat.gov.pl/obszary-tematyczne/transport-i-lacznosc/lacznosc/telekomunikacja-w-2021-roku,2,6.html.

Supreme Chamber of Control (Najwyższa Izba Kontroli). (October 2000). Informacja o wynikach kontroli prywatyzacji Telekomunikacji Polskiej SA, Warsaw October 2000.

Telecommunications Law of July 16, 2004. *Journal of Laws*, No. 171, item 1800.

Telecommunications Law of July 21, 2000. *Journal of Laws,* No. 73, item 852.

Telepolis. (2008). *TP zaczyna publikację KPI, żeby uchronić się przed podziałem*, 05.11.2008. https://www.telepolis.pl/wiadomosci/wydarzenia/tp-zaczyna-publikacje-kpi-zeby-uchronic-sie-przed-podzialem

Vass, P. (2006). Regulatory governance and the lessons from UK practice. In Crew, M. and Parker, D. (eds.), *International Handbook on Economic Regulation*, Cheltenham: Edward Elgar Publishing.

Vogelsang, I. (2019). Has Europe missed the endgame of telecommunications policy? *Telecommunications Policy*, 43(1), 1–10.

Williamson, O. E. (1988). The logic of economic organization. *Journal of Law, Economics and Organization* 4(1), 65–93. https://doi.org/10.1093/oxfordjournals.jleo.a036949

12 The Hungarian energy policy from the system change to mature EU membership – adequacy with regard to current challenges

Sarolta Somosi[1]

12.1 Introduction

The creation of energy policies should always take into consideration the different aspects of political, economic, security, and of late, environmental issues (Khan et al. 2021). After the evolution of energy policy goals within the recent decades, now the **energy trilemma** describes the challenges energy markets and policies should face when addressing conflicting challenges such as the following: ensuring energy security, providing energy equity, and achieving environmental sustainability (WEC 2022). It is about the constant balance between the three-fold priorities of the "holy trinity" of energy policy that sets the future course and policy formation guidelines for the member states (MSs). Following the outbreak of Russian aggression in Ukraine, this trilemma has turned into environmental, socio-economic, and (geo)political challenges. In the meantime, energy policy still relies on the geographical position, natural conditions, inherited systems, structures, and relations, in which any shift requires time and investments.

At the European Union (EU) level, the creation of a commonly acceptable policy was even a bigger challenge, having highly diverse domestic energy settings. Establishing the European Energy Union brought and continues to bring numerous difficulties. The EU MSs could so far keep important parts of their energy policies (such as the set of their energy mix) in their hands, resulting in a wide variety regarding resource endowments, national policy objectives, technological readiness, industrial reliance on energy, etc. Other fields, however, have been put under common regulations of the energy union and the climate-related common regulations.

Central and Eastern European (CEE) countries have made a big effort to overcome the historical dependencies, but their energy mix and energy sectors still rely on coal (Poland), natural gas (Hungary and Slovakia), and oil (Hungary and Poland). This determines local energy policies and the approaches of contemporary governments towards energy-related objectives, such as availability and accessibility (security of supply), affordability (for households with lower income compared to core EU countries), while also questions of competitiveness due to energy prices and Real Unit Energy Costs (RUEC) that significantly determines their future Foreign Direct Investment (FDI) attraction capability and export potential.

DOI: 10.4324/9781003425717-16

Several papers covered the Hungarian energy policy containing detailed criticisms of the overall energy policy (Szabo et al. 2021) or some selected fields such as energy security (Varró 2007; Weiner 2019) and the nature of diversification (Weiner 2019). Other papers have discussed the nature of the country's economic settings (Farkas 2018), which can now fit Baldwin's headquarters and the factory-economy model better (Baldwin 2012; Szalavetz 2017), or to patchwork capitalism within the CEE by Rapacki and Czerniak (2018).

Our chapter provides an assessment of the directions of the historical evolution of the Hungarian energy policy, with its embeddedness in the (changing) national institutional framework (state formation, main objectives, role of EU institutional impact). Hence, the evaluation of the last three decades of the Hungarian energy policy is based on the findings of the afore-mentioned studies, data from the Eurostat, while paying attention to the national institutional framework. We shall focus on Hungary's performance in the selected fields of the energy market and policy, but data from the Visegrad Group is provided as a comparison, as well as Austria being indicated as a benchmark.

The chapter hereinafter is constructed as follows. First, we shall briefly introduce the broader economic conditions that resulted in the dependent market economy (DME) nature of the country. Subsequently, we shall focus on the three decades-long history of the Hungarian energy regulation and settings with reference to the institutional perspective. The period we shall examine starts from the transition from socialism to present days and in our analysis, we identified four (plus one) periods. Subsequently, there is an evaluation of the institutional adjustment and readiness of Hungarian energy policy, while also its governance in answering the challenges of the trilemma. Finally, we shall put forward our conclusions.

12.2 The description of the approach: the institutional perspective

After the transition, all post-communist countries suffered from a lack of capital and had a weak civic society. The membership in the EU and in other international institutions exerted a strong impact on their economies (Farkas 2011). The negotiation period and then the EU accession had already commenced support of the building of the institutional and legal background of market-based economies (Bruszt and Vukov 2017). Business actors of the CEE region were to compete on an uneven playing field of the EU's single market, which through the EU's capacity for regulatory convergence and for empowering institutional change in the new MSs (Bruszt and McDermott 2014) created favourable conditions for those business actors that were better endowed with resources. Key domestic actors were incapable of providing economic dynamism, thus leaving that role to incoming multinational companies (MNCs). Without a substantial change from the established varieties of capitalism (VoC), and/or without the development of domestic competitive companies, CEECs were unable to catch up to the Western European economic level. Nölke and Vliegenthart (2009) described this as the **DME** model. They agreed with Bohle and Greskovits (2007) and Farkas (2011) that it was not a question of choice for CEECs, but rather a path dependence since the conditions were all set by different socio-economic and political factors, governance capabilities, participations in integrations, international institutions, global financial and goods markets, while also by FDI.

However, the DME model has its weaknesses. The overall economic development still relies on FDI (Bohle and Greskovits 2019), so the term FDI-based market economy (Drahokoupil and Myant 2015), or FDI-based economic growth model (Farkas 2018) is valid for the Hungarian economy, but some amendments are needed, especially because we believe that a country's (a region's) development path in its last three decades is hardly describable with the same theory based on a single dependence. This puts more emphasis on the dependence on MNCs and less on *the role of the state*. After the transformation of the system, an outlier increase in foreign ownership throughout the economy was visible with respect to other V4 countries. The range of net foreign assets as a proportion of GDP was an average of 81.9% between 1993 and 2015, while peaking in 2009. This brought a dual economic structure without bringing the highest economic efficiency and GDP growth (György and Oláh 2019). Since 2010, a reverse process has been noted in Hungary, which is evident with the expression of the will to increase the domestic ownership in banking, media, energy, and retail sectors. Due to this policy, in 2022 Hungarian ownership amounted to an average of 51% of the economy, with of course differences among sectors.[2]

Besides the role of the MNCs and FDI inflow, the state's role in redistribution and control of spending EU funds also became important (Bank 2017). They determine investment paths and attract private investors to participate in projects. This corresponds with the findings of Grieveson et al. (2021) in terms of the role of state in the growth model as well. The government also has a significant role in the coordination and support of innovation activities, especially in terms of defining R&D priority areas (Bank 2017). The share of government resources in Hungary has been significantly higher (range from 36 to 42%) for R&D compared to foreign (business and EU-related) resources (10% to 18%) within the period of 2009–2015.[3] Thus, besides the crucial foreign capital and EU funds to the economy (Myant 2018), local capital and the role of the state increased in terms of driving the political agenda. The gradually growing state ownership, while also the increasing role of state-owned enterprises in investments became visible, especially in the energy sector of Hungary. Amending the original concept with the role and influence of the state and at the same time by the implementation of contrasting constraints to them which arise from EU membership and participation in international institutions changes into "double dependence" (so DDME) in the extended version of the model (Lengyel and Bank 2014).

Another weakness of the DME theory is that it lacks *the acknowledgement of mutuality* in the economic dependence (Farkas 2016). According to the model, the CEE region's relative underdevelopment put institutional conditions and the growth possibilities through the necessary capital and technology import. The EU's internal market and its core principles work in support of keeping the most advanced activities in higher-wage countries since the incentives of MNCs to invest in CEE regions' innovations are missing (Ban 2017; Krzywdzinski 2017).

This results in the split of MSs within the internal market into *headquarters (HQ) and factory economies* (Baldwin 2012; Szalavetz 2017). The CEECs' regulatory environment fits the strategic relationships and/or attracting investments. However, in this relation the headquarters economies are also relying on the output of their factory economies, and temporarily they seem to have overcome the changing local institutional conditions until they are not in opposition to their economic interest. There has been no visible impact on inward FDI since 2010 (Greskovits 2015) when the Hungarian state started increasing its role in the economy and directly influencing the corporate governance or changing the operational environment of companies through regulations and distributive mechanisms (especially in the energy sector). It did not visibly affect the export-oriented sectors, but mainly those services where foreign market share was high even in an international comparison (Sass 2017).

The headquarters and factory-economies split of states is also supported by the low median wage structure of the country.[4] Keeping wages down, while attracting MNCs for less-skilled-labour-intensive activities is key to maintaining competitiveness based on low labour costs, and the low bargaining potential of employees therefore contributes to keeping those countries at a lower economic level (Myant 2018). Threats to reshore a plant figure persistently in collective bargaining, while encouraging moderation from employees (Drahokoupil et al. 2015).

Besides the strategic government decisions discussed and the relatively lower wages, cheap and abundant energy has supported FDI inflow for a long time. The RUEC between 2009 and 2015 has decreased from 14% to 9.5% in Hungary (Bartek-Lesi et al. 2019) (Figure 12.1).

The decrease had a wider impact even if industrial activities related to the HQ economy (machinery and automotive industry) are run by a low energy-cost ratio, so they are less sensitive to an energy price increase.

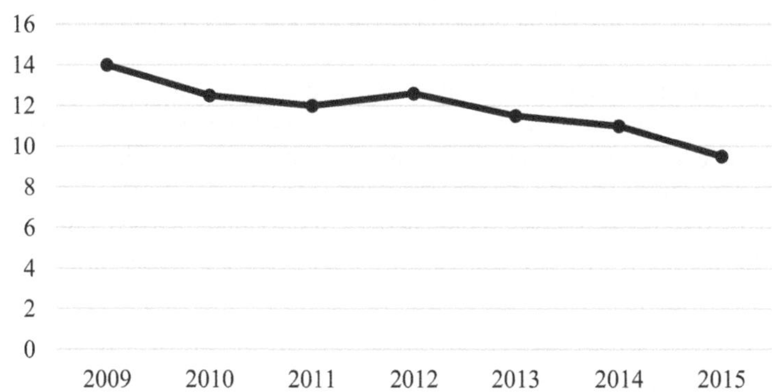

Figure 12.1 Real Unit Energy Costs (RUEC) in Hungary, in %.

Source: Self-analysis based on Bartek-Lesi et al. (2019)

The model of **patchwork capitalism in the CEE** (Rapacki and Czerniak 2018) is also a better description for the converging and diverging transition-specific and path-dependent development of the CEE countries. Hungary and some CEECs are closer to the continental European economic model, with Germany at its core (Rapacki and Czerniak 2018) but will probably never reach the "best practices" provided by Germany (Grieveson et al. 2021). They would be key in the development but set the dependence on foreign demands at a high level.

Overall, the FDI-based economic growth model and the factory-economy nature sets limits for Hungary to catch up to Western Europe. The Hungarian state's increasing role can support development and can also put the country in an unfavourable situation without any perspective. The state's direct involvement in the Hungarian energy policy is observed in terms of the energy policy. Currently, the situation has got worse with the energy market instability and price increases. Some factories and plants have already announced plans to move operations to countries with secure and cheap energy[5] which threatens the whole European industrial and broader economic landscape and the FDI-based growth model of the CEE region. Hence, Hungary must also react to this changing environment.

12.3 Hungarian institutional setting of energy policy with respect to the European Union

The EU's common energy strategy and policy has a real evolutionary path with its variously weighted contemporary objectives (Somosi and Megyeri 2022). When the CEE region's system change happened, the EU was already over its first phase in its common energy policy and strategy. Cooperation on an international level beyond the EEC level started with the handling of energy shortages in the 1970s to provide the **security of energy supply.** Strategic oil reserves, limiting energy consumption in case of shortages and disruptions of energy, while also acting according to the solidarity principle when necessary (Mittra et al. 1995) were all parts of the solution within the EEC. During the first phase of joint EEC-level actions on the energy market, the EU dismissed the importance of deciding about keeping strategic gas reserves (Austvik 2004) in a similar way to oil.

Hungary, being a relatively small, landlocked Central European country, with a low amount of domestic energy resources to meet its demand, while also a relatively unfavourable heritage, has limited possibilities. Since energy policy is designed for the long-term and is highly determined by the strategies and plans of the leading political parties, we set four (plus one) periods of the Hungarian economy in accordance with the work of Pelle and Tabajdi (2023) and we assess how they fit the emphasized objectives of the contemporary "common" energy policy of the EU.

12.3.1 From the point of the transition, the process of privatization and massive influx of foreign direct investment (FDI – until the late 1990s)

Before the transition, the energy market benefited from the secure and single energy supply from the Soviet Union based on "programs" like "gasification" and "energy rationalization" and missing market forces and the contact with the global energy market trends and world economic processes (Szabo et al. 2021). The energy import dependence was about 49.3% in 1990. Figures 12.2 and 12.3 show the final energy consumption and the sources of electricity generation in Hungary in 1990.

With the regime change, there was a need to change the previous centralized governance for a multi-level governance, while also the democratization of energy policy and regulation, albeit the environment was not suitable for doing this properly. The system change should have brought the establishment of markets and market processes, while also private ownership. However, weak legal frameworks, an underdeveloped environment, poor state support for local business activity, and economic development were all common themes for the CEE countries (Myant and Drahokoupil 2010). In Hungary, the well-established "transformational

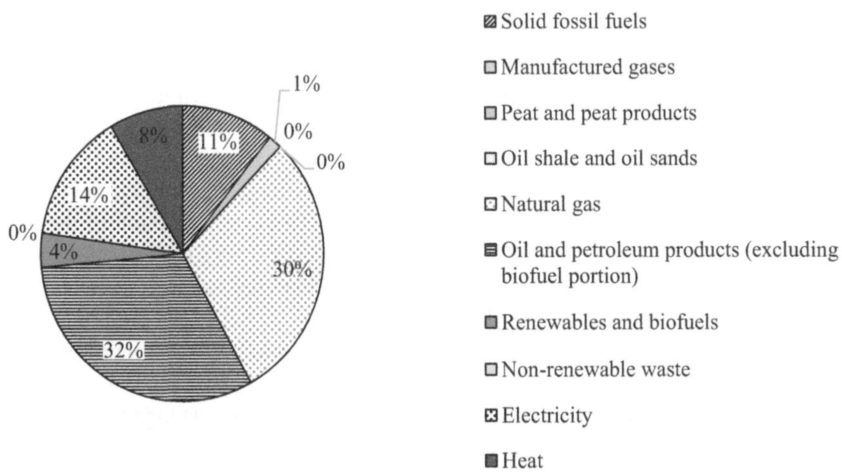

Figure 12.2 Structure of Hungary's total energy consumption in 1990.

Source: Self-analysis based on Eurostat data.

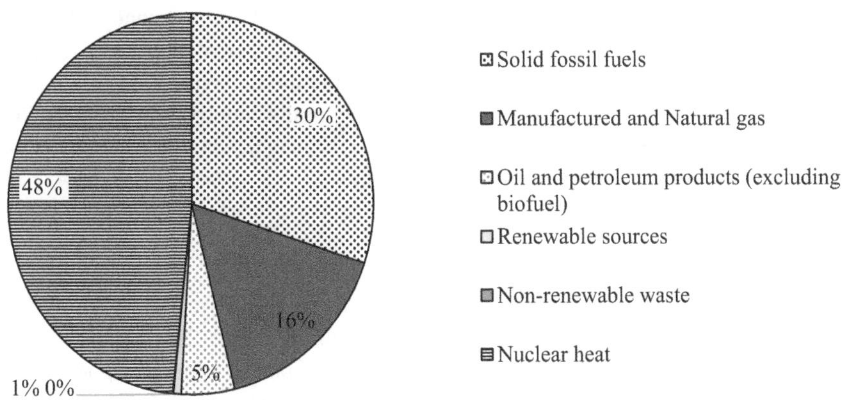

Figure 12.3 Gross electricity production by sources in 1990.

Source: Self-analysis based on Eurostat data.

privatization" of former public properties lost out to the truly slower establishment of the proper institutional background, relevant market regulations, and the foundation of new private enterprises/companies as counterparts of the public companies (Voszka 2018). This was the start of the period of massive FDI inflow into the CEE economies. The selling out of a significant part of state ownership meant that the private sector's share of GDP grew from 33% to 80% from 1991 to 2002. The share of state ownership also decreased in natural gas and electricity industry especially on the integrated retail company level (Felsmann 2014) with the purpose of financing the inherited high indebtedness (Voszka 2018).

Hungary started to create its own **independent energy strategy** in the 1990s. Soon after the transition, with the launch of the first energy strategy in 1993, the previously embedded, incumbent companies faced the loss of their markets which became privatized during the disruption of market integrations and recession, in an environment lacking strong institutions that could have handled and counterbalance the market disruptions. The state's weak position and withdrawal from the (energy) market and from the transformation process was also visible since the new owners of companies in the network industries could enjoy beneficial conditions such as tax allowances, guarantees for advantageous pricing, and future profitability. This situation lasted approximately until the introduction of the next strategy. Within this period, the sustainability aspects of energy markets and energy consumption were not emphasized in the Hungarian energy strategy, while also the security issues received attention later.

During these years, a **privatization and energy market liberalization wave** also started in Western European states, but its nature, objectives, basics, and the pace of processes were all different from those in Hungary. Hungary had shortages in terms of domestic investors, so most of the private ownership increase was backed by FDI and the impact of liberalization on prices (emphasized in Western European states) was not the most important objective in Hungary. Hungary signed the European Energy Charter in 1995, which was designed to improve the energy supply of CEE countries and to support sustainable development and energy efficiency. In 1997, Hungary also joined the International Energy Agency. Between 1998 and 2002, the Hungarian government had a different approach towards Russia, the largest exporter of energy sources, and the diversification of supplies started to become a topic within the energy policy of the country, albeit they lacked real financial and political support (Deák 2006). Hence, the energy dependence on Russia was not dealt with and did not decrease.

12.3.2 Pre-EU-accession (2000–2004) and the early years of EU membership (2004–2010)

At the end of the 20th century and at the beginning of the 21st century, while **embracing climate goals**, environmental issues of energy markets appeared on a EU level. This had a minor impact on the Hungarian system for a couple of years. With the enlargement, Hungary and other Eastern EU members brought new aspects into EU energy policy (a higher unilateral energy import dependence, a lower level of interconnectedness, while also a lower level of awareness towards climate issues, etc.), which already showed a colourful picture prior to 2004 (Deák 2006; Varró 2007).

Fifteen years after transition, Hungary was still vulnerable due to the lack of significant energy sources, having unilateral dependence on solely Russian imports and a lack of storage capacities. This was further intensified by the planning of the new nuclear investment with Russia as a partner within the Teller-Project and Lévai-Project[6] under the administration of 2006–2010. Most of the oil industry and the gas sectors were owned by a partially domestic private actor, MOL (Hungarian Oil Company Ltd), but a significant share of the company had been sold to Russian investors. The country had no significant role and ownership in storage capacities. Most experts urged the balanced, win–win relationship with Russia, while taking into consideration the transit countries. The shortages due to the Russian-Ukraine natural gas wars from the winter of 2006 drew attention to the risks of Hungarian dependence and of also missing the interconnection of networks on a broader EU level (Deák 2006). Albeit, this event (beside others, such as the war in Georgia, a new gas dispute in 2009) appeared as a geopolitical risk especially for CEECs, until 2010 there were no alternative pipeline infrastructures. Russia – without exonerating the participating private companies and contemporary governments – was able to undermine all the projects (Southern Stream, Nabucco Stream) aimed at the diversification of the origins of imported natural gas on a EU level. In the meantime, Russia in cooperation with EU MSs had started the planning phase (2005–2010) and then the establishment (2010–2011) of the Nord Stream I to provide direct access to the core EU countries. Their increasing concerns at that time unified the CEECs under the energy security threats.

The energy market liberalization process is also aimed at reaching the objective of energy equity and affordability by means of competition. By implementing every relevant EU regulation of energy markets, the background and conditions of competition within the sector were established. However, in Hungary, it functioned differently (Varró 2007) since there was no real chance of competition (Kaderják 2009) due to the mishandled unilateral dependence issues regarding Russia. Assets of electricity and gas distribution, while also power plants were sold to mostly European MNCs. Nuclear energy generation and the electricity transmission system operator (TSO) were the only fields kept in state ownership.

The volatile (increasing) energy prices at that time showed the weaknesses of the Hungarian energy system, namely, the dependence and lack of investments in handling the scarcity of resources, while also the lack of effective regulation (Kaderják 2009). A model change in the Hungarian electricity market brought significant changes. In this period, due to the fierce international competition for the investors in industrial production, the main point of the domestic energy policy started to be the maintenance of low utility prices (Szabo et al. 2021). Social aspects also became more important, hence, the price control remained for households, but other consumers had to turn towards the free market of electricity with limited space to modify contracts within the contracted one-year period. There was no liquidity and price transparency, and the system was often criticized for having a lack of planning opportunities. Hungary has also lacked the establishment of electricity stock markets, transparent pricing, and neither the market nor the regulator provided the necessary information for consumers and investors. There was a RES support scheme (the so-called KÁT) dedicated to handling sustainability issues, yet it also had a price increase impact since approximately 42% higher prices appeared on the increasingly supported market (Kaderják 2009, p. 3).[7]

Hence, two of the trilemma challenges were conflicting and for a while, the concerns about energy security were more important for Hungary and other EU-CEE countries than the issue of climate change (Grieveson et al. 2021). The economic crisis of 2008 brought a closure to the period by the decreased energy consumption and the cut or delay of energy-related investments with long-lasting impacts. This was like the case of the Western liberalized energy markets. The period from 2008 to 2010 was a temporary time for the domestic energy policy. The energy strategy accepted in 2008 was not successful partly due to the crisis and the change of the leading political party. Regarding the domestic energy policy and governance, until 2010 policy control over the industry was relatively weak.

12.3.3 The global financial crisis, gas disputes and their aftermath (2010–2013)

From 2010, energy sector became a strategically important branch of the economy and the new government's multi-level intervention determined this period with little autonomy for the regulator in management and planning. This **activism** was reasoned with the relatively high household energy prices (especially in PPS) compared to other EU MSs at that time. In 2010, Hungary had the highest prices, with other V4 countries among those paying the most for energy bills (Weiner and Szép 2022). At the same time, Hungary faced a high unemployment rate of 10.8%. Moreover, a wide range of households had to overcome the impacts of being heavily indebted in foreign currency-related credits with the rocketing exchange rates due to the economic and later Eurozone crisis (in 2009 this reached 70%).

Hence, the reason for introducing a *utility cost reduction programme* under the umbrella of energy equity was to improve the financial background of households. Its positive impact is visible in the change of the percentage of the population at risk of poverty due to having arrears on their utility bills, which reached 25% in 2013 and 9.7% in 2021.[8] Besides this positive impact on households, the measure was far from economic rationale or market conditions. Due to its neutrality to household incomes, the benefits of the system were unequally distributed among income deciles, upper-income households were and continue to be favoured the most (Weiner and Szép 2022). Consumers from the lower decile, who were not even connected to the energy services were subsidized to a limited level, namely, only through wood prices on a social basis. Its negative side effect was a substantial excess in residential energy use. The utility cost reduction also had an impact by means of delayed or cancelled efficiency or RE-related investments in the sector. Investment intensity per consumption practically halved after 2011, a decline that can be only partly explained by the financial and Eurozone crisis (Sebestyénné Szép 2018; Löschel and Managi 2019).

Another piece of evidence (or rather means) of activism on the market was the *increasing state ownership*. Partly because of the realization of projected future income, Hungary put pressure on companies by the activist measures (extra taxes, price squeeze, etc.) and bought back significant shares in energy companies (MOL and E.On gas division in Hungary) (Somosi 2012). Later, MOL also acquired significant shares in the Croatian INA. In 2012, Hungary could also buy back strategic gas storage facilities (21% from Russian Surgut SNGS).[9] Similar processes happened in Slovakia with the Transpetrol (Somosi 2012), in the Czech energy sector with ČEZ Group and EPH (Sass and Vlčková 2019), and in Poland (Pula 2017).

Regarding the **dependence** and security issues of this period, after the Russian–Ukrainian gas dispute of 2009, Hungary was an early mover to enhance natural gas interconnections and implement supply security policies, leading EU efforts and taking advantage of supranational support. Thus, Hungary's overall energy-related dependence has decreased since 2010. In the meantime, Hungary also retained the possibility of having long-term gas supply contracts to ensure the long-term security of energy supply even despite the increased conflicts with the EU. Short-term interests, deliberations, while also the threat of a shortage or future disruption of energy supply related to both energy sources and the origin of energy turned out to be stronger than the sustainability issues.

In the case of climate policy and energy transition commitments, besides some pressure from the domestic industrial policy, they largely relied on external pressure from mainly Western countries and the European Commission (Szabo et al. 2021). The domestic legislative background adjusted to the Europe 2020 Strategy and to the new rules of the third energy package (NES-2030), which was accepted in 2011 (Parliamentary decision 77/2011.).[10] It declared the will to create an increasing state presence in the sector and economic development based on cheap domestic nuclear power (Felsmann 2011; Szabo et al. 2021). It aimed to create a consistent structure of the energy sector and related fields such as climate, renewable energy, energy efficiency, transportation, and even educational strategies. During the assessment of the Hungarian performance in decarbonization, we should keep in mind that EU-CEE started the energy convergence process with flexible targets appropriate to their basic economic development (Wach et al. 2021). Subsequently, the implementation of the Treaty on the Functioning of the EU (TFEU2012) forming the European Internal Energy Market (IEM) also brought some new aspects and assessment into the national energy policies.

The overall EU energy policy created a detailed roadmap for 2030 and a draft strategy for 2050. The objectives of the Hungarian energy policy of 2011 related to the constant balancing within the framework of this roadmap and between the three ends of the energy trilemma: supply security, sustainability, and competitiveness. The strategy covered issues such as energy efficiency, support of renewable and low-carbon technologies, modernization of power plants and community district heating, improving energy efficiency and CO_2 emissions of the transport sector, while also greening of industry and renewable agriculture, waste treatment for energy purposes and the role of the state in achieving the objectives.

12.3.4 After a decade within the EU (2014–2020)

The Energy Union Strategy (EC 2015) aimed to give consumers secure, sustainable, competitive, and affordable energy. It was dedicated to creating a better integrated European energy market. Simultaneously, the EU's energy policy focused more on climate change and how the energy policy can contribute to mitigate it. Aligning to the Paris Agreement of 2015 (EC 2016), the Commission introduced its "Clean Energy For All Europeans" package. The **European Green Deal** (EGD) (EC 2019) provides a strategy for economic growth, environmental issues and has an impact on energy regulation and investments. It requires the active and real contribution of MSs through their National Energy and Climate Plans (NECPs), while targeting the transition to climate neutrality, energy efficiency, or energy poverty.

After several rounds of negotiations, Hungary's second **National Climate Change Strategy** was accepted (with four action plans amending it) in 2018, with detailed plans for 2030 and an outlook for 2050. The need for the submission of a new **National Energy Strategy** was also urgent in 2019 in line with the EU regulation. Hungary submitted its draft **NECP** to the European Commission with a delay at the beginning of January 2020 (ITM 2020). All these elements serve as phases of an integrated energy and climate policy strategy with its special Central European path of higher reliance on nuclear power providing cheap and climate-neutral energy (Kratochvil and Misik 2020). Besides the small wins, there are potential losses as well, especially in the CEE region. The **Just Transition Mechanism** and the **Just Transition Fund** are dedicated to assuring that those sectors, while also consumers affected the most by the structural changes in business models, as well as new skill requirements and relative energy prices will receive support to have the capacity to respond to the new challenges[11] (Overland et al. 2019).

Hungary's **net energy import dependence** has improved since 2005, but still reached 56.63% (2020), while the supplier concentration index has increased from 45.99% in 2005 to 70% in 2020. The IEA calculations show that Hungary's electricity interconnectivity reached 55% in 2020, which is substantially above the EU target of 15% by 2030. According to the EU's database, the ratio of electricity interconnection capacity of Hungary is 35.25% with relation to its total generation capacity, which showed a recent improvement of 6.25%. The n-1 rule for gas improved by 62 from 2009 to 2020, and it reached an infrastructure adequacy where 143% of total demand can be satisfied with the remaining gas infrastructure in case of a disruption of the single largest gas infrastructure element.

Regarding the physical access to energy, some projects (towards Romania and Krk LNG terminal, Turk Stream, etc.) improved the interconnection within the CEE region and Hungary declared its vision to become a regional energy trading hub (Szabo and Fabok 2020). However, the most important origin of energy source remained Russia, both for the EU and for Hungary. Overall energy import dependence on Russia regarding the selected countries and of the EU increased between 2014 and 2019, as seen in Table 12.1. This should have raised the security questions earlier.

Table 12.1 The change in overall energy import dependency and dependency from Russia in selected countries from 2014 to 2019

	Overall energy import dependency			*Energy import dependency rate from Russia in respect to the total import*		
	2014	***2019***	***Fuel type***	***2014***	***2019***	
Hungary	59.8%	69.7%	Solid fuels	2.57%	9.72%	↑
			Oil and petroleum	69.00%	51.42%	↓
			Natural gas	95.00%	95.00%	→
			LNG	–	–	
Czechia	30.2%	40.8%	Solid fuels	1.27%	9.40%	↑
			Oil and petroleum	38.8%	32.61%	↓
			Natural gas	90.36%	99.73%	↑
			LNG	–	–	
Poland	29.4%	45.2%	Solid fuels	60.51%	63.13%	↑
			Oil and petroleum	81.74%	63.79%	↓
			Natural gas	75.7%	55.02%	↓
			LNG	60.00%	1.15%	
Slovakia	62.1%	69.8%	Solid fuels	21.13%	33.66%	↑
			Oil and petroleum	80.37%	74.00%	↓
			Natural gas	100.00%	100.00%	→
			LNG	–	–	
EU	54.4%	60.5%	Solid fuels	23.66%	40.92%	↑
			Oil and petroleum	27.32%	23.06%	↓
			Natural gas	33.47%	38.35%	↑
			LNG	0.04%	16.84%	↑

Note: Energy import dependency equals share of total energy needs of a country met by imported fuels in total and/or from Russia.

Source: own calculation based on Eurostat data.[12]
Source: Self-analysis of calculations based on Eurostat data.[13]

Since the energy policy documents became linked to energy poverty, the household sector still enjoyed utility cost reduction. Approximately 26% of the total energy consumption belonged to the universal service and less than 60% of the total energy consumption was provided through market principles.[14] The impact of setting retail prices below production costs did not favour the locally active foreign energy companies. So, further takeovers happened, and state ownership increased in the Hungarian energy sector (Szabo et al. 2021). The Hungarian dominancy became visible on the TSO and DSO (distribution system operator) level, whereas E.On used to dominate the services market. However, this cannot be solely related to the Hungarian activist measures. There was a wave of asset sales and ownership restructuring reaching about 90 billion EUR on the whole EU energy market (both in the case of integrated companies and on TSO and DSO levels).[15] Many energy companies withdrew from Eastern Europe due to the worsening general economic conditions and unfulfilled expectations regarding the impacts of energy market liberalization (Székffy 2017, pp. 788).

Hungary could decrease wholesale prices of both electricity and gas, albeit, in the case of electricity, the drop in prices was not that significant compared to the EU average. On the consumer side in Hungary, there is no possibility to choose from the different origins of electricity (traditional, nuclear, or renewable), unless it is generated by the household itself. Despite every effort taken in the last decade, there was still a significant share of energy-related expenditure in total household expenditure (16.01%) for the poorest 10% of the population.

The recent Hungarian **primary and final energy consumption** has shown an upward trend since 2014. Within the final consumption, the share of different sectors is shown in Figure 12.4.

Even though from 2005 to 2020 the industry's share in energy consumption increased significantly, households still consume the most energy. Energy consumption is strongly related to output in the CEE countries (Table 12.2), so **energy (especially carbon) intensity**[16] improvements are important areas of the energy policy.

Table 12.2 Changes in production- vs. consumption-based carbon intensity of energy, energy use vs. changes in GDP per capita in selected countries (1995–2019)

Energy efficiency within the industry continues to mostly depend on the company level. After the financial crisis, Hungary introduced compulsory energy audits for companies established in the country, but most of the companies have only formally adjusted to the requirements (Szalavetz 2018). They did not find it necessary or were not incentivized enough to implement new energy management concepts and approaches into their practice because they have rather focused on cost-cutting measures instead of sustainability. A positive sign is that due to the tax allowances introduced after energy efficiency investments in 2017, higher energy standards, and the targeted support system, the newly built plants and factories generally meet the latest requirements, while they also implement new solutions. Hungary has done an effective job in channelling support from the EU and domestic budget,[17] which is evidenced by RUEC. The trend of decreasing RUEC is visible in the energy consumption related to industrial output within the CEE countries as well,

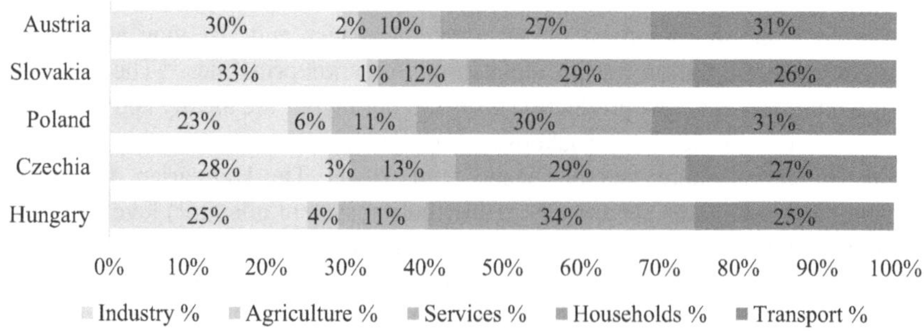

Figure 12.4 Structure of final energy consumption by sectors (%, 2020).

Source: Self-analysis based on Eurostat data.

Table 12.2 Changes in production- vs. consumption-based carbon intensity of energy, energy use vs. changes in GDP per capita in selected countries (1995–2019)

	Real GDP per capita change	*Production-based carbon intensity (kg/kWh)*		*Consumption-based carbon intensity (kg/kWh)*		*Change in domestic energy use, per capita*	*Change in consumption-based energy per capita*
		1995	*2019*	*1995*	*2019*		
Hungary	+152.82%	0.17	0.11	0.21	0.15	+31.10%	+27.46%
Czechia	+111.33%	0.28	0.18	0.30	0.19	+17.29%	+28.61%
Poland	+191.82%	0.32	0.26	0.30	0.23	+9.73%	+16.01%
Slovakia	+128.02%	0.22	0.13	0.21	0.18	+23.94%	+10.66%
Austria	+45.12%	0.22	0.17	0.24	0.19	+23.63%	+15.55%

Note: GDP per capita adjusted for price changes over time (inflation) and price differences between countries – it is measured in international-$ in 2011 prices.

Source: Self-analysis based on Our World in Data.

although they can still improve compared to Austria's performance (Figure 12.2). In 2018, Hungary had the lowest level among V4 countries in energy intensity (in kWh) per dollar (1.08) (Figure 12.5).[18]

Now, the rising energy prices can turn the focus of the companies to see the greater benefits of such investments, but with a big delay. Efficiency efforts can support the decoupling of energy demand from economic growth in Hungary, but notably due to consumption in transport and households (IEA) the effect is lower.

Besides security and availability, sustainability issues and indicators are also involved in the Energy Union Strategy. Regarding the targets, Hungary performed inconsistently, both with respect to the EU average and to the targets (Wach et al. 2021). In the case of the **decarbonization** process until 2018, Hungary (12) was in the second quartile (with Czechia (11), and Slovakia (14), while Poland (22) was in the third quartile). Decarbonization can happen mostly in the energy sector, as well as in household/residential, transport, and industry (Figure 12.6).

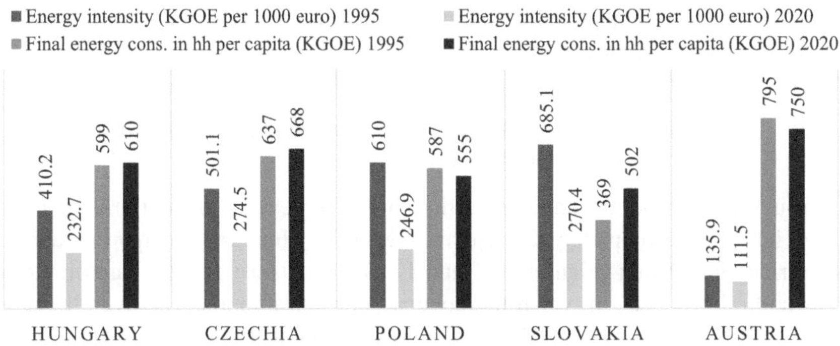

Figure 12.5 The change of energy intensity and final energy consumption of households in selected countries, 1995–2020.

Source: Self-analysis based on Eurostat data.

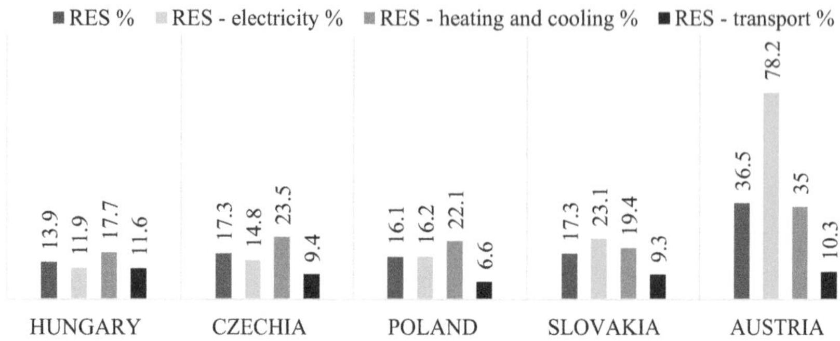

Figure 12.6 Share of renewable energy sources in total energy use overall and sectors (2020).

Source: Self-analysis based on Eurostat data.

In the **domestic energy strategy/policy**, both positive and negative elements are visible in this period. There was increasing support from the domestic and EU budget for the households in the areas of insulation, energy efficiency, while also installing RES capacity. For financial sustainability reasons in 2017, the regulator switched from the Mandatory Off-take Regime (KÁT) to the Renewable Support Scheme (METÁR). The new system puts less additional expense on the central budget and is more like a market-based approach internalizing RES use. The implementation of auctions in RE-related electricity generation was also a milestone in this period.

In the meantime, the missing regulation of construction of net zero houses did not result in a higher pace in the improvement of housing conditions, and the utility price reduction continued to stifle the energy investments of households. The disappointing results in decarbonization can be explained by the relatively low level of public investment and with the lack of incentives for private spending on Energy Union R+D priorities with respect to GDP. Hence, two objectives of the energy trilemma, namely, the level of affordability/competitiveness and the security of supply became weighted, and less focus has still been placed on energy transition and sustainability issues.

12.4 The settings and resilience of the Hungarian energy market amid a storm of challenges

Throughout Europe, we have faced the unforeseen events of the third decade of the 21st century completely unprepared. Regarding Hungary's energy mix and the electricity generation (Figures 12.7 and 12.8), we still see a huge share of natural gas and oil products, in which the country relies on imports. The overall energy import dependence was 54.1% in 2021 with a slight diversification only in the imports of oil (Table 12.1) and a stable situation in the case of natural gas which has 27% share of electricity production.

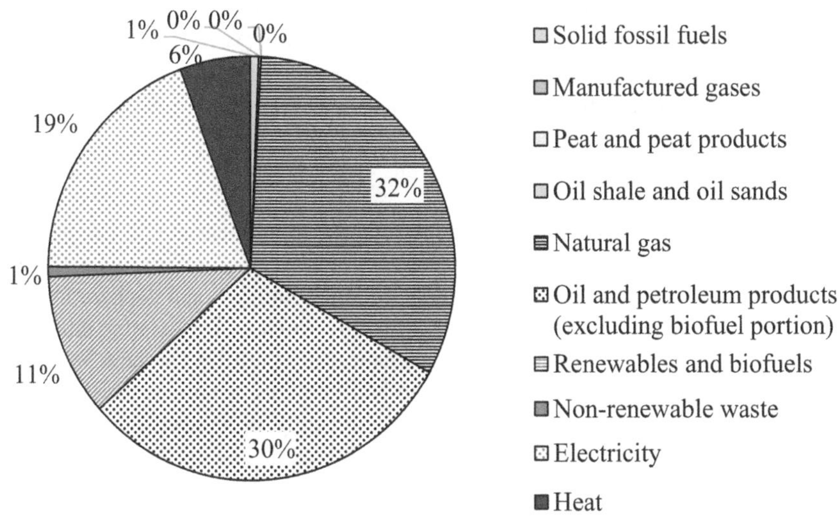

Figure 12.7 Hungary's final energy consumption in 2021 in terms of products.

Source: Self-analysis based on Eurostat data.

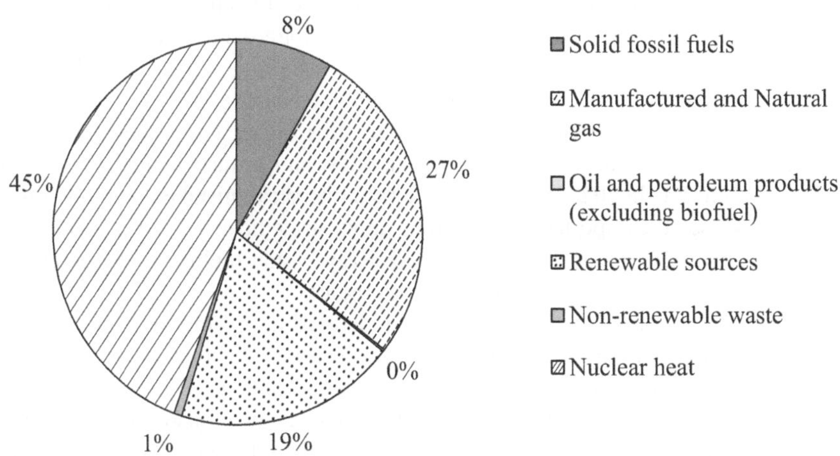

Figure 12.8 Gross electricity production by sources in 2021.

Source: Self-analysis based on Eurostat data.

Research also revealed that the Hungarian NECP underestimated the potential energy mix with respect to the expected future consumption and by 2030/40 Hungary may become the most exposed country to energy imports. Thus, the need for certain modifications and re-weighting in the Hungarian energy policy has already been identified (Aszódi et al. 2021). At that time, the impacts of COVID-19 were not measurable and the war's additional pressure on energy markets did not even exist, yet the trend towards the increased state intervention in energy sector proceeded. With relation to mitigating the impacts of the COVID-19, the Hungarian government introduced an "economic protection plan" in 2020, which also covered the rules of protecting strategic companies and sectors.[19]

12.4.1 Energy security

Although in recent years Hungary has introduced some measures to decrease its **net energy import dependence** on Russian energy, these efforts were limited both in their scope and their level of success. Regarding regional cooperation and its impact on dependence, the **infrastructure network** of the country improved through significant investments partially financed by the EU. The new NG pipeline towards Slovakia connects Hungary to Northern gas resources, while also the pipeline towards Romania, together with the recently introduced Interconnector Greece-Bulgaria (IGB), the Baltic Pipeline, and the Poland-Slovakia pipeline may provide alternative routes and origins of natural gas for Hungary.[20] Now Hungary has the fourth largest gas storage capacity within the EU.[21] The country is still heavily reliant on oil arriving from Russia within the energy mix, but with the stockholding system regulation that provides a level covering 90 days of net imports.

After the events of 2022, the **security of supply** again became top priority and urged the complex handling of economic challenges of keeping energy transition objectives on the agenda and decreasing the EU's long dependence on relatively cheap and abundant fuels of Russia. The RE Power EU plan (2022), together with the Recovery and Resilience Facility (RRF) and the National Recovery and Resilience Plans (RRPs), provide a framework for this by targeting energy savings, while also the diversification of energy supplies, and an accelerated roll-out of renewable energy. In 2022, it turned out to be a historical mistake that the EU had so far dismissed the importance of deciding about strategic gas reserves.[22]The Seventh Report (2022) about the State of the Energy Union highlights the perennial challenges for Hungary, which we share with the EU.

Since the beginning of 2022, Hungary requested an exemption from the EU embargo on Russian oil imports. However, this can only be a temporary solution. Witnessing the recent role and sensitivity of energy markets, Hungary has introduced some changes regarding responsibility issues. A new ministry was appointed for this area at the end of 2022, albeit there is still a shared responsibility with other ministries and authorities as nuclear development (Paks-II) and the negotiations of long-term gas and oil contracts still come under the jurisdiction of the Ministry of Foreign Affairs. This division of energy fields by political and technical borders does not support the complex handling of the area.

Hungary has also taken some **urgent steps** regarding the security of supply of other energy sources. They include the increasing of domestic gas production (to 2 billion m^3/y), while still securing additional gas imports from Russia, potentially banning exports of energy carriers and firewood, increasing coal production and power output at Hungary's lignite-fired power plant, while also extending the lifetime of the Paks Nuclear Power Plant (IEA 2022). These measures are easier to be taken with the increased state ownership and influence in the energy sector. Further steps in the future should cover the diversification of the routes and the energy sources. A recent study by Mayer et al. (2023) confirms that the decision to rely on a combination of nuclear-fossil-renewable energy sources in the Hungarian supply is justified and based on the local conditions. Furthermore, limiting oil consumption growth, speeding up energy efficiency investments, decarbonization of the transport sector, and the depletion of renewable energy sources would contribute to less volatile energy prices and to the lowering of unilateral dependence.

12.4.2 Energy equity

Together with the COVID-19 outbreak, we saw the break-up of economic ties resulting in an economic crisis. The electricity consumption faced high volatility in 2020 (ranging from 14% to +3% with respect to the year 2019) due to the lockdowns and later the rebound of certain sectors when only the residential consumption area remained stable or increased during this period (Morva and Diahovchenko 2020). At the same time, on the global market the energy prices also changed due to the average energy demand decline of 3.8% in Q1 of 2020 compared to Q1 of 2019. The report of 2021 was expected to indicate an energy price spike driven mainly by gas price increases across Europe only for a temporary period. This was further complicated by the events of 2022. The overall energy intensity of the economies and the amount of money spent on energy sources required to obtain one unit of value added for the manufacturing sector are receiving higher attention with the volatile energy prices and the insecure supplies.

In July 2022, within its new emergency legislation, the Hungarian government decided to re-structure the regulated gas and electricity retail prices under the utility price reduction system for households having above-average consumption and increase them towards market prices. Partly due to this measure, electricity consumption decreased by 5.6% in comparison to July 2021.[23] In the background, financial reasons and the sustainability of the budget are seen as priority areas. The state ownership in the energy sector holds the potential to withdraw only partially from the affordability or solidarity criteria.

12.4.3 Environmental sustainability

The economic turmoil caused by COVID-19 and the war provides an environment throughout Europe where green targets temporarily seemed to receive less emphasis and the mere physical availability and affordability of energy became prioritized. Furthermore, among the urgent steps to cover the European energy demand, we can see more details related to those exploiting already existing fossil fuel reserves compared to those investments targeting green solutions providing prospects only on a longer-term basis. This resulted in delays or cancellations of **energy-related investments** due to profitability reasons and their negative effect on the energy stock returns (Morina et al. 2022). After the sharp drop in 2020 in energy investments, it recovered by 8% in 2022 but as the IEA (2022) states, almost half of the increase is linked to higher costs due to multiple supply chain pressures, tight markets for specialized labour and services, while also the effect of higher energy prices. Overall, the climate goals set by EGD can hardly be achieved with current national energy strategies, which are not even harmonized (Aszódi et al. 2021).

Likewise, in the case of **greenhouse gas emissions**, in terms of the intensity of energy consumption, the biggest share belongs to the households in Hungary. However, there is a visible improvement in the overall level of GHG emissions and a significant part of this improvement is detected in the residential sector. Regarding the sectoral share of GHG emissions, energy industries, and transport are in the lead with 22%, followed by industry (19.7%), residential and commercial sectors (together 17.1%), agriculture (13.7%), and waste (5.4%). Thus, efficiency improvements in the industry, increased carbon neutrality in the energy sector, while also the electrification of the transport sector (Figure 12.4) and reducing building emissions are expected to have a positive impact on the overall emission performance (Figure 12.9).

Regarding the other area of the climate action, the share of **renewable energy** in the overall energy consumption is starting to increase again. In 2022, Hungarian primary energy consumption decreased, while carbon-neutral sources reached a higher level.[24] Power generated from renewable sources increased by 16.2% with relation to the same month of the previous year. Within this period, the electricity generated from solar energy could increase by 32.1%, which now accounts for approximately 20% of the overall power generation.

Regarding the future of decarbonization, there are some promising signs. The renewable energy auction announced in March 2022 was the fifth one in a row,[25] and it contained an additional requirement to also provide battery storage capacity. The participation of Hungary in hydrogen research is also a positive sign. The Hungarian Hydrogen Strategy was accepted in 2021, along with the EU's strategy from 2020 and research and professional facilities that already exist and are up and running. Hungary has a net zero target in place and its financial sector is working to stimulate the flow of capital to decarbonization efforts, but the National Energy and Climate Plan and the package of policies and measures should be updated.

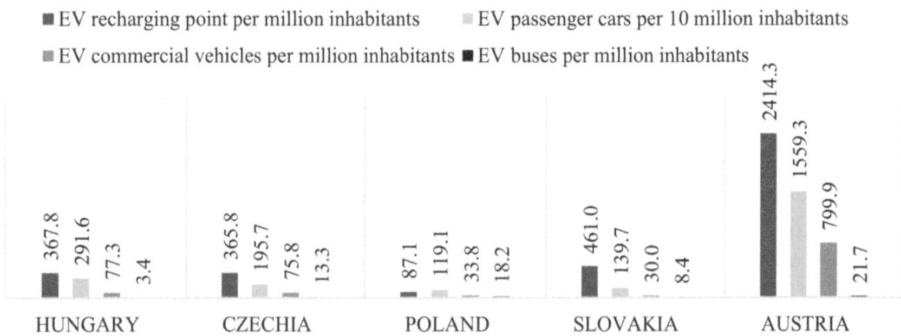

Figure 12.9 Figures of the EV (BEV, PHEV) fleet and infrastructure (per million or 10 million inhabitants) in 2022.

Source: Self-analysis based on European Alternative Fuels Observatory (https://alternative-fuels-observatory.ec.europa.eu/transport-mode/road)

12.5 Conclusions

In recent decades, CEE countries have followed their own development path with the necessary structural design, which led to a patchwork of conditions (Rapacki and Czerniak 2018). Inter-regional differences in the institutional settings are visible, but due to the necessity of relative proximity to headquarters economies (especially Germany), the variance is relatively small.

Hungary has a strong reliance on both economic relations from the EU, EU-based and MNCs, and although it has decreased recently, it still relies on cheap energy sources imported from Russia. **Energy policy became subject to competitiveness objectives** since Hungary still follows an export-oriented FDI-based growth model. The government had twofold objectives for a long time: maintaining the potential to attract more FDI and keeping the industry-based production within the country based on low wages and cheap energy. As the energy and the energy policy can underpin both economic and social development, the increasing role of the Hungarian state in energy policy became visible in the past decade. On the other hand, overall economic development could bring better consumption conditions through the ability of financing electrification, energy efficiency, and diversification improvements. Until this happens, the state ownership and the activism in the energy sector are visibly maintained, but with more difficulties due to recent events.

The attitudes and options of **CEE countries** towards mitigating the challenges of **energy trilemma** also show some differences related to each other and to core EU countries. These brought some **new aspects** into the EU. Nevertheless, they have a common interest in active participation in the EU energy policy. Soon after Hungary started focusing on the challenges of (among others) the energy trilemma, the COVID-19 outbreak brought **tensions on the markets** from pricing and sustainability aspects. Later, due to the events of 2022 security questions also arose.

At the beginning of 2023, Hungary was still highly dependent on a single supplier in natural gas and oil imports, and it is not so only by decision. Regarding **energy security**, only the recent infrastructure developments targeting the interconnection of the countries in the region can decrease the country's unilateral dependence on Russia and **increase diversity in terms of supplies**. However, in the meantime, the Russian natural gas and oil imports through long-term contracts maintain the country's dependence. Within the broader efforts towards **diversification regarding the countries of origin and the primary energy sources**, Hungary has chosen a **combination of electricity generation from nuclear-fossil-renewable sources**. This twofold diversification together with the technology neutrality accepted by the EU may provide **cheap energy, thus energy equity** in the future as well.

Concerning **energy efficiency and decarbonization** and their technological background, Hungary has much to improve on in terms of macro and micro levels as well. Domestic economic actors and the population are becoming more aware of the efficiency issues only now with the partial phasing-out of utility price reduction and due to some channelled government support in return of efficiency investments.

The security of supply, solidarity, and sustainability requires sensible, well-grounded, and well-thought-out government policies introduced in timely fashion both into the overall economy and in the energy policy to support Hungary in adjusting better to the twin (green and digital) transition. Tactical and operational answers regarding the recent issues of availability and pricing of energy were necessary, yet can have a long-term impact on the eligibility and the commitments towards the broader objectives of becoming carbon-neutral with the protection of competitiveness (that of the EU and Hungary as well). Thus, they should only be temporary.

Regarding **the long-term planning**, it is already obvious that the NECP(s) should be revised. Emphasis on expenditure is important and the budget should be restructured while keeping national priorities in mind. **Energy efficiency and decarbonization** should be **put at the core** of the Hungarian energy policy. These, together with **some measures** targeting vulnerable consumers, would facilitate the phasing-out of regulated end-user prices and reduction of energy poverty. The **review of the regulatory framework** to enable new investors to enter and the emergence of power generators from diversified sources, while also the establishment of energy communities, and services would also be beneficial. To strengthen the **security of supply**, it is required to prioritize investments in energy efficiency and domestic low-carbon energy sources by removing all barriers to the roll-out of renewable electricity and its system integration through the increased energy storage and demand response. As for the **financing aspect**, the Hungarian government should keep the country's risk at the lowest level possible. This can be done by a clear and consistent energy policy and strategy and by announcing well-based regulations and changes in advance. The current complex responsibility structures within the Hungarian energy policy do not support the adequacy, nor the clear and well-based planning, and transparent policy making.

We agree with Deák (2009) that Hungarian and the **broader EU-level energy policy** cooperation on the energy market and in energy policy is possible only in the case of win–win situations and by bringing these problems to the technical level instead of the political level. Without over-politicizing it, a national and political consensus should support the energy policy where the objectives and energy structure are set for the longer future. Thus, the role of energy in social development and competitiveness could also be handled and the political rent would be minimized.

Notes

1 I am grateful to Marcin Kędzierski, PhD (Krakow University of Economics, Poland) and to Maciej J. Grodzicki (Jagiellonian University, Krakow, Poland) for their insights and suggestions, and to Prof. Beáta Farkas (Faculty of Economics and Business Administration, University of Szeged) for her feedback during the writing of this chapter.

2 US State Department: https://www.trade.gov/country-commercial-guides/hungary-investment-climate-statement.

3 https://stats.oecd.org/#.

4 The Hungarian median gross hourly earnings of 7 EUR, in PPS, in 2018 it was approximately one third of the highest (19.2 EUR) in Denmark, but also about half of the EU average.

5 https://www.spiegel.de/wirtschaft/soziales/energiekrise-jede-zwoelfte-industriefirma-will-produktion-verlagern-a-6a1d507b-fc77-4fe1-b0e1-d9029737d3d9 and https://

english.news.cn/20221006/1abe4e909b8949d0a84f14d7437f37b2/c.html and https://www.irishexaminer.com/business/economy/arid-40968869.html.

6 http://www.nubiki.hu/content_en/referenciak.html.

7 With the increasing share (from 13% in 2007 to 17% in 2008) of supported power generators within the overall market, the level of competition decreased. This caused a 42% increase in prices under KÁT-system (25.6 HUF) compared to the average price of 18 HUF during January to November 2008.

8 https://appsso.eurostat.ec.europa.eu/nui/show.do?dataset=ilc_mdes07&lang=en.

9 https://www.reuters.com/article/uk-hungary-to-take-over-mols-gas-storage-idUKBRE89C08L20121013.

10 http://www.european-council.europa.eu/media/171257/ec04.02.2011-factsheet-energy-pol_finaldg.en.pdf.

11 Based on the main version of the index, Slovakia is ranked in 53rd position, Hungary in 92nd, Czechia in 107th and Poland in 109th position on the list of 156 countries where the first is the absolute winner of the energy transition and the last one is predicted to become a potential loser if nothing changes. (https://www.linkedin.com/pulse/gegalo-index-all-countries-ranked-indra-overland/).

12 https://ec.europa.eu/eurostat/cache/infographs/energy_trade/entrade.html?geo=PL&year=2020&language=EN&trade=imp&siec=C0000X0350-0370&filter=all&fuel=solid&unit=THS_T&defaultUnit=THS_T&detail=1&chart=

13 https://ec.europa.eu/eurostat/cache/infographs/energy_trade/entrade.html?geo=PL&year=2020&language=EN&trade=imp&siec=C0000X0350-0370&filter=all&fuel=solid&unit=THS_T&defaultUnit=THS_T&detail=1&chart=

14 https://hugas.met.com/hu/energiapiaci-betekinto/magyarorszag-energiatermelese-fogyasztasa-eromuvek/8?fbclid=IwAR1_A_xuCHjkVn9qB3Vtjp9RjimTKIdCwoGFDGuqitoCydVLoad2pmVhgF0.

15 Among the new owners, we can find local municipalities (Germany), professional actors (local and Chinese too), financial investors (Australian and Canadian), as well as states (Finland).

16 In carbon intensity (the quantity of carbon dioxide (CO_2) emitted per unit of energy) we must distinguish the consumption and the production-based metrics. Consumption-based metrics contain production-based emissions and energy minus exported goods, plus the energy or emissions from imported goods.

17 https://home.kpmg/…/2021/09/net-zero-readiness-index.html and http://forrasfigyelo.hu/palyazat/meg%FAjul%F3%20energia/osszes

18 https://ourworldindata.org/grapher/energy-intensity-vs-gdp?country=HUN~CZE~POL~SVK~AUT

19 The Government Decree Nr. 227/2020. (V. 25.)

20 https://ec.europa.eu/energy/infrastructure/transparency_platform/map-viewer/main.html

21 https://hungarytoday.hu/hungary-has-fourth-largest-gas-storage-capacity-in-the-eu/

22 It received significant attention only in 2021: https://www.bruegel.org/event/developing-eu-approach-strategic-gas-storage,
https://www.spglobal.com/commodityinsights/en/market-insights/blogs/natural-gas/092721-natural-gas-reserve-iea-europe After the events brought by 2022 this turned out to be a historical mistake.

23 https://www.mavir.hu/web/mavir/adatpublikaciok-es-kiadvanyok

24 http://www.mekh.hu/juliusban-is-nott-a-napenergiabol-termelt-villamos-energia-mennyisege

25 https://www.pv-magazine.com/2022/03/04/hungary-launches-fifth-renewables-auction/

References

Aszódi, A., B. Biró, L. Adorján, Á. Cs. Dobos, G. Illés, N. K. Tóth, D. Zagyi, and Z. T. Zsiborás. (2021) Comparative analysis of national energy strategies of 19 European countries in light of the green deal's objectives. *Energy Conversion and Management X*, 12:100136, ISSN 2590–1745. https://doi.org/10.1016/j.ecmx.2021.100136

Austvik, O. G. (2004) Strategic gas reserves and EU security-of-supply. *Energy Studies Review*, 12(2): 192–207.

Baldwin, R. (2012) Global supply chains: Why they emerged, why they matter, and where they are going. CTEI Working Papers CTEI-2012-13, Geneva: The Graduate Institute, Centre for Trade and Economic Integration.

Ban, C. (2017) *Dependent Development in EU's Extreme Periphery: Industrial Growth, Finance and the Great Recession in Romania.* Paper presented at EUSA Fifteenth Biennial Conference, Miami, Florida, United States. https://www.eustudies.org/conference/papers/download/283

Bank, D. (2017) The double-dependent market economy and corporate social responsibility in Hungary. *Corvinus Journal of Sociology and Social Policy*, 8(1): 25–47. https://doi.org/10.14267/CJSSP.2017.01.02

Bartek-Lesi, M., Á. Beöthy, E. Kácsor, L. Kerekes, and P. Kotek. (2019) Energiaköltségek hatása a feldolgozóipar költség-versenyképességére. *Közgazdasági szemle*, LXVI. évf., 2019. március (256–285. o.)

Bohle, D., and B. Greskovits. (2007) The state, internationalization, and capitalist diversity in Eastern Europe. *Competition & Change*, 11(2): 89–115. https://doi.org/10.1179/102452907X181929

Bohle, D., and B. Greskovits. (2019) Politicising embedded neoliberalism: Continuity and change in Hungary's development model. *West European Politics*, 42(5): 1069–1093. https://doi.org/10.1080/01402382.2018.1511958

Bruszt, L., and G. A. McDermott. (2014) Transnational regulatory integration and development: A new framework for institutional change. *Revista de Administracao de Empresas (RAE)*, 56(4): 447–455. https://doi.org/10.1590/S0034-759020160408

Bruszt, L., and V. Vukov. (2017) Making states for the single market: European integration and the reshaping of economic states in the Southern and Eastern peripheries of Europe. *West European Politics*, 40(4): 663–687. https://doi.org/10.1080/01402382.2017.1281624

Deák, A. (2006) Diversification in Hungarian Manner: The Gyurcsány government's energy policy. *International Issues & Slovak Foreign Policy Affairs*, 15(3–4): 44–55. https://www.jstor.org/stable/26590938

Deák, A. (2009) Is there a Central-European energy market in the making? *Research Center of the Slovak Foreign Policy Association (RC SFPA),* XVIII(1): 3–14.

Drahokoupil, J., and M. Myant. (2015) Putting comparative capitalisms research in its place: Varieties of capitalism in transition economies. In M. Ebenau, I. Bruff, and C. May (eds.), *New Directions in Comparative Capitalisms Research: Critical and Global Perspectives.* Basingstoke: Palgrave Macmillan, pp. 155–171.

Drahokoupil, J., M. Myant, and S. Domonkos. (2015) The politics of flexibility: Employment practices in automotive multinationals in Central and Eastern Europe. *European Journal of Industrial Relations,* 21(3): 223–240. ISSN: 0959–6801 (print); 1461–7129. (online) https://doi.org/10.1177/0959680114546437

EC. (2015) A Framework Strategy for a Resilient Energy Union with a Forward-Looking Climate Change Policy. European Commission (COM(2015) 080 final), 25 February 2015, Brussels. Available: https://eur-lex.europa.eu/resource.html?uri=cellar:1bd46c90-bdd4-11e4-bbe1-01aa75ed71a1.0001.03/DOC_1&format=PDF

EC. (2016) Clean Energy for All Europeans. Communication from the Commission. European Commission (COM(2016) 860 final), 30 November 2016, Brussels. Available:

https://eur-lex.europa.eu/legal-content/EN/TXT/?qid=1512481277484&uri=CELEX:52016DC0860b

EC. (2019) European Green Deal (EGD). Communication from the Commission. European Commission (COM(2019) 640 final), 11 December 2019, Brussels. Available: https://eur-lex.europa.eu/legal-content/EN/TXT/?uri=COM%3A2019%3A640%3AFIN

EC. (2022) Seventh report on the State of the Energy Union. Report from the Commission to the European Parliament, the Council, the European Economic and Social Committee, the Committee of the Regions and the European Investment Bank.

Farkas, B. (2011) The central and eastern European model of capitalism. *Post-Communist Economies,* 23(1): 15–34.

Farkas, B. (2016) *Models of Capitalism in the European Union.* Basingstoke: Palgrave Macmillan.

Farkas, B. (2018) What can institutional analysis say about capitalism in Central and Eastern Europe? Results and limitations. *International Journal of Management and Economics,* 54(4): 283–290.

Felsmann, B. (2011) Közgazdasági dilemmák a megújuló energiatermelés támogatásában. Working Paper, Corvinus University, Budapest. Available: http://unipub.lib.uni-corvinus.hu/1366/

Felsmann, B. (2014) Winners and losers in the liberalized energy retail sector in Hungary: A co-evolutionary approach. *Theory, Methodology, Practice,* 10(2): 25–36.

Greskovits, B. (2015) The hollowing and backsliding of democracy in East Central Europe. *Global Policy,* 6(1): 28–37. https://doi.org/10.1111/1758-5899.12225

Grieveson, R., A. Bykova, D. Hanzl-Weiss, G. Hunya, N. Korpar, L. Podkaminer, R. Stehrer, and R. Stöllinger. (2021) Avoiding a trap and embracing the megatrends: Proposals for a new growth model in EU-CEE. WIIW, Friedrich Ebert Stiftung, *Research Report* 458, November, Vienna.

György, L., and D. Oláh. (2019) The model of capitalism of Hungary's dependent economy as compared to other Visegrád countries. *Public Finance Quarterly,* 1: 7–29.

IEA. (2022) *Hungary 2022 Energy Policy Review.* Paris: International Energy Agency.

ITM. (2020) Magyarország Nemzeti Energia-és Klímaterve. (National Energy and Climate Plan of Hungary.) Innovációs és Technológiai Minisztérium, (Ministry of Innovation and Technology), Budapest, Hungary.

Kaderják, P. (2009) Energiapolitika – a 2008. év fejleményei. Műhelytanulmány, 2009–5, Regionális Energiagazdasági Kutatóközpont, Budapesti Corvinus Egyetem.

Khan, I., F. Hou, M. Irfan, A. Zakari, and H. Phong Le. (2021) Is energy trilemma a driver of economic growth? The roles of energy use, population growth, and financial development. *Renewable and Sustainable Energy Reviews,* 146: 111157. https://doi.org/10.1016/j.rser.2021.111157

Kratochvil, P., and M. Misik. (2020) Bad external actors and good nuclear energy: Media discourse on energy supplies in the Czech Republic and Slovakia. *Energy Policy,* 136: 111058.

Krzywdzinski, M. (2017) Automation, skill requirements and labour-use strategies: High-wage and low-wage approaches to high-tech manufacturing in the automotive industry. *New Technology, Work and Employment,* 32(3): 247–267. https://doi.org/10.1111/ntwe.12100

Lengyel, Gy, and D. Bank. (2014) The 'small transformation' in Hungary. Institutional changes and economic actors. In K. Bluhm, B. Martens, and V. Trappman (eds.), *Business Leaders and New Varieties of Capitalism in Post-Communist Europe.* New York: Routledge, pp. 58–78.

Löschel, A., and S. Managi. (2019) Recent advances in energy demand analysis—insights for industry and households. *Resource and Energy Economics*, 56: 1–5.

Mayer, M. J., B. Biró, B. Szücs, and A. Aszódi. (2023) Probabilistic modelling of future electricity systems with high renewable energy penetration using machine learning. *Applied Energy*, 336: 120801. https://doi.org/10.1016/j.apenergy.2023.120801

Mittra, B., N. Lucas, and I. Fells. (1995): Balancing markets and policy. *Energy Policy*, 23(8): 680–701.

Morina, F., K. Lyroudi, and C. Balomenou. (2022) The economic impact of the Coronavirus pandemic (COVID-2019): Implications for the energy sector. In S. A. R. Khan, M. Panait, F. Puime Guillen, and L. Raimi (eds.), *Energy Transition. Industrial Ecology* (193–213). Singapore: Springer. https://doi.org/10.1007/978-981-19-3540-4_7

Morva, G., and I. Diahovchenko. (2020) Effects of COVID-19 on the electricity sectors of Ukraine and Hungary: challenges of energy demand and renewables integration. 2020 IEEE 3rd International Conference and Workshop in Óbuda on Electrical and Power Engineering (CANDO-EPE), 2020, pp. 000041–000046. https://doi.org/10.1109/CANDO-EPE51100.2020.9337785.

Myant, M. (2018) The limits to dependent growth in East-Central Europe. *Revue de la Régulation. Capitalisme, Institutions, Pouvoirs,Capitalismes dépendants*, 24: 2. https://doi.org/10.4000/regulation.13351

Myant, M., and J. Drahokoupil. (2010) *Political Economy of Russia, Eastern Europe and Central Asia*. Hoboken, NY: Wiley and Blackwell.

NES-2030. (2011) National Energy Strategy-2030. Ministry of National Development, ISBN 978-963-89328-3-9.

Nölke, A., and A. Vliegenthart. (2009) Enlarging the varieties of capitalism: The emergence of dependent market economies in East Central Europe. *World Politics*, 61(4): 670–702.

Overland, I., M. Bazilian, – T. Ilimbek uulu, – R. Vakulchuk, – and K. Westphal. (2019) The GeGaLo Index: Geopolitical gains and losses after energy transition. *Energy Strategy Reviews*, 26: 1–16. https://doi.org/10.1016/j.esr.2019.100406. Available at SSRN: https://ssrn.com/abstract=3506677

Pelle, A., and G. Tabajdi. (2023) The role of manufacturing in the Central and Eastern European countries in the various periods from transition to mature EU membership. In J. Ricz and T. Gerőcs (eds.), *The Political Economy of Emerging Markets and Alternative Development Paths* (pp. 119–142). Switzerland: Palgrave Macmillan, Under publication. ISBN: 978-3-031-20701-3.

Pula, B. (2017) Whither state ownership? The Persistence of state-owned industry in post-socialist Central and Eastern Europe. *Journal of East-West Business*, 23(4): 309–336. https://doi.org/10.1080/10669868.2017.1340388

Rapacki, R., and A. Czerniak. (2018) Emerging models of patchwork capitalism in Central and Eastern Europe: empirical results of subspace clustering. *International Journal of Management and Economics*, 54(4): 251–268. https://doi.org/10.2478/ijme-2018-0025

Sass, M. (2017) Is a live dog better than a dead lion? Seeking alternative growth engines in the Visegrad countries. In B. Galgóczi and J. Drahokoupil (eds.), *Condemned to be Left Behind? Can Central and Eastern Europe Emerge from its Low-Wage Model?* Brussels: European Trade Union Institute (ETUI), pp. 47–79.

Sass, M., and J. Vlčková. (2019) Just look behind the data! Czech and Hungarian outward foreign direct investment and multinationals. *Acta Oeconomica*, 69(2): 73–105. https://doi.org/10.1556/032.2019.69.S2.4

Sebestyénné Szép, T. (2018) A hatósági árcsökkentés lakossági energiafelhasználásra gyakorolt hatásának vizsgálata indexdekompozícióval. *Közgazdasági Szemle*, LXV(2): 185–205.

Somosi S. (2012) Áldozat vagy haszonélvező? A válság hatása az európai energiapiacokra. *Külgazdaság*, LVI. évfolyam, 7–8. szám, július-augusztus.

Somosi, S., and E. Megyeri. (2022) A moving target: Changing priorities in the energy policy of the European Union. *International Journal of Energy Economics and Policy,* 12(4): 542–552.

Szabo, J., and M. Fabok. (2020) Infrastructures and state-building: Comparing the energy politics of the European Commission with the governments of Hungary and Poland. *Energy Policy*, 138: 111253.

Szabo, J., Cs. Weiner, and A. Deák. (2021) Energy governance in Hungary. In M. Knodt and J. Kemmerzell (eds.), *Handbook of Energy Governance in Europe* (1–32). Switzerland, AG: Springer Nature. https://doi.org/10.1007/978-3-319-73526-9_13-2

Szalavetz, A. (2017) Industry 4.0 in 'factory economies'. In B. Galgóczi, and J. Drahokoupil (eds.), *Condemned to be Left Behind? Can Central and Eastern Europe Emerge from its Low-Wage Model?* Brussels: ETUI, Chapter 5, pp. 133–152.

Szalavetz, A. (2018) Úton az energiahatékonyságtól az energiarugalmasságig. Magyarországi iparvállalatok tapasztalatai. (On the way from energy efficiency to energy flexibility. Experiences of Hungarian manufacturing companies) *Vezetéstudomány / Budapest Management Review*, XLIX(6): 13–21. https://doi.org/10.14267/veztud.2018.06.02.

Székffy, K. (2017) Vagyoneladás és a tulajdonosi struktúra változása az európai energiaszolgáltató szektorban 2010 és 2016 között (Changes in asset sales and ownership structures in Europe s energy sector, in 2010 2016). *Közgazdasági Szemle*, LXIV(7): 774–804.

TFEU. (2012) Treaty on the Functioning of the European Union. Available: https://eur-lex.europa.eu/legal-content/EN/TXT/?uri=celex%3A12012E%2FTXT

Varró, L. (2007) Az energiaellátás biztonsága és a magyar külpolitika. (The Security of Energy Supply and Hungarian Foreign Policy) *Külügyi Szemle – Foreign Policy Review*, 1: 64–78.

Voszka, É. (2018) *Az állami tulajdon pillanatai. Gazdaságtörténeti és tudománytörténeti nézőpontok.* Budapest: Akadémiai Kiadó.

Wach, K., A. Głodowska, M. Maciejewski, and M. Sieja. (2021) Europeanization Processes of the EU Energy Policy in Visegrad Countries in the Years 2005–2018. *Energies*, 14: 1802. https://doi.org/10.3390/ en14071802

WEC. (2022) World Energy Trilemma Index. World Energy Council. Available: https://www.worldenergy.org/assets/downloads/World_Energy_Trilemma_Index_2022.pdf?v=1669842216

Weiner, Cs. (2019) Energiaellátás-biztonság és gázdiverzifikáció Magyarországon: elmélet és gyakorlat. *Köz-gazdaság*, 1: 168–189. https://doi.org/10.14267/RETP2019.01.19

Weiner, Cs., and T. Szép. (2022) The Hungarian utility cost reduction programme: An impact assessment. *Energy Strategy Reviews*, 40: 100817.

Index

Note: **Bold** page numbers refer to tables; *italic* page numbers refer to figures and page numbers followed by "n" denote endnotes.